Fifteen year old Mariah has nothing to live for.
No friends, a neglectful mother and an abusive brother.
But on the night when she decides to end it all,
she finds Toby in her room.
Just his appearance isn't enough to deter her from her plans.
It's only when he tells her that he died that very night
that living feels important.

Published by Orange Monkey Publishing

P.O. Box 43
Langdon, Alberta, Canada TOJ 1X0
E-mail: Aviva@abnet.ca
Internet: www.avivabelharold.com

First Paperback Edition – March 2009
13 12 11 10 09 — 2 3 4 5 6 7 8 9 10

Library and Archives Canada Cataloguing in Publication

Bel'Harold Aviva, 1972–
Safe : a novel / Aviva Bel'Harold. — 1st pbk. ed.

ISBN: 978-0-9811144-0-8

I. Title

PS8603.E443 S33 2009 JC813'.6 C2009-900573-5

Technical Credits:

EDITING: Allister Thompson, Toronto, Ontario, **www.altereditorialservices.com**
DESIGN, PRODUCTION & PRINT MANAGEMENT: Jeremy Drought, *Last Impression Publishing Service*, Calgary, Alberta
PROOFREADING: Barbara Russo, Calgary, Alberta
COVER ART: Heather Reinhardt, Calgary, Alberta, **www.heatherreinhardt.com**

Printed in Canada by *Houghton Boston*, Saskatoon, Saskatchewan

Dedication

THIS BOOK IS DEDICATED TO MY DAUGHTER AMALLY, because she (like most of us) faced dark days. It was in those moments that my idea of Mariah had life breathed into it. It was from this that hope for her story was born.

Don't be afraid to face those dark times, just remember that they are not the end of time...Life will go on. It will get better. Brighter days will come again. And my advice would be to gather up all the good—you may be surprised at how much you end up having!

Safe
DAY 5
DAY 6
DAY 7
DAY 8
DAY 17
DAY 18
DAY 19
DAY 20
DAY 21
Friday...
Wednesday...
Saturday...
Thursday...
Friday...
Saturday...
Tuesday...
Sunday...

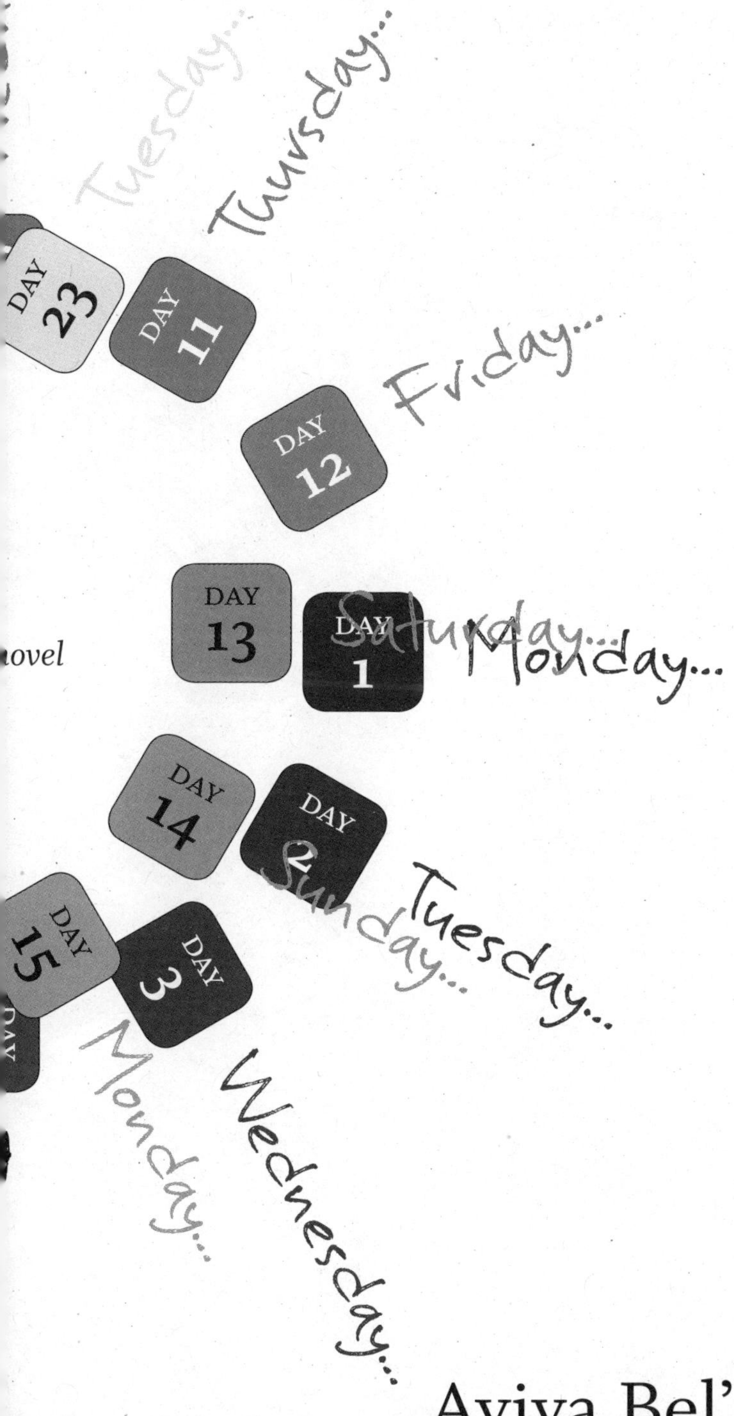

novel

Aviva Bel'Harold

DAY 1 Monday...

You know those life-changing moments? Everyone has them: getting married, having a baby, a promotion, winning the lottery, moving. . .you get the point. Though not all of them are good, they all affect you forevermore. Even if you wanted to, you could never go back. You are changed, permanently different, yet you are still you.

Everyone has had at least one life-changing moment, but I'd wager you that *no one* has had one like mine. . .

I was a naïve fifteen-year-old girl, way too much into myself and especially my problems. That was it, I had problems. Before I continue, I know everyone has problems, especially in this world, where we are continually on the move and always striving for more; but my troubles were far too big for me to see past them, and that became life threatening.

My father had walked out on us when I was nine. He just packed his bags and left. No forwarding address and no backward glances. I was dumbfounded; it came as a complete shock. My mom didn't seem phased, and instead of mourning or getting upset, she just kept on going like he'd never been there in the first place.

"Why do you care?" She stood towering over me, dressed in a crisp business suit, her hands placed firmly on her hips. "He was a ghost of a man when he was here… Which, let's be honest, wasn't all that often in the first place! There is really no difference between that and just being gone, so stop your crying and go to your room." *But it felt different to me!* Life seemed colder, darker and depressingly lonely.

My brother, on the other hand, raged. He was just over eleven at the time, and he got so angry that I was afraid to be anywhere near him. He stopped listening to our mother and started yelling at her instead. Then he began to stay out late and started getting into loads of trouble: punching holes in our walls, coming home with black eyes, new scars, or even worse, open wounds. The friends he hung out with were even more frightening than he was. I learned to live in my room and like it.

I felt lost. Mom was right in some ways: Dad had been preoccupied, and he never seemed to be around, *but he was my father.* I guess I missed the stability he brought, because with him gone, suddenly Mom was busier, had to work more and later, and when she wasn't doing that, she was dealing with my brother's problems. I just kept getting quieter and quieter; I didn't want to be a bother to her or anyone, so I stayed out of the way and made as little fuss as I could. It worked. She didn't have any problems with me, but the less of a pest I was, the less I felt like I was anything. If my father was a ghost dad, would that make me his ghost daughter?

My friends started to notice changes in me, but I couldn't tell them—how could I trust them with my problems? My troubles were so big, they were beyond me! How could any of my friends help? Instead, I shut them out, and they stopped hanging around me. I felt like I was becoming smaller and smaller and was going to disappear right out of existence, when in reality I actually started to get bigger. I started to eat my long afternoons away, and my lonely evenings, and my quiet mornings, and just about any time I could, I had something in my mouth, or in my hand ready to put in my mouth.

Not surprisingly, I gained weight, but this didn't help me to hide from my problems. *If anything, it made things worse.* To add injury to insult, I was betrayed by my body. It started to develop in ways that I was seriously embarrassed about. This elicited teases and chants from everyone around me. *I wanted to die.* Just when I thought I couldn't handle it any more, my mom announced that we were moving. She was tired of hauling my brother out of trouble, so she thought that a new location would fix all our miseries. That's what she said, but there was a big promotion that went along with it—more pay for her, less time for me.

One day she turned to me and said, "And perhaps now you can make some friends. All you have to do is be happier and lose all that weight so people will like you more." She fixed a smile on her face. "Now we can all have a fresh start." As she was walking away, she added, "Mariah, darling, haven't you looked in the mirror lately? You've gotten REALLY fat." And that was the end of any discussion. We moved three weeks later. That was the year I turned thirteen.

We were shipped halfway across the province to this new and improved neighbourhood. I couldn't see the difference. My brother, Jake, who sworn he'd run away back to our old home, changed his mind, since it only took him a few weeks to find new friends to get into the same old trouble with. As for me, I got all the tricks and tests of being the new girl, all of which I failed miserably. It was the same old story for me too.

I am shocked that I made it to my fifteenth birthday. I had planned to end it long before that, but I chickened out each time, or things would come up, and I wouldn't be able to complete the task. It was two weeks after my birthday, which had passed without a celebration. My mom said I had to have friends to have a party. I had no friends, so no party! She wouldn't even take me out to dinner with Jake when I asked. Instead I got a bag of extra large clothes, some too big even for me, and a handful of money that Jake took before I had a chance to go out and spend it.

But now the opportunity finally arose. I had it all planned out; it was Monday evening, so my favourite television shows would be on. It was the beginning of the fall show season, and all the cliffhangers from the last season were finally being worked out. My mom called to say she was working late again, and then she'd have to find my brother and haul him home. He'd been gone for two nights, so I shouldn't expect her until very late. *Perfect!*

"Order a pizza if you have to," she said in parting. With what money, I wondered? Her stash of "emergency" funds had been depleted just before my brother took off—and I highly doubted she would have noticed. But I didn't need pizza, or any dinner. I had my last meal planned: pills and alcohol. She had a good stock of both, even though my brother liked to help himself on a regular basis. She seemed to keep a better eye on *them* and always replaced whatever was needed.

So that was that—I watched a drama and two sitcoms. The first I could have skipped, but I really enjoyed the second. Then I poured a sixteen ounce tumbler of vodka and gathered up the contents of three bottles from my mother's "over the counter" drug collection. *I found it odd how calm I felt.* I had thought that getting this close to the end, I'd be more sentimental, like looking through all our old photo albums to see the good old days one last time, or crying over how horrible things had become...but instead I just wanted to go to my room and get it over with.

As I passed back through the living room, the TV screen caught my eye for just a second. It was the ten o'clock news broadcasting a tragic scene from a local car crash; flames from the exploded vehicle were seven feet high. I hit the off switch and marveled at how quiet our house now seemed. "I am truly all alone in this world," I said to the empty house, with not a sound in reply, then headed down the stairs to my room.

But I stopped just as I was about to walk in. I stopped because someone was sitting on my bed. *A boy!* He sat there silently, looking down at his hands. He wore a black shirt with the name "The Fray" (the popular band) smeared across its front and washed-out black jeans. He had short brown hair jelled up in spikes. If the situation had been any different, I might have laughed at how out of place he looked against my pink floral bedspread.

I froze. I was so startled to see someone in my room, I almost spilled the vodka... *This was my room, my sanctuary—what was this stranger doing in* MY *space*! It wasn't much; my single bed fit snugly against one wall, the desk and dresser opposite leaving barely two feet of space to walk. Beside my door, facing my bed, was a small closet. There was a window just above my desk. It was open, and my pink satin curtains were fluttering in the breeze. I could see the crabgrass growing in the dirt, just inches from my windowsill.

I steadied myself, and my grip tightened around the pills. I was determined. *Nothing was going to sway me from my plan!*

"What are you doing here?" My voice shook. I was sure it was one of Jake's friends (or "J-boy," as my brother liked to be called). He continued to sit in silence, slowly looking up at me. "This is my room, not my brother's!" I said, shocked to hear the cutting edge in my tone. He flinched as I raised my voice, but he didn't budge. "Get out!" I hissed through clenched teeth with such rage that my glass shook. When he still didn't respond, I finally said in defeat, "Who are you?"

His voice was so quiet, I wasn't sure I'd heard it right. When I didn't react immediately, he repeated himself, and though his voice was louder, it sounded hollow, as though he were speaking through a tunnel. "Toby."

"Well, Toby," I said, hardly restraining my contempt, "as I already said, this is my room. If you are looking for my brother, he's not here, but his room is across the hall—you are welcome to wait there." I didn't feel like he was welcome, but I had always been terrified of Jake's friends. They were not the kind of people you wanted to upset, though Toby looked very much less threatening than the ones I had met so far.

Regardless, he just sat there and stared at me. He had brown eyes the colour of chocolate milk that made him look dark and passionate. I was becoming unnerved and started to wonder if he knew what was in my glass or noticed how tightly I held on to the pills hidden in my other hand.

"What are you doing here?" I finally screamed out, irritated to have this disruption from an unwelcome guest. *I had a life to finish!*

After an eternity, during which he seemed to be taking notice of everything in my room—from the stuffed unicorns set up on the wall shelves above the desk, to the miniature glass figures my dad had given to me, displayed on top of my dresser, and the note I had left face down on the desk—he looked down at his hands and answered in that same faraway voice, "I'm not sure."

"Then leave!" I demanded, and stood to one side of the door so he could get by. Instead he just sat looking down at the floor. *Why wouldn't he leave?* I took several steps towards him and started to yell "Get out! Get out! Get out!" over and over again, but all he did was look up at me and shake his head.

"I don't think I can," he finally said, and this time his voice seemed to lose some of its hollowness. I took another step in his direction. Now I was only a foot from where he sat. His gaze was unblinking. "You see, I think I'm dead."

I lost all my energy and resolve in that moment, like a balloon filled to the top then let go. The pills fell from my hand, and the cup of vodka tumbled to the floor, shattering and splashing my toes. Now it was me who didn't move, not even to blink. I stood shocked to my core, staring at this strange vision that sat on my bed.

"What," I stammered in a voice no louder than a whisper, "Why? How?" Then the room began to swim, and for one short moment I was certain this was all a dream. *Had I actually taken the pills, washing them down with the alcohol, and was now hallucinating?* But I wasn't, because as I fell forward, Toby himself caught me, then gently lowered me to my bed, where I lay staring up at him.

"Are you an angel?" I asked, ready to believe almost anything, and wanting with every fibre of my being for it to be true. Could this mean that God cared enough about me to send me my very own angel?

"Far from it," he answered. With a hint of disdain, he stood up and backed away to my dresser. He looked like an animal trapped in a cage — *scared witless.*

My head reeled with possibilities, but the only thing that stood out clearly in all my thoughts was that there was life after death—suddenly I was very thankful I hadn't ended mine so swiftly. Who knew what the consequences of taking my own life would have been? So I looked over to this unknown boy and said in a soft, tearful voice, "Thank you."

He stared back, a half smile playing on his lips, "I didn't know if I could." Clearly he thought I was referring to him catching me. *Not stopping me from making the biggest mistake of my life.* "I've seen shows about ghosts," he continued, "and some can move things, but most go right through a living being…" He seemed more relaxed now.

I nodded as I pulled myself to a sitting position at the head of my bed and leaned on my pillow. "Um," I scratched my head, "what makes you think you really *are* dead?"

He shrugged and went over to the foot of my bed, where he sat back down, his hand only an inch from my outstretched foot, and though I saw him sitting, there was no ruffle of the bed sheets under him, and no creases where his weight should have pulled them down. He shrugged. "I'm not sure. But I know I am."

"Don't you think that's a bit unbelievable?" I asked, starting to lose the wonder he had inspired with his initial claim.

Then a horrible thought entered my mind. *What if this was just one of Jake's friends playing a practical joke on me?*

"I can understand your distrust," he said, reaching out to place one finger lightly on my big toe. A quick chill ran up my spine, while a realization raced like lightning through my mind. When was the last time anyone had touched me? Tears welled up in my eyes, which I quickly blinked back. *It had been far too long.* He pulled his hand back. Did he notice? He wore an expression of concern. "Sorry," he muttered, looking away to my open doorway.

"You're not dead," I said, feeling certain I was yet again the victim of an elabourate prank. My curtains fluttered, as if to confirm my notion. I didn't remember leaving my window open…

"I assure you I am." I heard resentment behind his now fully realized voice, for any hollowness was completely gone, and he had a presence that couldn't be denied.

"Well, I don't believe you," I spat out, more certain than ever that this was a mean and malicious trick to make me miserable. Someone somewhere was at this moment enjoying himself or herself snickering over it. I wished harder than ever that I had the courage to have kicked Toby out before I even began to have this stupid time-consuming conversation with him.

Yet he continued to sit and look around my room. He looked at my blank walls and the closet with its door shut tight. My contempt grew, and I wanted more desperately to get him out and go on with my one and only plan of the night. *I was wrong; there was no life after death. There was no God!* For if there was, how could he let these horrible things happen to me over and over again?

"Get out," I said, sitting up and swinging my feet over the side of the bed. Toby stood up quickly and caught my legs before I could get them to the floor, which I now remembered was littered with shards from the glass I had dropped. As he held me, I was no longer worried about the glass, but I felt quite disturbed that he had his hands on me again, so I struggled and kicked out for him to let me go. My foot swung towards him, and I watched in amazement as it passed right through his chest, then fell to my bed.

Toby let my second foot drop beside my first. He cleared his throat, and though his voice shook and he looked paler than when I'd first set eyes on him, he said, "Now you have your proof that I must be dead." His dark eyes flashed.

I couldn't argue. We shared the silence that enveloped us, and as the tension evaporated from the room, he took a seat by my feet again. That's when I realized he had been standing and stepping on the broken glass without a cut to show for it, even though he only wore a pair of thin white socks, *and no shoes.* As the time passed, I started to think the oddest thoughts: *Can others see him too? Where did he come from? Why is he here? Can I use him to spy on my enemies? Do I actually have enemies? No one likes me, but does anyone really hate me, or is it more like everyone agrees that I shouldn't exist…*

Toby made a motion to stand once or twice but then he settled back on the bed again. Finally he turned and looked at me full on, not removing his gaze until I finally returned his gaze, and we found ourselves locked eye to eye.

"What?" I blurted as I felt the tension rising once more. The smell of vodka had permeated my room.

"I don't know how this works," he said, not looking away, "but I feel that we are stuck together, somehow."

"You feel? You don't know?" I was irritated, and I struggled to tear my eyes from him, which I eventually did.

"No, I don't know, but I'm quite sure." He took a deep breath. "Like I was saying…" he paused, and when I didn't turn to look at him, he placed one hand around my foot. Again I felt a shiver; it was like my foot was touched by a slight draft, and yet it warmed as he held on. When I finally looked back at him, he didn't take his hand away. "I am sure we are connected in some way."

"Why?" was all I could manage. I felt trapped and enraged. *Who was he, and what gave him the right to infringe upon my privacy?* He let go, but even so, I still felt a whisper of his hand around my foot, and it stirred up all my feelings of loneliness and despair and made tears well in the corners of my eyes, like flood waters threatening to break the dam holding them in place. *I won't cry! I can't let him see me cry!*

"I'm sure of it, because twice I've tried to get up and leave, and I just couldn't. Also, I don't remember anything except being here; in fact, my memories only go back to the moment I saw you walking down the hall. Before then, everything seems black, as if there was nothing." He smiled. His teeth were white and perfectly aligned, and he wouldn't remove his piercing eyes from me…

He was quite breathtaking. "Maybe you *are* an angel," I said, a feeling of awe and wonder filling my chest once again as I thought of the idea of having my very own guardian angel. Then it sank, as I remembered his response: "Far from it." *What had that meant?*

"No, I know I'm not." His voice was completely flat. His smile faded, and he looked down at his lap.

"But why not?" I demanded. I was quite upset. I sat forward and grabbed his arm, confused, because this time I was able to hold on to him. "Why couldn't you be?" I wanted to believe he was, because it meant he could save me. If an angel had been sent to me, then that made me special beyond a doubt. Otherwise I felt worthless, like I did every day of my life!

"I'm sure I'm not, because I'm sure," he said, taking his free hand and removing my hand from his arm. His eyes were wide. I retreated onto my side of the bed and held myself as tightly as my oversized arms could. *I wasn't worth anything.* "But I am here to help," he said.

I could feel his eyes on me, but I didn't look. I was regretting ever going down to my room. Perhaps I should have taken my life in the kitchen. That would have showed my busy mom and…my brother.

"I want to help you," Toby said.

I hesitated. Then, gathering myself and wiping my bleary vision, I asked, "How?" Not a tear had managed to fall on my chubby cheeks, but they had left their presence in the corners of my eyes, and I now blinked them back, taking full stock of the mess I had made.

I thought of the broken glass on the floor. The smell of vodka was rising from where it had splashed. And the pills, over fifty of them, now just little gobs of melted mush, mere shadows of their former dangerous selves. How would I explain it to my mother, now that I hadn't gone through with it? *Would she even notice? Would she care?* Or was it just one more thing she'd have to handle before she would lock herself in her room and disappear into the cases and files that she always brought home from work?

It was nearing midnight. Surely she would be returning home, and I'd have to either hide what I'd done or be able to tell her something, truth or not. To me, the first option was looking like the easiest way out. I just felt so tired. *This was supposed to be over!*

"Well, I could help you clean."

He seemed to have read my mind, and I was unnerved by it, but I kept that thought to myself, and he didn't say anything more.

"I'll get some paper towels and a bag for the glass," I said, then I climbed past Toby over to the foot of the bed, where there was less glass, and picked my way out of the room before he could respond. I wanted to get away from him. When I got to the top of the stairs, I looked back and had to catch myself. He stood just a few steps behind me, silent and still. "What are you doing?" I asked, my shock a little too clear in my voice.

"We seem to be connected a little more than I thought," he said, looking just as put out and disturbed as I felt.

"Fine," I shrugged, though I didn't feel fine. Then I distracted myself by concentrating on cleaning. With paper towels and doubled plastic bags, we returned to my room. Without a word, I set to picking up the broken glass. Toby proved to be a bigger help than I would have thought. He was able to pick up most of the larger pieces of glass. He was also able to tell me if there were any under my bed or desk and even my dresser, without looking. I found that slightly irritating, especially because he was right every time.

Before long, we had the floor completely clean, with all the glass in the bag, all except one piece that had skidded into the hallway. That one I found with my foot. I recoiled so quickly that I lost balance and fell backwards, only to discover that Toby was again directly behind me. He caught me before I hit the floor, like he was waiting for me to fall. He guided me to a sitting position and raced around to my foot. He gently took it in his hands and started to doctor it without uttering a word. I also said nothing. Who was this boy, dead but not, and why had he come to me? And why a boy? Boys made me feel very uncomfortable!

Finally, he got the minuscule piece out, for that's all it was, smaller than a sliver, and stopped the bleeding with a spare paper towel. It was then that I was able to find my voice. "How come you could see all those other pieces, every last one in my room, even the dust finer than sand behind my laundry basket, but you couldn't see this one, and I ended up stepping on it instead?"

Hurt was clear in his eyes, but not in his voice. "I don't know. I was trying to figure that out myself. I would have loved nothing more than to save you from this latest misery of our first evening together…but the best I could do was catch you as you fell. I don't think I get to save you from everything, just certain things."

I was about to ask how he knew this, but he cut in, "I don't know how I know." He put my foot gently back on the floor and sat up on his knees. "I just do."

I could feel my heart sink. "Our 'first' evening together? Just how long do you think we are going to have to be 'sort of' stuck together?"

Toby rubbed his neck. "I don't know." He shrugged. "As long as it takes?"

"What takes?" I asked as I stood up, careful to keep my weight on my good foot.

Toby stood too. "I'm not sure." He took a deep breath. "Whatever stuck me here in the first place."

"Do you happen to know what that is?" I inquired angrily. *It didn't feel fair! No one asked me if I wanted this!* His only response was a shrug. Getting nowhere and feeling immensely annoyed by it, I limped upstairs.

We'd cleaned up every bit of evidence. I even took the garbage out, with Toby right behind me. Now we sat in my kitchen, not saying a word, and waited. It wasn't a large kitchen, by any means—it would barely fit my mom, brother and me, if we had ever eaten together. It was a U-shaped space, with a large window on the opposite side of the room from an archway into the hall. It had a small fridge and portable dishwasher along one wall, and the sink and stove along the other. The only place the small oval table fit was under the window, and as long as we kept the chairs tucked in, there was a little over two feet to navigate on all sides of it. The nice thing was that I could reach across from the stove that stood on one side to the fridge on the other without taking a step.

I sat and gazed out the window that dominated the outer wall. It didn't open, being made of a single pane of glass, and through it I could see the tops of the bushes that grew outside my mother's bedroom below. They grew beside the path that ran along our row of buildings. I took a moment to admire the huge planter boxes that lined the other side of the path, with their flowers still in full bloom. Beyond that and down an embankment lay the street that wove through my complex, and behind that was the low-rise building that housed an old folks' home. If I went up the hill, I would see nice family homes. The reason it was my favourite view was that our window wasn't obstructed by much, and I was able to gaze up into the night sky.

I didn't know what I was waiting for. Perhaps I wanted my mom to return so I could confront her? Or maybe I just wanted to see her, so I would feel like this was really happening. Since Toby's appearance, things seemed a bit like a dream. I also waited because I had never had a boy in my room, and though Toby was sure he wasn't alive, he still felt very real to me, and that made me nervous and self-conscious. So we just sat in the kitchen. For twenty minutes, nothing changed except the numbers on the microwave clock, and they simply marked off the passing time.

It was getting close to two a.m. when keys rattled in the front door, and in stomped my brother. He was madder than a hornet whose nest was being attacked; he swore and punched out at the wall. I shook a little where I sat. I'd forgotten that my mother had been out to get Jake. *Why hadn't I remembered that very important fact!* I desperately wished to not be so close, when he and my mother looked as if they were about to fight it out.

"Trafficking drugs!" Mom yelled from behind him. "I'm not going to be able to bail you out much longer, Jake!" The hurt was so clear in her voice, and I felt a pang of resentment. *When was the last time she had sounded that worried about me? When was the last time she had even thought of me?*

"How many times do I have to tell you, Ma? It's J-boy!" He kicked the closet door as he came up the hall to the kitchen. Then he stopped in his tracks as he caught sight of me. "Little sis," he said, the malicious joy all too clear on his face.

Toby stood up protectively, but if Jake could see him, he didn't acknowledge it. Instead Jake turned back to our mother, who was now just feet behind him, and watched her as she realized that I was sitting in the kitchen.

"Mariah? What are you still doing up?" She looked annoyed to see me.

"I couldn't sleep," I said, looking down at the ground, feeling guilty for being in my own kitchen.

"Well, you need to go to bed now. Do you really want to be tired for school tomorrow." It was a statement, not a question. I felt like I was a small child again, instead of the fifteen-year-old I had just become. I started to shuffle my feet as I headed down the short hall that led from the kitchen past the front door and to the stairs that led to our bedrooms. Even though my foot stung, I tried hard not to limp or show any sign of weakness.

As I drew level with my brother, he threw out an arm, barring my way. “Let her stay up, Ma, she’s a big girl now.” He looked at our mother, baiting her for a response. Fear flooded my heart and rang out in my ears.

“Jake, you’re still high. Let her go to her room so you and I can discuss what I dragged you home to talk about in the first place.” She sounded tired, but she was clearly angry. *Angry because of me?* Toby let out a soft noise in my ear, but I was paralyzed and didn’t dare try to look his way.

“I’m not so easy to push around without the police to back you up!” Jake leaned toward me to punctuate his statement.

Mom was about to answer when Toby walked past me and pushed Jake’s arm away. It was unmistakable that Jake couldn’t see Toby, because he clearly wasn’t expecting anything, and that caused him to lose his balance and stumble back into our mom. She put up her hands to protect herself and Jake rebounded off her, staggering past me toward the kitchen. I took that opportunity to duck out of his way and raced down to my bedroom.

Toby was right behind me, and I knew that if I stopped, he would have to stop too. That gave me a strange sense of power for a fleeting moment. Once I got to my room, I slammed the door shut, hooked my chair under the knob and fell onto my bed, burying my face in my pillow, moaning and complaining about my mother, brother, my life, without a single tear falling. I hated my life, I hated my mom, and I really hated my brother. *I hated being so afraid!* But most of all I was furious that it wasn’t over, and I’d have to continue facing more days like these, or worse.

Toby didn’t say a word, but I felt him sitting at the foot of my bed, watching and waiting. As the pain subsided, my anger became a hard mass that I could either set aside or bury deep down inside myself like I always ended up doing. I turned my thoughts to this puzzle of a boy/ghost sitting before me. *How was he truly going to help me, if that was his reason for being here?* He had helped me with my brother, but that seemed so trivial compared to all my troubles.

I wasn’t happy with the way I looked on my best of days, so now, after having a fit like this, I knew that I looked worse. My hair was tangled, my face would be full of red blotches, and my eyes were guaranteed to be bloodshot. I knew I was even more disgusting than I usually found myself. I mean, I was really fat, with a plump, rounded face, and hair that frizzed more than curled and was a horrible black colour, just like a Halloween witch costume. My eyes were brown with some green, but there was nothing noteworthy about them. I turned toward Toby, knowing that what he was looking at was an ugly, wretched mess, and I really thought he would flinch or hide his face in horror. But he didn't; he just sat there, yet in his eyes I saw… *Sorrow? For me?*

"Do you really think you're here to help me?" He nodded. I felt self-consciousness, a hopelessness over my life, but I was curious… "How are you supposed to help me?"

"I'm not sure yet, but I think I can." He too looked like he doubted his own words. "I mean, I must be able to, otherwise why would I be here?"

"Maybe you are here for no other reason than the universe being a cruel and horrible place where there is no hope even in death!" I breathed hard and waited for Toby to respond in some way… Instead there was a pause, which seemed to stretch on for hours, during which my words kept reverberating in my head. Finally, I sighed and asked, "So what now?"

After a moment's pause he said, "I don't know."

"You don't know!" *This was just too much.* "So you are just going to follow me around day and night, watching my life like it's an after school special to be viewed and judged, and I've just got to accept it! Should I make you some popcorn?" I stopped. Toby was trying not to laugh, and now that I thought it over, I *had* said something funny. I sighed. Then a horrifying thought hit me. "If we are stuck together, then what happens when I have to go to the bathroom?"

A small smile played on his lips, "I guess we'll just have to find out when the time comes." *Was he enjoying my misery?*

"I have to go now!" I said, feeling panicked, because once the thought had taken root, I couldn't get rid of it, and it pressed down on my bladder until I couldn't hold it a moment longer. His eyes danced. *I wanted to smack him.* Instead I crossed my arms.

"Then let's find out." He smiled widely, and for the first time I got a sense that he was a real teenaged boy, or at least the ghost of one. I braced myself. *A boy in the bathroom with me, what a complete invasion of my privacy*!

"If you get stuck following me into the bathroom, then you have to promise you won't look." I wasn't afraid of him looking at me, thinking he'd like it. Somewhere inside, I actually wanted to be admired and desirable, but I knew I wasn't anything of the sort. I was terrified that he'd look at my rounded belly, oversized chest, flabby arms and chubby legs, and laugh. I knew I was disgusting, but it would be unbearable having him know this too! Every time he'd look at me, I would see in his eyes just how putrid I really was.

"Mariah, I promise," he said gently. "However, for your sake and mine, I really hope it doesn't work that way." Did he already see how detestable I was, or was he trying to be kind? I had no way of knowing…

"What?" I teased. "No insights on this one?" I stood up and waited for him to do the same. Hesitating one last moment, I muttered, "I really wish you had some kind of knowledge about how this works."

He smiled widely, and I was taken aback by how handsome he really was. "Sorry, no helpful feelings on this."

He *was* cute. His lips were a thin line of pink, his nose perfectly centered, his cheeks high-boned, his chin rounded, and his ears didn't stick out too far and were even. He had wavy brown hair spiked at the top and no sign of any facial hair, which made his olive skin look smooth and clear. He had broad shoulders and a muscular chest with a slightly bulky frame, and his deep brown eyes seemed seductive.

In everyday life, he'd be a boy that I would have a crush on, but I would never admit it or ever let it show to anyone! I had made the mistake of liking this boy or that, or letting it slip that I thought a certain boy looked nice, or sometimes without uttering a word, they'd just know… Yes, I had learned my lesson well, and the hard way that it always came back to haunt me in the end. I didn't admire boys any more. I tried not to even look at them.

So now I made my way slowly to my door and listened for sounds. I could hear the far-off voices of my mom and brother screaming it out in the kitchen above, and feeling sure that they would be busy for quite a while, I rushed out of my room and into the bathroom. Our bathroom, the only one in the house, was fairly small; no room to really do more than a bathroom was built for. If I wore makeup, I'd have applied it in my room like my mom did everyday, because it was too small to even do that in the bathroom. I shut the door and scanned the room to be sure I hadn't been followed in. I had thought I might have to tell Toby to wait in the shower, but he was nowhere to be seen, so I did what I had come to do, as speedily as I possibly could.

As I stood looking at my reflection in the mirror and washing my hands, I slowly thought over the night's events. *Why is this happening? What can an invisible boy do that could ever possibly help me! People take their lives all the time, what is so different about me?* Deep in thought, I took longer than I had planned…

When I heard a voice in my ear, I jumped and hit my elbow on the towel rack. "You might want to move faster. I don't hear your mother's or your brother's voices any more, but I thought I heard steps in the hall above." Toby appeared so close to me, he was almost pushing me over. He turned and examined his reflection in the mirror. "Huh, I guess this means I'm not a vampire," he said, but he sounded shaken as he stared at himself.

Back in the safety of my room, I sat down at my desk. *What was I to do now?*

"Not tired?" Toby asked. He was sprawled across the end of the bed with his shoulders and head resting up against the wall.

"Too many questions." I found it hard to look at him too long.

He brought his hands up behind his head and said, "Shoot, but I may not have many answers."

"You're not an angel," I said, feeling sure of it now, though saying it made my heart sink.

"Sorry to disappoint you," he replied. "It means so much to you that I wish I was. Plus it would make this a whole lot easier. I might just know what I'm supposed to be doing here."

I shifted uncomfortably.

"I've upset you—I'm sorry." The compassion in his voice was unmistakable.

I don't ever remember a time when someone was this concerned for me. "Why do you care?"

He stared as if he could read my soul. "Our fates seem to be tied together right now."

"Oh, you care because you have to care," I said, feeling like I'd been slapped across the face. *He cared because he was stuck with me! How was that caring?*

"I wish that weren't so. But," he paused to sigh, "it is."

I felt so humiliated and ashamed that suddenly I knew he really had been alive once—he had been a real boy of about my age, for no one else could be quite so cruel and cutting! It took me a while to calm down, and then I did what I always ended up doing. I decided to make the best of it. *I had no other choice…* I tried to change the subject. "Tell me about your life."

He looked at his hands and seemed to search for answers there. Finally he looked up and replied, "It's over."

"That's all?" Wasn't he going to tell me anything about himself? He'd already seen my life, every part of it, and he wouldn't even give me a smidge about his! That didn't feel fair.

"That's all I get to know right now. Again, I don't know why it is this way. I'm not making up the rules, they seem to have been set out for me, and I just can't…" He looked flustered for a moment while he scratched his neck, then his face cleared. "I don't get to know anything I want, just what I need to know."

Now I started to feel sad for him. "But your life! Your family! Your friends? You don't get to remember a thing? Surely someone as good-looking as you had bunches and bunches of friends! And the most perfect life." Toby blushed slightly at my words, and I felt shock for having said it. Yet I was sure it was true.

"My life, as important as it may feel to you to know about right now, is not. It's over, and so whatever was, is no longer, and that makes it unimportant, at least for now. Maybe later, who knows? All I get to know is that it is fully and completely ended."

"I'd feel ripped," I said, then I stretched and yawned. "I think I am tired now." I stood at my dresser and pulled out my pajamas. "Can you leave while I change?"

Toby looked longingly at my closed door. "Not even if I tried," he said. But I'll close my eyes and promise not to peek, like in the washroom. *He had been there!*

I was so shaken, I dropped my nightshirt. "You were there!"

"You didn't see me?" He ran his hand through his hair. "Oh, try this," he said, and then he just disappeared.

"Did you go?" I asked tentatively, not allowing myself to be relieved yet.

"No," came a reply from so close, it felt like he was in my ear. He reappeared mere millimeters from my side, so close for a moment, I felt like he was attached to me.

"I just closed my eyes."

"Why are you so close?" I asked, feeling claustrophobic and swallowing hard.

He took a step back. "Seems when I close my eyes, I lose all sense of space, I guess because I feel as if I'm tied to you like the moon is to the earth. When I have my eyes closed, you seem to affect me with a sort of gravitational pull."

I felt sickened. I knew I was overweight, but to be referred to like a planet implied a new kind of largeness. I unconsciously pulled at my shirt and looked down.

"I've upset you."

"What do you care? It's only because you are stuck to me somehow." I choked on my pain and anger.

"But that doesn't make me care less," he said in his defense. "I'm sorry for whatever I said. Do you want me to close my eyes now?"

"NO!" I yelled. The thought of him being a helpless object in my gravitational pull was more than I could take. "I'll just change under the blankets." Then I moved my desk chair back to my door, something I'd learned to do whenever my brother was home, and dove into bed.

Toby came to sit at the foot of my bed, and I kicked out, going right through him once more, making both of us flinch, but I remained upset. "You go sit on that chair," I said, referring to the one I'd placed against my door. He nodded and went over to it.

I fought with my pajamas for only a moment, then huffed out all my frustration from the day's events and rolled onto my side. I was convinced it would take a while to find sleep, but it came to me instantly.

DAY 2 Tuesday...

As I slept, I dreamed the most vivid, beautiful and baffling dream: I was in a meadow, with the softest grass I'd ever felt under me. I sat there in the warmth of the sun, a sun that shone brightly, but it did not feel too hot on my skin. I had on my shortest sleeved shirt and a pair of shorts that I normally wouldn't have felt comfortable in, but they didn't feel too bad, and looking down at myself, I saw I wasn't overweight. I looked great, like I remembered myself when I was much younger. Suddenly someone was approaching. It was Toby, but he didn't look like himself either—he looked much younger, and he glowed slightly. He came and sat down right next to me, a wide grin on his face.

"He's not mad at you," Toby said, and he kept smiling an animated smile.

I was confused. "Who?" *Who'd be mad at me?* I felt momentarily panicked, but that quickly faded, as it was too difficult to hold on to such a negative feeling in this warm and wonderful place.

"And He loves you," Toby added, "He loves you, and He loves me."

"Who? Who? Who is he?" I sounded a bit like an owl. But all Toby would do was smile, he was so happy. I wanted to get angry, but it was too difficult, since the sun warmed my skin and the grass felt exquisitely soft, like it was giving me a hug.

Then I heard a far-off noise. I knew it was a loud and jarring noise, even though I could barely hear it from where I was, and I wanted it to go away, but it persisted. Slowly the meadow vanished, as did the warmth of the sun, and finally Toby, or at least this dream Toby. Because when I woke up and opened my eyes, I found myself staring right into the face of the real Toby, as real as someone who's dead can be. Somehow, in the night, he had come to be right next to me, and now he was here just inches from my own face, looking over at me. I quickly put together what had happened. He'd closed his eyes to sleep, and my gravitational pull had moved him over to my bed, so close I could have felt his breath. *Did he have breath*?

I was furious and pushed out at him. This time my hand did not go through him. It made contact with his chest, but instead of pushing him back, I managed to push myself right off the bed and onto the floor. I fell with a loud thud, and felt not only angry now, but also foolish. I was stuck between my bed, dresser and desk.

Toby brought his head over the side of the bed with that stupid odd grin and asked, "You alright?" I glared up at him, wishing him gone. He just shook his head. "I'm going to take that as a 'yes.'"

"I didn't go through you," I finally muttered as I collected myself and started getting up. *Why was it that sometimes I did and other times I didn't*?

"I noticed that too," he said, offering his hand to help me. This made me feel even more rotund, so I refused to take it. "I found that a bit shocking and a little amusing," he said, stifling a laugh.

I finally managed to stand, only to elicit more laughter from Toby. I had put my PJ bottoms on backwards under the covers, and now I was wearing big letters across my front that said, "stretch". Why pajamas for oversized girls had to be so degrading, or why my mom had bought me this precise pair, I'll never understand, but if I had been uncomfortable with the word "stretch" across my bottom, I was downright ashamed to have it go across my front.

Toby quickly gathered himself together. "How about I just turn my back this time when you change," he offered.

I was too out of sorts to give any answer but a short nod, in response to which he turned around. As I got dressed, I felt as if I was returning some unkindness and torture by taking extra long, but Toby did not utter a single word the whole time. When I was done, I raced upstairs, and then turned to see him just a few feet behind me, despite my best efforts and deepest wishes.

The kitchen was littered with bowls and cups. Clearly my mom and brother had resolved their differences, and she was now on her way to work, and he was either sleeping in or had headed back out to his friends on the street. Regardless, no one was left to clean the mess, so I started on it. While I cleaned, I nibbled on the half-eaten pizza someone had left out. By the time the kitchen was done, so was the pizza. I sat down and had a full bowl of cereal, but I had to eat it dry because the milk had run out. *Typical.*

I added both milk and cereal to the shopping list, as well as some other items, and then I looked in the cupboard in our special spot for my lunch money. I was relieved to find it there, because that meant my mom had remembered, and my brother hadn't found our new hiding place yet, like he had the emergency stash.

All the while, Toby just stood nearby and watched. I felt as if I wanted to say something to him; yell at him to go away or explain myself to him, but I kept busy by doing my daily routine until it was time to go. It had become apparent that I was the only one who could see him. This didn't seem to bother him, but I wondered if when he spoke, I'd be the only one to hear, and if that were the case, then I would look like a nut to everyone else when I responded. I was a big fan of the TV show where a very big comedian plays the only guy that can see or hear this imaginary person, and he always ends up making a huge fool of himself. But they get paid to do it, and I wasn't interested in looking so foolish, especially without some sort of payoff at the end. I made up my mind then and there; no matter what, I wasn't going to respond to Toby! *But how could I let him know this?*

For the moment, he seemed to just be along for the ride, and perhaps that was what it was like for him. We sat in an overcrowded public bus. It took two buses to get to school, but depending on how much walking I felt like doing, I would sometimes skip one, and some days I would walk the whole way, about four kilometres, if I was in the mood and on time. Today I was neither, so we crammed in with the rest of the morning rushers. Toby barely fit, and there were times when he was all but not there as people stood in him and walked right through him.

He seemed a bit put off by his lack of presence and made a point of standing extra close to me, which made me uncomfortable. As the ride continued, I caught him staring at me from time to time. He wouldn't look away until I finally acknowledged him with a nod or a blink. I guess that was the only way he could feel like he was real. Suddenly I felt an overwhelming sense of sorrow for him. Here he was, for whatever reason, tied to me and unable to do or go anywhere he desired or even remember anything that would have mattered so much to me if I were him, yet he just kept on silently standing near enough to be seen by me, the only person who knew he was real. *How hopeless would I feel*? Then I wondered if this would have been my fate had I been able to complete my suicide, and again I felt a wash of gratitude for him showing up just in time. I wanted to encourage him somehow. I ended up flashing a smile that was misinterpreted by another passenger, who smiled back. Toby chuckled quietly, but only I heard him.

At school, it was a little less crowded, especially because everyone would clear the halls to show me how big I was. My school was a three-storey grey brick building, or actually two buildings attached to form an L. Then there was a third building, the newest addition that housed the two gyms. The building looked a little like a straight-angled horseshoe or three parts of a rectangle. Only the gym building was just one-and-a-half storeys high. My locker was located on the second floor of the middle wing, right beside my homeroom.

I tried to ignore all the calls of "Here comes Godzilla," which I usually had to endure each day, or "Earthquake! …Oh, phew it's only Mariah." Today, however, I found it extra hard, because as I heard each comment, some quiet, some not so much, I'd see Toby flinch. He stopped trying to catch my eye and instead looked squarely at each person who insulted me, as if he could inflict some pain through his invisible stare. He didn't even get flustered when a guy walked right through him. He pushed past with an unsuccessful shove and kept following me. I saw him flex his jaw and square his shoulders. *How could he have so much confidence? He was nothing to anyone but me.*

At my locker, I collected my book and wrote a quick note to flash at Toby. It said, "Not gonna talk to you. Don't want to look insane… Smile

—this isn't your life." I casually put it on top of my books in homeroom. He read it over my shoulder, nodded and even bent down to give me a quick forced grin. Then I slipped the note into my desk and proceeded with the rest of my day.

Toby was like my shadow. He was never more than three steps behind, and whenever possible, he was glued to my side. I felt jittery. He watched me so closely— it was like my life was on display. I was so much more aware of things; the names I was called and the looks other students would give me. But I also had a hard time doing things I usually did, wondering what Toby was thinking of me now... Having him watching me made me start to look at things differently, like did I need to eat the chips between classes? And why did I only watch the ground when I was walking through the halls? Slowly I became more and more comfortable with him standing closer to me, so much so that by the time I took the bus home, which was even more crowded than in the morning, I didn't object when he was pushed right against me, his chest pressed into my side. He stayed that way for three stops.

"I'm sorry I had to hold on to you at the end there," he said once we were on our own, walking the rest of the way home. He sounded genuine.

"It was packed," I replied. Honestly, I had only taken one of the two buses, because even though I tried to act casual, I still felt squirmy when Toby was pressed tight to my side. Now we were walking down an embankment that led to a quiet neighbourhood, and through that we'd meet up with a walking path that would take us to my townhouse complex.

He nodded. "Well, I'm still sorry I had to. I know how uncomfortable you are with me being so close."

"No, it's not that. It's just..." I had to stop myself. *What had it been... just that!* "I'm not comfortable with my size, I guess. When anyone gets close to me, it makes me remember just how fat I am." *Why had I said that?* It was true, *but why!*

Toby came to a sudden halt. I kept going, sure he'd have to catch up eventually. I was shocked when I couldn't take another step. I looked back to where he stood, seven feet away, and I felt a little shaken by this new advantage he had on me. I folded my arms.

He looked a bit surprised too, but overriding that look was his resentment about my previous statement. I guess it had bothered him, and he was going to speak his mind. "Ever since I first saw you, it has been clear that you aren't happy with your size. I know I even made some mistake in referring to it, and that got you really upset. But the truth is, I look at you now, and I don't see you as any larger than most of the girls…" He paused to take a breath when I made a face. "No, Mariah, you're no larger than the full-figured girls at your school!" *Full-figured was just a fancy name for fat.*

"Then you must not have been looking hard," I said, pushing at the invisible wall that stopped me from taking even one more small step away.

"In case you didn't notice, I didn't have anything else to do today, and so all I was doing was looking! You think you're so big? Well, I spotted several other girls in EACH of your classes that were way bigger than you." He stood waiting for my response.

I didn't want to hear it, but what he said was true. I knew it. *Why was it so hard for me to believe? Why did I feel like I was the fattest of all?* Then a new thought ran through my head. *I might not be the fattest, but I was surely the most ugly!*

Toby slowly came forward until he was by my side again. "Now, I'm not going to mince words. You could use some toning up, I guess, but it's really nothing and other than that, you don't look so bad." He looked as if he wanted to say more, but he just shook his head and waited for me to make the next move.

I felt…confused. I turned and started to walk. *He said I didn't look so bad… but he was dead…he was also a boy… He didn't mean it, he just said it because he was stuck with me. But there were a few girls fatter than me…* "Did you notice Effie?" I shyly asked.

"How could I miss her?"

Effie was in my grade. She was almost three of me put together, but she was friends with the "in" crowd. In fact, she was at the top of the pecking order, the queen most high. She was loaded, rich enough to be able to buy the most expensive in-style clothes, get the top name brands and even start a few trends herself. Everyone acted like she was the only authority at our school. No one wanted to cross her, not even to disagree, because she called all the shots, and if she said anyone was "out," then they were. Ever since day one, she'd made it perfectly clear that I was "OUT."

"She's over twice your size, and she had the nerve to call you a fat…well, you heard what she said." Toby ran his hand through his hair.

"Ya," I hung my head low. It was what she'd called me at least once a day since I'd moved to her school just under two years before. "But she has a thyroid disorder, so she's allowed to have weight problems." I remembered the first time she'd called me that name, I'd asked her how she could justify it, when she was clearly bigger then I was. One of her friends had attacked me, saying that it was medical, and what was my excuse? That had shut me up for good.

"Well, she's got attitude," Toby added. "She's confident in her status."

"That's easy with enough money," I retorted. I was getting tired of the subject. *It just reminded me of everything I was not.*

"It's not her money, it's her." Toby slowed to walk a pace or two behind me. "She knows who she is and what she wants. That's what makes her. You could have that too."

I stopped dead in my tracks. "What do you mean?"

"You know I'm the invisible one here, but you act like *you* are."

I narrowed my eyes. "What are you saying?"

"Well, you have a personality that is quite special. That's why the kids pick on you so much—your potential scares them."

"You *are* full of something, and it's starting to smell," I said and walked the rest of the way home without uttering a word. *How could he think I was special? I was nothing! I was nobody! I wasn't worth the saliva that the kids used to spit on me.*

Toby honored my vow of silence, though he wore a pained expression. Once home, I helped myself to an extra amount of after school snack to spite him, and sat down in front of the television. I was just contemplating a second helping when the front door slammed.

"Honey, I'm home!" came Jake's loud, obnoxious voice down the hall. I tried to scoot out of the living room and make it down to my room before he could see me, but I was slower than him. He barred my way down the stairs. "Mom says I've got to be a good boy, so you sis, is gonna have to help me!"

"What do you want from me?" I asked, looking for an escape route. Panic making my breath come fast. I looked to Toby, hoping he'd push Jake out of the way again.

"You gonna have to cook me and my boyz some suppa." Jake's breath reeked of booze.

"Jake, your friends don't like me, remember?" I whined. My heart sank, and my mind raced for something to do to keep me away from Jake's "friends." My skin crawled at the idea of being in the kitchen surrounded by his gang. They all liked to stare at me, and some even grabbed at me if I got too close.

"Ya, well not allz them hatez ya, and sides, you cook and weel all lovez ya," he said in his mocking voice as he put a hand on my shoulder. His voice hardened. "But, if you don't cook, I'll let ma boyz lovez ya in a whole new way, and don't think that chair is gonna stop some 'em from getting inta your room!"

My flesh crawled under his hand, and I recoiled from him like someone trying to step away from a cobra. His fingers bit into my neck muscles, and I could feel his nails breaking my skin. Toby just stood there wide-eyed and watching!

"We got deal, little sis?"

I nodded obediently. "What do you want me to cook, J?" I asked, turning away from Toby, who was no help at all.

"What is there in this dump? Who cares, just make me a meal fit for a king!"

"For you and…" I questioned. "How many should I prepare for?" My mind raced, trying to think of a meal that I could make before Jake's friends even started to arrive.

"Everyone! I've invited them all. Boy, is mom gonna be sorry she made me come home!" He turned and headed down the stairs, releasing me so I could scamper into the kitchen.

Toby was still behind me as I turned around. "You still here?" I spat out. *I wanted to hit him! I wanted him to hurt as much as I did inside!*

"I can't go anywhere else," he said. I saw my pain reflected in his eyes.

"Oh, I just thought you came to help me! Well, if you didn't notice, I needed your help just now!"

"No, you didn't," Toby said, sitting down, but his voice held no confidence. I glared at him until he squirmed. "I couldn't do anything," he admitted, slapping the table in frustration. "I tried, and I just couldn't."

"Not good for much of anything, are you!" I snapped, and then spent the whole time I was making supper in a huffy silence.

Jake came back up and sat in the chair across from Toby. He watched me as I fried some ground beef for the sauce and chopped vegetables. Occasionally he'd make a comment about hurrying up. This just made me clumsy, and I took twice as long. Then his friends started to show up: Roc, Ed and Nick. They all piled into the kitchen, where there wasn't enough room to begin with.

I was pinched and slapped on the bottom at least five times before I was finally released to retreat to the privacy of my room. I could feel all eyes upon me as I walked down the hall and turned the corner to go downstairs. I heard the doorbell ring and more friends arrive. I shuddered and ran to my room.

Once we were down there again, Toby said, "You know upstairs?"

"Ya, living room, dining room, kitchen...what about it?" I said. I was not interested in discussing it, and I sat at my desk skimming over my English assignment.

"I've been thinking it over, and I haven't got it yet, but I know I'm here to help you. It's just not in the way you think you need help."

"You sure know how to talk in riddles, don't you?"

"Believe me when I tell you there isn't anything I'd like to have done more than push your big jerk of a brother down the stairs!" His hands shook as he held them out.

"You know, for his age, he's not so big," I said, feeling nervous.

"Well, you know what I mean." Toby rolled his eyes. "My point is: how would that have helped anything? He would have thought it was you who pushed him, then you'd be in more trouble, and I believe he was right about the lock on your door not being good enough to keep his friends or even him out."

"No lock can keep him out," I said, returning my attention to my work. I was terrified of Jake. Would I ever be safe from him? Toby was right, it wouldn't have helped, but it didn't make my whole life feel any better knowing it. For a moment I strained my ears, listening for what was happening on the floor above. Jake and his friends were still up partying, and I could hear the occasional smashing of a glass, or more likely a bottle. It was nearing nine at night, and I wondered when Mom would be getting home, and how she would face this new challenge. Then I returned to my

English assignment and the safety of my own room. Though I knew it wasn't truly safe, it still felt better to pretend it was.

Toby left me to my homework and rifled through some of my books. I was embarrassed at the collection of romance novels I owned. When I was finished, I couldn't deny the need to use the washroom any longer. It had grown as the hours dragged on, but I didn't want to leave my room. The extra chair was pressed up against my doorknob, as I'd seen in many movies where the occupants of a room wanted to keep something out. It seemed to work fifty percent of the time on those shows, so it seemed something worth using, despite my brother's insistence that it wouldn't. To remove it willingly seemed like asking for trouble.

I stood up and stretched, wondering if I could get away with quickly zipping to the bathroom and back before my brother or his wild friends made it down to check on me. I crossed my legs tight, holding against the mounting pressure, and hoped for relief.

"You have to go, don't you?" Toby asked as I looked in the direction of my barred door. I nodded slightly. "You know, I think I actually feel it too. Wow, you can hold your bladder a long time!" I looked over to my door again, not sure I was willing to risk it. Toby shook his head. "Listen, it's either this or crawl out your window and beg one of your neighbours to let you in to use their washroom, and that's if you make it out of the yard without being seen."

I knew he was right. My bedroom was just under the living room, where I could hear Jake and his friends hanging out. The living room had a huge bay window that the back door was right next to—I'd be seen in an instant and caught almost as quickly. My legs still shook with the idea of leaving the safety, imagined or not, of my room.

"Trust me," Toby insisted, "nothing bad will happen."

"Are you sure?" I asked, biting down hard on my lip.

"I promise."

I didn't think that was really good enough, but I had to do something or suffer the consequences. I decided to chance making a run for the washroom. Once there, Toby stepped into the tub and pulled the shower curtains closed. As soon as I had my pants down, I heard two loud voices on the stairs.

"Toby, you promised!" I said in a panicked and squeaky voice.

"Just relax, I've got your back on this one," he assured me.

I heard the two outside the washroom. They were both guys that had been Jake's friends from the beginning, and one of them would stare at me and make kissing noises whenever I looked his way. My gut squirmed. Someone tried to open the door.

"Don't make a sound," Toby instructed from behind the curtain. "You will be fine if they don't think it's you in here."

Make a sound? I couldn't even breathe.

"Hey!" one of them yelled as he pounded on the door. I kept my mouth and eyes shut tight. *What would they do if they caught me? Would Jake stop them?*

"Maybe it's J-boy's pretty sister," the other said. That was Nick. I could tell by his high-pitched, whiny voice. The pounding got louder.

If I could have stopped my heart from beating, in case it was at all audible, I would have, but then the knocking stopped, and I heard someone say, from further down the hall at my bedroom door, "You in there, pretty?" I heard a scraping sound and a bump as they tried to open my door, and for some reason they didn't get in.

"Aw, she's hiding in there." Nick sounded disappointed. "Must be Bib in here," he said, giving the washroom door one last thump.

"C'mon, lets get outta here, before J-boy thinks we were trying to mess with his baby sister again. He'd kick us right out on our asses like Mims." Finally I breathed a sigh of relief as I heard their heavy steps going upstairs.

"Now, hurry up and do your thing before anyone else comes!" Toby said.

"Who was Mims?" Toby asked as I was getting comfortable under the blankets. My homework now lay finished on my desk.

"A friend of Jake's." I was taken aback by this question and stammered a moment, trying to find my breath. "Why?"

"Well, because I heard them say something about him as we hid in the washroom." *Why did he have to bring up Mims?*

"So what?" I snapped. I didn't like where this was going, and I really wanted Toby to stop. I blinked back the memory that threatened to surface through my thoughts.

"Well, your brother kicked him out." Toby squinted like he was trying to see me better.

"Ya, again I say: so!" This time I was begging him with my eyes to stop, but he might have missed my look in the dusk darkness that filled my room. It was closing in on eleven. My mom had finally returned, and after some loud words, Jake's friends had left. As far as I could tell, he had come down to bed. His music beat through the wall that we shared.

"Why did he kick Mims out?" Toby reached out and gave my knee a nudge.

"Toby, it's late, and I really don't want to be talking about my loser brother and his gang of loser friends." I crossed my arms.

"But I wanted to point something out…well, two things."

"Why?" I felt like I was close to crying again. Mims smiled and leered in my mind's eye.

"Because I think you missed them, and you really need to know."

"Fine. Make your point so I can go to sleep." But by now I was so far from tired, I felt I could have stayed awake all night and not had to sleep again until the next evening.

"Alright." Toby shifted. He was sitting at the foot of the bed. My legs were behind him, and though he still didn't crease the bed sheets, I could feel him move against my feet. "First, this proves that you are worthy of admiration."

"What?" *I mean what! How could he really believe that? He'd seen more of me than most, and that only gave him a bigger picture of my flaws!*

"Well, forgive me, but your brother's friends, scummy though they are, do live in a very real world, and a lot of them, believe me, *a lot*, seem to be interested in looking at you. I was watching tonight as you made their meal and cleaned up before they started to get too rough. I'm not saying you should go for any of them. They're scum, and you'd be safer if your brother didn't bring them around, but if you weren't pleasing to their eyes in some way, they wouldn't be acting that way."

"I'm not so sure," I huffed. "They seem to be the type of boys that like to get a rise out of anyone they can. They could just be trying to have fun with me, making me think I'm all that."

"Doesn't make sense to me," Toby argued. "No, guys will hardly ever say a girl is pretty if they don't believe she is. In fact, most often they are willing to lie the other way around! A lot of the time, we guys will say a girl is downright ugly, even though we don't think they are."

I sat up so quick it made him jump. "Why? Why do you do that?"

"Because we are just as insecure as anyone. If our friends don't like a girl, or if we like her, but just don't know how to approach her, we'll put her down. It's not the smartest plan, but we're not so smart all the time."

"So, what you are trying to tell me is that if I'm being lunged after by my brother's druggy friends, that means I look good."

"Ya, and also that you shouldn't believe everything the boys at school say. At least half of them are probably lying."

"No way!" I shook my head so hard it made the bed shake.

"Believe me." Toby slapped my foot, and the chill raced along my spine. "You just trust me, I'll tell you tomorrow all the boys that are lying. I seem to be able to sense these things now." He smiled like he was proud of this ability. His perfect and straight teeth shone in the dark room.

"I don't know if I can trust you on this one," I said. "Not now, and not tomorrow, even if you point them out to me." I lay back down and got my head comfortable on my pillow. "What was the second thing?"

"Oh ya, your brother cares about you a lot."

I shook my head and laughed in disbelief. *Ya, threatening me and treating me like I was his own personal slave maiden, sure he cared for me!*

"What did Mims do to you?"

"Why do you think he did something to me?" I blinked. Mims was waiting on the inside of my eyelids; it gave me a chill.

"I know he did." Toby placed his hand around my toes.

I shook my head. Even thinking about it now, nine months after the fact, made tears leap to my eyes. "It was nothing," I said, turning so that I wouldn't be noticed wiping my eyes on my pillow.

"No it wasn't, it was something, and you didn't deserve to be treated that way, but I won't bug you any more tonight." I felt his fingers close around the toes on my left foot; quickly the chill from his touch subsided and was replaced with soft warmth, and as I drifted off to sleep, that warmth seemed to envelop my whole body.

DAY 3 Wednesday...

THIS NIGHT'S DREAMS WERE FILLED WITH DREAD AND HORRORS that I had endured in the past, without uttering a word to anyone. Mims visited me several times as the night wore on, first in the kitchen, where he used to sit with me while he waited for my brother to get home. He'd watch me with those piercing eyes, narrowing — never giving a clue to what he was thinking about, just staring relentlessly. Then he followed me through my dreams to school, where he stood behind bushes, trees and around corners just watching, never stopping. And finally, when I couldn't hide from him at school, he followed me home, where he cornered me in the storage closet. How I wanted to scream, to shout out, but I couldn't. Mims had his hand too tightly over my mouth, and what good would it have done? There was no one else home to save me, there never was...

I woke tangled in the bed sheets from thrashing about all night. Toby sat atop my desk. One leg dangled off, and the other was perched so his knee came up to his chest. His elbow was on his knee, and his face rested in his hand. He was wide-eyed and seemed to be watching me closely.

"What time is it?" I asked, turning to see my clock radio, but it was facing away from my bed.

"Six," Toby answered, not removing his hand. It concealed his whole right cheek, and as I looked closer, there seemed to be a light grey outline under his hand.

"Something wrong?" I felt like I was missing something important.

"You punched me last night." He said with a hint of shock.

"I did not!" I retorted indignantly. *I would never do such a thing!*

"You did, in your sleep," he argued but kept his face hidden.

"Oh?" I sat up.

"And," Toby lowered his hand to reveal a dark bruise that covered much of his whole cheek, "well, you were able to hit me."

I was aghast; I didn't know what to say. I felt guilty and ashamed, and I wished more than ever that I could get away from him. How was I going to look at him ever again without feeling horrible for what I had done? Toby moaned and looked away as if to punctuate my sentiments.

"I was sleeping, quite nicely," he started to explain, touching his jaw tenderly from time to time. "I think I was dreaming about me, my life, but it's nothing I could remember now, even though I'm trying. Anyway, suddenly I feel this whump, and I mean it was like someone had hit me with a brick. You know, you got a lot of strength behind your punch." He flashed me a smile. "So I get up, and you're just going at it, punching and kicking. I moved away before you could clip me again." He rubbed his jaw again. "I tried to wake you, but that just got you more upset."

"I'm sorry," I said, lowering my eyes. *I'd never punched anyone before in my life!*

"No worries, the pain makes me feel real." I snuck a glance to see that he was smiling when he said this. "Besides, no one will see it and bruises go away with time."

"I guess they do," I said. I didn't want to face him, or the day that lay ahead of me. Dread made my heart feel heavy.

"Well this kind of bruise goes away." He hopped down from my desk and held out a hand to help me out of bed. I accepted it wearily. "Oh, I took the liberty of picking you out some nice clothes for today," he said once I was standing. "I put them on your chair."

I looked over at them. It was my tightest pair of jeans; the ones that made me feel like I couldn't hide in, as well as a shirt with a plunging collar that had a fanned waistline. I didn't want to even try it on. I knew I'd feel too exposed in them.

"Give it a shot, and if it doesn't look good, I'll tell you." He continued to hold my hand. "I just think that if you were to wear more stylish clothing, you might get a different response from your peers. You do have some positive features. It would help if you showed them off a little."

"I don't want to," I said, pulling my hand from his. I looked at the pile of clothes in disgust. "I don't think dressing like the girls in my class will make me any better off."

"These are not to make you look like the girls in your class." Toby seemed offended. "I wouldn't want you to try and show off like them, I just want you to look like a girl."

"I *am* a girl." *I didn't need to expose my breasts for people to know I was one!* "I have all the right parts, and I don't need to show them off to look like I am one." I heard my voice getting louder and worried that I might wake my family, so I tried to speak more quietly.

"You don't look like a girl when you wear baggy sweatpants and oversized sweaters. You look like a very chunky boy!"

I couldn't believe he said that! I was hurt and offended. "Turn! I'm changing," I spat. He obliged. And instead of putting on the outfit that he had picked, I deliberately got back into the clothes I'd worn the previous day. When I let him turn back, he was obviously disappointed, but didn't say a word.

Upstairs, I started to clean up the mess from my brother's party, and Toby asked, "Why do you clean up when it isn't even your mess?" I had a bucket, and I was collecting bottles and broken glass in it.

"Because if I don't, then no one will," I answered bitterly, hating my life. There was a soft tinkling sound as I threw another piece into the pail.

"But that's not your problem," Toby said, standing right where I was trying to clean. I stopped and looked up at him. "Stop," he said. "Just have breakfast, and let's walk to school."

I couldn't understand myself, but I listened to him. I had always wanted to do that, but I knew there would be consequences. I ate only one bowl of cereal before I packed my bag and headed out the front door to school.

I thought of how Toby couldn't eat, him being… *A ghost?* Well, him being not alive at the least. "Do you miss food?" I asked.

"What a weird question," he said, looking over at me. "But come to think of it, not really."

"I would, I think."

"Why's that?"

"Because it's so good, I mean c'mon, doughnuts! And ice cream, and gummy bears and soda pops. They are about the best tasting things in the world, not to mention fudge and cola, and best of all, licorice. No. Popcorn. I could eat popcorn for breakfast, lunch and dinner!"

"But nothing you just mentioned is actually food," he said.

He was right, and I knew it. "Well what about spaghetti? Or burritos? I'm not talking the kind you get at 7-11. My father once took us out for a real Mexican meal, and it was so great. He used to take us out once a month." I paused. "Have you ever had sushi? It's the best…" I trailed off, because that was the last place he had taken the family to eat out. Since he left, Mom, Jake and I hadn't ever gone out for dinner again. I missed those meals with everyone together, and thinking about it made my thoughts dark and cold.

"Okay, I see your point." Toby's soft voice broke into my misery. "I don't need food, so I hadn't really thought of it."

"It doesn't matter." My heart ached and I wanted to get away. "You probably can't remember eating, so what would you miss about it?" I asked, quickening my pace.

"Actually, I remember pizza." I stopped and turned. He went three steps, then slowed down and looked back at me. "Coming?"

"Pizza?" I quizzed as I came alongside of him again.

"Ya, yesterday morning, when you were eating that leftover slice." He scratched the back of his neck, ruffling the hairs around his hand. "There used to be this really great pizza place near my school, and I would go there…with friends…ya, and they served one of the best deep dish pizzas you could ever imagine."

"Do you remember your friends? Do you remember where you went to school?"

"Nope, just the pizza. It was really good."

"Better than your friends!" I knew I liked food better than friends, mainly because I didn't have friends. "And if it was that good, don't you miss it?"

"I think I had good friends, but I still can't remember them. And no, really, I enjoyed the pizza, but I don't miss it. I can enjoy the memory of something and not miss now what I had then."

We neared the schoolyard. My two most dreaded places at school were the front steps, where all the "cool" kids hung out and smoked, and the girls' washroom. Both were "high attack" areas, and both had too many past incidents attached to them already. As we walked up the steps that day, and of course I say we, but no one there saw anyone other than me, I endured the same ridicule I'd heard for over two years, only now someone noticed that I was dressed in the same outfit as the day before. I think it was Effie. She didn't smoke because she had asthma, but that didn't stop her from being considered cool and able to hang out there with the rest of the "cool-junkies."

"Look, Mariah hasn't changed! She really is an elephant. Elephants don't change their skin, and neither does Mariah." This comment incited peals of laughter that followed me into the school.

As we got in, and the door swung shut behind me, Toby said softly in my ear, "You may be the one being called an elephant, but her saying it is like the pot calling the kettle black." I gave a sad smile and headed toward my locker. All I could wonder was whether it would have been better to wear what Toby had picked out, *or would it have been worse?*

It didn't take long before Toby was talking in my ear again. We passed a group of boys. They were the "techies," or "nerds," as everyone called them. To be honest, a few of them were not bad-looking. I mean some had zits and a few were too skinny, and one was too tall, but as outcast as they were, I still fell far below them in the social pecking order. So they too took their shots at me. "Godzilla approaches," was uttered a couple of times. I guess they hadn't heard "elephant" yet.

But as I thought that thought, Toby leaned in—I couldn't figure out why he was being so quiet about it. No one else could hear him—and he said, "The tall one likes you." This caught me so off-guard that I quickly glanced back at him. The tall boy was just as quick to look down the hall in the opposite direction. "I know you think this means he doesn't, but trust me, he was all eyes for you before you looked back. Maybe next time, don't be so obvious about checking, okay?"

I gave an almost unnoticeable nod as we stopped beside my locker. Then I grabbed my book and we made it to homeroom well before the first bell. Being my routine whenever I was early, I picked out a romance novel from my bag and started to read. I was the only person in the class for over five minutes, and then Elijah came in. He too was sort of an outcast, but still not as low on the pole as I stood. However, he was far enough down that he had never picked on me, at least not that I knew of.

It was less than a minute after he'd taken his seat that Toby was whispering in my ear again. "He really likes you." This time I took a moment, then snuck a glance over my book. I caught Elijah looking at me, but he quickly looked down at his desk. My heart skipped a beat. He was cute in a boyish way, with brown curls that fell like springs over his face and dark blue eyes. He was only an inch or so taller than me. I'd tower over him if I ever wore heels or platforms. He had high cheekbones and deep red lips, not a freckle on his face, but one beauty spot halfway along his right jaw.

I had to stop studying him, for I felt the colour rising in my face, but I positioned myself so I could watch him out of the corner of my eye and still look like I was reading. Sure enough, Elijah looked up from his notes three more times to stare at me for a moment or two. *It made my breath catch. Why?*

I wasn't sure if I was altogether comfortable with this. I suddenly thought of my hair, the black mess of tangles that cascaded down my head no matter how hard I tried, and never looked right to me. And my washed-out face. *I really should start wearing some make-up,* I thought. Then I desperately wished I'd worn the clothes Toby had wanted me to. *Why had I been so stubborn?*

As if reading my thoughts, Toby said, "Don't worry about it, you already 'wow' him."

Carefully, I took the paper with yesterday's note on it out of my desk, my fingers fumbling, and wrote, "What do you mean by 'wow' him?" Toby read it, and then I folded it up and placed it in my book.

"He likes you. That's clear, otherwise he wouldn't be looking at you. But he likes you for more than looks, although he notices them too." Toby looked long and hard at Elijah, like he was trying to read something from far way, then he continued. "He likes you because once or twice, when you were feeling brave, you made him laugh."

He really liked me? I blushed and hoped that Elijah wasn't watching at that moment. I took the paper out and wrote in my smallest writing, "How do you know this, and are you sure it's true?" Once Toby had read it, I hid the paper in my book again.

"I'm not sure, but I sort of get these flashes of memories, I think, just specific moments and sometimes a feeling. They are his, because it only happens when I concentrate on a specific person, and I've been kind of focusing on him for a while."

I took out the paper again and wrote smaller than I had before. "What sort of things did I do that made him laugh?" And as an afterthought, "Do you see or get those feelings from me too?" I wanted to ask him so much more, but the bell rang, and I got nervous having the paper out. I didn't even wait to see if Toby had read it all before I hid it back in my book and shoved it in my bag.

Toby waited for everyone to settle and all the teacher's announcements to be done, and then after she had dismissed us for our first period, he answered. "Were you ever in drama with him?" I gave a curt nod; I was one of the last ones to leave the class, so no one was behind me to see it. "Well, he really enjoyed a short monologue you did. And also there was a time when you had to be his partner for an improv. He found you fun to work with." We continued to walk down the hall, up a flight of stairs and over to my science classroom. "You didn't take drama this year," Toby said. "Why not?"

I turned to glare at him as I took my seat. I was not about to be baited into answering. I had taken drama my first year, because I had transferred halfway through the semester, and it was one of the few electives still open, and I had enjoyed it, so I had taken it again. However, at the end of the second year, I embarrassed myself so much in the class doing a skit that I vowed never to take it again. Now, in grade ten, I had opted for industrial shop and home economics. I sucked at shop and regretted ever choosing it, but it was too late now to do anything about it.

Toby pointed out three more boys that found me interesting during science, but not with quite as much detail. Two he flat out said were only in it for the looks. *What looks?* He said he just wanted to prove his point that

I was not as ugly as I perceived myself. *Even though he had said this morning that no one could tell I was a girl!*

I started to feel self-conscious and really began to wish he'd stop, as with each mounting "looker," I was finding it harder and harder to concentrate. Finally I became so distracted that I spilled the chemical mixture down my sweater, and the teacher had to send me to the washroom to get cleaned up. She was furious. My lab partner made a snide comment that was too low for the teacher to hear—"Clumsy elephant." I left feeling disgraced and wondered if those three boys were watching me leave. How did they feel about me now? Not so hot, I figured…

In the washroom, I sat in the stall. Toby was thankfully able to stand just outside, and I tried to calm my frayed feelings.

"Just take the sweater off," he said, tapping on the door. "The shirt you're wearing under it is very nice." I didn't want to listen to him, and I wasn't about to take his advice while I was feeling so upset. His voice whispered right in my ear, and I knew he had closed his eyes. "What is it really that has gotten you so upset?"

"You can open your eyes. I'm fully dressed," I said, not feeling comfortable with him so close again. He did and moved to stand against the inside of the stall door. We were still really close, but at least he wasn't able to touch me.

"You're making me feel all self-conscious with your reports about who is looking at me!" I said, quite a bit louder than I had intended. I guess all this holding my tongue had built up.

"Why?" he asked, looking innocent. His chocolate eyes danced.

"Because they *are* looking at me!" I said, exasperated. *Why would they want to look at me?*

"But they were looking at you before I said anything. I'm not making them look, I'm just pointing it out." Toby smiled.

I couldn't argue with that. "Ya, well!" was all I managed to say, and then I had to collect my thoughts. I pinched the bridge of my nose, something I'd seen one of my favourite actors do in a movie when she got upset. "I was blissfully unaware before, and now you have me doubting everything about myself." I crossed my arms.

"Does it upset you that I told you? Or are you more upset that they're looking?"

I wasn't sure which it was… After I thought about it, I knew it was the latter. *How could they find me attractive? I was ugly! They had no right to steal peeks!* But I couldn't be mad at Toby for their looking.

"Can I say something?" he asked tentatively. "I noticed these same boys looking at you yesterday, and I'm sure that it wasn't the first time. I just thought it would be good for you to know that you're being admired, even from afar. I mean, you are so down on yourself about your looks that I thought it would help for you to see yourself through someone else's eyes."

"But you're not giving a full spectrum. You only tell me when I'm admired, what about those that detest me?" The ones that recognized my true hideousness and thought I could be in a carnival where people pay to see the world's most ugly human!

"You'd be surprised—there aren't as many as you seem to think there are."

I breathed out a "humph" of disbelief. "You must not be paying close attention to everyone then!" I crossed my arms tighter.

"No, I've been watching everyone," he assured me. "I can even see the truth behind Effie and her lackeys. They don't despise you. In fact, as I explained yesterday, they're scared of you." He nodded, still smiling.

Now I knew he was wrong! "What?"

"It's true. Most kids don't even pay attention to you, and those that do are either trying to prove their status or are truly fearful of your potential. You have a lot to give, especially when you were in drama. You have so much more skill than Effie and any one of the kids that hang with her. You are also a better student in typing, and you have a wonderful smile. I've only seen it once, but it is killer. That is why they try to cut you down, they want to keep you down before you get a chance to get up!"

"And you know all this because you know it?" I scoffed. *Being dead must have addled his brain!*

"I know this because I see it in all the kids. When I pick them out of the crowd, I can sense it. But I also get the feeling that it was a part of my former life."

"You remember your life now?"

"Not yet, but what I told you feels familiar in some way, so I can only figure that it was a part of my life."

"Do you think you were scoffed at like me? Or perhaps someplace in the middle, not popular, but not the bottom of the barrel. Just low enough that you felt like an outcast too?" I found the idea of his life fascinating and a nice distraction from my own.

"I don't know. That doesn't matter right now. My life is over. Yours, on the other hand, is happening as we speak."

I didn't like how quickly we had gotten back to the subject of me again, but I knew the bell for class change was about to sound, and I had to gather myself together and get on with it. As I stood, I pulled off my sweater. The shirt clung a little at my bumpy waist, but it had a moderate neckline that revealed my chest. Toby smiled at this, like it was an improvement, but he kept his thoughts to himself. I stepped from the stall and went to wash my face in the sink. When I was finished, I tried to straighten my frizzled hair without luck, and headed for the door.

"You are going to have to face Effie now," Toby said as I reached for the handle. Within a moment, it was lurched out of my hand and opened up onto not just Effie, but also two of her friends. I gulped. I usually avoided the washrooms for this very reason.

For a moment Effie and I just stood looking at each other. She seemed slightly taken aback, then found her lost voice. "Godzilla," she said like it was a proper greeting, and for the first time it didn't seem as hurtful, or to inflict the kind of fear that usually shook me to my very core. I nodded then stepped past her and her friends into the hall that was filling with students off to their next classes.

Toby returned to my side a moment later. "You didn't get to hear what she and her friends said as you left, did you?"

I put my head down as I walked up the hall to the stairway

"You missed something great." Toby seemed excited, but he didn't say anything else.

I wanted to ask what, but I was still fearful of sounding like a raving lunatic, so I kept my mouth shut and went to my locker. I deposited my sweater; it was ruined, unless I could wash the chemical mess out. I was disheartened. That sweater was like my security blanket, and I was afraid to let it go, but I did. I grabbed my books for the next two classes, and Toby followed me there without uttering another word. It wasn't until I was in the lunch line-up that he found his voice again.

Our school cafeteria was located on the ground floor of the second building. It had one main entrance and five exits. Upon walking in, you had to pass the refreshments display, then the payment counter. You weren't allowed to leave through the entrance unless the bell sounding the end of lunch had rung. From the payment counter, the room opened to the size of three classrooms filled with picnic tables that could comfortably fit four students on either side. Some tables were pushed together so larger groups of friends could visit. Two of the walls had no windows or doors and were painted an awful green colour. The other two walls had windows that let in loads of natural light. Out of one group of windows, you could see the outdoors eating areas.

"In math you had three admirers," Toby announced as I was picking up my tray. "I decided not to tell you while we were in class, because you said that it distracted you, and I respect that. I'm not going to point out any more to you, but I wanted to let you know that they're everywhere. In fact, you had the most admirers in wood shop. Five guys; one was particularly into looking at you, but that could have something to do with losing that parachute of a sweater, so I guess I've proved my point now, and we don't need to argue about it any more." He wore a huge goofy grin, as if to say, "I win."

I shrugged as I took my favourite seat at a table in the far corner. I was beside a window that faced the track. I was usually never bugged there, so I could sit on my own. That was unless it was Thursday, and Ms. Telz was on duty. She never kept a good eye on what the kids were up to, so the bullies could really make someone like me miserable. I tried to avoid the cafeteria on those days.

I sat with one side to the wall, the other facing the rest of the room; this way I could watch the door, but I had my back to the window. I liked it when the sun was shining, because I would feel warmed, but it was a disadvantage, because sometimes the kids outside would try and scare me by banging something against the outside wall, if the teacher was far enough away not to notice. Yet all in all, this was the safest spot for me in the whole room.

Elijah and his group of friends sat three tables away. They were often referred to as "artsy-fartsy's," and sometimes the first part was left off their name to be a greater insult. Toby sat on the table with his back to me, facing the whole lunchroom. He seemed distracted by something. I figured he was just sneaking glances at the other kids' thoughts and memories, or picking out how many were admiring me, but no one I could see was looking my way, not even Elijah.

When I was done with my food, I pushed my tray off to the side and took my novel out of my bag, but I had no intention of reading. I slipped out our communication paper from the back of the book and started to write. "What did I miss with Effie and her friends?" Toby didn't seem to notice me. I sat up and looked right at him for what seemed like forever, but he didn't even acknowledge me. I carefully shifted over with my elbow to bump him. A shock shot up my back with the contact. Toby jumped from my touch and turned to face me.

I was really concerned now, knowing many people were secretively watching me, so I didn't want to make any sudden move that could be taken the wrong way. Toby turned but missed the note I had slid just slightly in his direction, so I rolled my eyes, then looked down at the table, tapping my pencil.

"Oh!" he exclaimed. He bent forward and read while I tried to look as if I might be working on some homework, something I often did. He straightened with a grin playing on his lips. "Got you curious, did I?"

I felt like I was a mouse, and he was the cat who had cornered me; or was I the cat and he a bear? Curiosity kills the cat after all. It wasn't a nice feeling either way. I took a deep breath and wrote "yes". I wanted to add "What did you think?" and a whole host of other things, but more than that I wanted him to get on with what I had missed.

Toby seemed to get the picture. "Well, Effie said to her friends, 'I guess I can't call her elephant any more.' And one of her friends, the other overweight one, said more under her breath, 'Ya, and probably not even Godzilla either.' But Effie didn't catch that. No matter what, you threw all three of them off, even her thin friend. She bit her tongue when she saw you."

"Why would she do that?" I questioned.

"Do I have to spell it out for you again?" he asked, sounding more than a bit disappointed.

"I really need to hear it again, because it would make me feel a lot better. You know how much Effie's hurt me, don't you?" I slid the note back and waited.

Toby sighed. "She's only hurt you as much as you let her," he said. Then he leaned back on his elbow and scanned the cafeteria. "They're mean to you because they're trying to make you feel bad so that you won't amount to anything." He breathed deep and turned to face me. "But you're the only person that can prove them wrong, by not letting them get to you and by being all you can be."

Tears welled up in my eyes. Not caring how I would look to others, I hid my face in my arms on the table and shook as I tried to regain control of my emotions. Did he understand how hard it was to not let them get to me? *I was only one girl, with no one, not one person telling me anything nice about myself!*

I heard the pain in his voice as he put his hand on my back and said, "Mariah, I'm sorry." He left his hand there, and it warmed me more than the sun shining through the window ever had. I stayed like that until the bell sounded, signaling the end of lunchtime.

Toby didn't touch me again, but he stayed glued to my side through PE, then during English he knelt by my desk and watched as I completed my assignment. "You have nice printing," he commented. *Like that was worth anything.* Or, "You are very creative in your writing." *I did enjoy writing.* I didn't acknowledge him, more for fear of being noticed than anything else, but he didn't seem to mind, and he kept making kind observations. "You got that right, no one else in this room did." I had to smile just a bit at that.

English was one of my favourite classes. Mrs. Lavender was always nice to me, and she didn't even dock marks if I misspelled a word. She had a strict "the content is more important" policy. It gained me great status in her class, but I had even learned to shy away from that, for when I seemed to succeed in an area, those around me would become even more intent on trying to take it away. This got me thinking about what Toby was trying to tell me, and as it resonated through me it started to feel more and more like truth.

When school was over, I decided to walk home. With my books put away in my locker and my ruined sweater in my hand, I headed out the front door, down the steps and past all the "in crowd" kids that had started to congregate there. I didn't try and dart past them as I usually did, but I took my time—not too much though, and I looked straight ahead instead of keeping my eyes on the ground. Well, I didn't have my head so high that I would be mistaken as pompous, and I did glance at the ground as I passed someone, but only because I didn't want to be tripped, a mean trick that they would play on any unsuspecting soul.

Once we were on a side street and I was sure we were alone, I started up a conversation. "I think I will wear the clothes you picked for me tomorrow," I said. My chest swelled with a feeling of confidence for the first time that I could remember.

"They'll look very nice on you, I'm sure," he said, and even though he seemed distracted I didn't care; I had to keep talking.

"But they won't show off too much?" I asked, feeling slightly less self-confident.

"No, they're still respectable." His eyes were filled with pain. It frightened me, but I didn't know why.

"Good." I breathed a sigh of relief. I didn't want to compete for attention, and I especially didn't want to look like some of the girls who show off everything. Those were the girls that I was sure were also letting the boys touch them everywhere, and I was a strict "hands off" girl, because I'd watched enough shows to see that doing that for attention didn't get you anything in the end. But more so, the thought of being touched in that way just made me ill.

"Why don't you have more nice clothes?" Toby asked. We were walking down a quiet street, with just a faint scent of late blossoms in the air. It was still nicely warm out; we'd had a very mild fall so far.

"I don't know," I answered. "Perhaps because I wouldn't wear them? I really feel safe in my sweat pants and loose tops, but my mom buys my clothes, so I don't get to choose much."

"Why does she buy your clothes?" He shook his head in disbelief.

"I've never thought about that before…she just always has, and I never asked if I could. When I was littler, we used to go together, but now she's just too busy to take me, so she gets me what I need if I put it on the list." *That's just how it had been since my father left.*

"How does she know your size? Or what you like to wear?" Toby seemed more concerned than I thought he should, which made me think it over myself.

"I'm not sure…Well, I sorta know. When I grow out of a shoe size, I'll just say 'sneakers' and put the next size up for her to get. Once that didn't work, so I went to the store and sized my foot, then I was able to tell her precisely 8½. For my clothes, I usually give her the size of my jogging pants. You can't go really wrong with an elastic waist. And for my tops, I always tell her two sizes bigger than I need. Sometimes she picks out things with the sizes I've given her, but that's rare. Actually, that's how I got those jeans. There was this one time when she was trying to encourage me to lose some weight, and she bought me everything one size smaller than I asked for, but I refused to wear any of those clothes, so she never tried that again."

"You really should go shopping and try on some of the clothes. I think you'd be able to find nicer things that you might like better."

"I don't know," I said again, feeling tired and wondering why it really mattered. *It was only clothes.*

"You are how old?" he asked.

"Just turned fifteen," I answered.

"Don't you think you should decide what you wear at your age, not your mother?" He sounded appalled.

"But she's got all the money." I was once told to be happy for whatever she decided to give me, and I remembered it well.

"That shouldn't matter. You could go out and get a job if you needed money of your own. Don't you want to be independent?"

I stopped and thought about what he was saying, and it all made sense. *Why hadn't I ever put this together?* I was fifteen, not a child any more! *Even though she hadn't celebrated my birthday for the last six years, that didn't mean I hadn't grown.*

Toby didn't notice that I'd stopped walking, so he made a sort of comical jolt as he reached seven feet away. He slowly retraced his steps until he was standing right in front of me. "What?"

I held up a finger to indicate that I was thinking. What I was really doing was scrutinizing my life. Why had I been so blind to my fate? I wasn't going to be stuck in that house with my overly busy, self-indulged mother forever, nor with my violent, verbally abusive brother. Why hadn't I been able to see that before? A distant light appeared, like I was on a train in a tunnel, and finally I could see the end, though it was still far away. Regardless, it now was in sight. I felt foolish for thinking life was so hopeless only two days prior. *Was it just two days ago*? Life had seemed so dark then, and now, in comparison, it felt bright and alive, with a flame—albeit a small one—of hope.

"You really don't even know yourself," he said. He looked at me with his dark, piercing eyes; Toby, in his tight black shirt, his loose pants and those threadbare white socks.

"Know what?" I said, shaken back to that moment.

"You don't know who you are, what you like, all your skills, anything that is good about you."

"You don't know anything about your own life!" I retorted.

"Yeah? But I'm not the one who's supposed to be living here!" he said, but he faltered. He ran his hand through his hair and licked his lips. "Mariah, you have so many skills, so many talents. I could see them the moment we met, but now I understand that anything outside of pain and misery are foreign to you."

He made my life sound so tragic, something they'd put on a daytime drama. I wanted to argue, so I said, "It's not all that bad."

"Really?" he challenged. "Give me three things that you can see are good in you or your life." He held three fingers up.

"There are some really good shows on TV," I said quickly, "and I know you don't miss the food, but it's really quite delicious!" I struggled for a moment, and then added, "And I've got some great books to read."

Toby shook his head. I was feeling feeble about my answers too, but if I dwelled on anything else, it just felt like I was falling down a cliff with razor-edge rocks that I'd scrape against, cutting me to shreds until my insides were out, and there would be nothing left of me.

"I understand now," he said softly, but it didn't feel like he was saying it to me. It was more like he was saying it to the air around us.

I hated the way he was looking at me; pity showed all too clearly on his face, but his eyes mirrored the deep well of sorrow that I could feel in my heart. "It's not that bad," I said, trying to ease his look.

This only made him look sad and more hurt. "No," he finally said. "It's worse. But I can help you, like I said. I know now that this is why I am here."

I wanted to get mad at him again. It infuriated me that he thought he could help, but an even more powerful emotion welled up from a deep hidden spot within: I felt like I was nine again, and I stood facing my father for the last time, his bags in his hand, and I wanted to cry out to him "don't go" and run to him and hug him so tight and never let him go.

Now I stood facing Toby, and I wanted to do the same to him. I could feel my eyes pleading with him, "Be right."

Toby closed his eyes against my stare, which made him disappear, only to re-appear within an inch of my face. I was so glad to see him that I reached out and embraced him, and though he seemed taken off-guard by my sudden action, the rigidity quickly melted away, and he wrapped his arms around me in response. I don't know how long we stood there. I wonder what it would have looked like had anyone come walking past, but I felt safe, and mercifully I was spared any intrusion on this tender moment. Eventually the feeling passed, and more importantly the need for it did as well.

I let go of him, my ghost friend who felt more real to me than anything in my life at that moment. He seemed to not want to let go, but he did. As we continued home I felt a refreshing of my resolve, like that hug had breathed life into me, and now I was more than an empty shell walking around just filling in time on this wretched earth. I called my mom's work and demanded to talk to her at once. *I was her daughter. I deserved at least a few minutes of her time!*

She sounded panicked when she came on the phone. "Mariah? What is it, are you all right?"

Slightly taken back by her response, I hesitated. Toby put his hand on mine, and that gave me courage to go on. "Yes, something is very wrong," I answered.

I heard the panic rise in my mother's voice, "What is it? Is it Jake? Does he need help?"

"No, it's me, I need something," I said, losing steam as she uttered each new word of worry and fear.

"What's wrong?" And now I heard the tone of frustration creeping back into her voice. She was returning to the typical tone of overwhelmed exasperation that she reserved just for me.

I faltered again, and Toby swept my free hand up into his. "Don't let her scare you into silence; you've been quiet too long! Say something; she needs to know how you feel."

Tears threatened to fall; I could feel them forming a bubble in my throat, trying to stop any words from spilling forth. *I wouldn't cry; I just wouldn't let myself!*

"Is anything wrong, or are you just wasting my time?" she said, not restraining the contempt in her voice. Then I forgot everything I wanted to tell her. All I could see was that I'd now used up two minutes of her important time, and I knew her time was much more important to her than I was. "I'm going to hang up if you don't say something right now, and we'll have to talk when I get home."

I was shaking so much that the phone didn't rest on my ear any more. "Mariah," Toby said, waving a hand in front of my face so I'd look at him, "Tell her you are tired of being quiet."

"I'm…t-tired of, of b-being q-q-quiet," I said as I tried to keep my composure. I could feel my eyes sting and my vision blur.

"What are you talking about?" my mom asked, her voice hard and threatening.

"Tell her 'you didn't want to make her life hard, because you understood how tough things were.'" Toby continued to feed me words. I repeated what he said, only this time it was just a bit easier to say it, not as much stuttering and stammering.

"Mariah, can't this wait until I get home?"

"No!" I demanded. "You won't listen!" I felt nervous for talking to my mother this way, but I kept going. "You are always too busy with Jake or your work or other things."

"Yes," she snapped, "I *am* busy, you know I work hard so we won't go hungry, and your brother keeps getting himself into trouble, so I've got to take care of his mess." If I made her too angry, she could take away so much from me. I lost my nerve.

"Yes, but…" I started to stammer again. Now I was losing confidence.

"Tell her you sometimes need help dealing with your stuff too," Toby prompted.

"Mom," was all I could manage to say. But she held on, silently waiting on the other end of the phone. "I need you too," I finally said, feeling so vulnerable.

"Well, I'm busy now, so you will have to wait until I get back home." Her snappy business tone had returned, and before I could say anything else, she said, "Now, goodbye."

I dropped the cordless phone and fled to the safety of my room and the comfort of my bed sheets. I buried my head in my pillow, feeling scared and frustrated. *Why had I even tried?* Tears stung at the corner of my eyes, yet I didn't cry. *I never did.* Toby just sat as the hours went by, holding my feet tightly on his lap.

It was almost eight thirty when I heard my mom get home. I quickly got up and barred my door. She came storming down the stairs, and when the chair worked to stop her from getting in, she pounded on my door. "Mariah!" she shouted, "Talk to me, tell me what's going on!" she screamed at the top of her lungs.

"We're done talking!" I screamed back, feeling so angry that I could melt the door right off its hinges if I wanted to. I stood in the middle of my floor with my arms crossed in front of me. But truth be told, *I was terrified.*

Toby came to stand in front of me, his eyes narrowed. I gave him a "What?" kind of look.

"Come on. Really?" he said, shaking his head. "You wanted her to talk to you. To listen. Well you've got her full attention, use it."

"I want to have money to go shopping for my own clothes!" I said, slowly going over to my closed door. There was no way I'd open it. I was too scared of what she would do if she could reach out and grab me. I knelt on the chair and stayed there.

"Really?" she replied through the door. "Is that what this is all about?"

"Ya," I said shakily. I avoided looking over at Toby to see what he thought about this. I knew, and he knew, that this wasn't the real problem; my real problem, *being so lonely*, was too hard to talk about, because I just couldn't take it if I told her the truth and she rejected me again.

"How come you didn't just say that on the phone?" The anger in her voice was subsiding, but I still didn't feel safe opening my door. "Why couldn't you wait until I got home?"

"I was afraid I'd forget," I said, which was only partly true. The real truth was that I knew I'd lose the nerve to tell her everything, as I had. Things like: "Why didn't she miss dad like I did?" or "How come she put up with my brother?" yet, "I wasn't allowed to even get C's, let alone drop out of school." Now was my chance, and I stood biting my lip when I should have been telling her how I truly felt.

But the relief in her voice was enough to buy my silence for a little while longer. "Okay, I'll get you some money tomorrow on my way home from work, how does that sound?" I didn't have a response. "Say about $150, sound like enough to get what you want?" How was I supposed to know? I hadn't ever shopped for clothes, but I agreed. "And I'll just give you that much each month, alright, unless you find you need more." This last statement made me feel somewhat happy inside, so I wholeheartedly agreed and even said, "I love you, Mom," through the door.

I returned to bed feeling relieved. Toby looked a little green, but he came to sit next to me. "How do you feel?" he asked as he took my hand again.

"Tired," I said, then I pulled my hand away and lay down on the bed. In my dreams, I replayed the whole day in my head over and over again: the look on Effie's face when I was coming out of the bathroom; Elijah sneaking glances at me over his book; my mom giving me money every month to go shopping for my own clothes. These were all good things, and every time I went through them, I felt a bit stronger, a bit freer, a bit lighter, and a bit happier about myself, until I woke the next morning ready to face a new day.

DAY 4 Thursday...

As I got ready for school, Toby stayed quiet. He looked as if he hadn't slept well, but his eyes brightened when I told him he could turn around and he saw me in the clothes he'd picked out.

"I was right," he said, nodding in admiration, "you look great."

I wasn't sure I thought so myself as I stood in front of the dressing mirror that I had to get from my closet, where I had hidden it. My bottom was just a little too round, if you asked me, and I wasn't able to hide my massive stomach. I expressed my fears to him.

"Mariah, I know how much you want to hide your flaws. But the honest truth is they're not so bad. Besides, you have some features that are quite admirable."

I decided to trust him on this, but I had to ask one last time. "I'm not dressing like a tramp though?"

He stepped back to view the complete ensemble. "No, just beautiful."

Did he call me beautiful? I half-smiled and looked back into my mirror. That's when I noticed my hair. It was way out of control. "I'll have to take a shower this morning," I said, trying to smooth down the mile-high frizz.

Toby nodded. "Can you make sure you stay outside the curtain? No matter what!"

"Oh," he said, grinning, "you mean no closing my eyes!" His teeth shone, and his deep eyes danced.

"You betcha, buster!" I said, placing my hands on my hips. *I didn't know what I'd do if he ended up in there with me—naked!*

"Hey, I'm the dead one here," he said. "This may be my last chance to catch a peek." But he smiled then added, "You can trust me."

I didn't laugh, and he stayed true to his word

I grabbed my lunch money and found extra, with a note from my mother: "Here is your money for clothes this month. If you ever call me at work again when it isn't an emergency, I will take it all away!" I shoved the money in my pocket, feeling guilty about disturbing her. *Still, I had been successful... sort of. Today felt like it was going to be good!* It was the first day I'd felt this way in a very long time.

On our way to school, when we had walked about halfway, and we were on a street that was mostly two-storey houses with fences, Toby said hesitantly, "I remembered something about my life yesterday, but I'm not ready to share it yet."

"Oh, what?" It took a moment for what he'd said to sink in. "And why not?" *He remembered something yesterday, and it took him until now to tell me!*

"I need to figure out what it means," he said, "but I felt I had to be completely honest with you, so I wanted to tell you."

Why did he wait until today? "I wish you hadn't. Now I'm always going to be wondering and worrying about what you aren't telling me." *If he wasn't going to tell me everything, why had he said anything at all?* I kept my pace brisk, even though my legs felt heavy.

"That's not fair. I told you so you wouldn't think I was keeping things from you." He sounded frustrated.

"Ya, but now I know you *are* keeping something from me." I knew he was trying to do the right thing, but I hated not knowing.

"No matter what I did here, I'd be wrong," he said in a defeated tone and ran his hand through his hair.

"Why don't you just tell me now?" It seemed the only way to make things better.

"Because I don't want it to ruin everything."

Ruin everything! My heart pounded. *Now I was sure I needed to know.* "Is it so bad that it will change things between us?"

"It might." His voice sounded strained.

I stopped dead in my tracks. "I need to know," I said, not willing to budge until I was told. The sun hadn't quite had time to warm the chill from the air, and wet dew was still thick in the grass. I crossed my arms and stared at him.

"Mariah." Toby had stopped a foot away.

"No," I said with great determination. "I won't be happy until you tell me, and it will bug me all day! You owe it to me. You get to know everything about me, so I deserve the right to know whatever you know about yourself—and don't give me 'it's over,' because if you've remembered something, then it might not be as over as you thought!" I was amazed at how brave I felt. Only three days earlier, I would have accepted his excuses and let him be, but I would never have been happy with myself.

"I'm afraid to tell you," he said softly. "You are all I've got. You are my world, and I'm scared that if I tell you, you won't think of me in the same way any more. And I don't want you to hate me." I could see him begging me with his eyes.

"It's something I could hate you for?" My resolve hardened. "I have to know!"

"Alright." It sounded like telling me would actually physically hurt him, but I stayed steadfast in my resolve. I needed to hear this, and that mattered more than his discomfort. "It was yesterday in the lunch room."

Those words delivered a real punch to my gut. *He had known since then, and he was finally saying something now!* But I kept my thoughts to myself. I was angry, but I didn't want to distract him from telling me.

"I was watching the table near the door, where all the in-crowd comes to sit. It started with a particular guy at the table who had noticed you for the first time; I think it was because I'd convinced you to lose the sweater. Anyway, he was goofing around. You weren't much more than a passing fancy, but his friend caught him gazing over your way and confronted him about it. This friend is the leader of the pack, just like Effie is with the girls, well, he's her equal for the guys. But he confronted the guy that noticed you and asked why he was staring in your direction, and well, I won't mince words, what he said wasn't pretty, but it was all an act, see? And I was going over what I had told you in the washroom about why everyone treated you so rotten, and that it's really up to you how bad they make you feel, and wondering why it felt so familiar. Then it hit me!" He paused.

"Because you used to be the equivalent of the male me?" I wondered aloud. I wanted him to say yes. I could see why he would think that I'd be disappointed in him. It would make sense; he would feel the same contempt for himself that I felt about myself everyday. I knew that wasn't what he was going to tell me from the drawn-out pause before he answered.

"No, not really." He looked down, typical of someone making a confession. "I was that popular kid, like Effie, at the top of the chain. I was the one who decided who was in and who was out, and if I wanted to make someone's life miserable, I could, and no one would ever try to defy me. In fact, I could get anyone to do just about anything…"

My head spun, and my knees wobbled. I couldn't look at him, I felt so sickened. I turned away and even bent forward, so if I became ill, I wouldn't get it all over myself. I stayed that way for what seemed like an eternity. I could feel Toby hovering just a few feet away, and I loathed him. *Why him? He was my enemy.* He was the one that held me down so I couldn't get up and kept me so low I had no place to go.

The faces of everyone who'd ever been mean to me flashed in my mind, but they were replaced by Toby's. I straightened up and started to run. I wanted to escape him, and all he represented. *He was the reason I felt so miserable every day!* I wanted to get as far away from him as possible, though I knew it was futile. As my pace slowed, I knew that he would still be mere feet behind me.

Now my legs trembled with the exertion, and my lungs fought to pull in enough air. I felt the sting of the cool morning air on my cheeks. I kept walking at a brisk pace, not even turning to see if he was there. I knew he was. I could feel him, and it made my skin crawl! Sobs emanated from my throat as I felt renewed grief over my life.

"I'm sorry," he said, a few steps behind me. I could hear real misery in his voice. I kept walking, not giving him the courtesy of a response. *I wanted to make him as miserable as I felt. I wanted to make him pay.*

I felt his hand catch my wrist, and with surprising strength he held my arm, forcing me to stop in my tracks. Still, I didn't face him.

"Mariah," he said through clenched teeth.

I wouldn't give him the satisfaction of an answer. Instead I pulled against his grip. I even used my free hand to try and pry his fingers off.

"Please, talk to me," he pleaded.

I managed to break free from his grasp, but I lost my footing in the struggle and fell into the grass that formed the divider between the sidewalk and the street. I sat there shaking, partly from my own anger, partly from embarrassment.

Why? I wondered again over the bizarreness of our situation as my body began to feel more normal. The true irony of all this was becoming increasingly clear. He was no angel, with that statement I wholeheartedly agreed now, *but why was he here?* I had this boy, almost my own age, glued to me by some invisible force, and he had to care, but in his life he would never have paid me a second thought, unless it was for malice.

As I sat, I felt the damp from the ground seeping into my pants. Finally I pulled myself up, not indicating my own feelings, for I wasn't certain how I felt about any of it. As I started walking I heard him take a deep breath, and I put up my hand to let him know I didn't want to hear anything. The rest of the walk to school was more peaceful, apart from my sore legs and damp pants.

As I made my way up the front steps, past Effie and her groupies, I saw her eyes scan me head to foot. She didn't say anything until I had passed.

Then she squealed with delight. "My, Mariah!" she exclaimed, "Did you pee your pants?"

I hurried into the school before I could hear any more, shooting Toby a fierce look, as if he had taunted me himself. *If he had been alive, it would have been him!* He bowed his head and stared at the floor.

He didn't utter a word all throughout the day. I noticed that he stayed extraordinarily close to my side but still managed to give me space. Only as the day went on and more and more of the school caught on to Effie's new claim that I was a baby who peed my pants—even though my jeans had dried before the end of the first period—did I feel an increasing need for Toby. Despite who he had been when alive, he was now the only person I could count on my side.

He kept a watchful eye on me while continuing to watch everyone else. I guess he used the time to set his own thoughts straight. As I thought about it more and more throughout the miserable day, I was sure that to discover this truth about his past was a shock for him as well, especially after spending some time intimately in my life, and I started to marvel at how painful it must be from his angle.

I decided to forgive him, because though he represented in my head everyone who had ever been unkind to me, he had never done anything to me personally. *I could see that now.* I also realized, with some reservations, that I needed him.

My last class of the day was home economics, and as we had just finished a lesson on baking bread, we had a lot of free time at the end. I sat down and jotted out a few words on my note page: "Still shopping, looking forward to your help." This produced one of the widest grins I'd ever seen on Toby's face.

"Yes, I'll enjoy helping you," he said with enthusiasm. "And now we know I have some knowledge about these things," he added, and I curtly nodded as the last bell rang. Then I quickly erased our note and headed down to my locker.

As we made our way to the mall on the bus, I pulled out the paper and scribbled: "Do you remember anything else?"

Toby answered, "No, and to be honest, I don't remember that much other than I *was* the popular kid. I don't know anything about what I did, though I feel it in my gut that I was just as slimy and malicious as the rest of them. I haven't got any specifics, and honestly, I'm almost afraid of them. Things look a lot different from this side of life." He fell silent then.

Inside the clothing store, I didn't know where to begin. I wanted to ask Toby all sorts of questions, but I didn't dare in fear that I'd look like I was talking to myself, so I chose my words carefully and wrote: "I trust your judgment completely, so you tell me what's first."

Again he grinned, then blushed, "Sorry, but this is personal—you need to start with good bust support," he said and led the way to the bras. "Now, again I'm going to be pointed, the nicer the bra, the better it looks, whether us guys can see it or not, so try this one and this...and that." The last was a neon pink bra.

'You sure about that?' I wrote on our pad.

"Yes," he answered.

So I went and collected the three Toby had pointed out. I took my choices to the change room attendant; she was a short, plump woman with graying hair and kind hazel eyes. I said aloud, sort of to her, but more for Toby's benefit, "Don't you think this will show under some of my shirts?" I caught Toby's eye and winked.

"Probably, hon, you might want to be careful what you put over it," the attendant answered. She led the way to an empty change room and clipped a number to the knob.

I smiled my gratitude, and then Toby stated, "I'm the dead one here, yet you walk around like you can't see. Haven't you noticed that it isn't uncommon these days for your bra to be showing?" I closed the door behind us, thankful that there was no mirror in the small space.

I had the first bra on and was adjusting the straps as I braved whispering, "But again I ask, isn't that too much?"

"Well, you'll have to be tasteful. You don't want to be hanging out, but just one bra strap is all right. And you wouldn't want to wear a thin white shirt, but a pale yellow one or a light grey, where a soft outline showing a bit isn't too flashy." Toby scratched the back of his neck. "I used to like it when girls hinted at their assets. I didn't like the ones that would put out all their wares for show and tell. But I was very hard on the girls who were clueless about their beauty; you know the ones that would hide behind their clothes like they had nothing good to offer..." Toby turned around abruptly after he made that last statement. When he realized I was in nothing but the new bra, he closed his eyes so quickly that I only saw him for a second.

I went red with embarrassment, but I didn't like him being invisible! I needed his help. Holding my arms over my chest I said, "You can open your eyes now!"

After a brief moment he did. "Nice," he said awkwardly, and then he turned to face the wall again.

I tried on the other two, but neither one seemed quite as impressive as the first. Toby helped me to find a pair of jeans that fit better than anything I'd ever worn, and with his input, I also got several shirts that completed the outfit. On the bus ride home, he said I was gonna really "wow" the boys now. I wrote my reply: "Absolutely, and won't Effie be shocked."

"Stop focusing on her so much. She's who she is, and there's nothing you can do to change that. I think it's time we start changing you, and I don't just mean what you wear."

I waited until we were safely inside my house before I replied. "What do you mean 'changing me'?" We were down in my room. I had put on my new clothes and was admiring myself in the mirror. I could see how easy it was to get vain about your appearance. I had curves, not like those girls that starve themselves, and the new bra defined my breasts, giving me an almost trimmer look.

"How many friends do you have?" he asked.

The question reverberated through me like a shot.

"None, then," he said when I didn't reply.

"I used to..." I answered slowly. "None since we moved," I added, even though I knew that wasn't the entire truth. *I had lost all my friends long before the move.*

"Good, then we can assume you are capable of making friends again," he smiled. "How long ago was that?" He stood next to the mirror, looking assured of himself. I could see how it would have been easy for him to be popular.

I pondered his question, trying to work out the math in my head.

"How old were you?"

I went over to my desk and sat thinking. I had friends when I was nine, and they didn't just disappear when my father had. When had I realized I didn't have any friends left? Was I still nine, ten?

"Don't bother, I can see it all," he said softly, coming to kneel in front of me and taking my hands in his. They felt warm and friendly, and that made me want to cry.

"Let's just say it's been too long." He nodded in agreement with his own statement. "Regardless, it's time to start making new friends."

"I don't know," I said, and a great mounting fear seemed to rise up from some unknown source, catching my breath. I looked away.

"What is there to not know about?"

"What if they don't like me?" I said. The memory of betrayal clung to the crags of my mind.

"What happened to your old friends?" Toby asked. His eyes were narrowed, making him look like he was trying to see far-off into the distance, and I could feel a tug on my own memories, from the time my father had walked out to the time I'd realized that I didn't have any friends left.

"They betrayed me!" I cried, shutting my eyes and trying with all my might to block out those painful memories I'd spent so long pretending didn't exist.

"Were you ever honest with your friends?" I could see, like a silent motion picture, my friends disappearing.

"What was I supposed to do?" I asked, feeling all cut open for him to see.

"Be honest," he replied, and I saw Stacy, my best friend since I'd started school, coming to me in tears, begging me to tell her something, but I didn't. Instead, I just turned and walked away. Her sobs followed me as I left.

"I was hurting!" I raised my voice and opened my eyes in hopes that the visions would stop.

"She knew about pain," he said, conjuring up a second vision of her crying, only two months before my dad had left, over her dog Champ. He had to be put down because they found cancer in his leg, and her parents wouldn't pay for him to get fixed. "Friendship is a two-way street," Toby said, his eyes drilling into me. "You can't shut out your friends and expect them to let you in. You have to be able to stand up for your friends and sometimes fight to keep them."

"That's enough, Toby!" I closed my eyes and fell to my knees. "I get the point." Visions of Stacy's tear-stained face danced in my head, along with some really great times we'd had together: going to the local pool, and the mall, and walking to or from school. Remembering these things only made me angrier with her.

Toby rested his hand on my shoulder. "You had good friends. They would have fought for you."

I looked up into his face and brought back a memory of Stacy taunting me outside on the playground at school. "My a, my a, baby Mariah!" she yelled when I had dropped one of my stuffed unicorns that I brought to school in the secret pocket in my jacket. She then tossed it around to all her friends until it was muddy from being dropped and torn from being fought over. Toby's eyes darted to my stuffy shelf. He knew the one I meant. It stood off to the side. I'd patched it up with rough stitches and washed it as best as I could. It was now my favourite, because it was an outcast; just like me.

"They betrayed me," I said with resolve in my voice. "I don't need friends." I stood up with determination. A friend could turn on me in an instant. *I was better off alone.*

"They didn't understand you," Toby corrected, his eyes pleading with me to listen. "She was scared of how much you'd changed and felt betrayed *by you* for keeping *her* out." He continued to kneel on the floor and looked up at me.

"That wasn't the only time!" I screamed. I stood *trapped*. I couldn't get past him.

"I know it wasn't," he said calmly. "But you know I'm right!" Toby shook his head and stood beside me. "You do need friends," he said, bringing his hand up to rub his sore cheek. It had seemed to be healing, but now it looked all freshly bruised again.

I felt terrible. I'd forgotten and gotten used to that bruise there, but now I remembered it was me who had put it there. "Does it hurt?" I stepped closer to him.

"Pain is sort of twisted for me." He looked down at his hands. "It's like it's somehow in its true form."

"I don't understand."

"You know the other night, you were having a nightmare. I could feel your pain like something was punching me. It actually took me a while to figure out that you'd hit me for real. Now, with this bruise, when you ache, it feels like I've just been punched all over again. This morning, when you were lying on the ground having that, I don't know, panic attack, I felt like I was being squeezed on all sides. It really hurt, and that's how I knew how much you were hurting."

"So just now?" I asked gingerly.

"It hurt. Whoever is throwing the punches has a fairly good arm. I feel winded a little, and my whole skull feels like something's going through it." He turned to me. "You want to know my theory?"

I shrugged. Somehow without doing a thing, I was hurting him, and I was scared I wouldn't be able to stop it.

"I think this is how you feel. Your pain is so sharp and so strong, but you swallow it, you push it off to the side, you make it evaporate. I get hit with the blows, while you stuff it down so it doesn't feel so real. But it's real, and it's there, and it's like a beast waiting for your weakest moment to come back and bite you." Toby rubbed his cheek again.

"Does it hurt right now?" I asked, afraid of the answer, because I knew what he said had made me feel upset, and I could feel the beast trying to escape as he spoke about it.

"Ya, quite nice and raw. This is the true pain, the pain you keep locked inside. I don't think it would hurt as much if you'd just let it out. But I can see it scares you. You aren't ready to let go of it yet." Toby put his arm around my shoulder and drew me against his chest. "If this is the price I pay to be your one and only friend, I'll pay it gladly."

I felt small. I wondered at how I could feel so small, when in comparison I was half again as big as Toby, but as he pulled me close, it was as if I were no bigger than a three-year-old, and I could climb into his lap if I tried. I knew I couldn't, and I also knew something else. "But the truth is that you have to pay it, you are connected to me, and until that goes away you are stuck here. Stuck caring, stuck hurting, stuck so it's not your choice."

"If I told you that I wouldn't leave now, even if I had the choice, would you believe me? No, I know you don't. However, believe me or not, it's true." I felt him lean over and kiss my hair softly. "The former me wouldn't, that's true." He sat up again. "But a lot of who I thought I was has disappeared in death. I'm glad I'm here with you right now."

I wrapped my arms about his waist as tight as I could and held on. True or not, it felt good being right here in this place, and I didn't want him to go. Time dragged on, and my stomach began to growl. I reluctantly let go of him and raised myself. *How could I be sure he wasn't an angel after all?* I wondered, and then I turned and headed for the kitchen.

"Right behind you," he said softly, getting to his feet more slowly.

I put together a real cooked meal that night, with a full salad and a side dish with some lamb chops I'd found in the freezer. I made sure that I cooked enough for Mom, whenever she got home, and for Jake, in case he bothered to show up. I didn't make anything for Jake's friends, because I hoped that them all coming over had been a one-time shot just to get back at Mom. *I hoped.*

Halfway through cooking, Jake emerged from the basement. I jumped a little as I heard him on the stairs and felt foolish. Jake always looked more like Dad than I did; his hair wasn't as dark as mine, and it only had a small wave to it, but he kept it long. His eyes were green, his cheeks sunken and his brows quite thin for a guy. His nose was flat on the bridge, and his chin had a dimple. Then there were the spacers he wore in his ears. He'd stretched them to two centimetres and had three piercings over his nose, two in his nose and three on his one brow. Jake was not tall, but he was skinny. When we were face to face, I stood taller than him by an inch or two, but I tried hard not to do so. I'd slouch because I knew it made him mad.

"You gots a friend over?" he asked as he drew level with me.

"No," I said, feeling a shiver of panic, "why do you ask?"

"Well, I thoughts I heard you talking to some-un earlier." He shuffled past me to the kitchen.

"Nope, no one." I scratched my head like I was pondering the question. "How do you know I wasn't talking to myself?" I asked. I stole a glance at Toby, and he smiled back as I followed Jake to the kitchen.

"'Cuz I thoughts I heard two different voices." Jake sat heavily at the table. He looked tired.

I felt my eyes widen. I didn't want to do anything to give myself away, but I felt them betray me. Jake looked around the room. For a moment he seemed to be looking right at Toby. He stood up and took a step towards him.

Toby must have thought the same thing, because he waved, but Jake didn't respond. He only went closer and said, "Iz that the real time?" He was facing the clock on the microwave that Toby was standing in front of.

"As far as I know," I said, trying not to let the relief show. I put the salad off to the side.

"You sure you didn't have a friend over?" I nodded. "'Cuz if yous did, I'd'a had to meet this guy and set him straight."

"Set him straight?" I asked.

"Ya, ya know, make sures he's the type that would treat me baby sista right." He went back to the chair and threw himself on it. Whenever Jake talked, it sounded like he was uneducated and dumb. I knew it was his street talk, but it sounded funny, especially when he said stuff like that.

"Well no, big bro," I said, trying to tease him back, "I don't got no one here with me…evah."

"Don't talk like that," Jake said, slamming the table and making me jump. "It don't sound right."

I sat down across from him. "Why not, Jake?" The timer said I had five minutes until the chops were finished, and then I could eat.

"You are way too pretty and smart to talk the way I do," he said, and even the twang of his accent had disappeared. He stared at me until I looked away.

"How do you know that?" *I never felt smart and far less pretty!*

"Because you always have been." He looked annoyed.

"But Jake, people change," I said. "I changed. Haven't you noticed how much I changed?" I could feel the pain welling up inside again, and out of the corner of my eye I caught Toby flinching.

Jake leaned back in his chair, his scarecrow figure draped all over it, and he looked at me, really looked at me for what I felt to be the first time in ages. "You've gotten prettier," he finally said. "And those clothes makes you look very fine. I can see why my boyz take an interest in you." He rubbed his nose with the back of his hand. "I don't think I'm gonna to let them hang about here any more." This last statement was more for his benefit than mine, but it made me feel uncomfortable nonetheless.

"I made dinner," I said, trying to change the subject. But Jake's eyes were glued on me wherever I went in the kitchen. I looked at Toby to see if he could help me. He shrugged and seemed to concentrate on Jake all the more.

Jake finally looked away when I put a plate before him. "You know, sis, you are some kind of wonderful," he said, and reaching over, he smacked my bottom.

I dished him out some food, and he ate it with several comments like: "This is delish" and "You're the best." And one that haunted me later that evening: "I still remember mom's cooking, but this is better." When dinner was done, Jake took his plate to the dishwasher and loaded it himself, then bid me goodnight and left for who-knows-where. I retired to my bedroom with Toby on my heels.

"Okay, tell me you weren't nervous when Jake said he heard two voices," I said, placing the chair up against my door.

"I was, but then I realized he was high." Toby stood only a foot behind me.

"No way," I said. "He was?" I went to my desk and sat down.

"Yup, didn't you notice how strange he acted the whole time?" Toby took up his spot at the foot of my bed. I looked at this boy, dressed in black, sprawled comfortably out on my rose-covered bed spread.

"Well ya, but that's just Jake," I said then added, "Lately."

"For about the last five years, am I right?" He stretched out, looking so relaxed.

I nodded. "Everything fell apart then. Or at least it did for Jake and me. Mom doesn't seem to have suffered as much." *I resented her for that.*

"She suffers, just in a different way," Toby said. *I didn't believe him.* "But I'm not worried about either of them, I'm worried about you!"

His words filled me with warmth. I moved over to the bed so I could lie next to him.

"Now, tomorrow you are going to make friends." His voice was kind but determined. *It didn't sound like he was giving me a choice.*

I rolled over onto my stomach, stuck out my tongue and put up my hands like a puppy, then panted.

Toby gave my cheek a push. "So, who do you want to be friends with?"

I rolled over to my back and put my head on his arm. "You," I answered.

"Alright, other than me." He rumpled my hair.

"No one," I said. *I just didn't want to be hurt again.*

Toby pulled his arm out from under my head and rolled onto his side. "Come on," he persisted.

"No, Toby, I don't want to come on." I said, crossing my arms and rolling away.

I think he could sense my frustration. After an eternity of silence, he said into my ear, "You do, you know you do, and you are just scared of trying."

"You bet I'm scared!" I said, more forcefully than I had intended.

"Don't let fear win. That is what gives bullies like me power. I know, I remember. You come across all weak in the knees, and we know you'll just let us do whatever we want to, because that's what you expect us to do." He reached out and touched my back. I jumped. *Would I ever get used to the initial shock of his touch?* "Break the cycle. I know you want to. And I'm here to help you."

"You are probably right." I felt overwhelmed at just the thought. "It's getting kind of annoying, you always being right." I got up and gave the signal for him to turn around so I could change.

"Sorry," he said softly. I didn't reply, but I crawled into bed and lay down. I fell asleep before I could think another thought.

DAY 5 Friday...

I WOKE WITH DREAD IN MY HEART. This was it, what I had feared forever. It was easy to be rejected, to walk through life expecting the worst of people, because eventually that's what you got. But to actually be hopeful, hopeful of a kindness that I didn't think I deserved, that was something that made me truly fearful.

Getting into my new clothes helped me think that I looked the part, but I felt like I would have nothing to hide behind if I failed, and I was sure I would. Toby seemed more optimistic, and he held the mood up for both of us. I don't know how I would have been able to even get up the nerve to try had he not been right beside me, prompting me and prodding me to continue.

"Now, I don't think you should try Elijah, he's got too much of a thing for you, and that could cloud his judgment and confuse his thoughts," Toby instructed as we walked to the school. We were on a quiet street, but I had to be careful to make sure we were absolutely alone, since the odd car would drive past.

"Don't you think I could use that to my benefit?" I asked, after a car backed out of the driveway behind us and sped away.

"Not unless you are ready to date him, which I don't think is the wisest move. No, you should try and concentrate on being friends before you move on to something greater. If you are friends with the whole group then you two eventually go out, you will not be known as Elijah's girlfriend, because if that were the case, you'd only be making friends by association. Then if you break up, as teen romances often do, they'd have loyalty for their old friend and be less likely to stay friends with you."

"Ooh, hoo," I said, feeling a bit testy. "And how many girlfriends did *you* have!"

"Several," he said as he rubbed the back of his neck again. He stopped dead in his tracks. "You said you wanted complete honesty from me?"

"Yes," I replied. The sun was just coming over the tall houses around us, casting long shadows and making the street feel like it wasn't quite awake yet.

"Well, I just got something, and it's not pretty."

"Shoot, you've seen mine," I said mockingly.

"I used girls," he confessed, his eyes clouding over. "I was not kind to any of them." He shook his head in disgust. I knew that look—I wore it often. "Getting the hottest girls was a sign of status, and I wanted to be the most popular. So I'd date any girl that looked pleasing to my friends' eyes. And we scored them by the amount of bases we could get to."

"I thought you said you liked girls that didn't show everything off or give everything away." I didn't like what he was saying, and it was making me feel insecure about trusting him with my choice of clothes now.

"I did say that, and I meant it," he said, looking into my eyes, "but it didn't matter what I really liked; what mattered was what my friends liked."

I tried to imagine him alive, in his tight shirt and baggy pants, and I knew who he'd be if he had attended my school—Max. Max was the boy who I'd heard rumours about him having slept with over half the girls in my grade! "So then you've been intimate? Like had..."

"Yes, more than once."

"How was it?" I was interested. I'd heard girls my age talk about it like it was something really great, then teachers told you to wait, making it sound extra special. "Was it all that everyone makes it out to be?"

"Surprisingly, no. But my circumstances might have had something to do with that." Toby held out his hand to me. "So are we still okay?"

I took his hand. *It was warm feeling, like a hug from inside out.* I held on to him in a way that would look natural if anyone passed by, without being able to see him. "How many times?" I asked as the thought entered my mind.

"Again, surprisingly not as often as I would have imagined I should have."

"Why not?" I could imagine being his girlfriend, and I would have willingly given myself up. That thought grossed me out, and I was happy to be distracted by his reply.

"Most girls, though they are trying to convince you otherwise, don't want to just do 'it' with any ol' guy. As cool as I was, I couldn't convince that many to sleep with me, mostly because it wasn't special. I didn't have very much to offer, other than becoming another notch on my bedpost. I'd date a girl until it was clear we'd gone as far as we were going to get then I'd dump her. If she went all the way, I'd keep her around until she stopped pleasing me." Toby tried to remove his hand from mine, but I held fast. "I was really not a very nice person."

"But like you said, that isn't who you are now," I said. I couldn't see him actually being that way.

He looked over to me and smiled. "You have such a warm and accepting personality, you will be a huge asset to anyone who becomes your friend. Ouch!" He put his free hand up to his bruised cheek. "What was that for?"

I didn't know, and I couldn't explain, but I saw his bruise spreading.

"Does it hurt so much to hear a compliment?" He still seemed phased by my pain, and it showed in his voice.

"Maybe," I said. "I don't know." And I really didn't, but something inside me felt like I needed to remember my faults so I wouldn't go off balance. *There's no way I was that great!* "Did you really mean what you said?" *He could only be telling me nice things to make me feel better.*

"Oh, that's it, you thought I was lying? That explains all the trouble you were having with Jake last night." I nodded. I could tell that each of Jake's kind words had caused Toby to jump, and it made me feel all the more miserable. "Well, I can understand why you thought he was lying to you, but don't you trust me yet?"

"I'm sorry," I said, feeling wretched. *I was causing him undue pain!*

"I know," Toby said, holding his jaw. "Now stop. Let it go. It's done." He fell to his knees and wrenched his hand from mine to hold his face.

I just couldn't. I saw his eyes welling up with the grief I was causing him, and the more I saw him agonize, the worse it made me feel. *I was such a bad girl.*

"You are going to have to let go of this sometime," I heard Toby's voice say more in my head than next to my ear.

"I want to believe you," I whispered, shutting my eyes tight.

"Then choose to believe me, and let's move on." Even so, his voice was still strained.

"Alright," I said in my mind, and I opened my eyes. Looking over at him, I saw the bruise was bright red, and it had cracked like someone had punched his face anew— only this person was able to punch right through his skin.

I felt a twinge of guilt, and Toby stepped back. "Listen," he said. "You hurt, I hurt, and it's just that simple. Don't get stuck in it, that's just how this works. Besides, this feels like a walk in the park compared to what I feel on the inside about who I used to be. That misery is way worse."

I turned away. "Fine," I said, but we both knew I still felt a bit bad over it all. He took my hand in his again, giving it a loving squeeze, and we headed down the road.

As we neared the school, he said, "I want you to take a different route to your locker. I want you to go in one of the side doors. I know some of the tougher kids hang out there." *He was right, the kids that looked a lot like my brother would gather by the side entrance.* "But they are kinder to kids like you, because they don't need to prove their status, they just have to know they intimidate you. Got it?"

"Be scared, not humiliated," I said out of the corner of my mouth. My heart pounded in my chest.

"Ya, that's sort of it." I knew that if I didn't have Toby's hand in mine, I would not have made it up the three steps that lead to the side door. But it wasn't as bad as I thought it would be. One or two leered at me, but most of them minded their own business.

Once inside, Toby stopped me. "Sorry to have tricked you like this," he said. "You see that girl to the right leaning on her locker?" I didn't say anything, but I squeezed his hand. "That's Rayla. She sits in Elijah's group, and I want you to go and talk to her." I felt my knees give. The floor was rising up to meet them. Toby held onto my hands tighter until I steadied myself. "You're going to need something to talk to her about." He wore a playful smile. "If you can't think of anything, I have something for you…" He waited for a moment, and when I didn't start forward, he said, "Ask her if there is still room in her drama class."

I cautiously looked over to him to see if he was serious. "You'll have to give up home economics, but you're really a whiz in the kitchen, so I don't think you'll miss much. I know you'd rather give up shop, but you can change that next semester. For now, this is the best solution. It's only four weeks into your term, so I'm sure the office will let you make the switch if there is room in the class."

I smiled at the thought. *I did miss being in drama.*

"But you are going to have to go over to Rayla and ask her if there is room." In this instance, I really found Toby's cocky confidence annoying, but at the same time I envied his ability to be so smooth. Again I could see why he had been so popular in his life.

I took one deep steadying breath and headed her way. Rayla was one of those girls that were short but could make being petite look cute. She had wavy auburn hair that she had cut into a short bob. Her eyes were more green than brown, and she had bushy eyebrows and long eyelashes that made her look mysterious. She was littered with freckles, and not just on her face. Her nose was small and a bit pointed.

As I neared, Elijah and another boy joined her. I tried to stop and turn away, but Toby held my hand tight and led me towards them. "If you hadn't taken so long at the door, you could have had a few minutes alone with her, but now you will have to face her and the boys." He finished his sentence just as I got within two feet of where they all stood.

I ducked my head and turned, trying to pull against Toby with all my might, when Rayla looked up and said, "Mariah? That's your name, right?"

I would have chickened out even then, had I looked to see the way Elijah was staring at me, so I focused on her alone and said, "Yes, and you are Rayla." Toby grinned ear to ear.

Rayla nodded. "I'm so glad you got it right; too many people remember me as Ray-Lynn, and I just think that is disgusting." She made a funny face.

I cautiously smiled back. "Um…" I stalled, hoping I'd feel braver in a moment. The thought of trying to escape still ran through my mind, but I figured if I tried to make a run for it now, I would only look even more foolish. So I kept talking, even though I was still terrified. "Ya, I was wondering if there were any openings in your seventh period drama class."

"You hear that boys, she wants to come back to drama! We were saying just yesterday that we were kinda sad you didn't come back this year." Again she turned back to say, "Isn't that right, boys?"

I gave Toby a quick glare. He smiled innocently back and shrugged. *Why did I feel like he had the whole thing planned out?* Then I snuck a peek at Rayla's boys; Elijah seemed distracted by the floor. His friend, who I later learned was Dan, kept his eyes on Elijah. Dan could have made a good football player. He was average height but with a bulky frame. He had tan skin which made me think he was part Native, and he also had the handsome, fine-cut features that often went with that heritage. His black hair was styled neatly short, and his eyes were light brown. Over all he seemed relaxed and carefree.

Before the pause could be drawn out too far, Rayla said, "Well I'd love to have you, even if my two yahoo friends can't bring themselves to say it!" She turned back to me. "And I'm sure we have two empty spots." Her hair bounced as she nodded.

"Thanks," I said. I turned to go but walked right into Toby, who stood as if glued to the spot. I crashed so hard against him that I slipped and sort of hung from his hand for a moment before I regained balance and straightened up.

"Stay and talk," he said, as if nothing embarrassing had happened. *I was humiliated!* Toby flinched. I grudgingly turned back to face Rayla.

She was laughing so hard, she held her sides. "I loved it, it was like an impromptu improv. You just pretended to crash against an invisible wall! Use that for your audition, and I'm sure you'll be able to get any part you want in our year end play." Both Elijah and his friend were applauding. "Hey, do you know the boys?" Rayla asked, "This is Dan, and the other one is El..."

"Elijah," Elijah finished. "We're in the same home room." He looked at the ground and shuffled his feet.

"I've seen you," I said, then feeling like I was being less than eloquent I added, "It seems we share a love..." Elijah looked up so fast, he might have gotten whiplash... It was like the cone of silence, all three faces were glued to mine, and I could even hear Toby suck in his breath; but that may have been because the pain of this situation was almost unbearable on me, so I could only imagine what it felt like to him. "What I mean is we share a love of reading."

Rayla was laughing so hard, she fell back against her locker. "For a moment I thought you were talking about something else, but this makes much more sense." Dan joined in her laughter.

Elijah just looked away and said, "That was kind of funny." His ears turned a bright shade of pink. "I'm sure if it was someone else I'd think it was funnier."

I chuckled at his comment. He turned back with a grin, the colour rising on his face. I looked down the hall. *What was I doing?*

The first bell sounded, and Rayla grabbed my free hand, thankfully not the one I still held Toby's with. "You will come and sit with us at lunch?" she said. "I want the whole gang to meet you!"

I nodded, almost dumbfounded, and then started down the hall. This time Toby followed, though I heard him say through the noise of the crowd, "What, you're not going to wait to walk with Elijah?" I couldn't figure out if he was teasing or serious. *Why did I say I'd join them for lunch?*

When we got to my locker, Toby put his hand on it and said firmly, "You can't open it." His face was set.

"Why?" I said out loud, flustered, before I could stop myself. But taking a quick glance around, I was relieved that no one was paying attention to me.

"There's a booby trap waiting for you." I waited for Toby to explain, but he said, "Go to the office and tell them you think your lock has been tampered with."

I did. As the second bell sounded, the halls quickly filled with kids, all trying to get somewhere. By the time I was finished in the office and the trap had been removed, I'd missed home room. Someone had rigged a bottle of shaving cream to explode as my locker door was opened. The janitor got the full force of the explosion. Had it been me, my clothes would surely have been ruined. As it was, everything in my locker was soaked from the blast, and I felt relieved that I hadn't left anything I cared for in it overnight.

When third period ended, Toby informed me that I was going to the lunchroom, and I'd be eating with Rayla and her friends. It was clear I had little choice, so I followed Toby through the halls. He tried to explain that I'd be fine, but his words fell on deaf ears, since panic had a choke hold on my senses.

I arrived at the cafeteria a bit late. As I walked in, Rayla waved and patted the seat beside her. I nodded numbly and bought myself some time by pointing to the food line. She gave me a thumbs-up. I went through the line up and then over to the table.

"Mariah, this is Charlie, and Cindy, Dan you know, Ted—but he likes to be called 'Teb', and that leaves me." Rayla turned to all her friends and said, "She got my name right first try." Then she added, "Oh, and let's not forget Elijah." I continued to stand next to the table. "Well," she said, "sit!" and with stiff legs, I did.

"Were you able to change your seventh to drama?" Dan asked.

After the locker incident, I'd asked the office, and I relayed their reply. "They said it looked good. They'll just have to check with both teachers, and I should come back after school to find out."

"Aw, that means you've got it," said Charlie, a girl with straight black hair. I'd seen her around the school. She was quite tall for her age, so it made her easy to spot.

"I hope so," I said quietly. *I really did hope so.*

"Hear, hear," several at the table cried.

When I looked puzzled, Rayla explained, "We're studying Shakespeare, and everyone always said 'hear, hear' when they agreed. You'll get used to it." I smiled. With Toby at my back, I could feel myself starting to relax, ever so slowly.

"Where were you during home room?" Elijah asked, but he seemed like he was trying to look as uninterested as he could. I turned toward him. A curl dangled in front of his face. To avoid my gaze, he busied himself with his food.

"Told you," Toby whispered in my ear, which made me jump.

"I went to the office and I asked them if I could change my seventh period." I wasn't sure why I wanted to leave out the booby trap in my locker. Maybe I felt embarrassed, like it proved what a loser I was. *So far none of these kids had noticed that!*

"That's not the only reason," Cindy piped in. She was very short for her age. It didn't help sitting next to Charlie. They both looked as if they could be in a circus show. Cindy had hazel hair, cut short like a boy's. She wore one earring that dangled down to her shoulder and none in the other ear. She had green-blue eyes. But most stunning was her warm smile, with plump pink lips and soft milky-white skin. "I heard someone tampered with your locker and tried to give you a nasty surprise!" She paused for dramatic effect, something I learned quickly that everyone in the group enjoyed doing. "Well, they didn't get you today, did they?" she finished with a note of excitement.

"No," I said. I didn't know why I felt sheepish. The way Cindy was telling it, it was like I was a superhero who had stopped a horrible crime. With a sudden rush, I was glad I'd sat there. My lonely table stayed empty, but I no longer missed it.

"She saw that someone had tampered with her lock," Cindy was explaining with great enthusiasm, "so she told the office, and they sent the janitor to check it out. Poor Gus, he got shaving cream head to toe! But at least he has extra suits to wear. If it was you, Mariah, you would have had to go home to change."

"That was really lucky," Teb, as he liked to be called, said. Several of the kids at the table "hear, hear"-ed.

"Well, I had a bit of help from my guardian angel," I said and leaned back into Toby.

"Thanks, babe," he said. I smiled, and I didn't care if I looked goofy doing it. At that moment, I was feeling a wealth of joy.

"Guardian angel, where could I get me one of those?" Teb asked. Teb had long, dirty blond hair, light blue eyes and a light completion, with a healthy dose of freckles and beauty spots.

I shrugged and said, "Couldn't really tell you, even if I knew." Teb touched the side of his nose and nodded knowingly. "But, Teb," I added, "Where do you come up with a nickname like that?" *I couldn't believe I was actually conversing, and it was fun!*

"Ah…" Teb seemed elated at my interest. "Glad you cared to ask. Have you ever seen *Galaxy Quest?*" When I admitted that I hadn't, he went into a lecture about the movie, trying not to give away the finer points of the plot, and after what seemed like a five-minute speech, he concluded, "Well, I like the movie so much, and I love that character, so I figured my name, 'Ted' is not so far from 'Teb', and though 'Ted' is quite plain and ordinary, 'Teb' on the other hand is not." He flashed a wide grin, showing off a chipped front tooth. "So I begged all of my friends to change my name for me..."

"You wouldn't let us call you anything different," Rayla said.

Teb nodded. "So, after three years of hard struggling, and some steep bribing, I've got everyone I love and care for to call me Teb, and never again plain and boring Ted."

"What about your parents?" Cindy asked.

"Right then..." Teb looked over the table. "Did I not say everyone I *loved* and *cared* for?"

"Oooow, snap," Charlie said. I had to laugh. *I was laughing, and it felt so good!*

"Hey, your parents are nice," Dan piped in.

Charlie leaned over and said softly, "This is where we compete over who has the worst parents." Her nose wrinkled as she smiled.

Teb added, "But you can't play if you like your folks." He said to Charlie, "Not everyone gets to pick their parents like you, darling."

"I'm adopted," she explained. I was intrigued at how casually she said that. "But if you want to play 'who has the worst parents,' and we're talking biological, I'd win hands down!" she said.

I stayed with them through the rest of the lunch period, though I quickly ran out of conversation pieces. I sat and listened to them with their quick-witted conversation, snappy phrases and one-line comebacks. And while I sat there, I tried to picture myself as a part of their group, friends. *And you know, I actually could.*

As the lunch hour was coming to a close, everyone was standing and collecting their stuff. Toby had come over to take his place beside me. Rayla turned to me and said, "I have next period with you; we can sit together and share a book. I heard that yours were just freshly washed this morning." I agreed, and we said our goodbyes. Everyone begged me to promise I'd come back on Monday to sit with them again.

As we headed out, I asked, "That reminds me, how did Cindy know about the janitor and my locker?"

"Oh, that's easy," Rayla answered. "She volunteers one of her spares in the janitorial office. She's probably the one that washed out Gus's uniform."

"Was he mad?" I had to ask. I hated the thought that he had to endure what was meant for me. Toby shook his head.

"Na, just glad it wasn't you. You know, Cindy was telling me what Gus said about pranks, and the reason behind them. They used to be in good-hearted fun, and never would they purposefully physically hurt anyone. But now he feels like kids are getting more and more malicious, like we have to stake out our claim on some invisible piece of the pie… crazy, I say." I followed her down the hall; she was exceptionally good at weaving through the other students.

We reached the classroom with a few minutes to spare. Rayla said she needed to study, so I took out my book to read. I wanted to thank Toby, who continued to stand just a little behind me, but I didn't dare with Rayla so close by. Rayla proved a good potential friend, because she made me laugh, and I was shocked to see how nice it felt to do that. *When was the last time I'd felt so carefree?*

I entered my last class of the day with a lighter heart than I had for years. I wasn't even bothered as I passed by Effie and her gang of hyenas. I headed to the desk I usually sat in and took out my book with the idea of writing Toby a gushing note, but he cut me off and said we'd talk about it later tonight. He seemed agitated, and I took a good look at his bruised face to see if I had been sending him blows again. I was relieved to see it looked to be healing quickly. But he was obviously upset. He kept rubbing the back of his neck like he had hives there or something. Before I could do anything more, the teacher walked in and class started.

I didn't forget to check at the office. When I got there, I saw Cindy, Dan and Elijah standing outside. *They were waiting for me*! I was almost knocked over to see all of them there. *They actually cared!* I found that thought almost too hard to believe…Toby's face showed my internal turmoil.

"Rayla wanted to wish you luck. She has to go straight home because she watches her little brother and sister, but she told us she's here in spirit."

I felt shy having them watch through the window as I stepped up to the receptionist's desk and asked her if my request had gone through. When she nodded, a great cheering broke out in the hallway. I blushed apologetically. The secretary, Miss Rose, gave me a warm smile, and I left before the noise from my three new friends got us all in trouble.

"Come with us to D.Q. to celebrate," Dan said. "Teb and Charlie are probably already there, and we can tease them if we catch them holding hands. And then you can tell them the good news yourself." I wasn't sure, but before I could answer...

"And I'm buying the ice-cream for the newest member of seventh period drama," Elijah said. I could see he was trying not to blush. *Did he really like me? Why?*

"Well, you'll have to go find him," I said, "because just after I switched, a new kid came in and signed up too."

"Really?" Elijah asked.

"No."

"O-Ooooo. She got you good!" Cindy said, roaring with laughter.

Dan joined in and slapped Elijah on the back. *I hoped I hadn't hurt his feelings.*

Toby leaned close to me and said, "Don't worry so much, this is normal."

We went out to the ice cream shop. Elijah ended up paying not only for my snack, but everyone else's. We had a lot of fun. I even joked a little, but I laughed a lot, and everyone got teased, in good fun, at least once. It felt like a happily-ever-after moment if ever there was one. On the way home, I felt so light and confident, I could barely feel my feet touch the ground. I was filled with wonder over the whole day, and I couldn't stop rehashing it.

"Did you hear what Dan said?" I asked.

"Which time? When he said you'd make a great Juliet? Or when he asked if you'd ever considered joining Thursday lunch time choir?"

I'd forgotten about choir... "Well then, both," I said and did a small skip.

"How come you can't just be happy?" Toby asked, rubbing his face.

I stopped. I was happy, but he was right. I was still worried about my life. *What if I let these new friends down?* There was so much that could still go wrong.

"If you keep waiting for the worst to happen, then it will."

"What does that mean?" I'd lost the precious bubble that had formed that afternoon and was feeling a bit mad, because it was Toby that seemed to be taking it away.

"Listen to me, because I don't know how I know this, but I do: there is good and bad in the world, but there is more good, if you look for it. Good may appear small, and it can often be missed quite easily, or swept away.

But it's up to you! You have to want it, and believe in it. If you walk around always waiting for the worst to happen, it eventually will, but if you seek out the good, all the small pieces of good, like the hidden shards of glass we cleaned off your floor, they will add up, and if. . .or more certainly when bad comes your way, you will have enough good moments to hold on to, so that the bad can't get in."

"Do you believe this?" I asked. *It sounded a bit unbelievable to me.*

"I have to. I'm stuck here between then and now, not quite real but yet most certainly not unreal. I don't have much good, but if I try, if I concentrate really hard, I realize I have a lot more good than what I first noticed."

"What's good about where you are right now?" *If anyone was worse off than I was, it was he.*

"I'm going to answer, and I want you to try really hard not to let your negative thoughts take over, alright?" I nodded, but I wasn't sure I could control it. "You, Mariah, you are something very good to me." He flinched and put up a hand as I tried to apologize. "It has been my honor and pleasure to share your life with you, and even more wonderful to watch it improve in just four days. I'd like to take some credit for it, but I can't. It was all in you to start; you just needed some help to unlock it. So I consider my being able to help you a very good thing. You have made me aware of so much that I missed when I was living my own life. And your kindness is an overwhelmingly good thing in my existence." He flinched at his last statement. "Why can't you accept a compliment and just leave it at that?"

I shrugged. As I started to walk home slowly, he followed. I could feel him dragging up times in my past when I had been kind, and it made me a little embarrassed, which I covered with huffiness. He pulled up the incident in my old school, where everyone was being rotten to this new kid, and I'd offered him a piece of gum, but it had backfired. He'd ended up spitting it out halfway through class, into my hair, then he'd become popular, and I'd stayed a social outcast.

"Just because he repaid your kindness with unkindness doesn't erase your good heart." Toby put a hand on my shoulder. "You're not tied to the actions of those around you, only to your own actions. And just because you were caring doesn't mean that you can make others care. Is it not enough that you care? It's not your job to fix everyone else, and you don't fail when anyone else chooses to stay stuck in their ways."

I knew he was right, even if he sounded like a Hallmark card or an after school special, but I didn't know how to accept it in my heart. Too long I had been carrying around the belief that it was my job to fix people, or more like it was my fault if they weren't fixed. Just like I felt I had to clean the house when my mother or brother trashed it. *Why did it bother me to leave things alone that I knew I couldn't change?*

I wondered about this the rest of the way home. I walked through my house looking around at the mess that had stayed untouched for over two days now, and I kept repeating the question in my head, "Why did it bother me to leave things alone that I knew I couldn't change?" Quickly a new question formed: "Why did I feel responsible for the actions of others?" Then the deepest, most painful thought erupted. "Why did I feel guilty when other people tried to hurt me?" Too many memories exploded, like fireworks on Canada Day, or a thousand tourists taking pictures at the same time. They fought to be the seen, heard, rediscovered, and dealt with. But I couldn't pick one out from the other…

Toby's voice reached my ears, and I turned to see him writhing on the kitchen floor. "Turn it off, Mariah!" he yelled, his body twitching as if it were being kicked from all sides. "Turn it off!" And I could see that my pain was his, for as he received each new blow, I felt it resound through my mind and emotions.

I turned slowly back to all these images, all these realities I'd endured, and I said in my head, "Not my fault, let it go." As each new situation arose in my mind, I said again, "Not my fault, let it go." And as more and more raced to the front of my consciousness, I found that I was able to be more confident. "Definitely not my fault…let it go," I'd say. Until only two memories remained: the first my father walking out the door with his bags in his hand. I lost my voice.

"Not your fault," Toby said. He had picked himself off the floor and was standing behind me. He took hold of my shoulders, making me feel stronger.

"But…" I went to protest.

"No." He cut me off in a firm voice. "Not your fault, and not your brother's fault either."

"Not my fault," I said meekly, and then breathed deeply. I could see it all play out. "Not my fault," I repeated with more conviction, "letting it go."

The last vision started to play itself out: Mims cornering me in the storage closet. My knees buckled, and a wave of nausea washed over me.

"Not your fault." Toby said into my ear. I started to shake, as if it were happening to me all over again. "Not your fault."

The memory continued to unfold: Jake opened the closet. If looks could kill, I would have fallen over dead.

"Not your fault," Toby said.

Jake took Mims by the collar and used his fists and his feet to strike out. Jake inflicted so much damage, he had to drag his friend to the front door.

"Not your fault," Toby reassured.

Jake threw Mims out, and I heard him stumble down the steps.

"Not your fault."

But the way Jake looked at me, he had such rage, such fire, *surely he felt it was all my fault.*

"Still, not your fault," Toby whispered.

"But Mims died," I screamed. My body shook with the pain of this memory. *How could Toby stand it?*

"I know, still not your fault," Toby said yet again.

"Jake had to go to court, he had to prove that it was self-defense." My knees gave. The only thing keeping me from collapsing to the floor were Toby's strong arms.

"This was not your fault, Mariah, you didn't do anything wrong."

"He had to go to juvie for three months and take an anger management course," I said, tears welling up. I held them back, and they made me shake and shudder.

"Not...your...fault," he said, sounding like he was being choked.

"How could it not be?" I moaned. *I had let him in. I had gone to the closet to get something from the bottom shelf...*

"How could it be?" Toby rebutted.

"I enticed him!" I insisted. *Mims had told me how irresistible he found me as he cornered me and pressed me against the shelf.* "I let him in." As I said it, I could almost feel Mims' hand unzipping my pants.

Toby shook his head.

"I wanted him to like me." *Mims had been kind to me, he kept me company while he waited for my brother, he talked to me, and he listened...*

Pulling me away from his chest so he could look deep into my eyes Toby said, "Absolutely, most certainly, and unmistakably—not your fault."

But I remembered that afternoon. He'd forced my pants to my ankles and pulled my shirt over my head. *I didn't want that!* I knew Toby was right, and from somewhere inside, I found the strength to say in a meek whisper of a voice, "It wasn't my fault?"

"No, it wasn't."

I continued to shudder. Toby followed me to the floor, no longer able to hold us up. As we stayed wrapped together on the floor, I felt a calm fall over me. The world was going into twilight, stars were breaking through the inky sky, and inside me hope breathed as if awakened to take fragile root in a heart that had been broken for too long.

I'm not sure how long we stayed that way, but my mother coming through the door at about seven interrupted me. As per her usual routine on Fridays, she'd hurry home to go out with the girls for drinks in the evening. She seemed surprised to see me sitting all by myself on the kitchen floor. It was dusk, and the light had faded away, but I hadn't bothered to turn the switch on. Normally by now I would be deep into watching some show on the television, a pizza on the go.

"Are you alright?" she asked, coming in cautiously.

"Not really." It was odd to hear my voice; it sounded flat and lifeless.

My mom seemed at a loss for words.

"Mom." I had a bizarre thought and an ounce of bravery. "Why don't we go out to dinner as a family any more?" *I missed our family meals. Life seemed better when we had them.*

She narrowed her eyes, gazing down at me with her hands on her hips. *What did she suspect was going on?* Surely she couldn't have come up with anything close to the truth. Toby sat calmly beside me, giving me strength to wait out her stare. She stood over me, unblinking. "That's a good question," she answered slowly. "Where did you come up with that?"

I sat up straighter. "I just miss our family meals."

She busied herself, looking through her purse, "I guess we aren't much of a family any more now, are we."

My heart sank, but Toby cut in with, "Define family!" I didn't know what he was trying to say. "Family is what you make it."

"What would you call us then, Mom?" I asked, feeling strengthened with Toby there.

"Well..." she stammered, still rummaging.

"Even if it's just you and me, what does that make us?"

"Family, I guess," she said off-handedly, pulling out a cigarette.

"Then can we start going out once a month to eat dinner together again?" *I felt like I was holding my very heart out in front of her,* and she had the ability to toss it aside if she wanted.

"Mariah, that was really your father's thing," she answered after a long pause, then she put the cigarette in her mouth and started to look through her bag again.

"So what?" I said with a fire in my voice that I wouldn't have thought possible after everything I'd already been through. She stopped and looked at me. "Why can't we just do it!" I persisted. "It doesn't matter who thought it up, it was a good idea, and it's important to me!" *I hated how needy I sounded.* But it might have been just what got my mother's attention.

"It matters that much to you?" she inquired slowly, looking around the room. "It wouldn't make you all depressed again about your father leaving?"

"I don't feel depressed about him leaving," I lied, "but I feel like when he left, you left too." My voice cracked, and I started to choke. *Why did I say that?*

"I didn't leave," she snapped as she pulled her purse from her shoulder and dumped it out on the table.

"No, but you're never around," I replied in an undertone that I hoped she didn't hear as she located her lighter and lit up her smoke.

"I have responsibilities; you know the bills won't pay themselves!" She took a long puff on the cigarette and seemed to relax a bit.

"I know," I said, dropping my head.

"Don't let her bully you," Toby said, rubbing my back. "You aren't asking for too much, you have every right to want this, she's your mother!"

Though I was wondering if I did want to eat a dinner once a month with this woman I called Mom, I knew it meant something, and I would have liked it even more if Jake was also able to be there. So I took a deep breath and asked, "So can we make a date sometime this month to go out to dinner together?"

"Alright, fine," she said in a tired voice. "But I need something from you."

Toby shook his head in disbelief, but he said, "May as well ask her about it."

"What do you want me to do?" I cautiously got to my feet.

"I work hard all week, and it isn't easy to come home to a messy house like this."

I almost fell back to the floor. *The mess wasn't mine!* Then guilt started to set in. I stopped as Toby flinched. I wasn't the cause of the mess, *surely she knew this… I was the one who always cleaned up, but I never made any messes!* "Mom, don't you notice that I try to keep things clean?"

"I'm not asking much," she continued, oblivious to my protest. "Just take care of the spills, the bottles, the dirty plates, vacuum a bit…" *Basically everything…*

"Haven't you noticed that I do that already?" I said and stood tall to face her. I was even with her height. Soon I'd be taller then her.

She looked at me in disbelief, the cigarette hanging out of her mouth. "Then what do you call the dishes all over the living room?"

"Your mess," I said. Toby gave me a thumbs-up by bringing one hand around in front of my face. "That was from you and Jake," I persisted.

"Was it really?" For a moment she looked confused.

"It was," I said confidently.

My mother took a long puff. "Oh well, is it really too much to ask you to clean that up, too?"

I took a step back and felt Toby standing behind me. "Be brave," he said, his cheek next to mine. "I've got your back."

"I usually do clean up after you two, but it's a really big mess," I said, trying to calm my thoughts. But I couldn't stop myself from adding more. "And it hurts that you never notice."

Mom put one hand on her hip. "What do you want from me?" she said, making it sound like I was asking too much from her already. "I mean, Mariah, you want money to buy your own clothes, you want lunch money, you want everything you put on the stupid shopping list, and now you want a dinner out once a month. You really *are* spoiled. What else?"

I actually fell against Toby. I would have fainted right to the floor had he not been there to catch me. *Was I asking too much*?

"Nothing else." I swallowed hard, wondering if I'd regret saying it.

"Do you promise? I mean, do you really swear you won't keep asking for more?"

"Yes," I replied, knowing that I was trapped now if I ever needed something else, but I felt desperate for a sense of value. That was what I missed from those dinners! *I'd do anything to get it back.*

"Fine," she snapped. "Are we done? I have friends waiting for me."

I nodded, and she walked away. *I had had to buy my value…*

"Not your fault," Toby whispered.

I was glad he was there to reassure me. I might have faltered and let everything return to the way it had been. It didn't take long for Mom to get herself together and head out for the night. She left a mess in her wake, though, and I grudgingly started to clean it up. To make me feel worse, Toby was watching my every move.

"I am cleaning it up because I want to go out to dinner with my mom, and she said I had to do this to get it. If I don't, she might take it back." *Why did I feel like no matter what, I was going to loose?*

"I didn't say anything," he replied. "But I wanted to tell you that what you did with your mom was a very brave thing, and I commend you for it."

"Well, I didn't feel brave, and if you weren't here, I wouldn't have been able to say anything. I would have chickened out altogether." I looked at the sea of mess and wondered how long it would take me to get it done.

"Well then, there is some good right there."

I smiled and continued cleaning. Once I was done the kitchen, I started to work on the living room. The broken glass was the worst, followed by the spilled drinks that had dried to leave sticky stains. *I should have cleaned it right away.*

Toby flinched but didn't comment. Instead he asked, "What do you do for fun?" He sprayed cleaner on the stains to help them soak.

"Pardon? What?" It was a simple question, but it felt more complicated.

"Fun," he repeated. "Do you go out anywhere, do anything on the weekends? What do you like to do?" His dark eyes penetrated me.

"I watch TV," I answered feebly. *I knew it was pathetic*, but that is what I did.

"Aw, girl, we've got to get you out of the house! Your life can't just be work and television." He was trying to be lighthearted joking about it, but there was just too much truth in what he said.

The living room was tidied, and all I had left was to sweep, then mop the sticky spots. Toby followed me to the closet while I got the mop and broom. "Now, think, some sort of activity you like doing, or want to try?"

I shook my head. "I've got nothing," I said, leaving the closet quickly.

"Alright, play it that way. I'll pick for you." This statement frightened me, but I couldn't deny the feeling of shy curiosity.

We finished the cleaning in comfortable silence.

As I sat up in my bed later that night, I came back to it. "Toby?" He looked over at me—he'd been reading one of my books. "Do you know what you're planning for me this weekend?" *I kind of hoped he'd say he wasn't going through with it.*

A playful smile appeared on his face. "Wait and see." *What could he be thinking?*

"Ya," I said, "so you are really planning something for me? Like what?"

"Good things." He looked back to the book. "I know where I want to take you tomorrow," he said firmly.

"So, what sort of thing will it be?" I asked again.

"Mariah, you're just going to have to trust me. Can't you do that?"

"Well, is it like a sport? Because I am not really good at that sort of stuff." That was the truth. "Or is it something I need to be part of a team for? 'Cause we don't have anyone to go with. Will I look foolish being there all alone?" *My nervousness mounted.*

He laughed. "Well, again you'll have to trust me, so wait and see." Then he put the book down. "Mariah, I have something to tell you." His voice had become so serious, it scared me. I didn't know if I could handle anything else that night.

"Well, actually, it's something I need to ask from you," he corrected. "You see, I have realized some mistakes that I made in my life, and now I think I know a way I can correct some of them. But I need your help."

"You want me to help you to make amends?" *I could help him fix his life! That would be more fun than him trying to fix mine.*

"Yes. I want to undo some of the damage that I created in my former life, but I can't do any of it on my own, so I was wondering if you would be willing to help." *I liked that idea very much.*

"Oh, Toby," I gushed, "you've been such a lifesaver to me and helped me out so much! I'm willing to do anything you need to return the favour."

"Good." He breathed a sigh of relief. "You don't know how much this means to me." *Had he been afraid I'd say no?*

"So, what do you want me to do?" It's funny how even the thought of helping someone else out can make you feel immensely better about yourself.

"I'm not sure yet," he replied. "I'm still trying to figure out the details. But as soon as I've got it, I'll tell you, alright?" *Interestingly enough, everything did feel alright.*

It was late, so we went to bed. I still felt apprehension over what he had planned for my Saturday, but I wanted to trust him. I tossed and turned a bit. "Toby?"

"Ya?" he answered sleepily.

"Today in the kitchen, I was in so much pain, how come you were so calm?"

I felt him roll. "I was hurting, but not as much as when you ignore it. I think it was because you were facing your feelings, so it felt painful for you, but it was healthy, instead of pushing it away and pretending it didn't matter."

DAY 6 Saturday...

In my dream I returned to that wonderful meadow, where the sun shone bright and warm, and the grass was like a velvet hug on my skin. Toby was there. He held my hand as we lay on the ground, looking up into the sky, a sky that was the most welcoming blue and twinkled like a shimmering pond.

"I wish I could stay here forever," I said, but I didn't even recognize my own voice. It sounded more like my childhood voice, full of innocence and wonder at the world.

"One day you will," Toby answered. His voice sounded younger too, and more free than I'd ever heard it before.

"Will we be able to stay here together?" I asked.

"That's the plan," Toby said, "but not for a very, very, very long time. And you are going to have to be braver and face even more trials until that day arrives."

I squeezed his hand, for I was not fearful now. How could I be when I was in such a peaceful and safe place? Then, as I felt myself leaving, I heard

Toby say, "I love you." But when I opened my eyes and stared at the here and now Toby, I wondered if I'd just imagined that last part.

"Ready for your fun day?" he asked. He was clearly itching to go.

"What time is it?" I wondered, feeling snug in my bed and wishing I could return to my happy dream.

"Almost noon." Toby sat up and stretched restlessly.

"Too early for Saturday," I said, starting to roll over again.

"Not this Saturday!" He pulled off my comforter so only a thin sheet covered me. I shivered and sat up, so I started the day with nervous dread.

With a bit of breakfast in my stomach, my hair fixed and my new clothes on, I caught a bus to who-knows-where, as per Toby's instructions. It took over an hour to get there. He had led me to an area of town that I'd never ventured to before, and when he told me to get off the bus, I looked up to see a huge grey building with the words "Mack's Bowlaramma" written across the top.

I quickly checked to see if I was on my own then said, "Bowling? Is that the plan? Are you crazy?"

He wore a huge grin. "No, I'm not. I used to love to toss the ball down the lane on the weekends, so I thought you might like it too. If you don't after one game, then we'll leave, and you can choose what you'd like for the rest of the day. I won't interfere again."

Again I checked about me. "But I'm all alone!" I was embarrassed at the mere thought of walking into the building alone, but admitting I didn't know how to play and setting up a game by myself was beyond my ability. I didn't budge from the spot.

"Lots of people bowl alone." Toby took a few steps towards the front door.

"Really?" I said unbelievingly, slowly following.

"Actually, I don't know," he admitted. "I can't lie; I don't remember much other than that I loved it. I gotta figure there are lots of people who bowl alone. I might have been one of them. I figure everyone there will be so into their own game, they won't pay much attention to anyone around them. Come on. I have such good and strong memories of this place, and I really want to share it with you!" He seemed so excited, he couldn't get there fast enough. *I found it annoyingly contagious.*

I followed more out of curiosity than belief that I'd enjoy myself, but I kept my steps slow and even. I was going to tell him that I felt like this was a long shot and we should maybe just look then go somewhere else when another bus came and several passengers disembarked. A few rowdy boys pushed past me and headed into the bowling alley. I followed them in. I had never been in a bowling alley before, so I didn't know what to expect.

It was well lit, making it brighter than I thought it would be. With public smoking banned, the atmosphere was less hazy than it could have been. It reminded me of the school gym in its size and ceiling height. There was a carpeted area with several tables and benches in the middle of the room behind an administration desk/concession stand. Along the two sidewalls were several clusters of benches around what looked like computer screens. Each was at the top of a bowling lane with its own number hanging above it, under a television set showing animated pins dancing, arguing and sticking out their tongues.

"Can I help you, young lady?" the attendant asked as I neared the counter. Toby's eyes widened as he looked everywhere, almost as if it were *his* first time in the place.

"Um," I stammered, losing bravado as I stalled, "I want to bowl."

"Well then, you've come to the right place," the attendant said. He seemed friendly enough. He was a large man with a big gut and greasy hair, but when I answered, he smiled to reveal that he still had all his teeth, even if they were slightly discoloured.

"That's Mack," Toby explained while he rubbed his neck. "He's a really nice guy, like a second dad to me…" He looked very pale as he watched Mack. I figured it was because we were so close to his past life. *How would I feel if the tables were turned?*

A boy with brownish-red hair and an olive complexion pushed past me. Mack turned his attention to this new customer, holding his finger up for me to wait. Toby watched as they interacted. I welcomed the break as I checked out the place myself. I saw a few other single bowlers and, as I watched, each one seemed to be enjoying themselves. *This might not be so bad.* I turned back to the counter as the boy strutted away. Toby narrowed his eyes, then when he noticed me, he relaxed and smiled.

Mack returned to me. "Sorry about that. He's our star player."

Feeling a little less nervous, I admitted, "I've never played before."

"Well, I wouldn't kick you out for that." His voice was gruff but kind. It sounded like it should be coming from someone older-looking.

"Thank you," I stuttered. Toby gave me a gentle shove, so I stepped up to the counter.

"Don't worry, we'll get you all set up." Mack smiled again.

"Thank you," I repeated a little too happily. I was ping-ponging between tension and relief.

"You betcha," he said, and then when I continued to stand there, he added, "I need your shoes." I could tell he was having fun with my inexperience.

"What for?" I asked

Toby chuckled. He seemed to be enjoying himself too now. "You need bowling shoes."

"Why?" I asked, and I was relieved that it made sense to Mack as well.

"Well, to tell you the truth, I don't like these shoes much myself," he admitted, fanning his hands at the shelves of bright red shoes behind him. "I bought my own, but if you don't have the right footwear, you could damage our floors.

I removed my shoes and placed them on the counter. He took them and handed me a pair of stiff, worn bowling shoes. "If they don't fit, just bring them back, and we'll get you set up right. And if they do, come on back still, and I'll get someone to show you the ropes. It's really easy, and once you've played one game, you'll be an addict.

I took the bowling shoes over to a nearby bench and tried them on. They felt uncomfortable, and my feet were cramped in them.

"Sometimes they don't fit the same as regular shoe sizes," Toby said. I got the impression something else was on his mind, and I wanted to ask what it was. I felt a strange feeling at the pit of my stomach that I was beginning to suspect was actually Toby's feelings, but I didn't want to say anything, because I knew I was too close to other people, and I had no paper to use. So I lingered, hoping he'd say something, but he didn't. That feeling continued to gnaw at my intestines.

After returning the first shoes for a second, slightly bigger pair that fit as well as they ever would, I went back to the counter where Mack was waiting. He stood on the outside of the desk, and when he spotted me, he waved for me to follow.

"I got the perfect person to teach you about bowling." He was heading deeper into the building toward the lanes marked one to five. He stopped at lane three and called out, "Yo, Tony!" The red-haired boy looked up. "He's sort of our bowling alley's mascot, if you know what I mean," Mack said. I hung back and watched as they spoke.

"Got a problem, the kind you're good at," Mack was saying. Tony was standing with three other guys. They all looked up and looked me over. I felt a bit like an animal on show, but more upsetting was the way Toby stepped in front of me in a protective way, *as if he could stop them from being able to see me: he was air to everyone but me!* He was also facing away from me, so I couldn't read the expression on his face.

"What's up, Mack?" Tony asked, peeling away from the pack and following Mack to where I stood. Tony didn't know it, but he ended up stopping in the exact spot where Toby stood rooted to the floor. I thought I saw Tony shiver just a touch before Toby stepped to the side and pivoted on his heel to face me. He wore an expression of great discomfort, but I had seen him look just as put out when other people had walked through him.

"Well, Tone, this lovely young lady has never experienced the pure joy of bowling, and we want her to like it so she'll come back..." Mack gave me a wink. "So, I was thinking you'd take a few minutes to run her through the drill, teach her a trick or too, maybe?" Mack studied Tony's face while he took a moment to ponder the request.

My gut started to tighten as he scanned me head to toe and back up again. A tiny sparkle sprang into Tony's eyes, and he gave a sly grin. "Sure thing." He turned to Mack adding, "It would be my pleasure." Then he quickly took three steps to close the gap between us. Behind him I could see his friends giving each other high fives. *Had someone scored?*

I quickly glanced over at Toby, not knowing what to do, or how I felt, but he didn't look at me, so I was stuck with the events that had been set in motion. *Is this what Toby thought would happen?* Or did he want to teach me himself?

"I'll put her on this lane then, and I can trust you to take good care of her?" Mack said as he turned to leave.

"You have my word on it," Tony replied. He had deep brown eyes that felt vaguely familiar.

"You're in good hands, young lady," Mack said without turning back. "Just give me a few moments to get her set up."

"Yup," Tony answered, and then said to me, "Never played before?" I could tell Tony wasn't a shy guy.

"Tone?" one of his friends called, but Tony just gave them a shooing wave.

"Never even set foot in a bowling building before."

"Alley." Tony smiled at me, and suddenly all apprehension or nervousness faded, replaced with a feeling like tiny champagne bubbles popping in my stomach—but in a good way.

"Well, this is like a second home to me. By the way, my name is Tony." He put out a hand.

"I'm Mariah," I answered, and taking his hand, I realized that I felt really comfortable with him, like he was an old friend I had already known from somewhere.

"Don't worry, Mariah; bowling is one of the easiest games to learn. I can tell you're going to be a pro by the end of the day."

I blushed and thanked him, aware that he hadn't released my hand yet. I stole a glance in Toby's direction. He had taken a seat on one of the benches nearby. He looked lost in deep contemplation, his hand on the back of his neck.

"Looks like your scoreboard is ready," Tony said, finally dropping my hand and going over to a chair in front of the computer screen. "How do you spell your name?"

I spelled it out. He complimented me on having such a beautiful name, and I could feel myself blush harder. After a few brief keystrokes, my name came up on the computer and the TV at the top of lane three, with a line of numbers and columns under it.

"'Kay," Tony said, swinging around to face me.

He was interrupted immediately by one of his pals. "You're up, Tone."

"Ya. Get Larry to take my turn," he called back. But he didn't remove his eyes from me. His friends left him alone after that.

"Why don't we go sit on that bench, and I'll explain to you how the game works."

I was the first to sit, and even though the bench was big enough for four adults to sit on it without touching, Tony sat so close to me that our knees touched. I felt a tickle working its way up my spine, something I'd never experienced before in my life. Toby took a seat on the other side of me and put a hand on my arm. He glared past me at Tony the rest of the time. *Was he jealous that Tony was teaching me?*

"Alright." I was amazed at how just Tony's gaze could command all my attention. "Bowling is all about balls…" He brought his arm up and slipped it behind my head. "You'll get three balls to try and knock down those pins over there." He pointed down the lane then started to fiddle with a loose strand of my hair, making me feel off balance. "Knock down all the pins— that's really the goal of the game." If you do it with just one ball, it's a strike, and that's the best score to have." He continued on to the finer points of the game, the scoring and the strategies. I tried to listen but found it hard to keep track, since I was preoccupied by his touch and smell; he smelled like old spice (what my father had always worn), and I was lost in it all.

"Got it so far?" he asked, bringing me back to my senses. I nodded, though I wasn't sure I did. "Good, I knew you'd be a quick learner." His compliment made me beam, even though I knew in the back of my mind that he was just giving me a line.

I could see Toby scowling out of the corner of my eye, but I was quickly distracted by the lesson. It took almost fifteen minutes to explain everything, in which time Tony had missed three more throws in his own game.

"Can I show you how to throw the ball?" he asked, holding out his hand to me. I took it and was surprised when he continued to hold my hand all the way to the top of the lane. Toby followed and sat on the chair at the computer screen. I had thought Tony was going to do the first throw for me to watch, but I was mistaken. First he led me to the top of my lane, then he let go of my hand and grabbed my hips to direct me into the exact spot he wanted, and finally he came directly behind me, so that his front rested against my back, and he walked me through the steps of set-up and release.

I felt torn between two emotions: discomfort over being so intimate, yet elated over having this attractive boy enjoying my company! *Why?* Yet a third, strong and unpleasant emotion would wash over me whenever I caught sight of Toby: *guilt*. I tried hard not to look in his direction.

After walking me through the motions three times, I got the impression that Tony was stalling to spend more time with me. *Why would he do that?*

Even so, my chest swelled at the thought, and I blushed. With Tony at my back I picked up my first ball, pulled it back and swung it forward, releasing it just as Tony had instructed. It hit the lane exactly where he said it should, but by halfway down, it ended up in the gutter.

"No big deal," Tony said.

I saw his friends signaling to him to let him know he was going to miss his fourth turn. "You can go back to your game now if you need to," I said as I stepped away from him. I felt bad at how much of his time I was dominating, especially since his friends seemed less than thrilled now. *I hated feeling like I was making anyone unhappy.*

"Yes, go," I heard Toby breath from the chair he was sitting on.

"Or I could stay and play this game with you," Tony rebutted.

I wasn't sure what I should do next. In desperation I looked to where Toby sat, hoping he'd give me a hint. He shook his head and crossed his arms, narrowing his eyes at Tony. *Was he trying to read Tony's thoughts?*

Tony took my hesitation as a need for more convincing. He took me by my waist and turned me around. *Surprisingly, I didn't feel so uncomfortable with his hands on me…* "I'll help you more." When I still didn't answer, he asked, "Do you want me to stay? Please say yes."

I wanted him to stay, heck, I'd have run away with him in that moment because of the way he was looking at me like I was the only girl on the planet. But I was having trouble with the way Toby seemed to be taking this turn of events. I didn't want to hurt him, so I shrugged my answer.

"Alright," Tony said, "how about a bet? If I can throw a strike with this one ball, then I'll join you, 'kay?"

Was I being set up? I didn't care. This way I could say yes without intentionally hurting Toby's feelings; I could only imagine how he felt not being able to be seen by anyone but me, but I was quite enjoying interacting with someone real.

Tony didn't hesitate, and within a few seconds, he had all five pins knocked down. "Wow," he said with less than genuine shock, "I guess I *am* good." He had a triumphant look on his face. "Guess that means I get to stay." He swept my hand up in his and held it to his chest while he said, "Don't go anywhere, I'll be right back. I'm gonna tell Mack to put me on your game card, then we can have some real fun." Releasing my hand, he walked off confidently.

I sat down in the chair next to Toby. He was in front of the computer screen for lane 4, which was empty. I brought my knees up to my chin and hid my face in my arms so I could whisper. "What's wrong?"

"He's playing you." Toby was picking at his threadbare socks. They were the same he'd had on since the first day he'd come into my life. "He's trying to soften you up and swoop in. I've seen it many times before." Beyond Toby I could see Tony's friends sneaking glances at me sitting all by myself.

"What should I do?" *I didn't want to tell Tony to go away! I liked being with him. Even if he was softening me up, it felt good.*

"I don't know," Toby replied, and he looked completely defeated. "Just be careful. We can talk more when we get back home; we'll have lots of time then. Have fun, that's what I brought you here to do, just be careful." He looked like he wanted to say more, but instead he fell silent.

I gave a jerk of a nod as I caught sight of Tony returning. Looking up at the television, I saw that Tony's name had been added under mine. My first box had a strike in it from Tony's throw, and I could see I still had one ball left to go.

"You gonna take your last turn?" Tony had gone straight to the alley and was holding out a green ball for me to take.

By halfway through our first game, I was sometimes able to hit a few pins down on my first ball, and more on my second and third. However, the only strike on my scorecard was still the one by Tony. He would have creamed me if we were playing for keeps, but it wasn't that kind of game. Instead it was fun right to the end.

On his final frame, Tony turned back and said to me, as I stood off to the side behind him, "If I get three strikes in a row, you play another game with me." When I didn't answer, he threw the ball and got his first strike; then his second ball and a second strike.

Just as he pulled back for his third, Toby came to my side and said, "He's going to do it."

"Hmmm," I said low so that no one could hear me.

"He's done this before." Toby didn't seem impressed in the least. I wondered if he knew because he was glimpsing into Tony's life or for other reasons, but I never got a chance to ask.

With a thunderous clap, five pegs hit the polished surface of the lane. Tony turned, triumph in his eyes, and ran over to me, sweeping me up in his embrace. There was a moment where I thought he might kiss me, but his friends coming over to us interrupted it. As they neared, Tony gently released me. I thought I saw disappointment in his eyes, *or was that just a reflection of my own thoughts?*

"Nice score," said one, who was just a bit shorter than the other three, with a round face that looked like his skin was a bit too loose. He was plump, his eyes were brown-green, and his hair was light brown, with frizzy dry ends, giving him a fuzzy peach look.

"I've seen him play better," said another, standing next to his identical twin, both with short blond hair and tanned faces.

"Mariah," Tony said, sweeping his hand towards his three friends, "this is Larry," the plump one smiled at me, "Sam and Sean, they're twins, in case you didn't notice." I wasn't sure which was which and never got it straight for the rest of the afternoon.

"How about we all play this next game together?" Tony offered, and when I didn't agree immediately, he added, "My treat." This got a good response from the three boys, and I couldn't think of any reason not to, so Tony set it up with Mack, and soon we were all taking turns.

It was different playing in the group, a lot more sitting around and waiting. I was struck with the realization that this was the first time in my life when I'd been alone with a group of boys other than my brother's thugs. I marveled at the difference, though as different as it was, I still felt nervous.

Tony seemed to play even better than in our first game, which came as no shock to any of his companions. My turn was just after his, so he'd wait for me and help me with my throw. In time I was able to get two spares, but no strikes. When he wasn't throwing, Tony stayed glued to my side. I liked the way that felt.

None of his three friends seemed interested in talking to me, so I used the time between my turns to just sit back and observe. The four of them seemed close, the kind of closeness you get from years of being together sharing experiences and adventures, although it can sometimes happen much quicker. It was interesting to watch; they seemed to have a lot of inside jokes, so I felt constantly like I was missing something. They even spoke with the same catchphrases. And they were very physical with each other, giving rambunctious high fives and rather rough looking slaps, pushes and the odd noogie. Yet as tight as they seemed, it felt like something was missing. They would awkwardly pause mid-sentence from time to time or fall quiet for no reason, and a couple of times they would crack a joke then turn to Tony with apprehensive looks. I wondered if it was me that caused such subtle discord.

Toby, my shadow friend, stayed quiet, but extra close. He seemed to be even tenser initially when Tony's friends came to join us, but as the game got on its way, he relaxed slightly. I continued to marvel at the similarities between Toby and Tony: just the similarity of the names was enough to get me intrigued, but even more interesting, they both seemed to have the same walk, same talk, and even the same way of sitting. It gave me chills, and I wondered if it was just because I liked them both, *or did I like Tony because he was a bit like Toby?*

The boys ordered fries for us to share, and Tony bought me a drink. I came in fifth, but it didn't seem so bad, this being only my second game. Larry suggested we go and hang out at the food court in the adjacent mall. This made Toby so tense, he made fists and his fingers turned white. Only when I declined did he seem to relax.

I watched all four boys remove their shoes and head out the front door, and then I had Mack set me up for my third game, finally all by myself. Toby seemed much more light- hearted as I stood at the top of the alley lining up my ball.

"You really are doing good for your first time," he said. I smiled in his direction and took my shot.

The ball glided gracefully up the alley and didn't sway one bit from the course I had set it on. It hit the lead pin just perfectly off centre, and down tumbled all five! I jumped for joy and saw Toby do the same. I wished more than ever that I could have run to give him a hug, but instead I got embraced from behind.

"Way to go," Tony said softly in my ear. I turned to face him. Looking down, I saw he had put his bowling shoes back on. "I didn't feel like going to the food court if you weren't going to be there. Mind if I join you for another game?"

"Okay," I said, wanting to be kissed right there, but Tony let me go and threw his coat over the empty chair. "I'll tell Mack."

"Remember, he's playing you," Toby said softly from right beside me, causing a sense of reality to come crashing down on me. I didn't want to hear it, so I moved over to the seat and breathed deep the smell that wafted up from Tony's jacket.

"You can't get away from me," Toby said, sitting in the empty seat beside me but looking dejected. I gave a quick shrug and looked over at Tony as he talked to Mack. "Please be careful," Toby pleaded. I pretended not to hear him. When Tony returned, I tried to stay as far away from Toby as I could.

It was a wonderful game. I got two strikes in total, and with each of my victories, Tony celebrated with me. He said that my success made him look good as a teacher. Toby kept trying to warn me, and he made it a practice to stay as close to me as Tony did, which meant that at times I was being book ended by the two boys.

I didn't want the evening to end. Tony tried to entice me into a fourth game, but I was feeling like it was time to go home. It was getting close to dinner, and I could feel myself becoming distracted by hunger. On top of that, Toby was getting quite insistent, and I was finding it hard to think past him.

As we sat on the bench changing our shoes, Tony asked, "Where do you live?"

"Near the creek," I answered, distracted by a knot in my laces.

"That's a ways off. Did you drive?"

"No." I pulled and tugged at my lace. "Took the bus."

Tony, who had already managed to get into his street shoes, moved to kneel in front of me. Taking my foot, he set it on his knee to work out the knot himself. He had it untangled in seconds, and then he looked up and my breath caught. "I could give you a lift."

"I need to talk to you," Toby said in a commanding voice and placed a hand on my shoulder. "Now!"

I jumped slightly at the urgency of his tone. "Where are the washrooms?" I asked Tony, and he pointed down to the back of the bowling alley. "I'll be right back." I excused myself while Toby dragged me away.

He was agitated; he paced back and forth as I leaned with my back against the row of sinks. He took a few seconds to collect his thoughts, while he kept glancing at himself in the mirrors and shaking his head or rubbing the back of his neck. Finally, he stopped and turned to face me. "Don't let Tony see where you live."

"Why not?"

"I'll tell you everything at home. Just please trust me. Tony is not the kind of person you want knowing your 411."

I nodded, wondering if Toby could sense what I was feeling. I felt intoxicated, giddy, and very alive. Toby however looked a complete wreck; his eyes darted all around the room as if he were trying to see something that wasn't there. I waited to see if he had more to say, because it looked like there was more, then I finally asked, "Anything else?" My voice was just above a whisper.

When I got out, I couldn't see Tony and thought he had left. Disappointment fell like a lead balloon in my chest, but in moments he came sweeping up behind me.

"Coming, beautiful?" he said, catching me around the waist and starting for the door. I thoroughly enjoyed the feeling of his arm around me as we walked. But the more I enjoyed it, the guiltier I felt, and it didn't help to have Toby sigh whenever my feelings started to overwhelm me.

Tony led me to an olive-green car—he said it was a Lincoln Continental—in the parking lot. With an air of pride, he told me his wasn't in too bad a condition, and he was always improving it. He opened the front door for me to get in, and I was surprised to find the front was a bench seat. The back door opened out backwards. Tony explained that it was a suicide door, but Toby didn't have to open it to slip into the car.

Tony was quiet on the ride home. He made the occasional remark and took directions when they were needed. Otherwise he seemed focused on the traffic, checking in his rear view mirror often. I guided him to a guest parking lot two blocks from my townhouse, the closest free parking near me, far enough away to keep Toby happy. It was surrounded by high cement walls, with a flight of hidden stone steps that went into my complex.

I thanked Tony for the ride, and he said, "My pleasure." He said he hoped to see me again. "Perhaps this Wednesday? At the alley." I assured him that I'd try and slipped from the front seat.

Toby acted agitated for over an hour after we were home. Figuring I wouldn't like what he had to say, I allowed him as much space as was possible. I didn't ask any questions or say a word while I made myself a light dinner. As miserable as Toby seemed I, on the other hand, was elated when I thought about the day. I'd blush at the memory of Tony helping me aim the ball; I'd catch myself smiling at the way he gave me a huge hug when I knocked my first pin down, and so on…then I'd check to see if Toby knew what I was thinking. *Surely he could feel my good mood.*

Finally he was calm enough to talk. We sat in my room with the door protectively shut. Between my four walls was a secret, private world, where Toby was very much real, and I was not afraid to talk with him freely.

His tone sounded like he was making a confession; he said, "Tony used to be my best pal." My eyes widened until they felt like they might fall out of their sockets, but I kept my mouth closed as he continued. "I was sorta the leader." He rubbed the back of his neck, a habit that I was slowly discovering meant he was having a deep thought or a memory. "Tony was my right-hand man. Together we were the toughest, meanest bullies of East Ridge High. I can't tell you all the things we did, and I won't. The list is too long and horrible to recount. But believe me, I'm sickened by it now." Toby closed his eyes and ran his hand through his hair.

"It all seemed so damned important at the time: social standing, keeping others in their place, the parties, the girls," here he glanced at me, "the stupid, mean and dangerous pranks done in the name of fun." Toby leaned heavily against the wall and rubbed his face in his hands as if trying to wash it all off him.

"It's all meaningless now," he said, taking his hands from his face and looking at them. I could see the remorse on his fine facial features. "I wish someone would have been able to tell me before now." Then he rolled over onto his side and curled up into the fetal position.

I was filled with such compassion. *He seemed to be hurting so deeply.* I lay down next to him and rubbed his back. He rolled over to face me. "Why are you being so nice? How can you care about me? I would have showed you no mercy. I would have used you for my own selfish pleasures then tossed you away like a Kleenex, or worse, hurt you so badly, you wouldn't have been able to live it down." His voice shook as he choked back tears.

I brought my hand to his cheek and wiped at a tear that clung to the corner of his eye. *I'd never seen a boy cry before.* "I care because we are connected."

Toby tried to sound casual. "You mean you care because you have to?"

I smiled "But you haven't done any of those things to me." *And even though I knew what he told me was true, somehow I just couldn't believe it about him.*

Toby rolled away and buried his face in the sheets. I left my hand on his head, gently caressing his hair. I could feel his pain in the pit of my stomach like it was my own. As I tried to comfort him, I wondered what regrets I would have faced had I been the dead one. *The regret of not truly living—of hiding myself away from the world?*

Toby pushed himself up to kneeling and caught both my hands in his. "I know what I want to ask you to do," he said with determination, though his hands shook slightly.

"Yes?" I said with mounting excitement, ready to face any task he asked of me.

"I need you to give Tony a message…from me."

"What?" I gasped, for it felt like all the air in my lungs had disappeared. All I could think of was how much I had enjoyed being with Tony, and that would all change once I told him I had a message from his dead friend. *Why had Toby asked me to do the one thing I didn't want to do?*

"It's really important for me to tell him what I know before it's too late for him!" Toby squeezed my hands. "You see, I'm responsible for Tony. I'm the one who taught him everything about living wrong."

I nodded. *I said I would do this for Toby, and I would*, despite how much I didn't want to. I didn't have to like it; I just had to do it. "I'll go on Wednesday. He invited me, so he should be glad to see me." *Until I tell him I am haunted by the ghost who was once his best friend, then he'll call the cops on me, and never kiss me*, I thought miserably.

"Thanks." Toby let my hands drop as he sat back down. He seemed like he wanted to say something else, but we were interrupted by the phone ringing.

I raced up to the kitchen, Toby in tow, and answered only slightly out of breath. "Is this Mariah?" a familiar voice asked after I'd said a greeting.

"Yes," I said, trying to place the voice.

"This is Cindy."

Cindy from school? "Oh." I was taken aback.

"Don't get mad," she said breathlessly. "But I snooped for your number in the janitor's report about your locker."

"Oh." I was flabbergasted. She had gone to the trouble of seeking me out. *Why?*

"Um," Cindy's voice faltered, and she sounded flustered. "I was wondering what you were doing tomorrow."

"Me?" I looked to Toby.

He smiled. "See, someone is interested in being your friend."

A bubble welled up inside. Something I hadn't even dared to hope for, for over six years, was unfolding right in front of me. It made me beam, *but was it too good to be true?* Toby fell to the floor as if something had knocked him over the head. He sat up to reveal a bruised cheek with a splatter of blood in one spot.

"Ya, you," Cindy answered.

"I'm sorry!" I whispered as I covered the phone so Cindy wouldn't hear.

Toby shook his head while he held his damaged cheek. *Always the same side*, I thought, feeling even more miserable.

"Answer her!" Toby said, pointing to the phone.

"Well…" I started hesitantly. I didn't want to sound too eager. "I might have plans already." Toby did a double take, looking shocked, and then he shook his head.

"Oh." Cindy sounded crestfallen. *Was she disappointed?*

"No, hold on, I think I'm free," I added quickly as she was starting to say her farewells.

"Really?" Hope returned to her voice.

"Yes. I couldn't remember if I had something planned, but I've checked now," I added lamely.

"Oh, so then you aren't busy." She hesitated then said, "Because I called to ask: do you want to meet up with me at the mall?"

"Absolutely." And I couldn't help myself smiling so widely that I felt my lips cracking. Toby grinned at me. After planning it out, I hung up and said, "Did you hear that? She wanted me, ME to hang out with her."

"I heard. That surprises you?" Toby asked. He was back on his feet, and he reached over to give me a slap on the back.

I steadied myself and confessed, "It does."

"It doesn't surprise me." Toby flinched and rubbed his jaw.

I looked down at the ground. A guilty feeling squirmed like a fish swimming upstream in my belly. "I'm really sorry about that."

"I know." *He never got mad.*

"Why does it keep happening?"

"I have a thought." Toby put his hand on my cheek so that I'd look at him. "Don't worry, it's just one aspect of our time together, and I wouldn't trade it for anything… Now, what are you going to wear tomorrow?"

We spent over an hour picking out my clothes. It was only after my teeth were brushed and I sat in bed under my covers that I came back to his bruised face. He was sitting at the foot of my bed, his back against the wall, staring at my stuffed unicorn collection.

"What's your theory?" I asked with my head heavy on my pillow.

"Actually, I'm still trying to work out all the points," he admitted. "Can you give me some time to put it together? I promise to tell you as soon as I've got it."

"Alright," I answered, finding it odd how comfortable I'd become with Toby, *a boy!* In fact, I was really beginning to like it. As I was carried off into dreamland, I had one fleeting thought: I wished Toby was a real boy, and he could be my boyfriend. Rolling over, I felt my foot rest against his leg. Warmth spread through the sole of my foot as my wish played itself out in my dreams.

DAY 7 Sunday...

WHEN I WOKE, I FELT NOT EXACTLY CONFIDENT, but a bit bolder. *I had friends! I was going to go to the mall!* Toby was quite hard to read, but he'd return my smiles when I looked at him. I was so giddy, I almost forgot to tell him to turn around as I undressed for my shower. "Whoops," I said with my shirt in my hands, "turn, please."

I was halfway through my shower, warm water running through my hair and down my back, enjoying the tranquility, when Toby spoke again. "I have a test for you," he said casually.

I lathered soap in my hands, worry creeping into my body. "What is it?"

"Just a test."

"Do we have to do this now?"

"Ya, I think this is the best time." *Now? I was in the shower!*

"Alright then."

"But first I need to tell you that I think you are quite beautiful, and I have to confess that I find myself attracted to you."

He had said exactly what I wanted to hear...then I looked down at my arms. They wobbled as I scrubbed them. *How could he be telling the truth?*

"I've seen the way others boys check you out too."

I put my hands on my belly and squeezed it then shook my head in disbelief.

"And your eyes…" Toby's voice broke, and he cleared his throat, "when you smile they seem to sparkle."

I felt it, more than I heard it: Toby being slammed across the room, the bathroom door rattling as he fell into it. I stuck my head out a crack in the curtain, being careful not to expose myself and looked sternly at him. His lip had started to bleed, but I almost felt he deserved it. "What are you playing at?" I snapped, and then softened as he looked up into my face.

"It's easy for me to see why Tony likes you." He braced himself, then relaxed when he wasn't hit again.

"What are you trying to do?" I didn't realize how close to tears I'd been until I heard it in my voice.

Slowly he pulled himself up. "If you are given a true compliment that you can't believe, you let it beat you up inside." I could see the bruise on his face starting to set in.

I pulled myself behind the shower curtain and hid under the water, but his words continued to bother me. "It turns to poison in your mind. You'll pick it apart and rip it into shreds, then glue it back together so it becomes twisted, something that was never meant to be. When that doesn't work, you'll actually attack yourself until you are so low, the compliment has nowhere to go, and it slips away."

"I don't understand."

"Your negative self-image runs so deep that it overrides anything anyone else feels about you." I started to lather my hair. "Like when I said 'I could see what Tony likes about you,' what was your immediate thought?" I hesitated, and the shower curtain moved inwards with a thwack, as if Toby had hit it.

"I figured he just thought I was easy," I said.

"Ya, you already think the worst of yourself, so in your head you'll twist comments into agreement with your own marred image. But what happened when I said your eyes sparkled?"

"I felt sick," I replied, trying not to get too close to the actual emotion, for fear it would knock him right out of the bathroom.

"You couldn't handle it. And I think if you were really honest with yourself, you'd admit that you run a recording in your head of all your failures just to completely degrade yourself."

I leaned further into the water. I could feel myriad negative memories dancing and teasing me just beyond my thoughts. *How was I supposed to overcome that?* "What can I do?"

"Stop listening to those lies."

That was easier said than done. I turned off the water and wrapped myself in a towel, stepping from the shower. I brushed my hair in silence and thought about it more and more. I wondered what it would feel like if I could actually do that. It was impossible for me to imagine. "What do you think that would look like?" I said more to myself.

Toby stepped behind me, his reflection crisp in the freshly wiped mirror. "Well, for starters, I wouldn't have a black eye." I subconsciously put my hand on the top of my towel so it wouldn't slip down and stepped away from him.

"I need to change." I choked over my own feelings. "Please turn around," I said more strongly as he continued to stare. I could see his good cheek turning bright red, and then he shook his head and shut his eyes, disappearing.

•••

As I stepped down from the bus, I saw Cindy walking my way. I was excited, nervous and a bit shy as she approached. She wore a pair of loose slacks with a pink T-shirt from a popular band, and she had sparkles on her cheeks that enhanced her innocent appearance. Standing in front of her, I became tongue-tied and couldn't think of a single thing to say.

She fixed that in an instant. "Listen, I hope you don't mind, but I also invited Rayla and Charlie to join us." I nodded, not sure if I did mind. "We'll meet up with them at the food court in an hour. They were both so happy to hear you would be joining us." I smiled at that, even though I had a hard time believing her. I started to follow her down the street to the mall. She linked her arm in mine as we went. Her head only came to my shoulder. We had to walk through the parking lot to the massive shopping mall with over four hundred stores and shops, a movie complex and an arcade.

"I think I've figured out a way to work on your self-image," Toby said in my left ear. *Now, why now!* Toby appeared and walked in stride with me. "I know you think this is extremely bad timing, you just want to hang out. But I think this is the best way to tell you." Sneaking a look, I saw his face was serious. *At least he wasn't taking pleasure in this.*

I turned away from him to show how disgusted I was. It felt like blackmail. Cindy was one of those people who could take a mundane thing and turn it into a great story. Right now she was embellishing her last time at the mall in one of her favourite clothing stores. I tried to concentrate, but it was hard with Toby walking so close that he almost tripped me twice.

"Listen, I know you aren't going to like what I tell you to do. So I figured this way you can't argue, but I was hoping it would also give you an opportunity to not think about it too long and just be able to do it." I felt cornered, and I hated that feeling. *What if I didn't want to?*

Cindy was recounting how she got an item discounted ninety percent when it was fresh on the rack just that day. She had a good nose for discounts and deals, and she liked to show off a little. Toby stuck his hand in front of my face, making me lose my footing and almost twist my ankle.

"Whoa," Cindy said, steadying me. "You just might be more clumsy than me… I trip on most everything: dogs, cats, other people, gum wrappers and cracks in the sidewalk, but I didn't see anything there." She looked down carefully.

I forced a fake smile. "I think I felt the wind kick up."

This elicited a gale of laughter from her. I used this opportunity to turn and glare at Toby. He gave me an innocent puppy look and shrugged.

"I am soooooo glad you came today. You know, Rayla told me how witty you are, and sometimes she can be a bit over the top, but I do believe she was bang on about you." Then she was off on a new topic.

"Here's what I want you to do." Toby's voice cut over Cindy's. I swatted my hand at him like I was trying to flick at a fly, but that didn't faze him. "Every time someone gives you a compliment today, I want you to answer 'yes, that's true,' got it?" I didn't respond. "Or we could go the other way," he said threateningly. Anger welled up, and for a moment I forgot that I was the only one who could hear him.

"What other way?" I said before I could stop myself, and immediately bit my lip.

"The other way is around the building to the back," Cindy answered, pointing. "It's much closer to all the good shops, but you have to walk outside most of the way." We were approaching the east entrance, the one she had said was the main entrance.

I breathed a sigh of relief. Toby pulled on my arm, and I stopped dead in my tracks. "This," he answered, pointing at his discoloured cheek.

"What?" Cindy asked. She stood staring at me, eyes wide and looking shaken. When Toby stopped me, my arm had been yanked out of hers.

"I, ah," I turned away from Toby and looked down to the sidewalk, "thought I saw an ant on me." Cindy gave a nervous giggle. "Or some other kind of pest," I added under my breath.

Cindy scanned me up and down. "I can't see anything." Then she linked her arm in mine again and started towards the front doors. "You sure it was an ant? Not a spider? I don't like spiders at all."

"Well, anything that's crawling all over you can't feel that nice." I hoped Cindy wouldn't notice how angry I sounded, and I hoped Toby would.

"Except boys," she interjected.

I smiled and added, "Except *certain* boys."

Cindy nodded. The smile faded from my lips as Toby caught my free arm and began walking in step with me again. "Do we have a deal?"

"So your phobia is ants," Cindy had just finished asking.

I figured my answer could cover both conversations. "I've got no choice." This miniscule success made me swell with cunning pride. Toby backed off.

"I guess not," Cindy said. "Any reason for it? I mean, I'm a little jumpy around spiders, but that makes more sense than ants."

I shrugged. *How quickly I could lose confidence in myself.* "Nothing, really. Do you have any specific reason?" I wished I didn't have this new fake phobia. Somehow I felt like it was going to come back on me in the end.

"Na, just my brother did a book report on them when I was nine, and he showed me all these close-ups of spiders. Then he collected a jar of about seven and didn't make sure the lid was on properly, so three escaped. I've been jumpy about the little suckers ever since."

Remembering a time when Jake had left his empty pop bottle on the living room floor and I had woken up the next day to a whole colony moving into it, I recounted that story, trying not to embellish, for I knew that if I did, I'd have to remember what I'd made up so I could be consistent in the future. I hated that I had to lie so early in our new friendship.

"That's alright," Cindy said, as we reached the front doors. "We've all got our own quirks."

Toby mercifully left me alone while we shopped. We did three times as much looking as trying on, and twice as much trying as buying. When we did end up purchasing, Cindy was able to haggle and persuade the sales clerk to drop the price. I got a few really great deals that day, one a beautiful pink sweater with a raised knitted pattern. It wasn't quite form fitting, but I didn't look like a balloon in it, and the cotton against my skin felt nice and comforting. It was the last one, so Cindy was able to bargain for half off. I was impressed, because it was from a posh high-end store.

At three, we met up with Rayla and Charlie in the food court. Rayla wore a pair of overalls that were lime green and a neon yellow shirt. She had her short hair in several ponytails all over her head, and she had on bright pink lipstick. Charlie, in contrast, who was almost twice Rayla's height, wore a long dark maroon shirt and pants that flared past her ankles. Her long black hair was pulled back in loose braids. We made a motley bunch sitting together.

I saved the table for everyone while the other three went to buy their food. They had all intended to get separate meals from separate vendors but ended up going to Burger King together to wait in line. I swelled with joy at the success of my day, but when I watched the three laughing as they waited, I still felt a little bit like an outsider.

The food court was at least three times bigger than our school cafeteria. It had over thirty different places to buy your meal. It was packed with people of all ages: families, other groups of friends, couples and hungry children.

As I sat, I could smell fresh cinnamon buns from one vender and fries being cooked at another. My stomach growled.

"What are you planning to get for lunch?" Toby inquired, kneeling down next to me so our faces were at the same level.

"I don't know," I whispered out of the side of my mouth. I wondered if all this practice would make me a skilled ventriloquist.

"What's your favourite?" My mouth began to water at the thought of it.

I already had planned out what I wanted; I just didn't want my new friends to judge me, thinking I was strange. I liked having them, and I didn't want to change their opinion of me, because I clearly had different tastes. "I might skip lunch," I said, trying to sound casual.

"Why? You are really hungry. Even I can feel it!" I didn't look at him. "Are you afraid Rayla, Cindy or Charlie will stop liking you if you don't get the same meal as they do?" I gave a curt nod. "You're being silly." I crossed my arms. "So you're willing to lie and say you aren't hungry and be the only one to sit here not eating? Do you think you'll feel more comfortable doing that?"

"That's my plan," I replied curtly, trying not to let what he had said bug me.

"It's not going to work." He shook his head.

What did he know? "What do you care?" I was still speaking out of the corner of my mouth and trying to keep my voice just above a whisper. "Your whole mission today is to make a fool of me anyway." Toby looked hurt, but he didn't say anything else. "Because of you, I had to lie, and twice I've acted like a moron."

"Why do you say that?" Toby sounded hurt. He moved to a seat where he could see me clearly, blocking my view of the girls, who continued to wait in a growing line-up.

"You humiliated me with Cindy on the way here. I had to come up with that stupid excuse about ants! And now you want me to say... What was it?" The family who sat at the next table finished and moved away.

"I want you to agree by saying 'yes, that's true' when you are given a compliment! How will that make you look bad?"

"No one else does that! I'll look either foolish or like a self-righteous prude." I kept my eyes on the three girls over Toby's head. They were one person away from being served. A woman wearing a uniform from one of the shops took the empty table.

"I just want you to stop feeling so bad." Toby turned and checked the situation with the girls, then looked back to me. The bruise on his cheek was still a bright purple.

"Or you don't want to feel so bad any more?" I accused. I looked back to my friends. The woman beside me took out a book to read. *Had she heard me?*

"I won't lie... these hits aren't pleasant!" He stopped to rub his cheek. "They really do hurt." I felt a momentary twinge of guilt.

"That just proves my point." Feeling guilty just made me madder.

"But…" Toby cut in. "It's your pain! Everything I feel is the physical equivalent to your emotional trauma. It's like the truer, tangible and unmistakable pain that you subject yourself to all the time. I am trying to do it for you, not for me!"

I wanted to keep fighting. I was ticked off. But I couldn't say anything more, since Rayla had returned.

She dropped her tray with an exaggerated thud. "Your turn." She sat in the seat where Toby had been moments before. By then he'd taken up his silent, invisible post behind me.

"I was thinking I'd skip lunch," I said. I felt like whatever I said or did, I was doomed to failure, and I would eventually be rejected. I didn't have to look at Toby to see he was feeling the stress that I tried to swallow.

Charlie and Cindy came to sit in the two free seats beside us. "Out of money already?" Cindy asked, nibbling on a fry.

I shook my head. "No, just wanted to watch my figure."

"Why, does it do something special?" Charlie asked, and then laughed at her own joke.

"Ya," I returned, "it expands."

Rayla put her hand over her mouth to keep the food from spraying as she laughed. Cindy wasn't as lucky; she ended up drooling her drink down her shirt.

"I bet it shrinks too." Charlie winked at me. "Please don't think I was trying to be rude. And honestly, I think you have quite a nice figure."

For a hippo!

Toby came to kneel by my side. He looked up at me with pleading in his face. I cleared my throat, trying to pluck up the courage to say those dreaded words, becoming painfully aware that the moment was quickly passing. "Yes…" I stammered, "that's true." It might have sounded more like a whine, but I had managed to say it.

My statement was met with a rousting chorus of "hear-hear" as Cindy, Rayla and Charlie all raised their drinks and clunked them together.

"Go get your food," Rayla said, "or you'll end up making us all feel like fat pigs." She snorted and took an extra large bite of her burger.

I nodded and headed straight for my favourite Japanese restaurant, Toby on my heels. As I was walking away, I heard Cindy starting to recount our success with my sweater. When I returned, all three leaned closer to investigate my choice of cuisine. I had purchased a roll of sushi, California style, as well as a beef and vegetable stir-fry with sweet, sticky gravy dribbled over it. I always got extra.

Rayla was the first to speak up. "What exactly is that?"

I explained, nervous the whole time. *What are they thinking of me now?*

"Oh, I've never had sushi before," Charlie said.

Feeling a bit braver, partly because they all seemed genuinely interested, I took it upon myself to educate them about the delicious foods they had been missing out on. They liked it so much that Rayla went to buy two more rolls, and Charlie ended up eating over half of my beef stir-fry.

"That was superb," Cindy said, leaning back from the table, a dark stain on her chest from the pop she had spilled earlier.

"Uh-oh," said Charlie, who was licking up any bit of sauce that was left on my plate. "I think you've started a new obsession among us."

"Yes," Rayla added, "Mariah has great taste."

Toby nudged me so hard, I almost spilled the cup of leftover ice I held in my hand. "Yes, that's true," I said, then quickly picked up a piece of ice to crunch on. This time my words seemed less forced, and again they were met with a rowdy chorus of "hear-hear" and the clinking of empty cups, but mine was half-full of ice, and in our high mood we ended up crushing it, so it tipped over and landed in Cindy's lap.

She leapt up from the shock, but she was still laughing too hard to talk. We were all holding our sides with excessive glee. Finally, she said breathlessly, "I think this shirt is a magnet for mess!"

Seeing as she hadn't bought any tops herself, I offered her my sweater to borrow. The rest of the day seemed to fly by. I ended up saying "yes, that's true" three more times, and it was always enthusiastically echoed with "hear-hear." I felt a lot better about it all, and looking over at Toby, I could see he was not getting worse. In fact, he might even have started to heal.

Cindy dominated the conversation, but it was a nice kind of chatter, and I enjoyed her stories, even if it meant her repeating them from time to time. We ended up watching a movie, something only girls would enjoy, and I quickly discovered that Rayla, Cindy and Charlie liked to comment on the show more than watch it, but that made the movie even more memorable. When we were done, we all went back to the food court. It was less full, as the dinner rush had ended and being a Sunday, some stands had started to close. Now only about one out of five tables was occupied, so in a way it felt like we had more privacy. The other three got what they deemed the "Mariah special," and I swelled with pride.

As we sat and giggled, for a moment I felt completely carefree, then Toby leaned over my shoulder and said, "My work here may be done."

Forgetting myself, I said aloud, "No!" *I had just gotten used to him, now he was going to leave me!* Then I began to stammer as three sets of eyes were on me, staring with mouths open.

"Everything alright?" Rayla asked, sounding worried.

I started to panic; I felt it moving like ice through my veins. I gasped. *How could I go from good to bad so quickly?*

"Hey, no biggy," Toby said, putting his hand on my back reassuringly. "Tell them you just remembered something—like your homework is due tomorrow." He tried to sound calm, but I could hear pain creeping into his voice.

"Not an ant?" Cindy chimed in. "I thought I saw one here earlier."

Both Charlie and Rayla turned to look at her with baffled expressions. "What are you talking about?" they said, sounding like they were in stereo.

I was still unable to utter a word, but as Toby rubbed my back, I could feel the tension slowly ebbing away. I was scared, but only a little over this embarrassment, more over losing Toby. *Things were finally getting good; if he left it would all go away!*

"Ants," Cindy explained. "You've seen me freak out when I thought there was a spider nearby? Well our good friend Mariah has an even worse phobia about ants."

"Ants?" Charlie questioned. "That must be a bit of a challenge."

I was finally able to answer. "At times." My voice still sounded a bit weak. *What a lame phobia!*

"What?" Charlie looked confused.

"Well, I can understand her completely," Rayla said. "I'm not afraid of all ants, but my Aunt Flo can be downright scary. And when she comes each month to visit, I think it's best to steer clear of her. Or perhaps when she visits, everyone should stay away from me." Rayla giggled at her own joke, shaking her head. Now one ponytail came loose.

Cindy brought her hand up to her mouth and held it there. She didn't make a sound, but her eyes danced at Rayla's statement. Both Charlie and I sniggered.

"You have amazingly quick wit," I said.

"Yes, that's true," Rayla answered, and now we were all roaring with laughter.

"Hear, hear!" Cindy, Charlie and I said, and we brought our cups together with a clash.

On the way home, Cindy caught the same bus I did, and we discovered we only lived seven blocks from each other, which was equal to two bus stops. She seemed to be running out of steam. She only recounted one story then became quiet. Finally she sat up straighter, and asked, "Do you want to have a sleepover next Saturday?"

I was so shocked, I didn't know what to say. Cindy looked back out the window and muttered quietly, "It's alright if you don't want to."

"Hold on..." I choked. Toby, who was sitting beside me, straightened up. "It's not that I don't want to..." I stammered, wondering if I should expose this truth about myself. Throwing caution to the wind, I admitted, "I've never been on a sleepover before. I haven't ever been invited."

"Holy cats!" Cindy whistled. "Never, EVER? Well then, you've just got to come." She was so excited, her whole face seemed to glow.

"I'll ask my mom," I said. But I wasn't as worried about her as I was about Toby... *How would he handle it?* He watched our conversation intently. Then a realization turned my happy bubble to lead, and it sank in my chest. I didn't know how long he was going to be here. He might be gone by then.

Cindy got off, and I sat in a somber mood for the rest of my short ride. Toby didn't say anything. As I exited the bus, I couldn't contain my grief any more. I felt hot tears make their wet paths over my face. *I was crying...* One slipped past the corner of my mouth, and I could taste the bitterness of salt on my tongue. *I was really crying!*

Toby leaned over close to me and said softly, "Its okay to be sad." *I hadn't cried in years!* That made the tears flow even faster. "You need to grieve for all the losses you've had to endure." By now I couldn't stop the tears, even if I wanted to. I no longer fought the pain, or tried to run from it, or hide. I simply allowed each new wave of sorrow to wash over me. This was new.

I'd never experienced pain like this before, and I couldn't have been able take it without Toby. Having him close, I knew I was safe.

My eyes were so blurry, I wouldn't have been able to make it home, but Toby knew the way. With my hand in his, he guided me safely to my door, unlocked it and took me right to my room. There I cried and cried for over three hours. I sobbed for all I'd had to give up, and all that had been taken from me, and all the times when life should have been good but ended up bad. And for all the people who were supposed to care for me and make me feel loved but had let me down instead.

As the night drew on, I wondered if I'd ever stop, or if I'd drown in a pool of my own tears. Yet I knew I would be just fine. Whenever I feared that I'd never feel happy again, Toby would reassure me with his words, soft and full of love and a deep hope that couldn't be explained, no matter how many words I tried to use.

Finally the tears dried, and I was left with a very empty but peaceful feeling. I also developed a very heavy case of the hiccups. The sun had set. It was late at night. My window was shut against the chill, but I could still feel it seeping into the house. The whole world seemed still, as if it were holding its breath to see what would happen next.

"You need water," Toby said once I was still.

"I don't want to see my mom." I felt split open, with all my miseries hanging around me like a heavy necklace. I also felt far too vulnerable, worried that she'd see this weak me as something to be attacked. *She had done that to me before.*

"I'll make sure you don't run into her, or your brother."

Why had I not thought of him? Was I more frightened of my mother than the raving madman my brother could be?

Toby stood and held out his hand for me to take. Up in the kitchen, he got a glass of water, and then he started to rummage for a snack for me.

I sat at the table, head in my hands, watching him from between my fingers. I found it odd how I didn't see his style and attractiveness any more, just my beloved friend. "Don't leave me," I said, bringing my hands down to look at him.

"I'm not going anywhere," he said as he cut up an apple at the counter.

"No," I repeated, "Don't *ever* leave me."

"Oh." Toby slowly put the knife down and came and to kneel where I sat. "Sweet Mariah," he took both my hands in his, "don't you know this isn't meant to be forever?" I looked into his deep, unblinking eyes and felt his soft, warm hands around mine.

"Why can't it be?" My voice began to quiver as I felt fresh tears welling at the corners of my eyes. *I had thought they were all empty, that there were no more to make…but there they were.*

"It just can't." He kissed my fingers and sighed. "But I'm certain that I will not be going anywhere until you are ready."

"What if I'm never ready?" Right there in my kitchen, as my mind filled with despair, I couldn't ever imagine a time when I'd be ready. I reached out and wrapped my arms tightly about his neck. Toby just leaned in and allowed me to put my head against his chest. I felt his warmth, but as I snuggled him close, there was not even a hint of a heartbeat.

"Believe me, beautiful," Toby said, and I felt his lips move in my hair, "you will be, one day." I didn't believe him, but I didn't argue any more. Though it felt like I spent years there, the moment was over in a blink of an eye. He waited upon me, making sure I drank more and ate a little. Then he got me back to the safety of my room before we could be disturbed. I slept with my feet against Toby's back. He insisted on staying put at the foot of the bed, *even though I wanted him next to me.*

DAY 8 Monday...

I WAS AMAZED AT HOW REFRESHED AND COMPLETELY ALIVE I FELT THE NEXT DAY; it was just like the world was crisp and new, full of great sounds and sights and the most wonderful smells. *Anything was possible.* I got up early with a huge smile. Toby echoed my good mood; his face was looking almost healed. I took extra care to get myself ready for school, then walked, more like skipped, all the way there.

On the way, I stayed in my thoughts. It felt good just to have Toby by my side, even if he didn't say anything. I remembered back to the previous Monday, the night he had showed up. How different things were for me. That Monday I had dragged my feet and almost been late to school. Now I couldn't get there fast enough. That Monday had felt darker, colder—today felt bright and beautiful. *I was so glad I had him!*

At school I hung out for the five minutes in the hall with Cindy (without sparkles today) and Rayla, her hair still in several ponytails. Cindy returned my sweater, and I stuffed it into my backpack. The day was nicely mild; no need for extra layers. I felt like I was beaming. Rayla even noticed it and asked if today was an extra special day. I explained that I was just having one of those perfect mornings, and we headed off to our homerooms.

Elijah sought me out as I sat at my desk and asked if I'd be joining them for lunch. I assured him that I would. *I was looking forward to it.* As he turned to leave, he added, "You look really great today."

I knew what I had to say, and though I said it low enough not to be heard by Elijah, as kids were starting to file in, I smiled at Toby and said, "Yes, that's true."

He bowed his head, pinched his now completely healed cheek and said back "Hear, hear."

I was so happy. I didn't remember anything from my first two classes. I wasn't even bothered by Effie in typing. When it came to gym, I didn't hide in the change room like I normally would, waiting for all the girls to leave. Instead I was one of the first on the floor to do my stretches.

Having picked a spot closer to the wall than the middle, where Effie liked to sit with her two cohorts, I was a little baffled when they came to sit opposite me and started warming up. We had an endurance run once a month; the teacher wanted us each to make a five per cent improvement from our time on the previous month, or she would have us come back during the lunch hour for detention. This usually made me nervous, because I was terrified of failing, but today I wasn't going to worry.

Effie sat with a satisfied smile on her face. Her gut rested on the floor like a Buddha, and I wondered why no one else noticed how comical she looked. She had shoulder-length blonde hair, almost too perfect, making it seem like it was bought and not natural. She wore contacts. Today her eyes were mauve. She had a real diamond in her pierced nose, the whitest teeth I'd ever seen, and her face was without a blemish. She tapped her acrylic nails on the gym floor as we stretched.

Beside her sat her friend Sara. She was a bit lumpy but not overweight, with obviously bleached hair, and she had an eggplant-shaped nose. On the other side of Effie sat Marika, who was tall like a model, but underdeveloped, making her body look like a boy's. But her hair was luscious brown and her eyes an aqua blue. She was really quite pretty, and I wondered if she downplayed it because she was afraid of Effie being jealous.

"Aren't elephants afraid of mice?" Marika asked, looking at Effie.

"That's what I heard." Effie looked smugly over at me.

Toby took a hold of my foot, and I looked in his direction, away from the three girls. "You may never be able to change those around you, but you can change the way you react to them." I blinked extra long, trying to tell him that that's what I was trying to do. *Something was going down,* but I didn't want to be scared…

"Hey!" Sara said commandingly, and without thinking, I turned back to the girls. "I know one that is afraid of ants." As she stretched forward, she gave a particularly nasty leer. *Why was I looking?*

"Remember that whatever they do has nothing to do with who you are and has everything to do with who they are." Toby squeezed my foot. I leaned over and brought my hand over his on my toe in a stretch and felt comforted by him.

"Well then, that elephant is a freak," Effie said, getting to her feet. She took something from Sara's hand and tossed it in my direction.

I flinched and jerked about, trying to see what they had thrown at me. Effie and her friends turned and left, a trail of evil laughter left behind. It was an ant, and it scurried about my thigh in desperation. *Poor little thing,* I thought, *even more of a victim than I was in this mess.*

"How did she find that out?" I wondered quietly as I hung back from the rest of the class.

"I'm not sure, but she didn't waste any time in exploiting it. She really must see you as a threat." I knew that was supposed to make me feel better, but it didn't. Instead I began to worry about what she might be planning next. *Would Toby be able to save me, or would I have to endure more humiliation?*

I was the last to leave the gym, out the side door into the bright sun and cool air. Being the beginning of fall, the ground was just starting to see the first layer of leaves. Our teacher told us to start slow and work ourselves into a run, otherwise we wouldn't have enough stamina to run the full race. She also pointed to the leaves and told us to take care not to slip, since she wouldn't excuse our poor marks on a skinned knee or a sprained ankle.

I stayed behind the pack, trying to keep my distance out of habit. But it felt as if everyone was running slowly today. I soon passed a group of girls as they chatted together; one said, "Ooooo, careful Mariah, there are ants under the leaves." I kept going, trying not to take notice. The next two were silent as I passed, then one called out to my back, "Mariah, you're about to run over an ant hill!" I didn't falter and tried to keep my pace. The third group chanted to the theme of the Pink Panther, "Dud-ant, dud-ant, dud-ant, dud-ant, dud-ant, dud-ant, dud-ant."

I was starting to feel ill, and looking to my right, I saw Toby was looking a little worn. "Hang in," he said through clenched teeth. *Why did this keep happening to me?*

The fourth group was quiet as I passed, and for a fleeting moment I thought the "fun" was wearing off. Then as I made it parallel with the fifth group, one screamed, "Mariah, you have an ant on your arm!" Her voice had such conviction and force that I brushed at my arm in spite of myself. Peals of laughter broke out, and I started to run faster to get away from it.

I slipped on a moist leaf and did a full body flop in the grass. I felt wretched. I could hear the snickers of several of my classmates as they ran past. I was prepared to stay in this position until I was sure everyone had left.

"Mariah," the gym teacher said, standing over me. "I meant what I told you. You will not be excused because you did not heed my warning."

"Yes, Mrs. Pain," I answered and wondered if it was poetic irony that our teacher had married a man with such a fitting name.

After a few deep breaths, where my nostrils were filled with the strong smell of fresh dirt, lush green grass and rotting leaves, I pulled myself to standing and started back on the run. I did miserably, so I was instructed to return the next day at lunch to retry, and every day following until I got a better score. I was the last to get to the change room, but to my displeasure, not everyone had finished changing. Several seemed to linger.

I slowly made my way to the very back row of lockers, noticing how everyone stared at me as I passed, and some even leaned in close to whisper to one another. A girl came running from my row, hands waving wildly and screaming, "Ants! They're everywhere!" I steadied myself, trying not to notice how much my skin felt like it was crawling.

It was like I was in slow motion as I rounded the corner and turned to face my locker… It was swarming with hundreds of tiny, black, six-legged ants. I shook and fell against the lockers opposite mine. Toby rushed to my side and held me up. I closed my eyes and tried not to cry. *This was not the time.* The locker room rang out with whispers from every direction. "Did she see them?" "Why isn't she screaming?" "Do you think she's fainted?"

"Wouldn't that be so great?" I heard Effie's voice. It sounded as if she was trying to peer around the lockers into my row. "Just imagine she faints, the ants crawl all over her, and she wakes up infested with them!" I could hear the sheer pleasure she was taking in her own story.

How can someone be so cruel? I wondered. I opened my eyes to see her pressed against the end of the locker row, staring straight at me. I glared right back at her, and for a second I thought I saw her falter. Then she blinked innocently and turned to leave like nothing had ever taken place.

I stood, Toby holding most of my weight, watching the small army of ants escaping from my locker, and listening to the girls as they finished up. I was in my gym strip; my clean clothes were in the locker that was filled with who-knows-how-many bugs. Effie really thought I had a phobia. *What if I did*? The first bell for lunch sounded, and I heard the last of my classmates rushing out.

Once I was sure there was no one left I went in search of Mrs. Pain. She called Gus, our friendly janitor, and he came as quickly as he could. I waited in the gym office, sitting on a hard wooden chair while Mrs. Pain filled out papers. Her office was a cozy room, with a row of filing cabinets against one wall, a desk in the middle and a window out of which you could see the larger gym.

"Is there anything I should know?" she said, looking up from her work.

"Know?" I asked, not sure what she was looking for. The volleyball team set up to practice. *Why did their lives look so much easier?*

"You seem very off today." She scanned the paper in front of her. "Are you feeling alright?"

I didn't know how to answer. The day had started so well, but somehow I had ended up in the same place. *I felt defeated.*

"Mariah." Mrs. Pain stood up and came to the front of her desk. "I just want to let you know that I've seen you trying; I do notice that…" She leaned against her desk, and a worry line appeared across her brow. "I wish I could have let you off, but if I did, it wouldn't have been good for either of us."

I nodded. *Yes, when teachers showed me favour, it didn't help my status one bit; it made me a bigger target.*

"I knew you'd understand. You're a good girl." Her words helped me just a bit. *Inside, she cared.* It really meant the world to me to know that I was recognized by someone who mattered, *but in the end it was no help to me.* "So you do know that I still expect you tomorrow promptly at the start of lunch."

I nodded, and before anything more could be said, Gus arrived. With big rubber gloves, he opened my locker to reveal a swarm of crawly black ants. I shuddered. He pulled the contents out and dropped them to the floor. My shirt, pants and undergarments were completely infested. Under it all was a pop can, which was deemed the source of the pest problem.

It was malicious, I knew it, but I couldn't prove it. Ms. LaKey was called down to see the mess, and she gave me a stern reprimand, telling me that this was precisely why the girls change room had a strict policy of NO FOOD. She wouldn't listen to my claim of innocence. It was clear that in her mind I was careless and had total disregard for the rules. She gave me detention for the last three days of the week (only because Mrs. Pain said I was already obligated to her for Tuesday).

Gus wanted to wash my clothes, but Ms. LaKey didn't think it was necessary. She insisted that he simply shake them out, and I could suffer the idea of those tiny creatures crawling all around the garments I now had on; this would be an extra reminder of my carelessness. I felt physically ill as I took my shaken stuff from Gus and went to the change room to get dressed. I checked, checked and checked again, and even Toby checked too. Not one little ant was left anywhere, but the thought of them made my skin twitch and tingle for the rest of the day.

When I left, I heard Ms. LaKey telling Gus that he'd have to spray, and the change room would be closed until tomorrow morning. Lunch was ending, and I just barely made it to my locker to get my books. I glanced at my lunch bag, but I was still too upset to be hungry.

"Who could have told Effie?" I wrote on the corner of my notebook. "Who knew?" I insisted. *The only people who knew I had thought were my friends!*

I walked to class with quiet chants of "ants" following me wherever I went. I couldn't help but feel that this was just like my problems with Stacy over six years earlier, and wondered why I'd ever been convinced that I needed friends.

"Don't jump to conclusions," Toby said, but he wasn't convincing me. I was quickly feeling like those new friends of mine were anything but friends. I entered the drama room with bitter resentment. Rayla, Teb, Elijah and Cindy all sat in a huddle at the far end of the classroom, and none of them looked over at me as I took a seat near the door.

We were to work on our improv skills during this period, so the teacher set us up with partners. I got paired with Sara. She smiled with glee. The object of the lesson was for one person to set up the situation and the second to go along with it. "For nothing ruins improv more than the inability to adapt to the situation, no matter how obscure it may feel." She started to walk about the room. "So partners, remember to try and come up with ideas your counterpart may not be adapted to dealing with."

Sara gave a vicious smile and said, "Mariah, you have an ant on your arm."

I stood stock still, even though every hair on my body quivered, making me feel like I was covered with several hundred ants. I balled my fists so tight, I could feel my nails biting into the palms of my hands. Toby tried to tell me to hang in, but I could barely hear him. It took all my energy to keep from completely losing my cool.

"It's going up your arm!" Sara yelled shrilly, cutting through the conversation around us. *No matter what, I wouldn't let her get to me!*

The teacher, Mrs. Kellee, looked over as I was shaking my head. *I wanted no part of Sara's fun.* "Remember Mariah, there is no 'NO' in improv, or it isn't improv."

I could feel a lump of frustration forming in my throat.

"It's crawling into your shirt!" Sara shrieked.

"Nice emotion, Sara," Mrs. Kellee said, coming closer. "Go on Mariah, what do you do now? Sara has set you up nicely, the next move is yours." She looked down her nose at me. Several other pairs of students had become distracted and were now watching me, waiting. *Yes, I had been set up, a little too well.*

I was trapped and powerless to change the course of this moment, so unwillingly and with great waves of nausea, I began by trying to brush at this imagined ant.

"An ant!" Sara yelled, which drew the attention of everyone in the room. "Down your shirt! Quick, it's going into your bra!"

"Mariah…" Mrs. Kellee kept watching. I begged her with my eyes not to make me do it. Instead she turned to the rest of the class. "Does this look natural? Does this feel like it flows? No." She answered herself. "When we come here, we put away our inhibitions. I don't care who you are outside of this class, but within these walls you are professional actors, and they can become anyone and do anything, so that we as the audience are taken on a magical trip called entertainment!" She pointed a long finger at me. "Mariah, if you would please demonstrate this for me."

"An ant?" I asked looking into my shirt, blinking hard trying not to show how scared I was that I actually might see one. *I could feel my hands beginning to tremble.*

"Yes!" said Sara. "It's in your bra…and another in your hair."

Then, like a bad dream, I played out every command Sara gave, from tugging at my bra to pulling at my hair, and eventually running in circles with frenzy over them crawling all over me. When it was done, I was so raw I could do nothing but stand and stare at the class who watched me. It was a sea of faces. I couldn't pick one from the other, and as far as I could tell, they all were laughing at me.

"Bravo." Mrs. Kellee clapped. "But next time I will expect a better performance from you." She dismissed the class to return to their own pairs and said quietly, "You really are quite talented, Mariah. Don't hold back so much, and you will excel in my class."

I shook from head to toe. "I need to go to the bathroom," I said, not waiting for a response. I didn't see Toby, but I felt him behind me, and that chased away all thought of ending my life right then.

Tears had already formed clear paths down my cheeks by the time I made it to the safety of the bathroom. My throat was constricting, and I felt dizzy. "Why does this keep happening?" I moaned as my knees hit the floor. Only because I was holding so tightly to the counter did I manage not to fall any further.

Toby massaged my shoulders as I leaned against the counter. "I don't know," he responded, pulling the hair back from my sweaty face.

"Why can't you make it stop?" I cried out and turned around, hugging his legs tightly, and then I slid to the floor.

The bell rang for the last change of class, but I couldn't bring myself to get up; I lay feeling the cool of the cement floor against the sticky heat of my face. I could hear the kids in the halls beyond making their way to their final period. I had no plans of moving. The last bell sounded as the noise died down. I felt my breath starting to return to normal, and then as I was just starting to sit up, Toby gave a twitch like a jolt of electricity had run through him.

"Someone's coming," he said, panic rising in his voice. "Get in the stall and hide!"

I didn't hesitate, and as I pulled my feet up onto the toilet seat, the door swung open. Three distinct voices could be heard having an animated conversation…

"…she was there," I heard Sara say.

"What's Mrs. Elephant Mariah doing at Mack's Bowlaramma?" Effie asked. "Are you sure it was her?"

"How many Mariah Lafonts do you know?" Sara answered.

"That Mariah is so annoying, even her name makes me want to barf!" Effie scoffed.

"Must suck having a name so close to hers, eh, Marika," I heard Sara sneer.

"Ya, well it must suck having a face that looks like that," Marika retorted.

"Girls!" snapped Effie, clapping her hands. "Focus! Sara, what exactly did your brother say?"

"He said exactly: you should have seen the girl Tony picked as his next project."

"Project? Did he actually say project!" I wasn't sure, but I thought I heard an edge of envy in Effie's voice as she continued. "Are you sure he didn't say 'play-toy' or 'sex kitten'?" Effie's voice was reaching desperation. "Project! Really?"

"Yes, project," Sara said quietly.

"This girl is starting to really bug me," Effie said with exasperation.

"Did you mention bug?" Marika laughed.

"Ya, B.U.G.," Effie said with such coldness that I actually felt a chill run down my spine.

My foot slipped from the toilet seat, and I only just caught myself with the toilet paper dispenser, which gave a quiet reverberating noise. I looked to Toby for help, and he put his hand up to his lips. I held my breath and waited.

"If I ever see her again, I'm gonna make her pay," Effie said, and though her voice was filled with new determination, she didn't seem to have taken any notice of me. "I'll squash her like an ant!"

"Good one," Marika said.

"I'll fix her up myself so Tony will have no need for his project!"

"Ef, she's gonna be so sorry she was even born," Sara added.

"Oh ya." Effie sounded like she was gleefully enjoying herself.

"So when are you planning to do this?" Marika asked.

"Now!"

Several things happened at once. Toby, who'd had been signaling for me to stay quiet, stepped away from the stall door and unlatched it. Effie pushed on it, and once it was halfway open, Toby rammed it back towards her. She fell back, holding her nose while blood started to pour out, and Toby yelled for me to run.

I was halfway to my locker when Toby told me to go directly to the office. "Wha…" I breathed, but he insisted. So I turned around. Within a minute, I was waiting in the school office to see Ms LaKey.

It was a long five-minute wait. My mind was still back in the bathroom. I was enjoying the sight of Effie's nose colliding with the bathroom stall door, but it sunk whenever I thought of the threats she had made and wondered what was in store for me next.

When I entered Ms. LaKey's office, her face looked hard and stern. "Well, Miss Mariah Lafont, twice in one day, what am I going to do with you."

"Tell her you'd like to report an accident." Toby calmly instructed. I was glad he could be so relaxed. I felt like my heart was going to beat right out of my chest. I narrowed my eyes, and he explained, "She won't believe that you were attacked, but if you tell her it was an accident, she won't expel you!"

Ice trickled down my spine at the word expel. *That was something my brother would do—I couldn't imagine what my mom might say if I started to do the same thing.* "Ms. LaKey," I said slowly, trying to calm the butterflies that had come to make a nest in my chest, "I accidentally bumped Effie when I was in the bathroom."

"Are you telling me that there is a student who's been hurt?" She narrowed her eyes.

"Yes. You see I was about to leave the bathroom, and Effie was coming in, but I didn't see her, so I opened the door into her by mistake." I found it hard to say those words, when it was me that was being threatened.

"And you left her there to come tell me this." Ms. LaKey had stood and was looking down at me, disappointment clear on her face.

"No, I left her with Sara and Marika."

She narrowed her eyes.

"It was really an accident," I said, feeling small.

Ms. LaKey crossed her room while I stayed facing the desk. She looked out her door, then came over to me and bent so she was speaking directly into my ear. "I will believe you for now." Her voice was low and hissy. "But you should believe me that if Miss Roosofe has anything different to tell me, then I will be wanting to see you again."

I nodded and sprang from the room, past the receptionist, who was trying to calm Effie and Sara down, out into the quiet halls and all the way to my locker. As I neared it I had to blink several time to be sure what I saw was what I really saw. It was! Hundreds upon hundreds of brown ants were emerging from my locker.

"This has got to stop happening," I said as I punched out at Toby. My fist sailed right through him, but he caught me before I hit the floor. "I want to go home," I muttered as he guided me down the hall. He took me out the front door and down the street. I walked in silence: *defeated— completely defeated*. Toby kept his arm around my back. Without it, I would have fallen down in my tracks and never bothered to get up.

"It will get better," Toby said. We were halfway to my house, walking along an empty street. All around me the world looked peaceful and livable, but inside my heart was dark and filled with despair.

"One part better," I muttered, "two parts worse."

Toby drew me closer and whispered into my hair, "Collect the good; it will outweigh the bad, I promise." I stopped and he asked, "What?"

"My backpack," I said breathlessly. "I left it in the bathroom."

"Consider it gone," Toby said. "We'll get you a new one."

"But all my stuff!" I slipped from his arms and found myself sitting on the cool pavement of the sidewalk. He squatted down to look into my face, concern all over his features. It was almost time for the last bell of the school day. In mere minutes, the halls would be filled with noise and commotion. But for me, where I sat, everything had come to a halt.

We sat on a relatively quiet side street in an upper-middle-class neighbourhood. It was here that people lived in houses they should be able to enjoy, but went away eight to ten hours a day to work. The front lawns were well manicured, usually by someone hired to do it, with pretty rock or flower gardens. The houses were sided in the brightest colours, and when I could see the backyard, it had perfect play structures and toys that were neatly put away.

Even the sidewalks were well cared for. No chalk left to be washed away by the rain or leaves needing to be raked and removed. The trees were tall, healthy and protected by iron bars that formed four posts around their trunks to keep them from being knocked over. Each was placed ten feet apart, and they grew from the ground under shiny metal grates so that the dirt wouldn't be able to get things...dirty.

I had sat down only a foot from one of these trees. It took all the strength I could find to shift myself over so I could rest my back against it. Toby moved closer and kneeled next to me.

"I can't go on like this any more," I said, staring at nothing in particular. I felt Toby's hand brush a strand of hair from my cheek. "You know..." I turned to face him. "I had planned to end my life the night you showed up, and now I can think of no reason why I shouldn't have."

"I can." He shifted and sat next to me. "You can't see it, but this is just one chapter of a long and full life." I closed my eyes as he continued. "I've often wondered about the irony of our unique situation. Often I don't understand one bit of it. But as I see more and more of my past life unfold in my mind, I'm weighed down by the regrets..." Toby's voice caught, and I heard him breath deeply before he started again. "I'm certain that if I were still alive, it would have actually been me with the bleak future."

"But you had it all. And you were happy; at least I think you really were."

"I have no doubt that I thought I was happy, on some level. But I wasn't, not really. I was constantly hoping for more, looking for it and never stopping, regardless of what the consequences were. But most of all, I was on a one-way track to loneliness and misery."

"That's where I am now!" My voice shook with fury. I wasn't mad at Toby, but I was so angry that I wanted to vomit.

"Please believe me." Toby took my hands in his. "This pain you experience is just a sliver next to the agony and utter despair I faced. The same pain Effie and Tony both face still. For our fates were destined to an eternity of sorrows so deep, there is never a way of getting free."

"But that's just how I feel now." I took my hands from his and covered my face: *more tears—if I could, I would flood the world with my tears.*

Toby respected my need for quiet. He neither spoke nor moved. Had he been alive, I'm sure he would have cramped from being so still for so long. I could hear birds twittering in a tree. The wind gently blew, and those spare leaves that had fallen into the grate fluttered up against it now, making a soft rattling sound. Somewhere down the block a dog barked.

"What am I supposed to do now?" I asked as I felt myself calm a little.

"Don't give up." Toby's chocolate eyes bore into me.

"It's too hard," I whimpered. The day played over again in my head. *It had started so well, things really did feel better...*

"Yes. But you are strong." Toby's face was filled with compassion.

"I don't feel strong," I complained.

"Well, you are." He stood up and held out his hand.

I'm not quite sure how I managed to get home; my whole body ached with emotions. I had no strength or desire for food, so I went straight to bed. *If Toby hadn't come to me, I'd be dead. Now that he was here, he wouldn't let me give up!* I saw Effie's face taunting me, Sara and Marika supporting her and a multitude of my classmates who joined in. *If I wasn't supposed to give up, how was I supposed to go on?*

DAY 9 Tuesday...

I SLEPT A DEEP, DREAMLESS SLEEP AND WOKE JUST BEFORE SIX the next morning, a full hour before I had to be up. At first I feared that Toby had left. He was nowhere to be seen. Then as I pushed myself to sitting, I thought that the air beside me felt heavier.

I drew my knees up to my chin and thought things over. *Don't give up — oh, how I wanted to, it would have been easier.* But as I sat, I gathered my resolve. *I would go to school, hold my head high and show them that they hadn't gotten to me, that they hadn't won.* As I thought this, I felt my jaw tighten, my bitterness turning to pure rage.

"Toby?" I asked, as I fanned my arms out, trying to touch him.

"Ya," he replied groggily. Even though I knew he hadn't gone, I was relieved to hear his voice all the same as he appeared beside me.

"I've been wondering," I said, while he rubbed at his eye like he had a bit of dust stuck in it. "Who do you think told Effie about the ants?"

"I..." he stretched, "I don't know."

"Because I've been thinking, and I figure it had to have been either Charlie, Cindy or Rayla, and if it was them, I don't really think I should be calling any of them my friends." Memories of Stacy filled my mind, and I felt determined not to have that happen to me ever again. *I would make sure it didn't!*

"Don't be so quick to jump to conclusions," Toby said, rubbing his eye again.

"Well, I don't feel like talking to any of them." Bitterness filled my mouth, and I felt like I was going to choke on it. *Or I could let them know just exactly how I felt about them. I wouldn't hold back!*

"You should at least listen if they have something to say to you." Toby's voice sounded odd, and looking over at him, I gasped; his eyes were bloodshot, his hair was in complete disarray, and his skin was a grayish colour.

"What's wrong with you?" I asked. *Could ghosts get sick? And if they did, who would fix them?*

"I'm not sure. I just feel…wrong." He stood up slowly, using my desk to steady and support himself.

"What now?" I asked, standing beside him.

"I think you should stay home from school today." He seemed to lean more heavily on my desk as he spoke.

"No," I snapped. *If I didn't show up, then it would look like they had won!* I was not going to let Toby or anything stop me from proving that they hadn't gotten to me, even though they had. *How could I be proud of myself if I stayed home now? How would I prove myself better than them?*

"Mariah, I can hardly stand." He wobbled as he said this.

"Toby, I have to go today. Otherwise I might as well paint a sign for everyone to see that says, 'loser walking.'" *Why did something have to be wrong with him today*?

Toby shook his head but didn't argue any more. Even with the extra time, we barely made it to the bus stop before the bus showed up. Toby held on tightly to my shoulders, making me feel tense and sore before I even caught sight of the school. I managed to avoid the gang of kids that I thought were my friends by walking up the main steps past Effie, with two bright black eyes, and her gang of wannabes. They all stared at me as if in shock, and not one said a word to or about me as I passed. I counted this as a small victory. I felt great satisfaction over Effie's eyes. Toby gave a moan and got heavier.

I took my seat in homeroom and felt a pang of regret that I had forgotten my backpack with my book the day before. I was tired and sore from Toby holding so tight, but an even stronger emotion overrode it: resolve to see this day through. I contemplated my triumph. *They hadn't gotten to me*! I was the only one in the room, so I lay my head on my desk and thought about how I could handle the rest of the day. *Pulling all of Rayla's ponytails out came to mind.*

"Not good," Toby said as he sank to the floor next to me and leaned on my leg. *He was heavy. How was I going to get around with him hanging off my neck?*

I lay there trying to work it out. *It's not like I could carry him.* Then I became distracted by a flood of memories of the two ant attacks from the previous day. My skin started to crawl at the mere thought. Opening my eyes and looking down at Toby, I wondered, *isn't he supposed to be here to help me?* His eyes were so swollen he could barely see, and his face had become misshapen by the swelling.

I opened my mouth to say something when I heard footsteps, and someone called out, "Mariah ants." I was crushed. After my success on the front steps, I had foolishly thought I had heard the last of these stupid pranks. I shook my head, trying not to react, but without explanation I began to itch and felt as if my skin had grown millions of tiny legs and was trying to walk away from me…

"Mariah!" I recognized Elijah's voice as I felt him tug at my shirt and pull me right from my seat. I landed on the floor and looked down. A black ant scurried all over my shirt. Up on my desk, several more were making their confused way about. Elijah brushed me off as I sat in shock, then he squished every moving bug and opened up my desk to find the source: a sandwich bag with the crust of a peanut butter and jam sandwich, and lots of ants still inside. The zipper seal was broken at one end.

Shivering, I stood and put out my hand to take it.

"What do you plan on doing with it?" Elijah asked. He kept looking me up and down, and I figured it was to be sure he got all the little pests. I couldn't tell if there were any left—my whole body twitched and crawled.

"I'll take it to Ms. LaKey and show her that I'm being framed."

"I don't think that will work," Elijah said, not handing me the bag. "I heard that Effie told her you're the one trying to use these ants as a prank on someone else, and you have been caught twice now. These will just prove Effie's right." He used his foot to squish a few ants that had made it past his thorough inspection. "Let me take it to Cindy. She'll give it to Gus, and he'll know how to get rid of it."

I didn't know if I could trust him. He sounded genuine, but if he was lying, then he was taking away my evidence. *How did I know it wasn't him who'd put them in my desk to begin with?* I was trying to come up with something particularly nasty to say when the first bell rang, and students began to come into the class. Without a word, Elijah stuffed the now-sealed bag into his own desk and sat down. I balled my fists as I too took my seat.

I was still determined not to let this get to me. *I would persevere!* Toby moaned again as he rested against my leg. During homeroom, I caught three stray ants and crushed them under my thumb but imagined it was actually Effie I was squishing to death. When the teacher left the room, I heard a whispered taunt coming from several of my classmates, "The ants go marching one by one, hurrah, hurrah. The littlest one stops to bite Mariah's bum, hurrah, hurrah." And on it went. They were creative and vulgar as each new chorus was added. The teacher came back by the third line.

When the bell rang to go to our first class, the teacher told me to hold on. "I've been up to talk with Ms. LaKey," she said once the room was almost empty. "She wants to see you in her office promptly at the beginning of lunch."

"But I'm supposed to retake my endurance run with Mrs. Pain," I tried to argue.

"Ms. LaKey comes first," she said and dismissed me without another word.

I nodded, getting to my feet slowly just in case the teacher had more to say, but also to give Toby time to stand up. He was like dead weight! As I made my way through the halls, I got more choruses of "ants marching," but I also heard "Attack of the Eleph-ant" and "dead ant—dead ant."

During wood shop, Toby lay at my feet as I worked on my bookends. In English, he moaned as he held my foot while I was trying to read from *Hamlet*. And in math, he shook so badly that I looked like I had a tremor in my leg. Finally, the lunch bell rang, and I was released to go see Ms. LaKey. The taunts of "dead-ant" made my heart fill with chills that only got worse as I neared the principal's office.

I was ushered straight into Ms. LaKey's office. She wasn't there yet, so I was told to take a seat facing her desk. Toby fell to the ground. His eyes were completely swollen. I wouldn't doubt that he had lost his sight entirely. "Mariah, I need you to take me home."

"Uh-uh," I said quietly.

"Please."

"No," I said with pride.

Just then the office door opened, and Ms. LaKey walked in. "Mariah," she said, "I have spoken with Miss Roosofe regarding the incident in the ladies' lavatory." She looked stiff and stern and came to sit across from me. "And from what Effie…I mean Miss Roosofe has told me, I have come to the conclusion that you are biased against her German heritage." I was shaking my head, but Ms. LaKey didn't take notice and kept on going. "She has filed an official complaint against you. It will be reviewed, and if it is found to be true, then you will have a permanent mark on your record."

My jaw dropped. I couldn't believe it. I looked to Toby. *I needed his help!* Reaching out with my foot, I rested it against his leg, but he just moaned. *Did he hear what was happening?*

"Miss Lafont, we have a zero tolerance for bigotry."

"I'm not a bigot!" I blurted out.

"What do you call the two attempts to infest Miss Roosofe's belongings with ants, something she had admitted to having a phobia about! Or the name-calling that several witnesses have reported, and what about this final attack, hitting her in the washroom where she was hiding, trying to get away from you!" Ms. LaKey ended in a shrill tone. "How can you still claim your innocence?" she added a bit more calmly.

"You believe her?" I said, barely above a whisper, because I couldn't get any more sound out of my shocked and constricted throat.

"I really can't see it any other way."

"What if they are lying?" I felt my body shudder, and I wished more than ever that Toby were coherent, because I missed his advice and his consoling looks.

"Are you claiming that Miss Roosofe and several other girls that attend this upstanding school are all collaborating on a false story against you? And pray, why should I believe they'd do that?"

That was exactly what was happening, but the look on her face told me she would never believe me.

"Well then, I've had quite enough of this," Ms. LaKey said with a chill in her voice. "I have called your mother regarding these incidents, and you will be required to serve detention with Gus after school for the rest of this term. I haven't expelled you, yet, for this is the first case of any kind of negative behaviour on your record." At this, she gave her head a small shake, as if she was surprised by it. "And you should really count yourself lucky that Gus was willing to take you. Now I do not want to see you in my office ever again!"

I nodded, completely shocked. *She called my mom…* My heart thudded painfully in my chest. *Is this how good kids go bad?* I could see no escape from this mess. I was at the mercy of the fools who believed the lies of those who were more powerful and had more influence. I was keenly aware that I had no voice.

"Mrs. Pain is expecting you tomorrow for that make-up run," Ms. LaKey called as I headed out of her office.

My steps were slow and laboured, because Toby was so out of it that I was practically giving him a piggyback. Yet it was my iron will to prove myself better than they thought me that kept me headed toward the cafeteria and not running in the opposite direction home. As I walked, my peers jostled me about. I was in a daze, barely taking notice of the people around me, or what they were saying. I missed Toby's calming words. Yet he had assured me that Effie would eventually have to pay for all her malice. *But when? And could I be the one to repay her?* Revenge is a powerful drug. If I had a gun right then, or even if I knew where to get one, I would have used it on Effie and ANYONE who got in my way! My jaw ached from clenching it so tightly.

I made a stop at my locker, relieved that it wasn't infested this time. Toby let go and leaned against the wall. *Was he looking worse?* The halls were starting to empty. Toby took hold of my shoulders once more, and I made my slow way to the cafeteria. *I should have skipped it… it was Tuesday after all, but I wanted to prove that they hadn't won.*

As I passed the washroom, I heard Effie yell, "Get out, Marika, now or you'll be the next elephant!"

Seconds later, Marika walked out in front of me. For a moment my heart stopped. Effie was still on the other side of the door, and she could have emerged too. But then I saw the look on Marika's face, and I was stunned. "Mariah," she said, looking strained.

"Dissension in the ranks?" I asked, feeling a sick pleasure from the sheer idea of it. Toby let go and fell to the floor in a ball.

Marika looked back at the door. She was completely pale. "Um," she stammered, looking down at her right hand, "I found this." She held it out for me; *it was my backpack!*

I was stunned, and it took me a moment to collect my thoughts. Marika continued to hold it out to me. Her sleeve fell back from her wrist to reveal three nasty-looking red marks. A wealth of self-satisfaction filled me. I took my bag, and she bolted down the hall. I swung my pack onto my back, then, checking that I wasn't being watched, I pulled Toby to his feet again and finally headed to the lunch room, frustrated at how unhelpful he was being.

I was one of the last students to enter, so the line was quite short. As I stood waiting to buy my meal, Cindy came over to me.

"You gonna join us for lunch?" She looked strained, like she knew something that I didn't.

A multitude of insults filled my head, but my tongue stuck to the roof of my mouth. Finally I answered sharply, "I don't know."

"Are you mad at me?" Cindy looked like a dog that had just been scolded.

I had no empathy; instead I felt a hot bitterness welling up from some deep dark spring within my soul. Toby gave a huge shudder, moaned and fell to the floor. Ignoring him, I accused, "How did Effie find out about the ants?"

Cindy's eyes widened, and she lowered her head, and then walked away quickly. *Confirmed.* I headed down the counter and picked out the daily special, tuna surprise. But the real surprise had nothing to do with tuna...

"Ants," someone whispered as they walked behind me. "Dead ants." Someone else walking the opposite direction said, "The ants go marching..."

I was about to push past her when I felt a strange pinching sensation on my neck, then an enormously painful feeling like a wasp was stinging me. I put my hand up and slapped my neck. Pulling my hand back, I saw a crushed brown-red ant. Then I felt three more pinches on my back, followed by the same stinging sensation; then the same on my left arm, then my right, and more on my back.

I clawed at myself like a madwoman! My pack fell to the ground, and I ripped at my arms and tore my shirt, trying to reach my back. The stinging didn't let up until I was able to reach the source. I couldn't reach my back!

I fell to the floor, landing on my pack and started to roll in agony. I felt like I was being poked everywhere by hot needles.

Effie came to stand over me. "Dance, Eleph-ant!"

"Get them off me!" I screamed. Effie stood above me with a malicious sneer. "Help! Help! HELP!" I yelled as I thrashed and tore at my body. I was on fire! I couldn't breath.

Effie was laughing, as were several other students as they stood in a circle around me. Then their voices died in my ears, followed by everything going dark.

• • •

I heard the paper crinkle under me as I rolled onto my back. The bed I lay on was made of vinyl-covered foam with a thin layer of stiff paper between me and it. There was a rough blanket draped over me. I could hear muffled talking coming from somewhere to the right, and though I had opened my eyes, it was just as dark as when I had them closed, but for a chink of light outlining the door to my right.

"They were fire ants," Toby said. He was close and sounded like his regular self again.

Once, when I was seven years old, my dad had taken Jake and me hiking. I had tripped and fallen into a patch of poison ivy. For three days after, my skin had prickled and stung. Lying here on my back now, I was surprised at how similar my back, neck and arms felt. I rolled back onto to my side, feeling my tears make moist paths over my face: *I had tried, and I had failed, yet again…so what was the point?*

"Mariah, will you forgive me? I let you down. I made a huge mistake," Toby said softly into my ear. More tears followed those that had already run down my face.

The voices on the other side of the door sounded more like a bunch of bees buzzing. I couldn't make out any words, but I could tell that there were several people talking. *Who was it? What were they saying?*

"I was supposed to stop you from coming to school today," he continued. "That's why I woke up feeling so miserable! It was supposed to be intuition. Didn't you feel it too?"

I had a sort of swooping feeling at the centre of my stomach, sort of like when you step off a curb, but you weren't ready for it. I had thought it was just me gathering my courage, but then I had felt something very different, a raw determination to prove myself. I felt embarrassed now as I remembered it.

"There is a difference between bravery and sheer stupidity. You are brave, Mariah, every day of your life, and you don't need to prove that to anyone."

The voices continued to buzz, and I put my arm over my ear, wanting Toby, them and the whole world to go away. Toby put his hand on my knee and held on as I tried to move away. "Go away," I moaned.

"You can't make me go away," he said softly.

"Then just leave me alone."

Toby squeezed my knee as he spoke. "You are grieving now."

"Again!" I felt my desire for vengeance starting to build again.

"Don't," he said, sounding as if someone were constricting him. "You have every right to grieve, so grieve away, I won't stop you. There is no shame in feeling sad. But don't let it harden inside you!" He sounded desperate. "When you don't let it out, it gets stuck and becomes something ugly."

"What are you talking about?" I hid under my arm again.

"I woke up sick with a premonition, but I got worse because of your resolve. It wasn't natural, it wasn't healthy, it was wrong, and just like I can feel your pain in a pure sense, I felt your desire for revenge in a very real form…it made me sick."

I swallowed hard. "So I'm not allowed to be mad?"

"Well…" Toby faltered, "I don't know if you can never feel angry. But what you were feeling wasn't anger; it was vengeance, and a desire to outdo those around you, or prove yourself. It wasn't a healthy anger; it was unhealthy. It was your pain turned around into something mean."

I exhaled slowly. I was feeling flustered, overwhelmed and like my life was entirely unfair. *How come Effie was able to get away with stuff like this?* I listened to see if Toby could pick up on my feelings, but he seemed calm.

"Mariah, just feel what you are really feeling."

More tears fell. I was sad, so very, very sad. I cried so hard, my whole body shook. Toby held onto my knee, and I was glad he was there.

From behind me, I heard the door open and two hushed voices. The first was my mother, the second the school nurse.

"I've already spoken to Ms. LaKey," my mom said, her voice edgy but low.

"Yes, I've spoken with her as well, but I reserve the right to form my own opinions about the situation."

"You said ants bit her?" I could tell my mother was standing over me, and then I felt the blanket being lifted. As a light breeze swept over my skin, I realized I didn't have my shirt on.

"Yes," the nurse answered. The blanket was dropped back over me. "A particularly hardy kind not found locally."

"Mmmm," I heard my mother respond as she walked across the room. "And this was the third time this week Mariah has been found harbouring them?"

"Not really." The nurse sounded exasperated. "This is the third time ants have been found in your daughter's property. But the first two times, there were just common black ants. This is the only incident of *Solenopsis invicta*, toxic red ants."

My mother sighed with disappointment. "Oh, Mariah."

"Gus was able to find the container they had escaped from. It was in her backpack wrapped tightly in her sweater, with no lid on it, and no lid to be found in any of her possessions. But luckily for your daughter, not too many of them had gotten loose." The nurse paused, but my mother didn't respond, so she continued. "She was in the cafeteria line-up when they started to swarm. Did you know that this type of ant can scurry over your skin undetected? It's that light-footed."

The thought made me shiver. I held my breath, hoping I hadn't been noticed.

"Where did they come from?" asked my mother.

"Originally Brazil, but since the turn of the century they were accidentally relocated to Texas and have since spread to other warmer states." The lights were flicked on and dimmed immediately. "You see, Mrs. Lafont, they can't survive here, as our winters are too long and cold."

"So you are telling me that Mariah had to send away for these ants from Texas?" I held my eyes shut tight; I didn't want anyone to know I was listening. But the disappointment in my mother's voice was so overwhelming that I felt a fresh tear slide silently down my cheek.

"What I am telling you, Mrs. Lafont, is that someone, with good connections and money, had these deadly little creatures brought here for the purpose of malice." I heard soft clinking noises, as if something were being moved about on a metal counter, like the one in our science lab.

"Oh, Mariah," my mother moaned. "Haven't you learned anything from your brother?"

I felt the covers carefully folded off me, and someone gently put their hands on my back—dabbing what felt like a wet cotton ball onto each of the areas where I felt pain and itchy.

"You see these?" the nurse asked, standing behind me. I heard my mother take a few heavy steps towards me. "Each of these is an individual bite." The nurse dabbed at several more spots on my back.

"Then what are those red marks around them?"

"That's the pattern they leave when they sting you. The ants bite down with their jaws and hold on with a super-tight grip. They sting you in a circular pattern, anchored with their teeth—they can sting several times in one minute, and they don't usually stop until they're removed. Effective little buggers, aren't they?"

"What are you doing now?" My mother's voice seemed just a tad less edgy.

"I'm applying Listerine…"

"The mouthwash?"

"Yes. I was told by a colleague that it will help the healing." There was a smile in the nurse's voice, "A friend of mine, the school nurse at North Hill High, had a similar situation a few years back. She told me that Listerine helps to alleviate the pustules that typically form about six hours after the initial bite."

"Pustules?" My mother sounded like she might be ill.

"Pustules are like small white heads, or the clear part on a chicken pox. They are quite sensitive, but you don't want to break them if they do appear, because it will create scarring, and it could lead to secondary infection."

"And this should stop them from forming."

"That's what my friend told me." The nurse started to dab at my arm, lifting it up to get the few bites in my armpit. "It's great having her as a friend; she's also a very good resource," she continued, more to herself than to my mother. "Kids these days are getting more and more inventive in their tricks and pranks, and we can debrief each other as well as encourage one another. You see, it's us in the trenches that see the real victims." She put my arm down very gently and gave my wrist a small squeeze as she did so.

"That must make it hard for you to have to treat the one who's been causing all the grief and harm." The edge had returned to my mother's voice.

"Trust me, it doesn't happen often." I felt her dabbing my neck and down my chest. "Mrs. Lafont, your daughter has just over fifty bites, with anywhere from two to ten corresponding stings. I suggest you give her plenty of care and allow her to rest for the next few days. I also strongly recommend that you give her Benadryl. She'll be immensely itchy. You need to watch for signs of secondary infections. They will look like a new rash, swelling or discolouration. Seek out immediate medical attention if she experiences dizziness, shortness of breath or is acting in any way out of the ordinary." The nurse moved around the bed to my front. "If you don't mind, Mrs. Lafont, I need to administer the rest of this, so could you please wait outside? I will send your daughter out in just a couple of minutes."

My mother didn't respond, but I did hear her walk out and the door snap shut.

"I need you to sit up, dear, to be sure I've gotten all your lesions." The nurse's voice was soft and sweet.

I had met the nurse before. Mrs. Kristy was in her early twenties. She had soft blue eyes, wavy brown hair and a long scar right along her jaw line. It was a running joke that she got it from her youth, when she was in a gang, but the truth was that she had lost most of her chin due to cancer, and it was only through the miracle of modern medicine that she'd been able to survive and could still look relatively normal. Perhaps it was because of this that she thought of life as a wonderful gift and always wore a smile, though sometimes it would seem sad.

I sat in only my bra, with the nurse dabbing at any spot that looked untouched, and watched Toby, who had his back to me and was rubbing the back of his neck like it was him that had been bitten, not me.

"Mariah." I looked at the nurse. She held up a cotton ball with green liquid between her fingers. "Go home," she said, but it wasn't unkind. It was said more with concern. "Take care of yourself." I nodded numbly. Her eyes spoke a story to me, but she said no more.

She handed me my shirt, and even though she assured me that there were no ants left, I had to check it over twice before I could put it on. My hands shook. The cotton against every sore was like rough grass scratching against me. I stood and wondered if I would collapse. Toby came to my side and lightly took my hand. I felt suddenly stronger with him by my side. I thanked the nurse and headed out into the hall, where my mother stood fuming. She gave me one hard stare then headed down the hall. I followed.

As we walked, the bell for class change rang. I was jostled this way and that, as the halls filled with other students. Each collision burned like a freshly made wound. Toby kept his hand firmly on mine and guided me through the fray. I passed Effie talking to Sara and Marika; Marika's wrist, where she had the three strange red marks, had puffed up into small white heads. She nervously scratched at it as I walked by.

A feeling of quiet resolve gripped my spin and gave me strength: *I had suffered, and I had endured, and I was still here.* I held my head up, not allowing anyone to make me feel bad about myself. I wasn't sure, but I thought I saw a look of nervousness from Effie as I passed her…

The ride home was uncomfortable. My mother didn't look at me even once. She pulled roughly over to the curb near our house and put the car in park, but she didn't take her hands from the steering wheel. She gazed out the windshield. "Where did I go wrong?" The sorrow in her voice made me feel panicked.

She looked down at her lap and took a Kleenex from inside the armrest, then started to dab at her eyes. "First my husband, now both of my kids!" I was opening my mouth to argue when she continued, "I'm a good person…" She blew her nose and took a new Kleenex as tears spilled from her eyes. "I pay my taxes. I am a good girl for my parents!" I wanted to point out that writing a letter once a year didn't make you a good daughter, but she went on, "I was a good wife. I supported my husband in everything he wanted to do." She went through three more Kleenexes. "I'm a good mother. I make sure my children are well fed and have clothes and a roof over their heads!" She blew her nose again.

Somehow I felt more vulnerable and afraid of her than ever before. She had yelled before, thrown things and threatened me, but there, stuck in the car next to her, I wanted to cower. Toby, who had been sitting silently in the back seat, reached over and brushed my ear. If he had not been there, I would have promised my mother anything just to get her to stop behaving this way. It gave me chills.

"So where did I go wrong?" She was shaking her head, and eventually she turned and faced me. The look in her eyes was like none I'd ever seen before. *Sorrow? Hate? Regrets. Broken dreams.* It was all there. She continued to stare, as if I should say something, but I didn't know what. Out of the corner of my eye I could see the minutes on the car clock change from six to seven.

"Just get out," she commanded.

I didn't hesitate a second. I was out the door and up the block before the clock could reach eight. Behind me I heard the screech of tires as she pulled away from the curb. Only when I was out of sight did I slow my pace. Toby put an arm around me so I could lean into him. It hurt to have him rub against my sores, but it was comforting too. He was beginning to feel like an extension of myself; I was getting quite comfortable with his touch and was far less jumpy when he did touch me.

Once home, I surveyed the damage. To do this, I needed Toby's help taking off my shirt again. He picked up the mirror and held it up, turning his head away. I gingerly slipped off my shirt and slowly examined each bite. I gasped at the amount. Toby turned back and echoed my disbelief. I had three on my chest, two on my stomach, ten on my left arm and four more under my arm, twelve on my right arm and six more on my armpit, but on my back I had eighteen, from my hairline all the way down to my pants.

"You were lucky," Toby said, leaning in to take a closer look.

I didn't feel lucky. I felt hot and prickly. "How can you say that?" I asked.

"Well," he held the mirror up so I could see better, "they didn't get into your hair, or down your pants or on your face… How do you feel?"

I turned to face him, and he shifted uncomfortably. "Awful."

He nodded. I searched through my drawer for a softer top and found one made from satin. I slipped it on. The coolness of the fabric felt nice against my raw skin. "You can look now. I'm dressed," I muttered.

Toby took his time turning back around. I slumped down on my bed and curled up around the pillow. "So what now?" I asked, trying to make sense of my life.

He sat down at the bottom of the bed and took my feet onto his lap and gently massaged them. “I don’t think it was any of your friends.”

“What friends?” I asked.

“Rayla, Charlie, Cindy, Teb, Elijah, Dan.”

“Oh, them. How can you be sure?”

“Well, when you yelled out for help, it was like I instantly woke up from a daze, and I was able to see clearly for the first time that day. I could also understand the mistakes you had made.”

“What!” I tried to take my feet away, but he held on to them until I relaxed again.

“I think I’ve put together everything that happened today. At first I just felt off and said that you should stay home. That’s what was supposed to happen, but you didn’t want to. You wanted to show the other girls up by pretending they hadn’t gotten to you, and that wasn’t natural. So, the more determined you were to stick it out for the day, for the wrong reasons, the worse I got. In the cafeteria, you became so livid I could feel the waves of vengeance emanating from you… But when the ants started to bite, you didn’t want to lash out. Instead you finally admitted that you needed help. So I was restored.”

“I need something to eat,” I said, sitting up. Toby followed me to the kitchen and watched as I emptied almost the entire contents of our fridge onto my plate.

“I wish you wouldn’t use food to hide your feelings.” He sat down in an empty chair.

“I wish you were easier to understand!” I said, and dropping the plate of food onto the table, I thrust myself into the chair opposite him. *He was right; I was feeling guilty. I had wanted to show Effie up. I had wanted to prove that she couldn’t get to me. And he was right; I wanted to hurt anyone I could, and I would have*! That thought made my stomach lurch. I brought my hands to my mouth and held them tight against my lips. My hate for Effie had turned me into someone just like her. I looked at the plate piled high with my favourite foods: brownies, cookies, cupcakes and doughnuts. None of it really looked appealing, so I pushed the plate to the centre of the table and turned to Toby.

“You really haven’t made my life much easier,” I said. “It’s confusing, because when you first came, you said you were going to help me, yet in the last week I've had to endure more hardships than in the two previous years." Toby smiled and nodded, but he didn't say anything. "Some of it has been a special brand of torture, because you represent everyone who's treated me badly. You even admitted yourself that you would have been no nicer to me if I had ended up in your school."

"You're right," he said. He stood up and went over to the fridge. Rummaging through, he found some leftover chicken and potato salad. "You really do need to eat." He placed a new plate in front of me. I slowly ate the meal.

"Effie might have gotten the ant idea from me."

Why did this not surprise me? I put my fork down and sat back, careful of my numerous bites.

"Mariah, you don't know how hard this is for me. I can see my mistakes so clearly now, but I feel powerless to stop the destruction I started!" Toby brought his hands up to his hair as if he were trying to wash himself clean. I felt his anguish.

"So what do we do now?" I asked, feeling resolved.

"Wait. Regroup." He looked deep into my eyes. "Give yourself time to heal."

I nodded then cleaned up my plate. Coming to sit back down, I asked, "Why don't you think Rayla, Cindy or the rest had anything to do with Effie and the ants?"

"Because of their reaction."

"Reaction?"

"Well, there I was, barely aware of anything that was going on. You fell down beside me, and I had no clue what was happening, then you yelled out in anguish, and it felt like a switch was flicked in my head. I sat up and took stock." He cleared his throat. "You were yelling, and Ms. Telz had come running over, all annoyed at the commotion. She is really oblivious, isn't she? So she completely missed the fact that you were on the ground, but by then you had gone unconscious. Effie took full advantage of that. She and several of her friends stepped in front of you, blocking her from seeing you. But your friends had come over to see what was going on, and it didn't take them long to figure out the real problem. It was Cindy who saw you first. You were twitching like someone having an epileptic fit, and she got so frightened, she let out a horrible scream. She ran to you, followed by Charlie, Rayla and all three boys. Rayla had thought you were having a seizure, Charlie thought you had choked on something… Cindy noticed the ants and saw the way they were attacking you, so she told the others, and all of them started to squish any they could see.

"It was Elijah who put it together that they were in your backpack, and in your state you had managed to fall right on it. So he pulled it out from under you and threw it right in the direction of Effie and her gang. They scattered. With her panic and screams about poisonous ants, the cafeteria emptied so quickly, several kids got trampled.

"Ms. Telz took some time dealing with the stampede, then she finally noticed you and your friends, who were desperately trying to help. She called down Gus and the nurse. Fire ants were escaping out of your pack. Charlie, Cindy, Rayla, Teb, Dan and Elijah were all keeping watch over you, making sure no more were able to get you.

"The nurse arrived, and even the paramedics. Everyone was very concerned that you were having an allergic reaction. Your mom was called. They wanted her to give permission for you to be taken to the hospital, but she wouldn't let them. They said you weren't hurt too bad, but they did want to keep you under observation. Your mom didn't see the need for that.

"Gus came dressed in a full nuclear waste uniform; he was prepared to fumigate as soon as you were moved. So the paramedics took you to the nurse's room, and all your friends came along to make sure you were looked after. They wanted to stay with you, but Mrs. Kristy wouldn't let them."

"After all this, you may not be the only one with an ant phobia!"

I smiled weakly. "But remember, I never had an ant phobia before this started."

"I know." Toby put his hand over mine. "And you don't really have one, not even now, with all you've been through." I nodded. "Well, Gus came to the nurse's office and explained what he had found. The ants had been stuffed into a plastic pop bottle, which was wrapped up tightly in your pink sweater, and there was no lid, not in any part of your pack. You were set up beyond a doubt."

"Well, I know that," I said with a sigh.

"You're not the only one."

"But Ms. LaKey," I protested, feeling hopeless.

"Well, she's wrong! And she may be the only one left who thinks that way. I heard them talking while you were still unconscious, and they'll be having an emergency meeting today after school." Toby gave a wide grin. "Things could be changing."

"And they might not," I said, feeling tired. I was surprised to see that it was barely after three. "I want to rest," I said, laying my head down on the kitchen table.

I think I would have slept right there if Toby hadn't gently pulled me up and guided me to the living room. He lay me down on the sofa then came to sit next to my head. With just a bit of shifting, I was able to use his thigh as my pillow.

I dreamed I was in that wonderful place, only this time, as wonderful as it was, I was angry. I was throwing rocks into the pond and yelling over all the heartaches and miseries I had to endure. I was really raging, screaming so my voice broke, and pounding my fists on the ground till they were tender and bruised. Finally Toby, the dream Toby, came to me. He stood next to me while I sat on my knees. My anger had diminished a little, and he said, "It's alright to be angry. But it's what you do in anger that isn't right." I was turning toward him to ask what he meant when a jarring noise interrupted my dream.

It was the doorbell. I slowly opened my eyes and looked at the time: four thirty. With great effort, I pushed myself up and, in an attempt to wake up more, I stretched. I regretted this immediately, for each of the ant bites stung separately from the other; it felt like I was being poked by over fifty pushpins at once.

"You going to answer that?" Toby asked.

"Who is it?" I wondered aloud.

"The only way to find out is by answering the door," he replied, but I wasn't sure he was being completely honest; I had a feeling he already knew.

I checked the peep hole and saw Cindy on the other side. Almost as if she sensed me watching her, she banged on the door with her fist and yelled, "We didn't do it!"

Toby came close to me, watching me for my response.

I turned to him and whispered in my quietest voice, "What if it's a trick?

"Seems to me that you have a choice to make." He leaned back against the wall. "You can either decide to trust and let her in, or you could choose to not trust, and they will go away. Then you'll never really know."

I chewed my lip. "What if I can't trust them?"

"You are going to have to trust someone, sometime, or you're going to have a very lonely life." When I continued to stand there, he added, "It's not rocket science, Mariah, think about it. What does your heart tell you?"

I looked back through the peephole, keeping my hand on the lock. Cindy shifted restlessly from one foot to the other. I tried to imagine her going to Effie and telling her. I couldn't see Cindy actually doing that, nor any of her friends. *But then how had Effie found out*?

I tentatively undid the lock and pulled the door open. I faced Rayla, Cindy, Dan and Elijah. For a moment no one said anything. As I faced them, I noticed Cindy had five red marks on her arm. Rayla had on a long-sleeved shirt, but I could see two on the back of her hand. Dan had six between both his arms, and it looked like Elijah had at least ten below his elbows where his jacket sleeves had been rolled up to. I felt gratitude wash over me. They sported these spots because of their kind attempt to save me.

"You guys look sore." It was all I could think of saying, but it did the trick, because all of us ended up laughing. I invited them in, and they followed me to the kitchen.

It was odd; with these four guests in my house, I was suddenly struck at how I had never had friends over before. The only other time I had spent in the kitchen with people other than my family was my brother's delinquent buddies. But I was no less calm at this point than if it had been the other scenario.

"Oh," Elijah said, pulling something off his shoulder. It was my backpack. "Gus gave me this to bring to you."

Panic gripped my heart, constricting my lungs and pressing down on my chest. *What if this was a trick? What if they had come to finish the job*? Toby stood next to me, invisible to everyone but me. I gave him a quick look before I walked the three feet to Elijah and took my pack from his hands. I was trembling as I walked back to my spot by the sink and slowly opened it up.

Reaching in, I found my sweater and pulled it out to investigate; it was stained red in places and ripped in others. I hadn't been able to see it before, because it had been bunched in a tight ball. Now it hung loosely in my hand, and I was stunned at the amount of damage it had sustained. I let it fall to the floor and reached in for my next article, my favourite novel. It had been blacked out by a black marker so that most pages were illegible. Only a few choice words remained legible, and they were not kind ones. I dropped it on top of my sweater and reached in again; both my math and science books had pages roughly torn from them. They too were added to the pile of my vandalized belongings, and I put my hand in one last time, thinking I'd find my notebook, but the bag was empty. I let it drop and, looking down at the heap, I felt a wave of relief wash over me… *no ants.*

"Gus kept your notebook," Rayla said in a choked voice. "He said it has evidence of your innocence as well as…"

"It was littered with death threats," Cindy added quietly.

I wanted to thank them for the return of my belongings, but I didn't know how to say it. The question of how Effie found out still lingered.

"Um," Rayla started cautiously, "we have something to tell you." The mood in the room became stiflingly heavy. Rayla started to play with her hands in her lap. "Well…we think we might have figured out how Effie knew." She looked quickly up at me and back down again. "You know how Charlie's locker is next to Sara's… Well, it is. And she was at it and talking to Teb about our trip to the mall. Anyways, she was telling him about you coming and stuff…" Rayla fiddled harder. "Sara might have heard her talking."

I put my hand over my mouth. I felt a bit ill. I was so certain that I had been set up, I had never considered that it might have been a mistake. I looked at all four in the kitchen. "Is that why Charlie didn't come?" I asked, wondering how I'd have felt if it was me.

Rayla nodded. "Charlie feels absolutely horrible. She was crying so hard, Teb had to take her home. She never knew this would happen."

Feeling the strength leave my knees, I pulled out the empty chair and sat down. I felt Toby place a hand on either shoulder, and as much as it hurt my bites, I didn't want him to let go. *How had I become so bitter? I had been so set on being the only one hurt in everything that I hadn't been able to see that others were hurting too.*

"She wanted us to come and tell you how sorry she is," Cindy added.

"It wasn't really her fault." My voice sounded so very small and broken.

"Tell them you aren't mad," Toby prompted.

"I'm not mad," I said more in response to Toby, but it worked. Everyone seemed to relax a little.

Rayla reached out and wrapped her arms around me; I was so surprised, she almost pulled me out of my chair. I don't know what felt worse: having her arms tight against several sores, or the sheer discomfort of having her hug me. *When was the last time I'd been hugged by anyone, other than Toby?* It stirred up new feelings, and as much as I knew I should reciprocate, I just couldn't, so I sat with my arms firmly by my side.

Rayla let go, and looking into my eyes, I think she caught sight of my unshed tears. "I'm so sorry," she mumbled. "I forgot you must be sore."

"Just a little." I gave her a half-smile. *I wasn't about to tell her the tears were there because I'd never felt friendship like this before.*

"Just a little!" Dan scoffed. "I've got six bites, and they're driving me crazy! You're a trooper, I'm telling you!"

This was a leaping point into a conversation about the "Great Cafeteria Ant War," as it was dubbed halfway through our talk. Through the telling and retelling of the day's events, everyone became a hero: the way Cindy finally got Ms. Telz to understand what was happening; Charlie's ability to squish seven in one swoop, and the best part, the way Elijah had thrown the pack right at Effie's feet, and how she'd fled screaming. I felt like a rookie learning a new skill being among so many friends—everyone trying to talk at once. *So this is what it was like to have a group of friends—it felt nice.* By the end, everyone was able to laugh at the whole thing—even me, a little.

The plate piled with baked treats still sat on the table, and as the afternoon wore on, everyone started to help themselves to it, as if I had put it there just for them. Our talk had eventually led to other topics: the mall, our teachers, the upcoming auditions for the school play, and other trivial things. I joined in from time to time, but mostly I listened. It was nice to hear their take on the world. They seemed to have a fresh and hopeful attitude, and I liked it. When I did say something, it was usually met with agreement, and at one point Rayla said that I was "deep," which meant I didn't talk much, but when I did, everybody should listen. This made me feel really great about myself. Toby smiled at me encouragingly.

It was after 6 PM when they decided that they all had to get home. I said I looked forward to seeing them again, though I had the rest of the week off, so it wouldn't be too soon. Cindy reminded me of her invite for the sleepover, and then they were gone. I was a bit disappointed as I turned back to my empty quiet house, but then I saw Toby standing beside me, and I felt my spirits lift.

I made myself dinner and ate it in front of my favourite shows. Toby seemed quiet again, but my head was so full of my own thoughts, I didn't ask what was on his mind. My mom breezed in around eight, barely taking time to say three words to me; actually it was five: Benadryl is on the table. Then she headed down to her room to lock herself in for the night. I cleaned up the mess she had left in her wake and went to my own room once my shows were done.

As I lay in bed, mulling over the day, Toby interrupted my thoughts. "You remember that tomorrow is Wednesday?"

"Ya..." I replied. "This is Tuesday; one week and one day ago you came into my life..."

"A week and a day...huh," he said.

"It's been a very full eight days." I reached out with my foot until it found his leg. Instantly the warmth that seemed to emanate from him seeped into my soul. "Feels almost like a lifetime."

Toby put his hand on my ankle. "Ya. But I was trying to say that tomorrow is Wednesday, and you promised to go to the bowling alley."

"Oh, ya," I said, mindlessly scratching at a bite on my arm.

"Don't," Toby said, pointing at me.

"Don't go?" I asked, confused.

"Don't scratch." I dropped my hand.

"But about the other thing—are you still willing to go?"

"I guess I am," I answered, though I wasn't so sure. I was intrigued by how Effie had reacted to Tony's interest in me, but frightened by it at the same time. Then I remembered something. "Do you remember what you told me in the nurse's office?" Toby narrowed his eyes. "About feeling sad then, because I wasn't going to feel it later?"

"Ya," he replied. "So?"

"Well, I think I sort of understand what you meant." *I did.* "You see I used to believe that if I was miserable, then I'd stay miserable forever, like my misery would swallow me up and never let me go. But it didn't, and this day turned out kinda okay."

"I'm glad."

Without realizing it, I brought my hand up to my arm again. "Stop scratching." Toby commanded.

I stopped but let out a frustrated moan. "They're just so itchy!"

"Take the Benadryl," he suggested. I had brought the bottle and a spoon down but hadn't taken any yet, so I did. I was still intensely itchy and getting worse. I sat at on the edge of my bed, holding the side with my hands, afraid that if I let go, I'd scratch myself raw.

Toby came to sit beside me. "I feel it too," he whispered consolingly.

I closed my eyes against the growing urge to scratch myself raw. "What does it feel like to you?"

"Different. I think I can actually feel the poison trying to spread, but I also feel your body's defenses working to eliminate the toxins. It's all really fascinating."

I gripped the bed tighter; it felt like millions of ants were crawling all over me again! This thought gave me a shiver, and I leaned into him as I shuddered.

"Don't worry, the battle is already won."

"I don't think I can keep myself from scratching much longer," I admitted, still not letting go of my bed.

"Here." He came up behind me so that his arms were around mine. Then, once I had finally let go, he pulled me down so that my head rested on his chest, but he still had his arms around mine so I couldn't scratch.

DAY 10 Wednesday...

I DIDN'T BUDGE FOR THE WHOLE NIGHT, AND WHEN I WOKE, I could feel that Toby hadn't either. In the few magical moments between sleep and waking, I felt more peaceful, calm and safer than I had ever before in my whole life. I felt protected in his arms, and I didn't want to stir because the feeling would end. Toby took a deep breath. I felt his whole chest expand, and he yawned loudly.

"Morning, beautiful. Did you sleep well?" He sat up with a satisfied grin on his face.

"Ya," I answered absentmindedly as I got up and went to sit at my desk.

"I stayed awake the whole night thinking, and I was reminded of this one dream I've had where I was in this meadow..." he continued, but I had stopped listening.

Instead, I was looking for an empty book to write in. I managed to find a half-used binder. "Oh, ya?" I responded as he paused for a response, but I was too busy removing the used papers from the book. I found a purple marker. On the inside of the front cover I wrote in bold print "GOOD", then on the first page I scribbled down my joy of waking in Toby's arms.

When I was finished, I swung around and he was saying, "And the best part was not feeling any guilt and no pain! It was like it was completely gone!"

"That does sound good," I agreed.

"It really was." His chocolate eyes danced.

The morning, at least that last half hour of it, went by without a hitch. After breakfast, Toby suggested that we take a walk. He seemed to be restless, so I agreed.

Mature trees and numerous green spaces surrounded the complex I lived in. There were large areas of well-cared-for grass surrounded by shrubs. In some directions we had hills to climb and in others it was flat, but in any direction we were well served with pathways and benches to sit on. Usually when school was out, they'd be filled with kids playing, and on the weekends people would gather in them. At the back of our building complex was the river, along which ran a path. We took this path.

About three blocks away, we were passing one of the many outdoor mini-malls. Toby scanned the shops, and grabbing my arm, pointed to the hair salon. "What about a haircut?" he asked.

"Haircut?" I repeated, catching sight of my frizzled hair as it lightly fluttered past my face from the breeze. "I don't cut my hair," I stated, "I only trim it."

"Why?" he asked.

I told him the only reason I had. "I was told once that fat girls look better with long hair."

Toby stood away from me and inspected me up and down. "I disagree on two things." He held his fingers up to frame my face. "First, you're not fat. And second, I think you'd look really great with shoulder-length hair." I wrinkled my brow; my hair reached all the way down to my hips, so I really wasn't sure. "Can you trust me on this?" he persisted.

"Well…" I began, but he cut me off.

"Please, Mariah. I know you'd look great. Your hair being so long makes you look too mature and serious. And I know if it was shorter, it would be easier to take care of."

Looking down, I caught my shadow. My hair was already a big mess, even with the minimal amount of wind that blew.

"Come on, just give it a try." He took my arm and started to guide me to the salon. "I know you're going to love it!" I didn't protest and allowed him to usher me forward.

As we stepped in the door, a bell chimed; it was a sweet inviting sound. At the front door was a waiting area, but instead of chairs there was an assortment of soft stools. A curtain that was only partly drawn sectioned off the waiting area. In front of the curtain was a small high table that barely accommodated the old fashioned cash register placed on it. A stool stood empty beside it. Behind the curtain I could see one salon chair with a large personalized mirror in front of it. The mirror looked like it had feather boas glued on it. It looked more like a room in someone's home than a professional boutique, and I think that was what helped me to relax.

"Hello. Can I help you?" a young woman said as she appeared from behind a curtain. She was just over five feet tall and very slender; her hair was red and very short. It looked to be only three inches long, and she wore it in spikes with several barrettes pinned all about her head. She wore bright pink and purple eye shadow, and her lips were covered with bright pink lipstick. Her cheeks sparkled with a light dusting of what looked like fairy dust.

I smiled. "I'd like to have a hair…" I choked out the word, "cut."

She smiled back. "Are you sure about that?" When I didn't answer right away, she said, "My name is Molly. Now, are you sure you want a haircut?"

"No," I admitted. "But my friend," I snuck a sideway glance at Toby, "says I'd look nice if I…."

"Got it cut shoulder-length and had it layered," he coaxed, and I repeated it to Molly.

She cocked her head sideways and squinted. "Yes," she finally said, "I agree. You would look absolutely stunning." She stood up straighter and asked, "Do you want to try?"

"Can I take it back if I don't like it?" I answered.

This made both Toby and Molly laugh, which helped ease the tension in my neck.

"No," Molly said. "I can't undo a haircut. But I will promise that I won't let you leave until you are completely satisfied."

I still felt nervous, but I allowed her to guide me to a chair in front of a porcelain sink that had an indented groove for my neck, and she began to wash my hair. She had a way of talking about nothing in particular but making it sound fascinating. She chatted about becoming a hairdresser—something she'd wanted to do since she was nine.

She explained that when she worked in other people's salons, she'd felt rushed to just cut hair, and now that she finally had her own, she really felt free to create—like she was an artist of people.

The more she talked, the better I felt, so when she was done washing and moved me to the seat in front of the full length mirror, and took my long swooping hair in her hand then held the scissors up to it, I didn't jump up and run out of her shop, but I did flinch.

"Are you ready for this?" she asked, swinging the chair around so I was now facing her.

"I think I am," I whispered. I looked down at my chest, where my hair fell in ringlets: my hair was my identity. I felt like I was losing myself. *Would it be so bad to loose my old identity?* I wondered. *Could I create a new one?* "I want to be," I said, bracing myself. "Just do it quickly."

"Alright." Molly stood back a moment. "Do you want to watch?" I shook my head, and she kept the chair where it was, then moved behind me and began. Toby kneeled in front of me and held my hand. I just closed my eyes.

"You have the most beautiful hair," Molly cooed as I felt her work a brush through the wet strands. "It must be a bit challenging to manage at times, though." I agreed. "You know, I could teach you some tricks and secrets to keep it looking controlled for longer." I liked that idea. "My sister has hair like yours, and she's always being asked to be a hair model. Once she let it grow long then darn near cut the whole mess off so she could donate it to be made into a wig; it was auctioned off for charity, and hers got highest bid."

I opened my eyes; a large amount of my hair lay on the ground, and more and more was being added to it as she worked. Toby watched her work. He seemed to be pleased with the progress. Finally Molly came to stand in front of me. She took a strand of hair from either side of my face and pulled them straight, and then she did the same several more times at different spots on my head.

"I think we're done," she announced. "Are you ready to have a look?" She didn't wait for a reply. Instead she gently swiveled the chair until I faced the mirror.

My mouth fell open. My hair seemed to be more curly, and less of a frizzled mess. It shone like happy, healthy hair, and when I moved my head, it seemed to bounce. But even more stunning was the way it framed my face so my cheeks didn't look as chubby.

"Oh, Mariah!" Toby exclaimed, stepping forward to stand beside me and look from my reflection to me. "You're so…"

"You seem to have a shadow on your shoulder," she said.

"A what?"

"A shadow." She moved to the side of me where Toby had been standing and brushed my shoulder. "Hmmm," she said to herself and stepped back. "I could have sworn I saw something…" With a quick shrug, she looked over at me. "Never mind—do you like it?"

I stood up and gave my head a shake. The Mariah I looked like now wasn't as frightened or quite as desperate as the one I had looked at for so many years before today. Gratitude welled up, and I gave Molly a hug. I was surprised at myself, but she took it in stride and hugged me back.

"Now my work is done," she said softly in my ear.

I would have paid her anything, but all she wanted was fifteen dollars for the haircut. Then she spent over forty minutes showing me how to style my hair and which products to use. I bought everything she suggested, and she insisted on giving me a discount.

As we walked home, Toby kept sneaking glances at me when he thought I wasn't looking. I beamed; *I liked it when he looked at me like that.* I tidied, organized, did my homework and took a long shower, then styled my hair and even applied a moderate amount of make-up. Looking at my reflection, I was impressed. Even with the red marks spattered across my chest and arms, I didn't think I looked so bad. But as I primped and prepared, Toby seemed to get more and more agitated. He rubbed his neck at an increasing rate. Finally, I was ready to get dressed, so we went to my room to pick out clothes.

"What about this one?" I asked, holding up the same shirt for the fifth time.

Toby shook his head. "We don't have any other options?"

We had only bought three shirts, and anything old he refused. "These are our only options," I assured him. "But are you certain about the pants?" I felt my face fall when he nodded his head. The pants were made of stretchy denim, so they clung to my every bump and flaw. I felt totally exposed in them. "What are you trying to do?" I asked.

Toby looked at me with an apology in his eyes. "I want him to look at you and be so distracted that he won't be able to think of anything else." He flushed and looked away.

"You must be dreaming," I scoffed, looking down at myself. I stood wrapped in a towel, and though I felt my upper body was improving, the bulge at my abdomen hadn't gone anywhere; it was still massive.

"No." Toby picked up the first shirt. "You can do it." He held it out to me, made a face and dropped it again. "It's just going to take you doing something that you've never done before." Toby looked over his shoulder at my door.

"What?" I picked up the middle shirt and held it up to my chest.

He shook his head again. "That one looks nice, but the collar is too low, and your spots will show."

"Then what?" I asked, feeling prickly, not because of my bites but because of the way Toby kept looking over at my closed door made me feel panicked.

"You are going to have to look a bit like…" he stopped and turned back to me.

"A hooker?" I asked.

Toby coughed so hard, he almost fell over. "No! No, not flashy. Tony would never be distracted by 'show'; no, you need to look classy."

"What do you mean?"

"Well, you need to wear something very much like what your mother does."

I slumped to the bed and held my face in my hands, a feeling of squeamishness dancing through my gut. *I didn't want to look like her. I'd rather look like a hooker!*

"The other night, you got Tony's attention. He noticed you, and I wasn't even planning it. I hadn't remembered him yet. But he didn't see you as anything more than a plaything; something to amuse him for the moment then discard when he'd conquered you. I want him to see you as the bright and sophisticated person you are, and for him to notice you that way, you've got to dress the part."

"My mom keeps her room locked," I said, hoping that would make him give up on the idea.

"Let's try it. If the door doesn't open, then I'll come up with a different plan."

"First tell me what you hope to accomplish tonight."

"Well, I want you to get him alone…"

"Alone!" I interrupted, feeling insulted. "I had him alone when he drove me home the other night! Why couldn't I have said something to him then?"

"Two reasons: first, I hadn't asked you yet; and second, that night all he had on his mind was how fast he could score. I need him to see you as something more." *I was offended by his accusation.* "Trust me, he's not interested in you in the right way, yet. If you were to tell him anything now, it wouldn't stick."

As if in a dream, I followed Toby to my mother's bedroom door. I couldn't remember the last time I had gone into her room, with or without her there. As he turned the knob and it opened, I held my breath. Walking over the threshold, I felt like I was breaking a law.

My mom's room was twice as big as mine, with a queen-sized bed centered along the wall to my right. There was a closet that took up a quarter of the room and a nook where my mother had placed her desk. Her room looked well lived-in, with clothes discarded all around and many books and papers among them. The huge window didn't let in much light because of the hedge that grew outside it.

Toby stood with his head in my mother's closet. Most of her clothes were formal suits and dress skirts for work. I rarely saw her in anything else. Once or twice she'd come out of her room in pajamas, but I couldn't remember her dressing up. She must have, since she would go out almost every weekend with her girlfriends. I sat gingerly on the edge of her mattress.

"Ah-ha!" Toby called out triumphantly. "I think I found it."

He pulled a red top from my mother's closet and held it up. It had shiny elastic material around the bust and looked like an empress waistline with several strips of material flowing down. I took it, feeling very unsure about the whole thing. Then without a word, I went back into my room to change.

The top was tight and made of Lycra that went from my wrists all the way up to the short V-neck. It clung to my skin, revealing my bust without actually showing anything. The strips of material turned out to look rather flattering. With the way they seemed to float, there was no real way of telling how much excess weight I had hidden under them. The pants did a good job of holding everything in place, making my legs appear shapelier than I had ever seen them. Overall I was really impressed with how I looked.

Finally I gave Toby permission to turn around; when he did, he just stood looking at me. I started to feel nervous. "Toby, am I going to be safe tonight?"

"Safe?" he asked, confused.

"Well, by the way you can't seem to talk your eyes off me, I was wondering if Tony was going to have the same response and try to act on it with more persistence then the other night?"

Toby finally managed to turn away. "You know I want him to take a real interest in you."

"But what if that just makes him want to score more?"

"He probably will," he muttered more to himself, and then turning to face me again, he added, "But I'll be there. I'll make sure nothing happens." I reached up to my arm and started to scratch. He grabbed my hand to stop me.

"How can you be sure? You've been there all along, and you haven't been able to stop everything every time!"

"This one is different," he assured. "I know that if you do what I tell you to, it will all work out."

I nodded as the memory of Tony's hand on my back, around my waist, and playing with my hair flashed in my mind. I still longed for him to kiss me, but just a kiss, nothing more. *What if he wanted more? What if I couldn't resist? Would one kiss interfere with Toby's plans?* I looked over at Toby—he was smiling at me. *Would he be smiling if he knew what I was thinking?*

I went to the washroom to get a better idea of how I looked: I stood transfixed in front of my reflection; it was like I had morphed into a whole other person. With my hair shorter, it made me look like a bouncy person. The make-up seemed to make my eyes sparkle. I couldn't help but feel prettier as I looked at myself.

The bus ride seemed to take forever. I quietly asked Toby when the bowling started, and he promised that I'd be late, but he wanted me to be, so I could make an entrance. And I did. It was ten past seven when I walked in, a full forty minutes after the games had begun. I had to concentrate hard just to breathe.

"Walk slowly," Toby said. "Go to the table just off to the side of Tony's lane." I looked around, taking slow steps. "He's at lane two—do you see him?"

Toby didn't need to point him out to me. I had caught sight of him the moment I walked through the front door, but despite myself, my breath caught as I watched him. As I passed each lane, everyone present would stop playing and look at me. I felt my knees wobble.

"Don't worry, just keep going." Toby reached over and placed his hand firmly on my back. It seemed to give me the strength I needed to steady myself.

As I passed the front desk, Mack looked up and whistled. I nodded and kept on going. I had my destination in sight, and I was silently coaxing myself to make it there.

Tony hadn't noticed me yet. He was too involved in his game, but as I drew closer, Larry nudged him, and he finally looked over. He was just standing to take his turn, but when he looked my way, he seemed temporarily paralyzed.

"Gonna play?" Sam asked. He had just finished throwing. "Come on, man! Grab your balls!"

Tony reluctantly tore his eyes from me and went over to the ball dispenser, but he looked back once he had picked one up.

"Beautiful, it's working." I could feel Toby's excitement.

I stopped at the table, and with a great deal of effort, gracefully sat myself down in one of the seats. Tony finally turned to take his shot. It bounced twice and hit the gutter before it had made it to the midway point in the lane.

"Yes!" Toby whooped and did a small jump. "We've got him now!"

I smiled, still looking toward Tony's lane. *I felt happy with who I was, sort of.*

Tony turned back to look at me quickly but didn't linger long. Instead he picked up his second ball and tried to recover from his first. This time he dropped it too early, and it veered off into the gutter instantly.

"Alright," Toby said, taking the seat next to me, "just sit here, and he'll come to you."

I sat facing Tony and his pals with my legs crossed and my back straight. Tony didn't look back at me for his third throw and managed to bowl a ten— low for him. I sat for three more rounds, while Tony kept checking over his shoulder. However his game continued to deteriorate, until in his last turn all three balls ended up in the gutter. Toby remained quiet the whole time; his eyes were glued to his old friend.

A boy approached me from another lane. Toby encouraged me to make small talk. Meanwhile, he watched, as Tony seemed to be unnerved further by this turn of events.

As the last frame was being bowled, Toby leaned over to me and said, "I've never seen Tony have such a lousy game." I blushed. *It was strange to have such an effect on someone else. Strange but powerful.* "When he gets here, keep the conversation light. I'll tell you what to do when the time is right." I felt a tiny bit of resentment that I couldn't just enjoy the evening. Instead I was going to have to ruin it all once Toby was ready to have me relay his message.

The game ended. Tony had come in third. His friends seemed elated by this and begged him to stay and play at least one more round. I could hear their conversation drifting over to me. Tony kept looking over at me and brushed his friends off with a wave as he came over to see me. I could hear taunts of "sore loser" and "chicken" from Sam and Sean. Larry sat back and smiled.

As he neared, he didn't look back once. At the table he took a seat directly across from me, and bringing his hand up to his chin, he leaned his elbow on the table and sat as if entranced by me.

I looked to see if Toby had anything for me to say. When he didn't respond, I said, "Wow, you sucked."

Finally Tony stopped staring and said, "They're going to print that off and have it laminated." He gave me a smile. "Must be something in the air tonight. I've never bowled so badly." The lights reflected off his brownish red hair, making it appear like as if it were flecked with gold. His brown eyes were actually mixed with streaks of copper, and with his olive complexion, he looked a bit like a Greek god to me.

"Just like I told you," Toby added.

I smiled, feeling self-satisfied. "You won't be able to say that again tomorrow."

I could feel Tony drinking me in. He stopped at my hair, then my eyes and my chest.

I turned away and looked at Toby. It was like I could sense Tony's thoughts, and they made me feel off-balance.

"Just hang in a bit longer," Toby said.

The more I looked from Toby to Tony, the more similarities I could see, and as I did so, the more confused I became as to who was who. They were both tall, almost six feet. They both had seductive brown eyes. Both were muscular in the upper chest but slim at the waist. Tony had reddish hair, but they both had the same cut and style. Tony sat back, and at that moment both had their left arms draped over the chair. And they both behaved in a way that made them seem like they were in complete command of the situation.

It gave me a chill, and I felt myself mixing up my feelings for each in my head. All this staring caused a primal emotion to well up in my chest; I drew back my shoulders and sat up a little straighter. Both boys seemed to take notice.

"I'm so glad you came," Tony said after clearing his throat.

"I wasn't sure I was going to," I answered, not really understanding why I would say such a thing.

"Well then, I'm extra glad you did." Tony's eyes danced.

"Thank you." I felt hot inside.

"How'd you get here?" he asked.

"The bus," I answered, looking away to his friends as they set up the next round.

"That must have taken over an hour!"

I nodded.

"All just to see me?"

"Um…" I faltered. I didn't want to give him the wrong idea.

Toby was staring at his old friend with narrowed eyes, but he said, "Tell him you thought you'd bowl today."

"I…" I stammered, "I didn't realize it was league practice. I thought you had invited me to play."

"I had invited you to play," Tony said softly. "Do you want to play?"

I didn't know how to answer. I felt like I was missing something. As Toby glared at Tony his hands clenched into fists. A shiver ran up my spine, and I leaned back in my chair, waiting for either Tony to talk or Toby to instruct me on what to say next.

Eventually Tony turned to me, giving me his winning smile and asked, "Hungry?"

I shrugged.

"I'm starved," he exclaimed. "I'm gonna get some fries. Do you want anything?" I shook my head. "I'll be right back." With that he was off to the front desk.

Toby followed him with his eyes. "This is good," he said, but his voice sounded otherwise. "You've just got to be careful, alright? Don't trust him at all, and don't let him get too close. You really are doing superbly," he said. I sat up straighter and shook the loose curls that had caught on my shoulders. "Absolutely superbly." Toby looked past me to where Tony was ordering food then back to the friends he had abandoned at the lane.

I too looked over at the boys. They continued to check me out from time to time; but now I wondered whether Larry recognized me, and if he did, would he tell his sister? Who would most certainly tell Effie! *Was I asking for more trouble? Was it worth it…doing this favour for Toby?* He rubbed his neck; I could feel his regret building. *I was the only one who could try to set things right for him.*

Toby was also distracted by the boys. "Larry never liked me." He laughed dryly. "He was terrified to death of what I would do to him, though. But he never trusted me or the things I did." He scratched the back of his neck. "Smart boy. He's a good friend for Tony."

Larry had just bowled a spare. Sam and his brother gave him congratulatory high fives. "As for those two, they're trouble: twin trouble!" Toby stood up and moved to behind my chair when he saw Larry making his way over.

"Mariah, right?" Larry said as he took the same chair Toby had been sititng in moments earlier. I nodded. "You were here last Saturday?" I nodded again.

I felt panicked. I had been prepared to talk to Tony, but I had never imagined myself talking with his friends. My apprehension grew.

"You had that loose black top on," Larry said, leaning forward in the chair. "I liked you better in the other shirt."

"So did I," I admitted, and I heard Toby laugh along with Larry.

"But you are funnier today." Larry smiled. He had a warm and honest smile. I grinned back at him. "Hey, don't you go to East Ridge High?"

The smile slipped from my face. “That’s right.” I felt my throat constrict around the words.

“My sister goes there too.” I couldn’t speak, so I nodded curtly. “Ya, she’s a real brat!” Larry looked over to the desk where Tony was waiting for his order to be filled. “She made this big fuss to be transferred there so she could be with her best friend, who we called a really spoiled effin’ princess… But it works for me. Now I don’t have to see her ugly mug in the halls of my school.” I pulled my lips together, trying not to smile. “Ah,” Larry continued, “I see I have amused you.”

“It’s just that I’ve never heard of Effie referred to unkindly.”

“Ya, well, she’s not all that.”

Tony returned with a tray of food: fries, jalapeño peppers, chicken wings, a pile of gummie candies and two drinks. “Dinner is served,” he said, and then added as Larry reached out to take a fry, “Not for you, you mooch!”

Larry took one anyway and popped it in his mouth.

“What were the two of you talking about?” Tony asked suspiciously.

Toby leaned down to my ear and said quietly, “This is working out far better than I thought it would have.”

“We were just discussing the love of your life!” Larry winked, then explained, since Tony wore an expression of confused annoyance. “You know her, Effie Rooster.” I stifled a giggle at the play on her last name.

“That witch!” Tony slapped the table with such force it made me jump. “Don’t even joke!”

Larry was laughing so hard he almost fell out of the chair. He tipped his head to me and gave Tony a punch in the arm, and then he walked away to the lane, where a not-so-happy looking pair of twins waited. Tony sat where Larry had been. Toby’s grip tightened on my shoulders, but he didn’t say anything.

Tony ate almost everything on the tray, insisting that I should have some, but I only nibbled on a few of the fries and drank the pop he had bought for me. He spent a lot of time telling me about his bowling trophies, and his other successes like pool and blackjack. “I’m second best to an old friend of mine!” he boasted.

“That’s true,” added Toby. “I was the only one who could outplay him game for game, and seemed better than him in everything he did.” Then he added more softly, “And it’s all meaningless to me now.”

I tried to listen, but I found it dull, so my mind wandered a little. I discovered that when I pulled my shoulders back and sat up straighter, then batted my eyes, cocked my head and gave a small smile, Tony reacted in the most amusing ways, stuttering, forgetting what he was saying, and he once stopped mid-sentence to clear his throat and wipe his forehead.

Larry came back over and stood between us. He wanted to know if Tony was going to bowl the last game, "Or have you given up completely?" he teased. Tony smiled but declined. "Well, I don't blame you, my friend." Larry winked at me again. "After such a crushing defeat, it's hard to get back into the game. Might have to give it up for good!" He pulled a sheet from his pocket. "First place, Sam. Second place, Sean. And third, THIRD, Tony…"

"Oh, get lost." Tony kicked out, but Larry was able to sidestep it. "You still lost!"

"Ouch, that hurt." Larry put his hands to his heart and went away.

"It's time to tell him about me," Toby instructed.

I faltered, unsure how to begin. "Do you know a boy named Toby?"

Tony's mouth fell open, but he quickly regained composure. "He was my best friend," he said, quietly staring off somewhere behind my head. "Why do you ask?"

"Um…" I stalled for an idea, or some help from Toby, but he stayed silent. "Well, I just met him last week, on Monday, and you sort of remind me of him."

"You met him last week, on Monday…" Tony repeated, robot-like. I nodded. "He, he…he died," Tony's voice was barely audible, "that night."

"I know," I answered, marveling at the irony.

"So you met him just…" Tony's gaze dropped to the floor. *He looked so sad and broken.*

"Ya," I said, and in spite of myself, I put my hand on his knee. Tony looked up at me sharply, his eyes narrowed.

"Excuse yourself to the washroom," Toby said, pulling me up by my armpits. I stood. My hand slipped from Tony's leg.

"Don't go." Tony reached up and grabbed my wrist; I felt the smoothness on the palm of his hand tight against my skin.

"I have to use the girl's room," I explained. He sighed and let my arm go.

"We have to talk," Toby said as he dragged me away. "Tony's going to want to take you into the storage room," he explained as we walked into the women's washroom. "I don't want you to go! So you'll have to stay very alert."

I stood at the mirror, looking at the girl who looked back at me. *Who was this fresh, attractive young thing? Was she really me? Was I really her?* "What if I can't?" I asked, fear of my own feelings taking root. I should have asked: what if I felt like I wanted to go? For when Toby had told me of Tony's plans, a spark of excitement had leapt up my spine.

"I'll be with you," he assured. I was certain he didn't understand what I had really meant. I was beginning to like the attention a little too much, and I wanted to just go with this new and wonderful feeling. "Mariah," Toby cut into my thoughts, "I know this is a lot to ask from you, so if you can't do it, I'll understand."

"I'll do it," I answered. "Just do me a favour and don't let go of me."

Toby followed me out of the room with his hand firmly on my back. I had gone no more than two steps when Tony came up from behind me and embraced me tightly—I couldn't feel if Toby's hand was still there. Instead I felt as if I were Jell-O melting into Tony's arms. "There's a closet back here." I could feel his breath on my cheek as if it were a tranquillizer. I leaned back and relaxed into his chest. "Let's go there, where we won't be disturbed."

I nodded, even though somewhere inside I wanted to scream no. My heart was fluttering in my chest, making my head swim. *Where was Toby? I couldn't feel him, I couldn't see him, he was supposed to help—but did I really want him to help?* Two strong emotions warred in my mind.

As Tony stepped back, leaving me to stand up on my own, I felt my knees wobble, and finally I could sense Toby's hands strong and hard on my waist. "Tell him no," he said firmly. I opened my mouth, but nothing came out. "Don't go!" Toby said, trying to hold me back, but as I started to resist, Tony simply pulled me tightly to him.

Tony led the way. I felt like I was in a complete daze. "It's like a drug," I murmured. I couldn't see Toby, couldn't feel him! But I did hear him.

"Believe me," Toby said with venom in his voice, "I know." Then he said with more disgust than I'd ever heard, "I taught him most of this stuff."

Like a puppet, I was guided to the storage room. *I wanted this...what was I doing?*

It was a small space, made smaller by the many stacks of boxes. There was a little over three feet of spare room between the storage and the door, but that seemed like plenty when we were pressed up against each other.

Only once as we walked in did Tony let go of me. I thought about making a run for it, but my legs barely had strength enough to stand. I ended up tripping in the attempt to flee and caught myself on the stack of boxes. Tony had turned back to the door, and I heard the click of the lock.

"For privacy," he explained. Then he stepped towards me and wrapped his arms around my back. For a moment he stayed with his chest pressed against mine, his face mere inches from my own.

Was he finally going to kiss me? All sense of time and space disappeared. Finally, he leaned in and kissed me square on the mouth—*my first kiss.* His lips were as soft as rose petals, warm and slightly moist. I closed my eyes and felt dizzy, like I had been twirling for hours.

Tony pulled back from me, and with a smile he said, "Oh, beautiful, you are so great."

It was the word "beautiful" that caught me—not just the word, but also the way he said it. I was instantly reminded of Toby, and my eyes swept the room to find him. When I didn't see him, I pulled out of Tony's embrace and turned to see if he was behind me.

Toby was there, shaking where he stood. He seemed paralyzed.

"What's wrong?" Tony drew me back into his arms. "Don't you want me?"

I didn't want to do this…or did I? "I can't," I said, breathlessly begging Toby with my eyes for help.

Tony spun me around so I faced him again. I melted. "Mariah, I want you… I need you," he said passionately.

I would have liked to have believed him. It would have been nice and convenient, but even though Toby wasn't holding on to me, I could feel him at the back of my thoughts; "watch out, he's a player" echoed in my mind. I tried to grip tightly onto that feeling as Tony leaned in and started to kiss me again. This time he opened his mouth a bit, and without thinking I did the same. A new wave of exhilaration ran through my veins. *This felt so good, how could it be bad?*

My mind began to scream. *I was behaving like a tramp!* I didn't want to be there, but I didn't know how to stop! I tried to pull away, but that made

Tony hold tighter. His arms were like a vise I couldn't squeeze out of. *Or maybe I didn't want to.*

He kissed me long and hard on the lips, then he kissed me on my ears, each of my cheeks, my nose, my neck, and drawing my hand up, he started to kiss me on each of my fingers. As wonderful as I felt, I felt a wave of nausea. My thoughts swam before my face: *I was acting like a tramp. I needed to stop! But I didn't think I could. Where was Toby? He said he'd protect me! But who was he supposed to protect me from, Tony or myself?*

Tony noticed my hesitation and paused.

In that moment I called out, "Toby, I need you!"

Tony dropped my hand. The colour drained from his face as he sucked in his breath. He even took a step back and leaned against the door. I finally felt Toby as he stepped closer and rested his hand on my shoulder. From the look on Tony's face, I wondered if he could also see the ghost of his old friend.

"I'm here, Mariah," Toby said softly.

Tony just kept looking over my head to the back wall. He looked like he was glued to the door. Then he cleared his throat and asked, "Did you just say Toby?"

I nodded, feeling a sense of safety and calmness return to me. *What had I been thinking before?*

"How well did you know him?" Tony asked, still sounding shocked.

"I think I've gotten to know him quite well."

"Were you with him that night?" Tony looked at me with awed appreciation.

"Yes," I answered. I was about to tell him that I'd been with him every day since, but Tony interrupted.

"You were the last person to be with him." Tony leaned more heavily on the door and stared at the floor. Again I felt sympathy for him; he had lost his best friend. I knew what that felt like, though mine hadn't been taken by death…

I reached out and brushed his arm. "I'm so sorry." I looked back at Toby, thinking that this would be the best time to deliver his message.

He ran his hand through his hair and said, "I don't know what to say."

"Why did you call me Toby?" Tony was looking up at me.

"I wasn't calling you Toby…"

"Don't," Toby said sharply. "He'll never believe you!"

"There is something Toby wanted you to know," I started.

Tony stood up straighter. "He told you something that night?"

"In a way…" I answered and reached out with my hand behind my back to encourage Toby to give me the words to say. He said nothing, and I couldn't turn to see him. I felt a like a fool. As the seconds slipped by, Tony seemed to relax and regain control.

Taking my free hand in his and holding it tight, he asked, "What is it?"

Tony's hand felt warm like Toby's, and it sent a tingle up my arm. "I…" I stammered, not knowing what to say.

Tony leaned in so close our noses almost touched. "Let me help you to remember." Then he kissed me before I could say anything more. It was more passionate and intense than before.

Pulling back I said, "But Toby wanted you to know something. It's really important!"

"It can wait," Tony replied, pulling me tight against him like an octopus trapping its prey. He moaned softly. Any feeling of nervousness left me as a mounting excitement raced through my body. *I liked this, I wanted it…it felt good!*

"Mariah." Toby's voice interrupted my thoughts.

"What do you want?" I moaned, my voice sounding almost like a whine.

"I want you," Tony said in almost the same tone as I'd used, while he planted kisses wherever he could reach.

I could feel Toby's hand heavy upon my shoulder. He was the only thing that kept me from abandoning all my resolve and giving in to every desire.

"Tell him he's making a bad deal," Toby sternly instructed.

"Now, Toby?" I asked.

But it was Tony who answered, "Yes." Then he worked his hand under my shirt and held it hard against my bare back. *Oh, that felt really good.*

Then he slowly started to slide it up my back. His finger brushed one of my bites, causing me to jump in pain and yell out, "Stop!"

"What?" Tony gasped and stepped away. He looked horrified.

"I'm so sorry, Mariah," Toby said, appearing beside me. "I shouldn't have asked you to do this. It was a bad idea. I don't think it's going to work." He took a deep breath and added, "It was too much for me to ask you to do this."

"No," I shook my head in response.

Tony held his hands up in front of his chest. "No, what?" he said.

My breath came heavy; I was angry, confused, sore and feeling ashamed of myself. *Where had things gone so wrong?* I spun around so I could face Toby. "I want to still try. What do I do now?"

Tony moved up behind me and wrapped me in his arms. "Let me have you like Toby had you," he said seductively into my ear.

I broke his embrace and held up my hand to signal for him to stop.

"He won't understand now," Toby explained. "It's no use."

"Tony, could you excuse me? I need a moment alone." Surprisingly, he left without a fuss. "Toby," I started once I was sure the door had been firmly closed behind him, "I don't care if I come off looking like a total loon," I said, feeling surprised at my own words, but certain that I meant them. "Just tell me what you want to tell him, and I'll repeat it."

"I'm so sorry I put you in this situation."

"What's so bad about this situation?"

Toby looked around the room. His hand had flown to his neck. "This room is trouble. I'm so sorry."

"I don't think it's your fault," I replied flatly. "You told me not to come into the storage room." I shook my head sadly. "I didn't listen to you."

"No, it's my fault. I knew Tony wouldn't take 'no' for an answer. I just thought if I could… I don't know—get him to trust you… I don't know."

"Well then, let's just tell Tony the truth." I suggested, and before Toby could argue, I went to the door and pulled it open.

"Don't worry," Tony said, sweeping me up in his arms as if nothing had interrupted us. I wondered if Toby had been this smooth. Or even better, as both seemed to believe he'd been.

"I think I know why you're so nervous." He pulled me extra close

I closed my eyes as we kissed. Tony ran his hand through my hair, and vibrant tingles shot down my spine. I gripped tightly to his neck. I fought the idea of stopping—*this felt good, and I wanted to feel good!*

"Let me make love to you like Toby did," Tony said as he tried to guide me further into the closet.

"What?" I screamed out. I felt like ice-cold water had been poured over my head. "No!" I snapped. "I didn't… he didn't… no." I said again, trying to break away from his strong grip.

"Then let me show you what he would feel like."

"No!" I said, and there could be no way anyone could think I didn't mean it. Tony didn't advance—he just stood staring at me in his arms, but when I didn't say anything else, he gently leaned in to kiss me again.

"Just listen to me," I said, placing my hand firmly over his mouth. His eyes widened but he didn't struggle. "You are right. I was the last person to be with Toby. But not while he was alive."

Tony pulled my hand away from his mouth. "What are you trying to say?"

"When Toby died…" *How could I explain this?* "The night Toby died…"

Tony waited patiently, never removing his eyes from mine.

"He died…and…and…he came to me." When Tony didn't say anything, I added, "after he died."

"Are you telling me that he's a ghost?"

"Yes," I answered.

"So he, like, appeared to you?" There was the sound of a chuckle behind his voice.

"Yes," I went on, "and he stayed with me."

"He doesn't believe you," Toby said, sounding defeated. "But thanks for trying." I smiled.

"You're just kidding," Tony said, a huge goofy grin spread across his face. "Who put you up to this? Sam? Sean? Surely not Larry…" Then before I could protest, he leaned in and kissed me again. My knees wobbled. *It still felt good.*

"Believe me," I insisted between kisses. I didn't want to say any more. I knew he didn't believe me, and he probably never would, but I had to keep trying. "He's here. And he wanted me to tell you that he died a horrible death."

Tony pulled away so quickly, I almost fell to the floor, but Toby caught me and held me up. "What do you know about his death?" Tony spat.

I was at a loss for words—I didn't really know anything about Toby's death.

"Now," Tony said in a frightening voice, "that's enough of that."

As frightened as I felt, I continued, "But Toby doesn't want you to end up with the same bad deal," I said, remembering the words Toby had wanted me to use.

Quick as lightning, Tony raised his hand and made a motion to punch me in the face—he might have, had his fist not been knocked off course by Toby's hand. In that brief moment, even though Tony's face was contorted with rage, his eyes were filled with pain and suspicion. "Leave me alone," he said, then turned and ran from the room.

I leaned even more heavily on Toby as he held me up. I was emotionally drained; if possible, I think I was even more exhausted than when I had cried for hours.

"Well, I think that went quite well," Toby said sarcastically as he slid to the floor with me in his arms. I repositioned myself so that I was leaning up against the stack of boxes, and brought my knees up to my chin to rest it there.

"I'm sorry I failed you," I whispered.

"No," Toby said while he shook his head. "No, I should have guessed that my problems would be harder to fix than yours." He rested his head on my shoulder.

I sat listening to the far-off noises of the bowling alley and I could feel my own heartbeat; somehow I found it soothing. I could feel Toby's regrets at the edge of my own frayed emotions.

"Are you alright?" A vaguely familiar voice called out, followed by quick footsteps. I looked up to see Larry rushing into the storage room. He fell to his knees in front of me. Toby moved away to give Larry space.

"Fine," I answered, trying to ease the concern I saw on Larry's face.

Larry brought his hand up to my forehead and looked into my eyes.

"I'm fine," I protested, pushing his hand away, then tuning to Toby I asked, "What is all this about?"

Toby opened his mouth and closed it like a fish out of water, but no sound escaped his lips. I noticed he was shaking a little.

Larry answered my question. "I just thought..." He looked at me more closely, narrowing his eyes, "Never mind." He sat back a little. "But you are sure you're alright?"

"I'm positively fine," I assured him, moving to stand up. Larry stood and offered his hand. Though I was standing, he kept a close eye on me, like he was worried something was going to happen.

"Come have a drink with me," Larry invited as he continued to watch me.

I just wanted to go home. I felt worn out from the day, but Larry seemed really insistent, so I followed him back to the table where we had sat earlier. He went and bought us something to drink.

The place seemed far less busy now. There were only a few people left bowling. Tony was nowhere to be seen, and it also seemed as though his twin friends had left too. I watched Larry talking with Mack, and then he carried back two bottles of apple juice.

"Interesting choice," I commented.

"Didn't you know that the health board has recommended that everyone should have seven to ten servings of fruits or vegetables every day? How else is a busy teen like me supposed to do that?" With a flourish, he drank down half the contents. "There now, I've already had at least two servings!"

I grinned, and Larry passed me the unopened bottle, and then sat down in the seat next to me. I drank and was surprised to discover how thirsty I had been.

"Better?" Larry asked as I put the container down on the table. I nodded.

He leaned back in his chair and scanned the emptying bowling alley, but I had the suspicion he was still watching me in his peripheral vision. I wished I could see Toby. I had a small uncomfortable feeling at the edge of my stomach, and I thought it might be coming from him.

"What happened with you and Tony?" Larry asked. I was struck by how much older and more mature he appeared than any of his friends, including Toby. I put them at about my brother's age, yet Larry seemed even…wiser? Calmer…

"We discovered that we had a friend in common," I explained.

"Oh…" Comprehension spread thought Larry's soft eyes. "Toby. Right? Tony was his shadow." Larry smiled sadly. "What's a shadow without someone to cast it?"

"A chalk outline." I spoke before I thought, and as I was saying it, I already regretted it. I felt Toby bang the chair. *Had he tried to hit me?*

Larry let out a hard, dry laugh. "You may have nailed it right there. Did I tell you how much I like the way you think?" His face turned serious. "You're too smart to be slumming with the likes of these guys."

"I could say the same thing about you," I retorted.

Larry nodded, still smiling. "What did I say, you're very smart." He took another drink. "Tony and I grew up together. We've been neighbours since before we could talk. Tony always hangs out at my house. He's sorta more like a brother than friend. I think he just puts up with me 'cause of our history."

"But why do you put up with him?" I felt a bit jealous. *Why hadn't Stacy just put up with me?*

"Well…I guess he's like family."

I grinned at the idea: a long-standing friendship sounded really nice to me. "I wish I had a friend like that," I said quietly.

"It has its nice parts."

"Ya," Toby cut in. He leaned on the back of my chair and caused it to start tipping back.

Larry lunged forward and caught my chair before I went completely over. The look of concern returned to his face. I steadied my racing heart. *I hated the feeling of falling!*

Toby went on. I didn't like his tone. "Larry does receive protection from anyone who would really want to mess him up, because he's Tony's friend." After that, he let go of my chair with a small thunk.

"I bet you know Tony better than anyone else," I commented, trying to ignore Toby.

Larry let go of my chair and turned away, his jaw flexed with tension. "Yup, you could say that."

"Sounds like you aren't happy about that." I was starting to wonder why Larry would still be friends' with him if he felt so negative about it.

"There've been some…moments," Larry said, his hazel eyes filled with unspoken sorrows. "But he's my bud—what else am I going to do?"

I continued to feel jealous, as I thought of how Stacy had so willingly sold me out for a higher notch in social standing. She'd been my buddy, yet she'd been the first to turn her back, and everyone else had followed her example. *Was I not worth it?*

Toby fell beside my chair like he had been knocked over the head. He was sporting a bright black eye. "I thought we were past this," he said through clenched teeth, pointing at his eye.

"Mariah, are you sure you're okay?" Larry asked, leaning closer. "You don't look so good…I mean, you look good…"

"Yes, that's true," I said from habit, then blushed.

Toby exhaled loudly as he was getting back to his feet. It unnerved me that I couldn't tell what he was feeling…*was he mad at me?*

"What I meant," Larry said, as a light pink spread across his upper cheeks, "is that you don't look completely alright."

"Thanks, but I'm okay," I tried to reassure, then I added, "Tony is lucky to have you as a friend."

Larry smiled sadly. "He really is a great pal. He was nicer before he met that friend you two had in common, no offence to the dead. Regardless, he's been nothing but nice to me." Finishing off his juice, Larry started to fiddle with the bottle in his hands.

My stomach lurched—it was Toby's emotions again.

"He wasn't anything but nice to me," I said, thinking back on the evening.

"I disagree," Toby said at the same time as Larry asked, "Are you sure?"

"Really," I protested, nodding, "I mean, he didn't do anything that I didn't really want him to." The honesty of that statement unsettled me. *I felt vulnerable.*

Larry stared harder. Feeling embarrassed, I leaned back against the chair. This was a mistake. Immediately I jumped forward, as an explosion of pain and itchiness broke out across my back. Checking the clock, I realized that it had been over four hours since my last dose of Benadryl.

"What's wrong?" Larry had sprung from his chair and was standing over me. Before I could explain, he pulled my shirt up my back and gasped. "What did he do to you?"

I pushed Larry back and snapped defensively, "It wasn't him." *Why did everyone think Tony was such a creep*? "Listen, he was nice to me, a bit insistent, but not too much. He stopped when I told him to." *At least he did stop when I really wanted him to!*

"But..." Larry sputtered.

"Just trust me, it wasn't him. I was already like this when I came here tonight." Looking into Larry's eyes, I wanted to add that it was the Effin' Witch from my school who had done this, but I was too embarrassed.

Larry seemed like he wasn't going to believe me, then his face changed as if he was remembering something, and he sat back down. Now that I had started to feel the itch, it spread until every inch of my body screamed out "scratch me!" I squirmed in my seat, trying to gently rub my back on the chair, while I also brought my hands up, crossing my arms so I could reach my biceps without really looking like I was.

"Did you bring the Benadryl with you?" Toby asked as he moved to my side and put his hand on my arm.

I tried to stop squirming. "I forgot the medication at home," I regretted aloud.

"Where do you live?" Larry asked. I told him, and he whistled. "That's really far."

"Two buses," I replied, knowing I wasn't going to make it.

"I'll call you a cab," Larry said. *Oh, thank goodness he had a solution.* He went to the front desk and made the call, then came back and walked me out to wait for it.

The parking lot was mostly empty. I stood with my hands in fists by my side. Toby stood behind me, holding my wrists so I wouldn't be able to scratch. My only relief was the cool night air on my skin.

"So, what happened?" Larry asked, standing to my right and keeping his eyes fixed on the busy street for any signs of my cab.

What if Larry knew? What if he was going to tell his sister all about me? I didn't think he would, but I still didn't feel safe enough to trust him with the truth, so I lied. "Allergic reaction."

"To ants?" he added, sounding so casual, but that didn't stop my pulse from quickening and my mouth from going completely dry.

Larry reached out and brought his arm up to my face, and then he pulled up his sleeve. In the dim light from the streetlamps, I could make out three white scars.

"Nasty little buggers," he said. "I kinda had a run in with them myself a few years back."

"Oh..." So many questions flooded my mind: *how, why, and who?*

"I came across a colony that Tony was keeping for a school project," Larry explained, but I wondered if half the story was missing, and if Larry was leaving it out to protect the illusion of innocence of his friend, or did he really not know?

Toby's grip tightened around my arms.

"I was lucky enough to only get seven bites." Larry dropped his arm while watching for my cab. "You must have quite a few more..."

"Fifty-five."

Larry whistled. "You're lucky you weren't hospitalized."

I nodded. "The school wanted to send me, but my mother wouldn't let them. She didn't feel it was necessary."

"Then you are very lucky." He seemed to know what he was talking about.

"I don't feel so lucky right now." I switched my weight from one foot to the other and added, "I just feel itchy."

Larry closed his eyes and roared with laughter. "I love your sense of humour." He opened his eyes and looked away. "Don't get mixed up with Tony," he said. "You deserve better."

I was filled with warring emotions: I still wanted to try and deliver Toby's message. His pain weighed down on me like a heavy jacket. But also I couldn't get the feel of Tony's lips on mine out of my head. Then there was another more scary thought, as Toby continued to hold my wrists so I wouldn't scratch. *What would Toby do if he knew what I was thinking?*

"Mariah, please believe me," Larry warned. "Tony doesn't love girls, he doesn't know how! He just uses them. Please, please just stay away from him."

"And what about you?" I asked. "Why do you hang out with someone you think so little of?"

Larry took a step away from me and shook his head. "Tony's my pal, I watch his back, and he watches mine."

"But what about you and girls?" I asked, wondering if Larry did anything but clean up from his friend's adventures.

"Me?" Larry stammered. He looked out over the parking lot and let out a soft sigh of relief, then turned to me with a huge grin. "Your cab is here."

"Alright," I said. Then I had an idea. I pulled my arm away from Toby and, rummaging in my pocket, I found a spare piece of paper and a pencil. I quickly jotted a note that said my name, my phone number and "call me—I enjoyed our time together." I handed it to Larry as the cab stopped in front of us, and I climbed in.

Larry was still looking at the napkin as the cab pulled away. Finally he hollered, "See ya!"

Toby sat next to me, his hands over mine in my lap. I told the driver where to go and sat back against the seat. The movement of the cab created a small amount of relief on my back, but everything else irritated me: the seat belt across my chest, the elastic in my shirt, the strap of my bra, the temperature of the cab, every bump, pot-hole, and red light I had to endure. I closed my eyes against the insanity of it all.

"Hang in there," I heard Toby say as he gave me an extra squeeze, but I couldn't respond—I was using every ounce of energy to keep myself from yelling in anguish or opening the door to throw myself from the moving car just to stop the pain. My skin felt as if it had taken on a life of its own and was now trying to walk away.

Finally the cab stopped—I reached into my pocket and found some money to pay the driver. Then I leaped out and raced all the way home. I headed straight to my room, to my desk where I had left the Benadryl. I took the maximum amount recommended then fell face down on my bed and stayed there, waiting for the drugs to take effect.

My mind raced with wild thoughts, and I know that had he not been there, I would have lost all my senses and perhaps gone mad with itchiness.

It was close to twenty minutes before I experienced some relief. Toby hadn't said anything the whole time. In order to keep from scratching, I had been in a spread-eagle position, with my arms straight out, and I had kept my face smooshed into my pillow to keep from screaming. Now I was able to roll onto my side and look at Toby.

He didn't budge. I registered his feelings; he was grief stricken. *But by what?* "I am so sorry," he said, still not looking in my direction.

"For what?" I wondered if it was an apology to me directly, or an overall statement of his sorrows?

"For..." Toby rubbed the back of his neck, and I actually felt my stomach lurch. "For everything," he finished in no more than a whisper. He removed his hand from my leg. *I didn't want him to,* but as I watched, he brought both his hands to his face and started to cry. This was the second time I'd seen him cry. *I thought boys didn't cry...*

"When I was alive, I thought I was so great," he lamented. "Now I can see how wrong I was...so wrong."

"What does it feel like..." to be dead, I was going to say, but Toby didn't let me finish.

"It feels like torture! It hurts, like my whole body is being twisted and squeezed." Toby slid from the bed to the floor on his knees. "I want to turn it off," he moaned. Then he pulled his hands away from his face so he could look at me. "But I don't deserve it to stop! I deserve to feel like this forever, and far worse!"

"No!" I reached out and touched him on the cheek. It pained me to see him like this. I didn't believe he deserved this; he had been nothing but kind and caring to me.

"You don't understand," he protested. "The more I find out about myself, the more I wish I hadn't. Do you remember our first night?"

How could I forget! I nodded slowly, still fretting about what he was about to reveal.

"All I felt was concern for you."

I remembered the pills and the eight-ounce tumbler of vodka.

"You were in so much pain. I didn't feel it physically myself that night, but it was unmistakable."

Tears leapt to my eyes. He had saved me in so many ways.

"Now I feel an even deeper connection to you and your miseries."

I took my hand from his face. The look in his eyes made me nervous. *Where was this going?*

"I can feel your pain in so many ways, and I feel completely terrible knowing that I've caused it."

I sat up and pulled myself into a tight ball, as far back from Toby as I could. "What do you mean?" I asked shakily.

"Everything in my life seems to have had a direct or indirect effect on your life! We are connected in more ways than I would have ever dreamed." Toby moved to reach out to me, and I jumped back. He looked hurt, but he sat back. "Through my pranks and games, I've hurt more people than those I had aimed to, and for all I had convinced myself that I didn't care while I was alive, now I know I *do* care! I care so deeply, it's making me feel like I'm splitting in half!"

I felt renewed compassion for him; he had saved me, but he hadn't been able to save himself. He had lived life oblivious to the chaos and destruction he had wreaked, but now it sat in his face, too plain to ignore. How would I feel, if I had made such terrible mistakes, and now I was powerless to do anything on my own to change them? And I could see that it would be easy to make those mistakes, had I been given the opportunity to be popular and adored.

"Shush," I said. "It's alright."

"No!" He swore and slammed his fist into my sheets, then brought his hand up to cover his eyes.

I slowly crawled over to him and placed my hand on his head. "Didn't you once tell me that everything is working itself out?" He didn't respond, but I felt him relax a little. "I believe that. You saved my life that night."

Tears fell as I continued. "I was going to kill myself. Life is hard. It's full of tough choices. I was all alone, and I would have ended it had you not shown up." Gratitude flooded my heart. "I owe you my life. Who knows what mistakes I faced that night? The mistake of suicide would have been one. To give up hope completely, I know now that that was wrong. It was you that kept me alive, and I'm glad." Toby moved up onto the bed, sitting on his knees while I collected my thoughts. Tears still flowed freely. "I will take you with every bit of your past, all the mistakes made on purpose or accidentally, because it is what brought you to me. I don't understand how or why, but I do know that we are meant to set things right together."

Toby's eyes were wide, but he didn't answer. When he finally started talking, it was in a low monotone that made me feel like interrupting him would be a big mistake. "I have a second favour to ask of you. I need you to find someone—a girl." He brought his hand up to his neck. "There have been many girls. Too many! But I need to find this one because," he faltered, "because I…" He looked away. "I raped her."

I brought my hand up to my mouth.

"It was five weeks ago, at the bowling alley, in the storage room…" Toby went on.

"Don't," I begged.

"I have to, you have to understand. It wasn't like tonight. You were right when you told Larry that Tony didn't do anything you didn't want him to." I felt my stomach lurch and held my mouth tighter. "Tony isn't like me—he couldn't ever do what I did. I took her, forced her to come into that room, and when she protested, I forced myself on her…"

As my stomach continued to churn, I felt acid climbing up my throat. I didn't hesitate a moment. I bolted from my room, heading straight into the washroom, barely reaching the toilet in time. When I finally stopped heaving, I sat down and rested my forehead on the bathtub, feeling the coolness of the porcelain soothe my throbbing head.

"Mariah?" Toby said softly from behind me.

I shook my head. "Don't try to explain."

"I don't need to explain. I don't have an excuse; I was wrong, and I know I was; even at the time I knew it." I heard a soft thud, like he was leaning his head on the wall.

"Then why did you?" I asked, my voice sounding more like a sob.

"I'm not sure now…" he sighed, and I wondered if he was rubbing his neck again, like trying to release a genie from a magical lamp; only it was memories from a reluctant mind. "I thought I could do whatever I pleased, and no one could stop me." I heard him slide down the wall, and I could feel his remorse weighing heavy upon him.

The bathtub surface had heated up under my head, so I moved over an inch to a cooler spot.

"Mariah?" Toby said once again. I wanted to scream at him. Didn't he know this was too hard for me! "She was victimized by me. I did a terrible thing to her. I want to try and set things right. I just have to try! But I can't do it without you."

My heart sank. I knew he was going to ask me something like that. I heard him shift about, then felt his hand on my back. I instinctively recoiled from his touch. "Please, Mariah," he pleaded but kept his hands off. "Will you look for her? Will you go to her and give her a message?"

"Oh, ho!" I snapped, "that worked so well the first time!"

"This time will be different, I know it will, Mariah, she was completely innocent—she was the victim. Can you find the strength in your heart to help me to try and fix this?"

Toby's desire to undo his past was so strong; I felt it pulling me down. I closed my eyes as a new wave of nausea pulsed through my veins. I thought of this girl. What if Mims had tried to apologize to me? *How would I respond if some girl came to me to say he was sorry? Would I believe her? Would it make a difference? Would I want to hear it? Yes, I would want that.*

"Yes," I finally answered. I wanted Toby to leave me alone. I wasn't going to do this for him. *I was going to do it for that girl!*

Toby took my hint, giving me as much space as he could; he stayed quiet as I washed my face and out of my way as I went to bed. I tried not to look at him, mostly because he looked so wretched; his eyes were red and swollen. Everything about him looked miserable: it reminded me of a puppy left in the rain. But somehow I knew this misery was necessary.

Toby had to stay in the moment, and I didn't try to distract him from it, or make it any easier.

As I lay in bed, Toby sat at my desk. Rolling away from him, I muttered, "'Night." I wasn't too concerned when I didn't get a response.

DAY 11 Thursday...

I WASN'T AWARE OF THE ACTUAL TIME, but it was early in the morning hours when I slipped into a new dream, like walking through a door. Now I was in my storage room. It was darker there than it had ever been before, and I was suddenly aware that I wasn't alone! At first I thought it was Mims. It wasn't uncommon for him to chase me through my nightmares—eventually, he was always caught by my brother and thrown from the house to fall in a heap and stay that way until some other nightmare.

Yet as this person approached, I realized it wasn't Mims; it was Tony, and I felt a rush of relief and mounting excitement. He leaned in, our lips met, and feeling completely free in this dream place, I enjoyed the memory of our encounter uninhibited. But it only lasted a fleeting moment, because I was suddenly ripped from Tony's arms and dragged into the storage room at the alley. When I was finally able to get a look at my attacker, dread trickled down my spine—it was Toby! He had me by the hair, and as I tried to struggle free, he pulled me up and pressed me against the stack of boxes.

I wanted to scream, but nothing came from my mouth.

"Please don't!" I gasped for air as Toby pressed himself against me even harder. I wished it was Mims, and Jake was about to rush through the door to save the day. But no one arrived. "Toby, I thought you're not allowed to!" I whimpered.

"Oh, but I'm a completely real boy!" he spat out and leaned in to kiss me.

"No, no, no!" I cried, thrashing out at this dream Toby in any way I could, but nothing seemed to dissuade him. "You're supposed to help me!" I whispered as our lips met…

Who knows how far my dream would have gone had it not been for my mother. I jumped out of bed: the shock of ice cold water being spilled over my head woke me instantly. My mom stood with the empty glass in her hand.

"Awake now?" she asked, looking annoyed.

I nodded, shivering as the wetness cooled my skin.

"Good, I'm already late for work, and I need to show you something."

Without argument, I followed her upstairs. I had my pajamas on, my top partially soaked; she was in her business suit. She went straight to the drawer in the far part of the kitchen, the one beside the sink. Pulling it out from the cabinet, she placed the drawer on the table and picked something up.

"These are shells," she explained emotionlessly. "If you look at the back of the cupboard, you will see a gun taped there."

Toby, who seemed just as groggy, had been following quietly; he now let out an exclamation of shock. Ignoring him, I asked, "But what are they for? Why do we need them?"

My mother returned the drawer and slumped down at the table. "It's your brother." She sighed. "He's done it this time. He's completely messed things up, and I can't bail him out any more." She seemed very upset, and I wondered if it was because of what Jake had actually done or because she couldn't save him…

Gingerly, I took the seat next to her. "But why do we need a gun?"

"Because, Mariah," she said with an edge in her voice, "he's desperate! He may come after us."

I wanted to be shocked. I wanted to tell her that I didn't think she was right. But I just sat, nodding, *because this was my life.*

She reached out and covered one of my hands with hers. "If he comes around, please, please be careful." *Did she really care if something happened to me? Or was it just another thing for her to deal with?*

I promised I would, though I had no clue how. Then she headed off, telling me to keep the door locked. I did, and almost as if Toby wasn't there, I headed back down to my room, took a dose of Benadryl and crawled back into bed.

It was nearly two in the afternoon when I woke for the second time with a start. It hadn't been the front door that alerted me to the presence of someone else in the house—it was heavy footsteps on the floor above my room. I sat up as Toby appeared beside my right shoulder.

"You locked the front door?" he asked, but I didn't know why he was whispering. No one, apart from me, could hear him.

"How was that supposed to help?" I answered in my quietest voice. "My brother has a key!"

Toby looked shocked. Perhaps he, like me, had only come to that realization right now. I scolded myself for that oversight. Toby flinched, but I couldn't be bothered with that now.

Turning, I looked to my window. *Could I make it out unnoticed*? Toby shrugged. *Where were his helpful feelings*? He seemed less and less able to really help me!

As I sat, contemplating my choices, I heard my brother's voice, along with at least one other. Even through the floor, I could tell he had Nick with him. Nick had a high-pitched, whiny voice that sent a chill right down my spine. With that I decided to make a run for it. I bolted from my bed, taking care to not make a sound. Then I pulled yesterdays clothes from my desk. I wasn't going to go out in my pajamas. I started to slip my bra on under my shirt.

"What are you doing?" I could hear the panic in Toby's voice, and it made me jump. "You don't have time!"

With my bra haphazardly on, I started to work on my pants. I had one leg in, and I was lifting my second up, when I heard the back door slam—*did someone go out*? Distracted, I lost my balance and fell into the dresser with a thump. Then I heard feet rushing down the stairs to my door. I barely had time to zip up my jeans when my door was thrown open. *Why had I not put the chair in the way! I always put it there! Careless!*

I heard Toby give a soft groan. But I turned toward my door and found myself looking at two of Jake's friends: Nick was tall and slim. He had a scar down the side of his face, big dark eyebrows and a five o'clock shadow on his face. His fingers were quite long, and he always liked to put them on me whenever he could. He had long, greasy blond hair and a lip ring.

Rock was about my height but built like a tank. He had thick, chubby fingers like sausages, but they were just as creepy when he used them to harass me. His face was round, and he had two teeth missing. His smile sent chills down my spine. He had a tear tattooed by the side of his eye. Their strange nicknames always frightened me, as if they weren't just boys any more, they were more like monsters.

Before I had time to react, Rock rushed toward me and grabbed my wrist, spun me toward him and grabbed my second hand. He had such amazing strength that I found myself powerless against his grip. He brought his thigh up against my pelvis and pinned me back between himself and my dresser. As he leaned forward, I recoiled back as far as I could, then shutting my eyes, I heard Rock smell me.

"Fresh meat," he said softly, but there was nothing soft about his voice. It was rough, like he had gravel in this throat.

"Quiet," Nick said in his whistly voice. "J-boy will hear!"

Before I had a chance to scream, Nick pulled a roll of duct tape from his coat and tore off a piece to place over my mouth—*what kind of person carries around duct tape*?

Rock chuckled, his voice gurgling in his throat.

I was scared out of my wits; panic ran so high, my heart felt like it was breaking out of my chest. My ears went numb, and my eyes stung. Then I felt something quite different—it was rage, boiling hot rage—and Toby leapt from the bed and started swinging! With no results, his fists made clear paths through both the boys, as if he wasn't even there. But he was, I could feel him, and that was enough to give me hope. I blinked thanks to him as he stood just behind Rock, *just as helpless as I was.*

"You go to J's room and get what he wanted," Rock commanded to Nick. "I'll stay with our sweet cherry."

"Why do you get to stay with J's sister!" Nick argued. "I'll stay while you get J's stuff." Nick tried to shove Rock away from in front of me, but Rock remained solid and shoved back at Nick. Then he leaned in for another smell.

Having him so close nauseated me. I kept my eyes fixed on Toby. Tears rolled down my face and fell from my chin, slowly soaking my shirt.

"Let me go first!" Nick pleaded. "I promise I'll leave some for you."

"Why should I? I'm here. I'll go first, then if there's anything left, you can have it!" Rock pried me off the dresser and turned me so he could force me down onto the bed.

"No!" Toby yelled so loud it hurt my eardrums.

"Why do I always have to take your leftovers?" Nick protested. "I'm tired of your scraps! I'm not your dog!"

Rock forced me to a sitting position at the edge of my bed. "Tape her hands," he commanded, and Nick obeyed.

"Good boy," Rock said as he held my wrists so tight, I couldn't feel the tips of my fingers. He forced my hands behind my back. Then Nick taped my fingers together. I tried to wiggle them apart and found the bond was impossible for me to break. With just my fingers taped together, Rock was able to push me onto my back, lying flat against the bed. I was stuck, but I drew my knees up to my chest and held them there with all my might.

Toby stood beside my bed and shook with futile anger. I could feel his frustration and his remorse, so I clung to his feelings because they made me calmer in a way.

Rock seemed amused. He grinned evilly. "Nothing can stop me now," he said, forcing his hand between my legs and grabbing my zipper.

As he did this, several things happened; Toby turned away and punched out at my window. His fist made contact, resulting in a loud bang that echoed through my room. This caused Rock to hesitate, and in that moment, Nick rushed him and tackled him to the ground. Then Nick stepped past his friend and came to lie down next to me.

"This time I'll be first..." Nick said as he pulled himself closer.

I turned away and held my breath, but the next thing I felt was Nick being pulled from me. I turned back to see a mess of fists and a blur of two bodies intertwined in a fight. Nick and Rock exchanged angry words, but they were too busy attacking each other to bother with me. *I was safe... for now...*

Toby sat next to me and pulled a strand of loose hair from in front of my face. "Help is on the way," he said calmly.

Looking up at Toby with my mouth gagged and my hands bound, I was reminded of my dream from the night before. I shivered, and Toby pulled his hand away as if he had received an electrical shock.

I looked past the two boys, who were entangled in a fight, and down my hall, where I saw Jake turn the corner of the stairs and rush toward them. He stormed in, looking larger than life. He pulled Nick and Rock apart, holding them both up by the scruffs of their necks. Looking from them to me, he said through clenched teeth, "I'm not going to ask what you were planning to do to my sister." Then he dropped them and continued, "Go do what I sent you to. And don't you ever, EVER try to touch my baby sister again!" *I'd never seen him so angry!*

Both Rock and Nick fled from my room as if their lives depended on it, *and I believe they did.* However, my relief turned to panic as my brother shut my door and came over to me. "Skipping school, Mariah?" he asked, sitting on my bed where Toby had been just moments before. He even pulled back the hair from my face in the same way. "That's not like you. You were always the good one."

I looked from Jake over to behind him, where Toby stood. *How could I need and despise Toby at the same time?*

"Even Dad knew that you were the better kid." Jake bent down close to me. My body went rigid as he neared. If anything, this was more uncomfortable than both of Jake's friends put together.

"It's alright, Mariah, he won't hurt you." Toby tried to calm me, but I didn't believe him. I had never felt comfortable around my brother; now, being tied up, I didn't feel calmer.

"Stay good," Jake said into my ear, and then he straightened up. "I'm sorry, little sis," he added as he got up from my bed, "I can't untie you now. But I promise I'll call mom later and tell her to come home." With that he left my room, shutting the door as he went.

All I could do was listen as Jake and his friends stomped about doing who knows what. Toby started to say something, but I shook my head and rolled to my right with some difficulty and stayed in that position. Tears poured out of me. It was well after I had stopped hearing noises that I rolled onto my back again. My whole right side was numb from the pressure of being tied up. There stood Toby, standing over me at the edge of my bed with a miserable look on his face.

"I think I can untie you now," he said. I didn't respond, but that didn't stop him from coming to my bed and carefully un-sticking the tape from over my mouth. It hurt worse than I could have imagined, but I didn't make a sound. Then he helped me sit up and slowly unwound the tape from my fingers. Once they were loose enough, I pulled them free and brought my hands in front of me to examine them. My arms tingled as the blood circulated down them. My fingers were white, and they had the marks where the tape had bit into them, making them look as if the tape was still there. It was quite a while before I could bend them properly again.

It was 5:30 PM. Parts of that afternoon were a blur. I was dazed and distracted. *Why was Toby even here? If he was sent to help, why did it seem that he was unable to the times when I really needed him? Yet he had untied me…* As the hours slowly ticked past, I wondered what it would have been like to still be stuck, bound and gagged. Because no matter how late it got, my mom didn't come home. *Had Jake forgotten to call her? How long would I have stayed stuck?* Yet despite my gratitude at being freed, I couldn't even look at Toby. *He had done that to someone else… Had he been alive, would he have thought twice about doing the same to me? But he wasn't alive, he was stuck, and despite my strange dreams, he had never once been unkind to me.*

I hardly ate, and I was too anxious to sit and watch television. Instead I wandered from room to room. Toby stayed a step or two behind me, never in sight, but I could feel his presence strong in my mind. Finally I settled down enough to take a shower, and then I retreated to my room to try and do some homework.

It was nearing nine in the evening when the phone rang. I turned to Toby wondering what I should do.

"You gonna answer that?"

"Who could it be?" I questioned. "Do you know?"

Toby just shook his head; *he really was getting much less intuitive the longer he stayed with me.* "It could be your mom…"

I sprinted up the stairs and into the kitchen. Despite all our problems, I needed to talk with my mother, to hear her voice, and to tell her I was alright. *That's* if *she was worried.*

"Hello," I answered, a little out of breath.

"Hi, is this Mariah?" a girl's voice responded. It was Cindy, and despite my immediate disappointment that it hadn't been my mom, I was glad it was her.

"Cindy!" I exclaimed, taking a seat at the table and looking out the window into the clear, star-filled sky.

"Hi," she said once again, only now she had a giggle in her voice. "I really miss you." *Just hearing that brightened my evening!*

I thought of that for a moment then said, "I've missed you too."

"So what have you been up to with all your time off? Bet you've been having a grand 'ol time!"

"Sure, I've been all tied up," I said, but she missed the sarcasm in my voice.

Toby gave a chuckle. "That's what makes you so great, your ability to find humour in truly horrible things."

I wanted to explain that that's what I had to do to survive, but I was trying to have a conversation on the phone, and for some reason I still felt a little prickly toward Toby. I turned my back to him and listened to what Cindy was chattering on about.

"I'd be sleeping in and watching TV all day…" she was saying enviously. "Oh, but I forgot, how are your bites, or stings? I can never remember what they really are."

"They're bites with stings," I said, quoting the school nurse. Then I thought for a moment; since that morning I had been too distracted by other things to really pay attention to my wounds. "Better, I guess," I answered. "How are yours?"

"They itched like crazy Tuesday night. My mom had to put a sock on my hands when I went to bed, but she wouldn't let me stay home. I only had five! I just can't imagine what you've been going through. The school nurse called us in yesterday morning and applied some sort of local anti-itch cream, and it really did the trick. Today they're mostly healed."

"Ya, mine have been about the same," I agreed. "So how is everyone else?"

"Well, Elijah stayed home on Wednesday. He got a secondary infection and had to go on antibiotics, but other than that we've all been fine. Oh, I was told to tell you that Rayla, Charlie, Teb, Dan and Elijah all say that they miss you, not just me. Rayla keeps asking if I know when you're coming back to school. Charlie wants to know too; she made you a get well soon card, but she's too shy to bring it to your house. You're not still mad at her, are you?"

I felt hurt because she thought that about me. "I never was mad at her," I replied softly. The stars twinkled. *Funny how things could feel so calm after the day I'd had.*

"So listen, you remember I invited you for a sleepover this Saturday? Well, I was wondering if you could come?" Her voice was filled with hope.

I hadn't thought about that in days. In fact, until this call, I had forgotten that I was making friends and had a life outside of my family and Toby. *Toby.* I shuddered again and gripped the phone tighter. Then I answered, "Yes" before I could think too hard and talk myself out of the idea.

"Really!" Cindy sounded overjoyed. "That is so great!" she squealed and went on to talk about her plans, including the menu, the movie choices as well as her address, and when this great slumber party was to start; though why it was called a slumber party, she had no clue. We certainly were not planning to sleep, she warned. Then she begged me to come back to school tomorrow. "You make the day so much more interesting."

"Ya, with me around you never know when you'll be attacked by fire ants or have to evacuate the entire cafeteria…or worse," I joked.

"I don't think you have to worry about those things happening any more. The teachers had a meeting, and things are already being changed."

I was intrigued; *perhaps I would go back to school tomorrow just to see what Cindy meant.* We said our farewells, and I hung up. No sooner had I pushed the off button when the phone rang again.

"Don't answer it!" Toby called out. His voice startled me, and something about it made my back stiffen. "Please, don't!" he pleaded a second time.

I turned to him, placing a hand on my hip. "Why shouldn't I?"

"Just don't," he said flatly, looking away.

I didn't feel like listening to him. In fact, I felt like doing the exact opposite of what he was telling me. I figured it had to be my mother. Who else would call me now? I was shocked when my greeting was answered this time by a male voice. I felt like I should recognize it, yet I was at a loss. Looking into Toby's eyes, I could tell he knew.

"Who is this?" I asked, and then before he answered, I realized who it was…

"It's Tony from bowling."

"How did you get my number?" I wanted to sound surprised, but my true emotions could be heard all too clearly. Despite myself, I was happy that he was calling me and excited with the idea of talking to him and possibly seeing him again.

"I got it from Larry." I heard amusement in his words.

"He gave it to you?" This time I did sound shocked. Larry had been warning me to stay away from Tony. *Why would he give Tony my number*?

"Well, not exactly." There was a small pause, and then he went on, "Now why would you give your number to him? Unless you wanted me to get it, eh?" He sounded so confident, so sure of himself. *But what about him getting mad at me in the storage room?*

I could feel heat waves coming off Toby. He was fuming over me talking to Tony, and somewhere inside, I was glad I was causing him such discomfort. At that very moment, I felt like Toby had been nothing but a discomfort to me! "So you found out that Larry had my number and made him give it to you?" This idea made my heart flutter.

"Something close to that," Tony said. "He always empties his pockets out onto his night table, so when I found your name and number on a piece of paper there, I just took it. I'm sure you wanted him to pass it on to me." I could feel my cheeks aglow. *Tony was really interested in me!*

Toby continued to fume, and as if he could read my thoughts, he said, "More like the thought of you with Larry made him jealous, and he had to get you for himself."

I waved him away distractedly and asked, "So what do you want then?" I couldn't deny that my feelings of elation had seemed to sag with Toby's input.

"Would you like to join me for a movie tomorrow?" Tony asked.

"Like after school?"

"No. Like a date, in the evening."

My stomach did a flip. *An actual date! I've never gone on a date before. No one had ever asked me*!

"Don't," Toby said through clenched teeth as he tried to step closer to me, but he kept his distance when I glared at him.

I thought of Toby and that poor girl. I thought of what Mims had tried to do to me. Then I thought of Nick and Rock. My fingers were still sore and had faint marks left on them from the tape. I thought of Effie and all those ants. Then I thought about the other night with Tony in the storage room…

"Yes."

"Mariah…" Toby breathed, but I turned my back on him.

"Wonderful!" Tony said excitedly; it was contagious, like a yawn, but much better. I felt giddy for the rest of our conversation.

We arranged our pick-up time and place, then I got off the phone and turned to Toby. "What?" I asked, all the pleasure seeping away at the mere sight of him.

He stood looking at me with his mouth agape. "I thought I explained to you how dangerous Tony is."

"Oh," I almost shouted, anger overflowing, "would that be more or less than you!" Toby looked as if I had slapped him. "Or would that be as harmful as Jake's pals?" Toby's mouth fell open, and his eyes widened, but he didn't utter a word. "At least when I'm with Tony, it's because I want to be!"

I stormed out of the room. I knew it was futile. He had to follow, but I did it all the same. Once down in my room, I paced back and forth until I eventually started to calm down; then I felt bad about the way I had talked to Toby. He was only trying to help, but I wondered if in some way he was just trying to keep me away from Tony because he didn't like seeing me with him.

"Mariah, I'm concerned for your safety," Toby said quietly as I finally took a seat on my bed.

"I know!" I cried. Toby had done nothing but take care of me. I brought both my hands up to cover my face. It all seemed a little too confusing. I felt his hand on my back, gently rubbing, being ever so careful of my healing spots. "But are you really concerned about me going out with Tony? Or is there something else?"

"I don't know," he whispered. "Whenever you're close to him, I get confused… Mariah, he's a player, he's never had a steady girlfriend like Larry told you. He doesn't know how. He'll just end up using you. Is that what you want?"

I shook my head. That wasn't what I wanted, but I found it hard for my heart to believe what Toby was saying. "But you keep telling me that he's not as bad as you were," I protested.

"No, he never was," Toby agreed, "but he's also not much better, especially when it comes to girls."

I wanted to go out with Tony! More than anything! I couldn't bear the thought of canceling, so out of desperation, I asked, "But what about your message? This will give me another chance to try and give it."

"He definitely wants you to give him something…" I think Toby could tell how much I wanted to go, because he stopped and gave me a sad smile. "Mariah, he's not going to…" He stopped and looked out the window.

As much as I wanted a date with Tony, I was now torn by my feelings for Toby. Suddenly it all seemed clear to me: Toby had a message for his old friend, Tony needed to hear it, and Toby needed me to give it. *Things wouldn't be right until that happened!*

"Don't give up," I said. "You haven't given up on me, and I'm not going to give up on you." I pulled at his shirt.

"How can you say that? After everything, everything I've done. I've felt the way you've despised me today." He tried to pull away from me.

"Yes." I shut my eyes and held tight. He stopped resisting me. "That's true. But most of it, I don't think, has even been your fault."

"How can you say that?" He pulled himself free, stood up and paced a bit. "Everything, all of it has to do with me, who I was!" He beat his chest. "I was a monster."

"Alright," I said reaching out and catching his hand, "That's what you *were*. But that is *not* who you *are* any longer! From the moment you've appeared, you have treated me with respect, kindness and helped me in ways that might not appear obvious but have been truly helpful."

He dropped to his knees in front of me. "But the longer I stay, the more I feel like the old me."

"What do you mean?" I moved back slightly.

"I remember myself, things I've done. And old feelings I used to have. They surface at the most inconvenient times, and I'm having trouble separating them from now."

"Like when?" I asked in a small voice, yet I wasn't sure I wanted him to answer.

"Like this morning, I was dreaming…"

I put up my hand to stop him. I didn't want to know. *Had he been dreaming the same dream?* Were our lives becoming too intertwined? *Why was he here?*

"Let's just go to sleep." I stood and started to do my evening routine. Toby didn't protest, but I heard him following me.

There was a time in my life when I felt so utterly alone that I longed for someone to be close to me, so I wouldn't feel so lonely. Now I felt overwhelmed by Toby and longed for just a few moments where I could be by myself to collect my own thoughts.

As I tried to relax enough to fall asleep, I heard Toby's breathing slow, and then I felt him shift and disappear. Now I could sense that he was just beyond my sight but right next to me, eyes closed, perhaps already lost in some dream. I pondered all the events of my life; taken in pieces, they were either horrible beyond words or more wonderful than imaginable. But put together, they seemed to even out. I wondered if life would always feel that way.

DAY 12 Friday...

Sleep finally found me, and again I dreamed of a wonderful meadow with velvet grass, a soothingly babbling brook and a glorious sun that shone down warm and wonderful upon my skin. Dream Toby approached and greeted me with a huge hug.

"I do love you," he whispered in my ear. "You are the one and only girl I have ever truly cared for." I knew that what he said was true, and though I found his words were sad at the core, they filled me with peace. He embraced me. I would have happily stayed in his arms for the rest of my life, but as dreams go, this too ended, and I awoke at 7 AM with the sun just starting to rise on a new day.

It's amazing how a good night's sleep can help you have a fresh attitude—like the once dark and gloomy world was now filled with hope and new possibilities.

I turned to Toby. He had his eyes open and his arms around me, but as I turned, he pulled his hands back and said with a sheepish grin, "Good morning."

"Yes," I replied. "Let's have a good day as well." I was feeling more confident than I ever had before in my life. I was determined to not let anything get me down this day. Toby seemed more optimistic also, and I took that as a good sign. *After all, I couldn't possibly have as bad a day as yesterday…*

I had eaten a healthy breakfast, dressed in my nicest outfit for school, done my hair, brushed my teeth and even applied a small amount of make-up. Every once in a while, worries tried to play at the edge of my consciousness, but I'd mention them to Toby, and his response would chase them away.

"What do you think will be different at school?" I wondered aloud.

"Perhaps Ms. LaKey has hired you a bodyguard?" Toby jokingly replied.

"Unlikely," I said, trying to picture it in my mind, "but wouldn't that be great…" Then I was struck with another thought. "What if Effie has found out I visited Tony on Wednesday? Or worse, that he's asked me out? What would her jealousy be like then?"

"She'd probably have to admit that you are the more popular one and ask you for advice," Toby smiled.

"You think?" I giggled.

"Well, no. But don't worry, Ms. LaKey hired you that bodyguard."

Our fun was interrupted by a sharp knock on the front door. Toby looked just as surprised to hear it. He shrugged when I mouthed, "Who is it?" I went to the door and opened it to find myself looking into the faces of two rather stern police officers. The first had sandy blond hair, and he looked to be in his early thirties. The second was older. He had a mustache, and his hair was graying. Both wore crisp blue suits and no-nonsense expressions.

The one with graying hair stepped into the house and asked, "Is this the residence of Jake Lafont?"

I had barely answered yes when he pushed me to the wall, and his partner ran past. "We have a search warrant, as well as papers to arrest one Jake Lafont. Any attempt to get in our way will lead to your own arrest, do you understand?"

"Yes," I said, paralyzed with fear. "But Jake's not here."

The officer stepped back, loosening his grip on me so I could face him. "May I ask who you are, and what your relationship is to the assailant?"

"I'm his sister," I snapped, feeling harassed. "My name is Mariah Lafont."

"Well, Miss Mariah Lafont, will you please take a seat at the kitchen table."

"Can't I just go to school? I'm going to be late now," I protested.

"No," he said commandingly. "Please take a seat at the kitchen table."

I went into the kitchen with a huff and sat down. The officer stayed at the door, and I could hear his partner searching through our living room. It took over an hour before his partner returned; he had looked through the cupboards and stopped when he discovered the gun.

Bringing it to the table, he dropped it in front of me. "And what is this for, young lady?"

I looked at the shiny, black, metallic, revolver; I had never seen one up close before. Even when Mom had shown me where to get it, I hadn't bothered to get a better look. It instilled fear so deep in me that I didn't want to be anywhere near it.

"My mom got it a few days ago," I answered in a small voice. "She said we needed protection from my brother."

"You are not allowed to own one of these without registration. Do you happen to know if this gun is registered?"

I shrugged. "She didn't say."

"Is there a number where we can reach your mother?" The first officer with the sandy blond hair was leaning so close I could smell his cologne. It made me cough a little.

I gave them my mother's work number, and once they started to talk with her, I stopped paying attention. It was then that I realized I hadn't seen my mom since yesterday morning. *Had she come home? Would I have still been tied up until the police came?* Now more than ever, I was thankful Toby was with me. I looked over at him. He was enthralled with the conversation the police were having.

"We understand, Mrs. Lafont," the sandy haired officer was saying. "There is really no other alternative, we are talking murder here… Yes, I understand that he is your son, but do you understand that it was nine other people's sons or daughters that we are talking about… No… No… No… Well, if that is how you feel… Fine then, we will just check out your registration papers and be on our way." He put down the phone and looked to his grey-haired partner. "Go check the mothers room, bedside table. She says you'll find a second gun there and registration for both weapons." His partner left.

Looking at me kindly, he said, "I am so sorry." I nodded. I felt numb. *Had he said my brother killed nine other children?* How could he? I knew him as a jerk, but never a killer. "Mariah?" he asked. I just nodded once again. "I'm sorry we had to detain you; we only came to arrest your brother and search for evidence." I blinked. "It's very rare that people like these still live with their parents. Usually by now they have a place of their own, with a few…roommates. We just had to be sure you were who you said you were."

I fiddled with my hands. My fingers still ached when I tried to bend them. "Did you say Jake killed…?" I couldn't go on as tears leapt to my eyes.

The officer just nodded sadly.

"Jake?" I whispered.

"Yes, through a bad drug deal he is responsible for at least nine deaths." That made more sense. I was sure he was into something like that. Somehow, knowing he hadn't gone out and murdered them himself made me feel better. Then I caught sight of Toby, and I realized that nine people were worse off than he was because of my brother. My heart broke.

After they found the registration papers, they returned the gun to its spot then told me that if my brother came back to not hesitate using it if I needed. I nodded numbly as I watched them leave.

So much for not let anything ruin this day. My legs wobbled as I stood up.

Toby also seemed to be shaken. "Do you still want to go to school?" he asked tentatively, holding his hand to his neck like it was sore.

I was up and pacing. "Sure," I answered. "I'll be late, but Ms. LaKey hired those bodyguards for me, and I'd hate to see their day wasted." Then I stopped and looked at Toby. "Honestly, I'd feel safer at school right now."

Toby stood up and smiled. "As always, you're a true trooper."

It was nearly nine when I walked into a quiet school. The hallways were deserted, and behind closed doors I could hear teachers giving their lessons. I felt a bit like I wasn't supposed to be there, but I walked with determination towards the office.

Miss Rose looked up as I entered, and her face brightened, "Feeling better, Miss Lafont?"

I nodded and smiled at her. "I believe I need a late slip; I got held up this morning."

"I'm glad you came to the office to sign in. We have something for you." She reached under the counter and pulled out an envelope with my name on it.

"Thanks." I took it and folded it into my pocket. "Can I have my late slip?"

"Of course." Miss Rose filled out a note and sent me off to my first class.

I got to the room with less than ten minutes before it ended. Toby suggested that I just wait out in the hall and continue on to my next class when the bell rang. As I peeked in, I agreed with him. It was typing, and catching sight of Effie, I wondered how she really would react to seeing me. But the teacher noticed me in the window and came over.

Mr. Brown was a short man with a large smile, and when he walked, it was more like he bounced. His room was the computer lab, and he made sure we all knew and stuck to the rules. There were three rows of tables, each with approximately ten computers.

"Mariah!" he exclaimed, pulling the door all the way open. Everyone in the class looked up. "My star student has returned." He ushered me in with gesture. "Please, your seat is waiting."

I moved awkwardly, aware that everyone in the class was watching me.

"Now," Mr. Brown continued, "we were just going over speed and complicated key strokes. I'm sure you haven't forgotten with all this time away how to do these most basic of tasks." I sat and placed my hands over the keyboard. "Bravo!" the teacher exclaimed, and he raced off to the head of the room to call out a few instructions to the whole class.

I actually found it soothing to hear him yell out random letters and just let my fingers find them. Something mundane to take my mind off the panic I felt. Effie and Sara sat a few seats away, and I could see them put their heads together while sneaking glances at me from time to time.

When the bell rang, I tried to get up and out as quickly as I could, but the teacher called to me and asked me to stay behind a moment. Once the class had emptied, he said, "I know you have had it hard. I remember being bullied when I was younger. I was the smallest in my age group, and I got called the meanest names. But I want you to know that if it ever gets bad again, please, please do not hesitate to come and talk to me about it. I'm on your side." I nodded. Then he added, "And by the way, you may have come to class late, but based on your seven minutes of typing, you got the top score in the entire room." He gave me a wink and sent me on my way.

"Not so bad," Toby said, trailing behind me. I wanted to say, "So far." But I didn't dare open my mouth.

The next class was gym. When I got there, the teacher called me into her office. Mrs. Pain leaned on the corner of her desk. "I think I owe you an apology. That other day, I didn't realize what was going on. Please, come talk to me in private if it ever happens again," she urged. "But now, you are all better?"

"Mostly."

"Can I see your bites?" I pulled up my sleeve. "Hmmm," she said thoughtfully as she bent to take a closer look. "I believe you are on the mend, but I must insist that you sit this period out; I don't want any scars to form on my account, and we're playing dodge ball today. So I am sending you to the library to study instead."

I smiled. I hated dodge ball; it was a wonderful game where it was acceptable for someone to openly attack you. I thanked her and headed off to the library.

"Oh," Mrs. Pain called out as I was leaving, "your detention with me is cancelled."

"So far, not so bad, eh?" Toby said as we walked through the empty halls.

Not yet…

Our library wasn't that big; with more and more information available quicker and easier off the Internet, the school was cutting back on books. The room was just a little smaller than two classrooms put together.

The library was quiet; just a few students were there. I took a table off in the corner and pulled out my book. I had just found my place in the story when someone tapped me on the head; I turned around to see Elijah.

As I lowered my book and turned towards him, he gasped, "Your hair!" At first I thought he didn't like it. "Wow! You look great!"

He smiled shyly at me. He wore a buttoned-up shirt and jeans. His curly hair had formed a ringlet between his eyes, which he tried to brush back. It just fell in front again, so he blew at it in an annoyed way and asked, "Mind if I sit here too?" I shrugged, so he dropped a pile of work on the table in front of him, then he sat opposite me. Toby was sitting on the edge of the table to my right.

"Now this boy," Toby said, "he would make a good boyfriend." I blinked and held my book up. *Elijah was nice, but he was no Tony.*

"What did you do on your sick days?" Elijah asked. He was staring at me as if he had never taken his eyes off me. It made me feel uncomfortable.

I lowered my book again, and answered, "I itched. I scratched. What about you?" I shifted a bit, feeling a twinge of guilt. Toby huffed noisily.

"About the same—want to see?" He pulled up his sleeve. I could see the place where his original bites were, but he was also covered with a small dusting of light red spots as if someone had taken a pen and tried to give him freckles.

"I'm sorry," I said. *It was because of me that he had those bites, and that infection. If he hadn't saved me…* Toby shuddered and brought his hand to his cheek.

"Don't be." Elijah smiled, and it made me feel better. "I got to stay home, play on the computer all day and eat ice cream for lunch. I was just fine. And I'm glad to see you're doing better too."

"Yes, thank you," I said, and I pulled up my sleeve to show him my scabs.

Reaching across the table, he touched one spot and said, "I got this one, and this," he moved to the next spot, "And this… and all of these." His finger tickled my skin, and it felt nice. I was reminded of the way Tony touched me. This was not as intense, but somehow exciting in its own way.

"This is what having a boyfriend would be like," Toby cut in, and again I found myself wondering if he could sense my thoughts. "Boyfriends are friends that you are supposed to enjoy being around, not just kissing."

I felt my face flush and pulled back from Elijah. He slowly sat back down.

"Don't," Toby protested, jumping from the table. "Don't ruin it. He really likes you."

I looked across the table at Elijah. He had concern on his face. "Did I do something wrong?" he finally asked.

"I'm not sure," I answered, picking up my book. Elijah lowered his head to work on his papers, looking dejected.

"Tell him you like him," Toby said. "I know you do, just tell him you are interested in him." *Did I like him?* Even if I did, there was no way was I going to say something as bold as that.

"Come on, Mariah!" Toby insisted, waving his hand in front of my face so I couldn't keep reading. "Don't stop talking to him! Ask him what video games he played! Ask him about his favourite ice cream."

But the more Toby pushed the idea of Elijah on me, the more I wanted to think about Tony. The way he had taught me to throw my first bowling ball, *the way his hands sent tingles up my spine.* I wanted to scream at Toby, but I didn't dare even glare his way. Instead I sat feeling more and more harassed and less and less interested in anything to do with Elijah.

Elijah worked in silence, stealing peeks at me; I could see him over the top of my book. When he wasn't looking, I would glance at Toby, who didn't stop badgering me; ask him this, tell him that, he prattled on the whole time.

I never got far in my book. In fact, I never turned a page, because I was too distracted to read more than three sentences at a time and often repeated the same ones. Finally the bell rang.

Elijah stood up and started to pack up his papers. "We may as well walk to our next class together?" He looked nervous.

"Say yes!" Toby insisted.

I was tempted to say no, like I had to go to my locker to get something first, just to spite Toby, but I decided not to be petty. I knew Elijah would be hurt if I did.

"May as well," I answered. Elijah cracked a grin.

I was instantly thankful that I had accepted; as we left the library, I caught sight of Effie and her two pals heading towards me. They turned away when they saw I wasn't alone. And as we got to the drama room, Cindy, Rayla and Teb joined us.

The drama classroom was odd. It had two floor levels, and the lower part was considered the stage, where students went down to do performances. On the higher part of the room were folding chairs. Students were allowed to sit in the chairs, on the floor in front or to stand at the back.

We found some empty chairs by the wall. I sat with the wall on my left and Rayla on my right, with Cindy next to her. Elijah and Teb sat on the floor in front of us. The classroom door was across the "stage" area, so we got a good view as our classmates slowly made their way in.

"Love your hair," Rayla commented.

"Thanks. I do too." *Was that too cocky to say?*

"It looks really great!" Cindy added, then she explained how she was envious of my curls, and how the cut really brought them out. "And how're your war wounds?" she added.

I looked confused, so Teb explained, "The wounds you got from the great cafeteria ant war." He said it like it was the title of an epic historical battle.

It felt nice to think of the ant attack as something more that a deadly prank. "They're healing. What about you guys?"

They all gave their own account of the healing process; Elijah had it the worst with the secondary infection.

"There was a small white mark under the scab. I wonder when that's going to go away," Cindy added.

"It may be a permanent scar for the rest of your life," I answered, remembering Larry's scars and feeling miserable for them about it.

Her response surprised me. "I'm so sorry for you, Mariah." When I didn't respond, she explained. "You'll be stuck with over fifty marks to remind you of this."

"I'm not so certain they'll be permanent," Elijah cut in. "My doctor seemed to think they wouldn't be, or at least that they would fade."

I pictured Larry's wrist. His had been unmistakable, even in the poor light from the streetlamp in the parking lot, but perhaps he hadn't had the attention from the school nurse that we had. I shrugged.

"Where did you hear that they would leave scars?" Teb asked.

How could I explain Sara's brother? I figured it was best not to mention him. "I just thought they would..." I answered lamely.

Toby sat looking up at me. "Why not tell them the truth?" he wondered, but I pretended that I couldn't hear him.

The bell for class rang, and the teacher rushed in, then stopped at the sight of me. "I think now is a good time to make our formal apologies to Miss Lafont," she said loudly, addressing the whole class. "I'm sure that many of you need to make amends. This way we can start off on the right foot. Yes?"

Several students answered, "Yes, Mrs. Kellee," less than enthusiastically. Some groaned, but not loud enough for her to pay attention.

"Come and sit here, Mariah." Mrs. Kellee pulled a chair down from the higher part of the room and extended a hand for me to come sit.

With shaking legs, I went over to the chair and lowered myself into it. Holding my hands in my lap, I looked up at all the faces of my classmates and wondered in horror if this was going to end well. Toby's hand was heavy on my shoulder. His lips were pulled tight into a thin line.

Mrs. Kellee came to stand in front of me, blocking out my view of the class. "I am sorry I was critical of you the other day. I was not aware that you had a phobia of ants, and that was why you were hesitating with the exercise. I was upset over your participation, and I doubted your acting abilities, but now I understand that there was more going on than I first assumed. I have reversed the initial marks I'd given you; you now stand at an A- for that assignment." Then she stood up straighter and turned to the whole class. "But I must caution that as aspiring actors, you must overcome your personal problems so you may immerse yourself completely in your character, and I strongly suggest that you learn to take all these troubles and grow from them, transforming them and adding them to your dramatic abilities."

I was beyond words. I just sat with my mouth open. Then someone else came forward, a pimply-faced boy who said he was sorry for calling me "elephant." Then a girl with short, spiky hair said she was sorry for the "dead-ant" chant she had sung. A boy who wore nothing but black said he was sorry for the joke that he had repeated, and behind him I saw several students stifle their laughter, then another and another.

I wasn't sure which was worse; being called these things in the first place or having it publicly announced that I was called them, even in the form of an apology. It took several minutes to get through every student who felt they owed me an apology. Sara kept hers short and sweet, saying she hadn't known I was afraid of ants. When everyone was finished, I wanted to flee from the classroom more than ever. Yet I was sure that no one would understand, because they all were being nice. I swallowed hard as I stood to go back to my seat, all the while trying to act like it didn't really bother me—after all, this was a drama class.

My feet felt heavy as I went to my chair. I heard Mrs. Kellee praise the whole class for such wonderful honesty. I stumbled as I neared my place, but Elijah stood up and caught me before Toby was able to. With Elijah's hand on my side, I sat down.

Mrs. Kellee started the lesson for the day. My stomach squirmed; I wanted to sink through the floor. Toby crouched next to me and put a hand on my thigh. "It might just be possible that they will kill you with kindness." Hearing his voice helped me to not go completely mad from the insanity of it all.

As I calmed down, I realized that neither Cindy, Rayla, Teb nor Elijah had stood up to say sorry, but when she got a chance, Rayla leaned over and said, "I'm sorry we couldn't convince Mrs. Kellee that this was a very bad exercise!"

Mercifully, I wasn't called upon to do anything more for the remainder of the class. I watched numbly as other kids were called to the front to do some improv skits. Everyone seemed to be enjoying themselves. Even Cindy seemed unfazed, using every spare moment to whisper her plans for the sleepover to Rayla or me. Elijah and Dan held their own hushed conversation, but I did notice that Elijah kept looking at me.

The lunch bell rang, and Teb jumped to his feet. "To the cafeteria!" he exclaimed.

"Coming?" Cindy asked.

"I might have a detention with Ms. LaKey," I remembered.

"Still? After everything!" Elijah's voice was filled with contempt. I smiled and wondered, *why not?*

"I don't know... I did get a letter," I said, thinking of it for the first time since I'd gotten it.

"Did you read it?" someone asked. "What did it say?" They all watched as I pulled it from my pocket opened it, un-creased it then read it aloud:

> Dear Miss Lafont,
>
> On behalf of all the staff at East Ridge High, we would like to extend our deepest apologies over your situation. We recognize that you have been the unfortunate victim of bullying. Due to the nature of this problem, we find ourselves unable to reprimand the guilty party. There are simply no guidelines to handle this kind of behaviour in our school's policy at this time.
>
> Those whom we know to be involved have been spoken to, and any future attempts to hurt you will not be tolerated. Having said that, we also ask that you cooperate with us in trying to keep yourself safe by avoiding this person as well as anyone who is affiliated with her. That way no more conflict should arise.

> Again, we are sorry for all you've had to endure, and we are sure that if we work together, we can keep our school a safe place for everyone.

I finished reading and saw that over thirty teachers and staff members had signed it, including the secretary and even Gus the janitor, yet I couldn't see Ms. LaKey's name anywhere.

Teb, Rayla, Cindy and Elijah all stood looking at me in shock. The classroom had emptied. Mrs. Kellee asked us to shut the door when we were done.

"Aw, that was nice…" Toby snorted. Shaking his head he added, "For all that, they didn't really help, now did they?"

I shut my eyes, trying to steady my aching heart. For all their lovely intentions, it all felt like another insult.

"Forgive me," Teb said, finally finding his voice, "why did they give you that letter?"

"I'm not sure." I folded it back up, placed it in its envelope, and returned it to my pocket, my fingers shaking a little.

There was a loud bang that made me jump. Looking up, I saw Elijah had kicked over one of the folding chairs.

"Alright," Rayla said, sounding anything but all right, "we need a plan."

"Ya!" Cindy piped up. "Like if the school isn't going to do anything to help, then ya, we need to."

A strange feeling began to grow in my chest, *not pride, or joy, nor contentment… I had friends that cared… they really cared! And they seemed outraged for me,* ME. I had felt this way for others, but there never had been a time when it had been returned. It was strange, but it was nice.

"Thanks, guys," I said, trying not to seem too emotional. My chest swelled; it was as if nothing could get me down now. "But the letter never said I was out of my detention with Ms. LaKey, so I'd better get to her office before I'm considered late."

No one wanted me to go. They all complained loudly about the injustice of it all. I thanked them again for their kind words, more like their unkind words against the school, especially Ms. LaKey. Rayla offered to walk with me to the office; the whole way I tried to think of something to say, but I couldn't. It was a bit weird, like I was on death row, and she was escorting me to the gas chambers.

Rayla stopped at the door, and holding it open meekly, said, "See ya."

I nodded and headed in.

Miss Rose gave me a sad smile as I entered. I took a seat like she instructed, and I saw Rayla wave through the window. Had Toby not been sitting next to me, I think I might have burst into tears on the spot. I was so happy to have friends, but now that they weren't standing next to me, nervousness enveloped me. His presence gave me the strength I needed to endure the wait. *I knew I wouldn't have been able to make it through any of this if Toby weren't with me.* Yet somehow I felt just a bit stronger.

With a flick of her hand, she beckoned me over. "Ms. LaKey has some photocopying for you to do. Once it's done, you may be dismissed for your lunch. Do you know how to use the machine?"

I shook my head.

"I'll show you." She led the way down a short hall to the copying room.

It was a small room, not much bigger than the school bathroom, and the same awful sterile green that made me want to go to sleep if I stared at it too long. One wall was lined with shelves, which were more like cubby holes, and each was tagged with a description of what was supposed to be in it: pink paper, lilac, blue, lined, white, off white and so on. The next wall had a long table pushed against it, but apart from a large paper cutter on one end, it was completely empty. The wall opposite the shelves had two machines, a photocopier and a laminator.

Miss Rose walked over to the photocopier and showed me how to work it, then left. It was a fairly simple procedure—three stacks: one that just needed to be duplicated, a second that was double-sided, and the third that was to be copied onto a very bright pink paper. I was warned that my biggest concern would be to change the paper and un-jam the machine if it got stuck. The problem was that our school had an older copier, so it would likely get stuck, almost every fifty sheets.

The next twenty minutes were a crash course on every place a paper could jam and how to locate it and remove the sheet. I'd have to reset the machine, recalculate how many papers were still needed and start the whole process again.

With each paper jam, Toby became more and more agitated, but I felt fairly calm—*I was safer here*, and the rhythmic whir of the photocopier was almost soothing.

He had spent the whole time pacing and finally stopped to rest against the wall. Leaning his head back, he closed his eyes. "If I was still alive, I'd be loving this." His tone was filled with contempt.

I watched the machine spit out copy number 37, 38, 39 and so on. *Almost done this batch.* Glancing at the clock, I saw that I still had 25 minutes left in the lunch hour.

"This explains a lot about how I was able to get away with everything I did." Toby ran his hand through his hair. "I don't blame anyone else for what I did—it was my choice, no one made me do those things. Now I can see how wrong I was… But I wonder if I would have been half as cruel if someone had stepped in and called me on all my…" He stopped. The copier had whined and shuddered with its eighth jam.

Slowly I searched for the location; there were seven spots that paper could get stuck. As I pulled the crumpled paper out of its hiding spot and replaced the cover, I laughed at the irony; just three more pages were left.

"This is no different than any other time I've been picked on," I explained with a shrug. "It's always: I didn't see her, or I didn't know it would hurt, or I was only joking, or can't she understand it was just a game? It's all the same believable excuse." *Only this time was different. The teachers knew there was a problem and didn't deny it.* Even if they only gave me lip service about it, the teachers finally recognized my problem. Just the thought of that made my spirit soar. Also, I had friends that cared: I didn't know that could make such a big difference. *But it did.*

The photocopier clicked to a finish. I gathered the three stacks and took them to the secretary.

Looking up from her desk and glancing at the clock, she said, "Well, at least you have some time left for lunch." Again she gave me her sad smile. "I've been informed that Ms. LaKey expects you every lunch hour next week."

I nodded and left. Walking from the office, I stopped and pondered what I should do; barely twenty minutes were left before the end of lunch bell, not enough time to buy and eat any food, and with no idea of where Rayla or the rest of my friends would be… I didn't know what to do. Toby tapped me on the shoulder, and I looked down the hall to where he was pointing.

Rayla was leading the way, with Charlie, Cindy and Teb following her. As they neared she called out, "Finally finished? Can you have your lunch now?"

"There isn't enough time," I answered, but I beamed as I looked at the gang.

"You've got plenty of time!" Cindy smiled then caught my wrist and headed in the direction of the lunchroom.

As we rounded a corner, I thought I saw Sara duck into one of the rooms. *Was Effie near?* My heart skipped a beat, but when we passed, I didn't see or hear anything.

Dan and Elijah had saved a table, and someone had taken the liberty of buying me the daily special. I was jokingly threatened not to waste the food, so I sat. The whole thing had me feeling euphoric, making it hard to swallow over a new kind of tears: *joy!*

Everyone had taken a seat, and I felt as if they were all watching me as I raised my fork. Instead of eating, I ended up breaking down and crying. Pulling my elbows onto the table, I hid my face behind my hands. *Why was I doing this now? It was embarrassing!*

"Just relax," I heard Toby say from behind me as he placed his hand on my back.

"What's wrong?" Rayla asked.

I couldn't answer; the tears were coming too fast.

"Was Ms. LaKey mean to you?" someone asked.

I shook my head behind my hands. *How could they understand? I'd never felt kindness like this before.*

"Mariah, don't push them away," Toby pleaded. "Don't shut them out!"

I shook all over, but not so much from my sobs. I was scared: here it was—they had proven they were true friends, yet I still didn't think I could trust them.

I felt someone put their arm around my back. It wasn't Toby, and turning I saw Charlie. Looking into her face, I suddenly felt braver.

"I'm really happy," I said. "I don't ever remember having friends as nice as you."

A tear ran down Charlie's cheek, and she hugged me fiercely. Rayla embraced me from the other side, along with Cindy. *And it didn't feel uncomfortable.*

Teb, Dan and Elijah, who all sat on the other side of the table, suddenly embraced each other, saying things like, "Man, I love you", "No, I love you", and "You're the best".

"Boys," Charlie muttered, "can't live with them…"

"Wouldn't be alive without them," I finished and snuck a look behind me at Toby. He chuckled.

"Well I was going to say 'can't shoot them,'" Charlie said, patting me on the back, "but alright, we'll go with survival of the species instead."

Everyone seemed to be in a better mood. Dan joked about not knowing that lunch came with a show. Everyone laughed, and then the subject changed. There were complaints about the letter I'd received and the general unfairness of it all. When interest in that topic died down, it became a conversation comparing TV shows and movies.

I was able to eat most of the meal while listening to them chatter before the bell to signal the end of lunch sounded. Elijah and Dan offered to walk with me to my locker, Elijah because he needed something from his own locker and Dan because he shared the next class with me. When that class was over, Dan walked me all the way to my final class before he left for his own.

"They're trying to keep you safe," Toby said as I took my seat. "It just might work." When the final bell of the school day rang, I jumped to my feet.

"What's the rush?" Toby asked as I hurriedly gathered my papers—*I didn't want to tell him that I was excited to get ready for my date.* "Just take your time." He kept looking over at the door.

I tried to slow down as I watched the room empty; I ended up being almost the last student in the class when Rayla and Teb showed up out of breath.

"That's what I figured," Toby said under his breath. I felt warmed just seeing them.

They walked with me to my locker, where Charlie, Cindy, Dan and Elijah all joined us, and we went out to wait for my bus. Cindy was the only one who lived near me, so she and I got on and waved to the rest.

Cindy kept talking about interesting facts she'd picked up. She was a self-proclaimed scientist; she explained that she loved finding information, then sharing it with anyone who would listen. I enjoyed the way she could keep the conversation going almost all by herself, and she didn't ask too many questions.

Toby stayed quiet, but he seemed amused. It was only for the last two stops, after Cindy had gotten off, that his smile began to fade and his mood became agitated. The walk from the bus stop to my house felt like it took an eternity, mostly because he was dragging his feet. I used the extra time to think about the events of the day, like playing a movie in my mind: my heart soared when I remembered the way Cindy had looked back as she was leaving and said, "Remember, sleepover tomorrow!" But when I thought of being tied up, my breath caught… *Were everyone's lives as crazy as mine? Was this normal?*

Toby stopped on the sidewalk in front of my home. "Are you still planning on going on this date tonight?"

Scanning around and seeing no one, I answered, "Do you have a good reason why I shouldn't?" *I really wanted to go!*

"Only the same as before: Tony only wants to use you."

I closed my eyes against the bluntness of his words. I could see Tony in my mind—he was leaning in to kiss me, and those familiar tingles raced up my spine. "What if I want to be used by him?" I asked without opening my eyes.

"No, Mariah," Toby said, and I could hear him move in front of me. "Believe me, beautiful, you don't want to be used like that."

Yet I couldn't believe him—*I didn't want to.*

Toby grabbed me by my shoulders. "I know what you're feeling! I remember, I remember a little too well now! I know he makes you feel special. I can see it clear on your face, and it feels good to him too…I remember!" His grip tightened. "But it's not good, it's not special, and when this feeling passes, it will leave you worse off than before!"

I pulled myself out of his grip. I didn't like what he was saying. *How could that be true? He's just jealous because he's not allowed to feel this way any more—he misses it!* I turned from him and headed into my house. Nothing he did or said for the rest of the afternoon could convince me otherwise. Finally he gave up and fell silent.

I choose to wear the tight jeans I'd worn the previous night and one of my new tops. It was a deep burgundy colour. I felt a twinge of guilt about my attire. *After all, it had been Toby who helped me pick it out…* But I didn't let that stop me. The shirt had a very low neckline, but now that most of my ant bites had started to heal, I had no reason not to wear it. I styled my hair the way Molly had showed me, so that my curls would be their most bouncy, and applied a smidge of flattering make-up.

It wasn't until I stood out in the parking lot where Tony had dropped me off before, and we were now supposed to meet, that Toby tried to talk me out of the date one last time.

"What about Elijah?" he asked.

"What about him?" I retorted, keeping my eyes fixed on the street, watching for Tony's car. "Weren't you the one who told me we should just be friends?" I knew I was taking Toby's words out of context. *But I didn't care right now.*

"Mariah, Tony's a dog! He doesn't care about you, he's only interested in how far he can score with you."

"You don't know that!" I spat. "This time could be different! He could be different with me!" I crossed my arms. *I didn't even want to imagine that Toby could be right.*

"We both know that's not true." Toby sounded defeated.

"Listen," I said, turning back and catching his hand in mine, "just let me have this one date. I've never had a date before, and who knows if anyone will ever ask me again!"

Toby shook his head. "That's a lousy excuse to let Tony have his way with you."

"I promise I won't let things get out of hand. I just…I just," *I just want to kiss him again*, I thought, but instead I said, "I just want to go to the movie with him. And besides, this gives me another chance to try to give him your message."

Toby tried to pull his hand away, but I held on, so instead he brought it up to my cheek. "He won't listen to you, not like this," he said quietly, his dark eyes looking sad.

"You don't know," I protested. Those eyes reminded me of Tony. *I couldn't wait for him to get here!*

Before Toby could say another word, Tony pulled up. He wore a loose button-up shirt and baggy jeans. His hair was slicked over to one side, and he wore his school ring. Toby looked green at the sight of him.

"Hop in, beautiful," Tony said as he reached across the car and swung the door open for me. I felt Toby squeeze my hand tightly as I tried to let go. In one quick jerk, I wrenched myself free and stepped up to the car.

Tony smiled, his eyes lingering on my plunging neckline. I felt myself blush as I climbed in. I was barely aware of Toby slipping through the back door and taking a seat behind me. Tony adjusted the mirror. I caught Toby's reflection. He wore a scowl. Tony's smile widened as he slipped the car into drive. We were off.

He seemed infatuated with me; he kept looking over at me as we drove to the movie theatre, like he couldn't get enough of me. He let me pick the show, and paid for the pop and snacks. As we entered the theatre, he asked if we could sit at the very back, because his eyes felt strained if he was too close. Also, this way we would be able to be alone, because no one else liked to sit so far back. I agreed, even though Toby was shaking his head.

Tony led the way down the back aisle and took a seat in the centre of the row. I sat next to him and placed my large pop in the armrest to the right of me. Tony put his drink to his left and suggested that this way we could keep the popcorn between us, and we wouldn't have to worry about spilling drinks. Toby tried to sit in the chair on my left, but it wouldn't unfold for him, so he ended up standing and leaning against it. This didn't improve his already dark mood, but I was too distracted.

There was a commercial for the latest video game console, and Tony started going on about how he was going to buy it. He loved video games, though they weren't much of a challenge. He usually ended up beating them in a few days. Luckily, his dad bought him every game he wanted.

"You impressed yet?" Toby asked snidely.

What's so bad about liking video games? I wondered, but instead I nodded as Tony droned on. I wasn't interested in most of the games Tony talked about; he liked the real blood and guts kind, and I was partial to the adventures.

"Oh ya," Tony answered as I mentioned one of the games I liked, "I've played that one. It's a bit slower-paced." Then he recounted one of the most gruesome games he'd ever played, a pirated copy out of another country because it was banned from ours.

"Still believe he's interested in you?" Tony asked quietly.

I was starting to feel less than special, but I didn't want to admit it.

The previews began, and Toby fell silent. He even seemed to forget that I was there. I was trying to figure out what I liked more about movies, watching them or seeing what was going to be released in the months to come.

As the opening credits began, I felt Tony slip his arm across my shoulder. A tiny shiver ran through my body.

"Cold?" he asked quietly, and before I could answer, he pulled me closer.

I liked the feel of his hand across my neck, but as the movie started, I got caught up in it, oblivious to Tony's arm or anything else. We had only been watching for about fifteen minutes when I realized that Tony had put the popcorn on the floor and placed his free hand on my knee. I could feel his hot breath near my cheek and, turning to him, our lips met, and he began to kiss me.

This is what I had wanted, and it felt every ounce as good as I hoped it would. Tony was passionate, kissing me for long periods of time and drawing me as close as he could. His one arm slipped down my back to my waist, and his other traveled up my knee to my thigh.

I felt good all over. I brought my left hand up to Tony's neck, and he moaned softly. Then he took his hand off my thigh, grabbed my right arm and pulled it around his waist. I grabbed him, and he returned his hand to my thigh. We kissed for what seemed an eternity. I was only mildly aware of the movie playing in the background, and I had lost all sense of Toby sitting next to me.

Tony stopped for a moment and looked at me. "I want you," he said in a seductive voice. "Let me have you."

These words excited me and scared me at the same time. *I wanted to be had; I wanted to give myself to him, I think…* Tony unbuttoned his shirt and pulled my hand around his back. I closed my eyes with the thrill of feeling his smooth warm skin against my hand. Tony's hand worked its way up my shirt until he was touching my bare skin, just below my bra. I felt dizzy, like I had been spinning a little too long. But before I could think or do anything else, Tony's lips met mine again, and he opened his mouth, causing our tongues to touch.

What was I doing!

Toby interrupted loudly. "Excuse yourself to the bathroom. Now!"

Tony's hand had just found my bra clasp, and I felt him working to get it undone. *I didn't want to leave. I wanted to see where this was going to go.*

"Now, or I make the pop spill onto your lap!" Toby said, giving the pop a push with one finger. The ice sloshed against the plastic sides.

"I have to..." I said as I tried to pull away from Tony's strong embrace and fought my own desire to stay. "I have..." Tony had unclasped one of my bra's hooks. I continued to struggle. "I need to..." Tony's fingers continue to fumble with my bra but the two remaining clasps were holding fast.

Then I felt Toby yank me up by my arm.

"I have to use the washroom," I said, shocked to find myself standing.

Tony had grabbed my arm as I stood up. He now held it with great force. "Hurry back," he said.

I nodded, not even wanting to go, but Toby held me under the arm and started to haul me down the aisle and out of the theatre, all the way to the washrooms. Walking me to the counter, he pushed me against the sink and turned the cold water on. Catching a bit in his hands, he splashed it up into my face.

"What are you doing?" I spat, anger welling up so fierce that I shook.

"Stopping you!" he said, anger in his own voice.

"I don't want to be stopped," I said, turning from Toby to my own reflection in the mirror. I was stunned at the sight; though my cheeks were flushed, I looked rather nice. I admired myself and marveled at how far I'd come in just over a week. What a whirlwind it had been, but here I was looking back at my reflection and enjoying what I saw.

Toby looked sadly at me in the mirror too. "Mariah," he started, sounding a bit calmer, "I need you to remember why Tony is in your life."

I bit my lip; *I didn't want to think about that*, because I knew it was Toby who had made it all possible.

"I needed you to do me a favour." The memory of Tony's hand on my back was more persuasive then Toby's words.

"I feel like this is all my fault. If I hadn't asked you to do me that favour, then you never would have gone to see him again. In fact, it was my idea for you to go to the bowling alley in the first place." His voice was full of regret.

I wasn't unhappy to be here. Toby took a step closer and put his hand on mine as I held on to the counter. The initial cool feeling of his touch, melting into pure warmth that traveled up my arm, was like an old friend returning. It chased away the thoughts of Tony's caresses faster than the wind blowing fog away.

I opened my eyes again to look at Toby in the mirror. "Believe me," he said, "I want you to be loved and experience the pleasure of someone who really enjoys being with you." I tried to pull my hand away, but Toby held fast. "Tony is not the boy to give this to you."

"Yes," I said, feeling my emotions choking me, "yes, he is!" Toby's sad eyes stared deep into mine, and I shook my head again. "Yes, he is. He has…he does," I argued.

"He doesn't love you. He doesn't even care about you," Toby persisted.

"I don't care!" I felt my voice break. *That wasn't true.*

"Please, please, Mariah, I know I'm the one who put you here, but please don't do this. I've taken this road, and I know it leads to heartbreak. Do you think Tony's going to want to be friends? Do you think he even cares about how you get home? If you give in to what he wants, do you think you'll ever see him again?"

I knew Toby was right, but that didn't make it any easier. I thought of Tony in the theatre waiting for me. *What would he do if I returned and didn't let him touch me, kiss me, undress me? Would he just leave me here?* I could imagine him getting forceful—what would I do? What if he became insistent? Could I stop him? Did I have the ability to resist him? I didn't think I did.

"You're probably right," I said, leaning forward and placing my arms under my head to half lie on the counter.

"I know I'm right," Toby said, but his voice was kind.

"It felt so good," I sighed. "I didn't want to stop."

"Believe me Mariah, this isn't right. I could see Tony's intentions—he was tallying up the points before you even got in the car. This whole night was a set-up to take you as far as he could go. He wears that stupid ring only on the nights that he intends to score!"

I did believe him, but it had felt so good. When I was in Tony's arms, I could believe that I was beautiful and lovable, if just for a moment. I hadn't realized until that night how much I ached for attention from a boy, any boy really.

Toby was still talking, and I listened as he said, "And if I hadn't stopped you, Tony would have had your bra off by now, and your hand would have been down his pants."

"What's wrong with me?" I asked, standing up but holding tight to the counter for fear I'd fall over. My knuckles turned white with the pressure.

"There's nothing wrong with you," Toby said, but he hesitated, his eyes narrowed. Looking at my face through the mirror, he added, "I think you need to sit down." He guided me to the floor.

As I went out of sight, I caught my reflection. I was as white as fresh-fallen snow. I sat and shook, wondering how this evening was going to end. The events of the other day came back crystal clear and washed over me like a flood. I leaned against the wall, where Toby had propped me.

I played out the scenario; I woke with someone in my house… *Why hadn't I run as soon as I figured it out? Why did I hesitate? Why was it so important to put my bra on? Did I deliberately delay myself and get caught? Why hadn't I called out for Jake right away, instead of allowing them to get their hands on me…? Had I wanted it?*

My stomach lurched, and I rolled to my side just in time to miss being sick all over myself, as the washroom door opened and an employee walked in.

She stopped, looking disgusted, then asked, "Are you alright?"

I couldn't answer, as visions of Nick, Rock, Mims and the dream with Toby got all muddled up on my brain.

"Do you need help?" The employee came next to me. "Are you here with someone?"

"Yes," I choked, and I told her which theatre she could find Tony in.

Looking relieved, she left to find him. I leaned over as I continued to shake heavily. It didn't take long for the employee to return, with Tony just steps behind her.

"Beautiful," he snapped as he rushed into the washroom; his tone was anything but kind. "I got it," he told the woman, and she left. Shaking his head, he leaned down and lifted me to my feet. I was shocked that he had the strength to pick me up. Once I was standing, Tony put my arm around his shoulder and guided me all the way to his car.

It was strange how just a few minutes ago I had wanted him to touch me and hold me. Now that I didn't care if he ever called me again, I needed his help. All I wanted was to get home. Though Tony couldn't tell, Toby was walking along on my other side, keeping me from collapsing the whole time.

Tony let me fall into the front seat of his car. "If you are going to be sick, try and miss the seats. They may be vinyl, but puke gets stuck between the cushions."

As he walked around to the driver side, I brought my knees up to my chest. I was still shaking, and the waves of nausea continued to wash over me.

"Mariah, you're going to be okay," Toby said before Tony got in. Then Toby reached over from the back seat and put his hand beside my head. I leaned my head over to rest on it.

"Home or hospital?" Tony asked curtly.

"Home," I moaned.

Without another word, he turned the engine on and sped out of the parking lot. I closed my eyes against the jarring lights. Tony stayed very quiet while Toby kept whispering reassurances in my ear. Though it felt like the ride took longer, I knew we had made it back to my complex in half the time it should have.

With the car in park and the engine off, Tony turned to me and sighed. "What did you take?" He sounded like he had calmed down a little.

"Nothing," I answered weakly.

"Ya right, nothing," he scoffed.

I was starting to feel more normal. I sat up a bit but kept my legs tucked against my chest.

"I'm no stranger to a bad trip…" Tony persisted.

"That's not a lie," Toby interrupted, pulling his hand away. "Come on Mariah, let's go."

But I wasn't sure I had enough strength to walk yet. "I don't do drugs," I protested.

Tony narrowed his eyes. "Then what? Are you an epileptic?"

"No," I said, but I continued to shake.

"Alright then, can you get yourself home?" He seemed anxious to get rid of me.

I still wasn't sure. Toby was insistent that he could help, and I should just get out, but I couldn't find the strength to even open my door.

Tony let out a sigh, then said in the gentlest tone I'd heard him use, "Alright then, I'll help you get home." I looked straight at Tony, and despite myself, I still found him attractive: his deep, soft eyes, his reddish wavy hair, his smooth olive completion. He got out and made his way around to my door.

"Don't trust him; once he gets you home he won't leave!" Toby protested. But he stopped when Tony had my door open and was offering me his hand.

I didn't know what to do. I was still nauseous and barely had the strength to stand. Tony leaned in and guided my feet to the floor, and then he held me around my sides and pulled me up. It still felt good to have Tony so close, but that thought only disgusted me, so I tried to push him away and walk myself, but I stumbled.

Toby sighed loudly. "It's alright, let him walk you. Clearly you need his help." I was shocked and confused, but I stopped fighting and let Tony help me.

"You know, I've done my share of drugs. I could even get you some if you wanted," Tony said as he helped me up the steps away from the visitor parking.

Toby, who had taken up his spot on the other side of me, only scoffed at his friend's comment, but stayed silent.

"Just level with me, you took something..." Tony insisted.

I shook my head then directed Tony down the path that led to my townhouse.

"You want me to believe that you're like this for no reason?" Tony chuckled. "Not possible, beautiful, you had to have taken something." I closed my eyes as we walked. "Just do me a favour. Next time you want something, use a different dealer."

I didn't respond, but I did open my eyes. I kept directing Tony until we made it to the bottom of my steps, but instead of walking up, I sat down on them. Tony followed suit.

"Don't let him into your house," Toby instructed, and I nodded. *I had no intention of that any longer.*

I was amazed at how quickly my lust had subsided. There was no shred of desire for Tony to kiss me or do anything of the sort. He brought his elbows to his knees and placed his chin in his hands. He looked out across the front walk, beyond to the road.

"You know how I told you that Toby's ghost had come to me," I said, leaning away from Tony and on the banister. Toby stood next to me, his hand on the railing.

"Ya."

"Well, it's true." I looked at Tony. He kept staring forward. "Do you believe me?"

"No," he said flatly, then he added, "It just proves that you're on something."

"How come it's so easy for you to believe I did drugs but not that the spirit of your best friend is trying to help you?"

Tony didn't answer, but Toby did. "That's his world," he said sadly. Toby squatted down in front of me, but looked over to his old friend. "He's more stuck than you are. I don't know if I can help him now." There were tears in his voice, and it made my heart break for Toby, and Tony.

Tony was oblivious; his whole world was the pursuit of more, but never the enjoyment of what he had. Feeling compassion for him, I placed a hand on his knee.

Tony slowly turned to me and looked deep into my eyes. "You should go lie down," he said softly. "I'll help you get in." He stood and held out a hand to pull me to my feet, and we walked the eight steps to my front door.

"Thank you," I said, feeling almost better. I slipped the key from my pants pocket, but before I could get it into the keyhole, Toby had put his hand over the door handle.

"It's time to say goodnight," Toby demanded.

"Why don't you give me a tour of your house?" Tony said, and I felt like he was slipping back into his commanding role.

"Maybe another night," I replied.

Tony looked disappointed, but he smiled and leaned in to kiss me one last time. My body trembled as our lips met. His were soft and warm against mine, and I suddenly wanted more than anything to invite him in, but Toby's hand stayed firmly over the keyhole. Eventually Tony stood back, and letting out a soft sigh, he gave his school ring a kiss, said his farewells then headed down the stairs. I watched him until he turned the corner, and I couldn't see him any more.

Toby snatched the key from my hand and unlocked the door. He took me sharply by the shoulders and led me into the kitchen, plunked me down on the only chair pulled out from the table, went to the fridge and started to rummage through it.

"You need to eat something," he said curtly. I watched him as he put some ham, cheese and crackers onto a plate and poured me a generous glass of chocolate milk.

I ate slowly; each bite helped me feel stronger. My nausea had completely subsided, and I wasn't shaking any more. As I chewed, I wondered what had happened to make me so ill? *I had never had a problem with this before Toby came into my life*, but now I'd had two, or maybe three, episodes when I'd just fallen completely apart. *What was wrong?*

Toby watched me as he stood with his arms crossed, leaning against the counter. "I feel so useless!" he exclaimed. "What am I doing here?" He pounded his fist on the counter. "Do you know?" he asked, looking to me.

I shrugged. *How was I to know?* "You're the one who's supposed to know these things," I said.

"This is getting too confusing!" Toby pulled out a chair and threw himself into it. "In the beginning it was so clear, I was here to help you…" He looked me up and down. "But now you don't seem to need my help, and you sure as hell don't seem to want to listen any more!"

"What do you mean?" I protested, putting down the cracker I had been nibbling on.

"I mean everything, Mariah!" Toby slapped his hand on the table. "I told you not to go tonight, but you didn't listen! I tried to stop you, but you didn't want to! So why am I still here?"

"Because I still need you!" I yelled. The thought of him leaving filled me with fear. *I wasn't ready; he promised he wouldn't go until I was!* I reached out and grabbed Toby's hand.

"Then why wouldn't you listen to me?" he asked, hurt all too clear in his voice, but he didn't pull away from me.

"Because…" I started thinking back on the whole night. "You don't understand how I felt. It was nice having the attention—it felt so good." I closed my eyes and thought about it. "And when he kissed me, and touched me…"

"Stop!" Toby pulled his hand back. "I don't want to hear it. I can feel it too."

I was shocked to the core. "Did you feel what I was feeling?"

"No, not even close." Toby ran his hand through his hair. "Like I told you, I do remember what it used to feel like. Only now, just like your pain, I feel your lust in its truest form. It felt like ice was pumping through my veins, making me so cold, it burned."

I didn't take my hand away from my mouth. I could barely breath. That's what he had to endure while I was enjoying myself? I wondered how something that made me feel so alive and wonderful could be so horrible, and then I remembered a secondary emotion that I had managed to ignore at the time.

I brought my hand down on the table. "I didn't like that he put my hand on his chest," I admitted. "I mean, it felt exciting, but somehow wrong. And I really felt a bit scared when he put his hand up my thigh, and worse when it went under my shirt." Tears came to my eyes as I continued. "And when he started to unsnap my bra…"

Toby reached out and placed his hand over mine.

"I felt like a trapped animal." I swallowed hard. "Why didn't I stop him? Why did I think I liked it?"

"Because you were trapped," Toby answered. "Tony had you cornered right from the start. And you were an animal, acting on instinct and emotion."

I didn't feel any better, and I wondered if Tony were to show up now, would I behave differently, or would I be just as easily preyed upon? I made a note to keep as far away from Tony as I could… *I couldn't trust him… And I couldn't trust myself to be around him!*

My brain felt full. I cleaned up and settled down to watch TV in the living room. Several hours passed while I did nothing but watch mind numbing shows. Toby stayed quiet. He seemed calmer now, and as the night wore on, I slowly leaned on him and rested my head on his arm.

"I'm glad you're here," I said sleepily as a commercial came on.

DAY 13 Saturday...

My mom came in at about three a.m., waking me, since I had fallen asleep on the sofa. She was drunk and talked very loudly as she explained about the great sale she had made and the celebration party that had followed. I came groggily into the kitchen as she made herself a snack and talked on and on about her great accomplishment. She gave me three hundred dollars and said it was my clothes allowance for the month. I didn't protest. She'd already given me money that month, but I took it and waited for her to go to bed so I could clean up after her. Toby watched bleary-eyed, not saying a word.

Sleep came quick, and it wasn't hindered by any memorable dreams. It was past noon when I finally woke and pulled myself out of bed. Toby seemed quieter than usual, but I was in a good mood. I had three hundred dollars and a yen to spend it. Putting together a snack on the run, I headed out to the mall.

As we shopped, Toby's mood seemed to lift. I tried on several outfits, shirts, pants and even a corset for fun. He gave me his opinion of each item. He was like my own private personal shopper, and it was especially great because he would know if the salesperson was telling the truth or not.

I had a meal in the food court. I was enjoying my "Mariah special"—as Toby reminded me it was now called—when a familiar voice called my name. It was Larry.

"Mariah." He took the empty seat across from me. Toby had just been recounting a memory of a pool game that had lasted all night, but he fell silent as Larry sat.

"Oh, hi." Larry's hair was just as dry and frizzled as ever, and his face was so round, it looked like a dinner plate.

"It's nice to see you again." Larry rearranged the contents of his tray so the burger was in front of him and the pop to the left, making me wonder if he was left-handed.

"Thanks." I pretended to be looking across the mall, but I was actually staring at Toby. He gave me a shrug in reply.

"Who are you here with?"

I almost told him Toby, but I caught myself in time. "No one. Who are you here with?"

"Tony." Larry nodded his head toward the Fry Shack. I turned to see him, and my heart jumped into my throat. I was torn—as much as my eyes enjoyed drinking him in and my whole body quivered with the idea of being close to him once more, I remembered the promise I'd made myself the previous night. *What was I supposed to do?*

"Um…" I stammered, looking all around for an excuse and a good escape route. I glanced at my half-finished meal.

"Need to go?" Larry asked. He had unwrapped his burger and started to eat it. I nodded vigorously. "Then go," he said with his mouth full.

I took one last glance at Tony, who was now waiting for his order in the pickup line. Thanking Larry, I went to grab my tray to clean up, but he told me to leave it, and I scooted away. As I walked, I saw Toby was looking very pleased, but he took one last backwards glance at his old pal, and I thought I could feel all his regrets weighing down on my gut: *He couldn't save his best friend… and I couldn't help him…*

With my new purchases clutched tightly in my hand, I headed home to pack for the slumber party. I had bought some new PJ's and undergarments. Cindy had mentioned a hot tub, so I also packed my swimsuit, though I wondered if I'd feel comfortable enough to wear it. Once my backpack was full, I went up to the kitchen to wait.

"How's tonight going to work for you?" I asked Toby while I sat on the counter.

He leaned on the table across from me. "I'm not sure. I'm probably going to have to keep my eyes shut for a lot of it." I felt bad for him, and I worried I might miss him, but I understood.

"Mariah, I'm glad you get to go on this sleepover, and I want you to have fun…" He looked down and ran his hand through his hair. "But I feel like I'm running out of time. I need you to start looking for that girl."

I nodded. "Alright." Hopping from the counter, I grabbed the phone book. "Just tell me her name, and I'll start looking for her."

Toby's face fell.

"What?" I asked, the phone book weighing heavy in my hand.

He brought his hand up to his neck and rubbed it so hard, it looked like he was trying to pull it right off. "I can't remember her name," he said, as if every word hurt.

I dropped the phone book, and it landed with a thud on the kitchen floor. I rubbed my eyes. "How am I supposed to find her if you don't have a name?"

Toby shook his head and slid to the floor on his knees. "I don't know."

"Alright, don't worry. We'll figure something out." I rushed over to him and put my hand on his knee. "Tomorrow, 'K? Maybe we'll be able to check out your school enrollment records or something…"

"I don't think she went to my school," Toby said, defeated.

I didn't feel like he was making this any easier. "I'm sure something will come to you, you'll remember something, I don't know…" *I didn't know,* and it felt pretty hopeless. *How could we find a girl without a name?*

"Oh, do you know where she lives?" He didn't, not the address nor even an inkling of the general neighbourhood. Defeat was creeping in, but I didn't want to give up. "How did you meet her?"

"Tony," he said brokenly.

I moved back a foot or two and sat shaking my head. "You don't… I can't…" *Why hadn't he thought of this before our date? I might have still been able to ask Tony it then!*

Toby looked up at me, his eyes filled with sorrow. "It's alright, Mariah. I don't expect you to see him again, not even to just talk. I don't figure he would cooperate anyway. I'll figure out another way. Like you said, it will come to me."

I got up and headed out the door, still early, but I needed the fresh air to clear my head—*too much Tony on the brain.* I wondered if I'd made the right choice to never see him again… I tried hard to not let Toby's misery permeate me.

Cindy's house was only two bus stops from mine, so I decided to take the extra time I had and walk all the way there. I was quite excited to be going on my first sleepover, and as I got closer, I couldn't wait to get there. As I neared the bus stop that we had all planned to meet at, I saw Charlie sitting alone. She was gazing down the street in the opposite direction waiting for the bus, but she turned my way and waved happily at the sight of me.

"It's so nice to see you!" she greeted as she walked with me back to the bench. "I'm always early—horrible habit of mine." She smiled. I admired her raven-black hair that shone in the sunlight. "Listen, I had told the others that I made you a get well card, but that wasn't the whole truth. I felt miserable, and I really wanted to make you a card, but I just didn't know what I should say, and I thought it was kind of a dorky idea. But I am really sorry, you know. I didn't realize Sara was standing behind me. I forgot her locker is so close to mine. Well, I never meant for Effie and her gang to find out, or anything that happened…" She bit her lip and shifted nervously from one foot to the other.

I put my hand on Charlie's arm. "It's all in the past. I was never mad at you, so don't worry." Somehow it felt nice to be able to tell her this. *It was freeing.*

"Phew!" she exclaimed. She seemed to relax and sit down. As we waited, she told me all about herself. She was an only child, sort of. She had eight brothers or sisters that she knew of. She had been adopted when she was seven, but she didn't remember much about her birth parents, or siblings. When things are too horrible to remember, sometimes your brain will forget to protect itself: at least, that's what her therapist had told her.

I found it unnerving to have her be so honest with me.

"She's being honest with you, you should try and do the same," Toby coxed.

I didn't know where to start. Charlie had run out of facts about herself and was looking down the road for the bus that would bring Rayla.

Eventually, I started by telling Charlie that I had a hard time trusting people who said they were my friends, and I told her all about Stacy: how she'd betrayed me, the mean tricks she'd eventually played at my expense, the name calling and even the mud she had thrown at me in front of her new friends.

Charlie gave me a hug when I was done. "That must have been really hard. Did you tell your mom?"

That launched me into recounting of how my father had left, my mother had become too busy and my brother's behavior had become scary. I didn't share everything—I kept some things out of the story, like Jake killing Mims, and the latest encounter with Nick and Rock. But she got the general idea of my life.

"Well, perhaps our lives aren't so different from each other in some ways." Charlie said. "Only I guess I'm better off because I'm happy with the parents I've got now." I laughed. *I didn't know why—it wasn't funny.*

Rayla arrived with her hair pulled back in a bandana. She squealed when she saw us and ran to give us each a hug, and then we all walked the three blocks to Cindy's house, our mood high.

Cindy hadn't lied when she said she had planned many great things for us. It started with pizza, only we had to make them from scratch. Cindy's mother, a health-conscious parent, had all sorts of alternative flours to bake with. I found this interesting, but I was at a loss because I hadn't even baked with whole wheat before. Cindy was the oldest of three biological siblings, and she also had other foster siblings. Her parents took the rest of the family out to dinner so we could make ours in peace.

Her house was huge, three stories, with five bedrooms upstairs and two in the basement, and a guest room on the main floor. There we were allowed to "set up camp," as her mother called it. The living room had a huge plasma TV, where the characters were almost life-size. It also had three comfy sofas that matched, with a piano off to the side, and everything was clean. *How'd her mom keep everything so tidy?* Cindy explained that everyone had chores and was expected to clean up after themselves.

I was standing admiring her television when Cindy came next to me and said, "Just wait till we hook up the video games."

Her backyard had a swing set, trampoline and the promised hot tub. As Rayla, Cindy and Charlie were chatting, I sat and watched, wondering how it would feel to grow up in a house like this, and feeling a bit like I was the only one with an unbearable home life.

"He's the dreamiest!" Rayla teased Cindy. She and Cindy were watching the pizzas cooking.

"Who?" I asked, tuning in. Charlie was washing the counter.

"Greg—he's in Cindy's gym class."

"Oh," I said, still not having a clue who they meant.

"Cindy's had a thing for him for ages," Rayla explained.

"And so have you," Cindy shot back, but it was plain they were just having fun.

"Well ya, but you saw him first, so it's your move, sista." Rayla gave Cindy's arm a playful push.

Charlie smiled, threw the rag in the sink and took a seat at the table with me. "We don't fight over who gets boys in our group. No, we fight over who doesn't get them."

"I don't," both Cindy and Rayla said

"That could be closer to the truth," Charlie said while she scratched at a bit of dried up food on the table. "Because they're going to take so long to make a move that Greg will already be snatched up by someone else."

"Well, that's easy for you," Rayla retorted. "Not everyone can get a boyfriend as conveniently as you got yours."

"Uncalled for," Charlie said and turned her back on the other two. "It wasn't easy. Once Teb and I figured out that we liked each other, we had to decide if our friendship could handle it. I mean, if it didn't work out, which one of us would leave the gang?" Her nail lifted off some of the stain. "But I think they're just jealous."

"Why would one of you have to leave?" I questioned.

"Come on, you couldn't see us both being in the group with that between us?"

She had a point. "I figured you'd understand, what with Elijah and all…" she stopped—my eyes had bulged. "Don't tell me you hadn't figured that out yet."

I had, and I told her, but out of the corner of my eye I saw Toby smiling. He seemed to only be paying half-attention. In the back of my mind, I could see him trying to work out the problem of his mystery girl.

"Well, you better decide real quick if you like him and if it's worth putting your friendships to the test."

Rayla came over and leaned on the table. "Don't listen to her. We wouldn't give you up if things didn't work out with Elijah." Rayla had such a nice smile.

Charlie shook her head. "So what, you would stop hanging out with him?" Her eyes, so dark they looked black, bore into Rayla.

"Oh, why does everything have to be so doom and gloom with you?" Cindy asked, coming up behind Charlie and putting her hands on her shoulders.

"'Cause it's the truth," Charlie said, crossing her arms.

"It doesn't have to be."

Before any more could be said, the timer buzzed, and we went to take our pizzas out. Forgetting all about the previous disagreement, we ate dinner. Everyone laughed and talked about the latest celebrity gossip. Then we cleaned our dishes and headed to the living room just in time for the family to return. Cindy's mother informed us that it would be two hours before we could "claim" the living room as "sleepover territory," so we hid in the guest room. It wasn't that private. The door to it had a huge glass pane almost the size of the door itself, and we caught every one of the younger kids with their noses pressed up to it at one time or another.

"Which one is that?" I asked as an adorable two-year-old boy with blond hair and light brown eyes, that reminded me a little of Toby's, peered in.

"Elliot," Cindy said. He was her foster brother who been living with them for six months.

"How many foster siblings have you had?" He kept his nose squashed up to the glass. "It must be hard when they leave."

Cindy's mom tapped on the glass. She explained that Elliot wanted a goodnight kiss. I watched Cindy go to him and embrace him, place a kiss on his cheek then airplane him to the stairs. "It's always been this way," she answered as she came back in. "I was five when they started. Goodbyes are hard, but they're normal around here..." She glanced at Charlie. "There was only one sibling that I tried to convince my parents to adopt. She was my sister and my best friend." Cindy took a few steps and put her arms around Charlie, "But we couldn't adopt her. They had already found good parents, but I was promised she'd still be close enough to visit all the time!"

My mouth fell open.

"See, this is why we've got to keep you in the group," Rayla said. "Otherwise I'm the third wheel." Everyone laughed, but I felt like Rayla believed there was truth behind what she said. *Everyone feels lonely, I guess…*

Changing the subject, Rayla said, "Let's do the hot tub." Cindy and Charlie agreed, but I hesitated. All three girls started pulling their swim stuff out.

"You packed the suit, what's wrong?" Toby said when he saw the look on my face. I couldn't answer, but I looked down at my body. I wasn't as thin as any of the other girls. "Oh," Toby muttered, understanding my gesture. "Well, I'm sure they don't care." *But I did.* "Come on, what are you going to do, stay here? Where's the fun in that?" I didn't budge. "Listen, you're going to have to get over this. No one else thinks you're that big, and Mariah, you aren't…" But he stopped as Rayla, who had been standing behind me, pulled off her shirt. In a split second, he was gone, but he kept trying to coax me in my ear.

I smiled. I found it amusing that I wasn't the most uncomfortable one in the room, even if no one else knew he was here. Then I wondered what the other girls would think if they knew Toby was there, and that thought almost made me laugh out loud.

"Gonna change, Mariah?" Charlie asked.

I shrugged and then went to my bag and pulled my swimsuit out. *Why not?* It was only us girls. Timidly, and with the towel that Cindy's mom had given me to use wrapped around myself, I changed. I could feel Toby just outside of my thoughts. I wondered if he knew we were all dressed again and heading out to the tub.

We had been sitting in the tub for only fifteen minutes when Cindy's mom called from the balcony. "Girls, are you decent? The boys are here!" Out tromped Teb, Dean and Elijah, already in swim trunks.

"Oh, Cindy said slyly, "I might have forgotten to mention that Mom said they could join us for a while."

Charlie almost threw herself onto Teb as he climbed in, which Dan complained loudly about. I wanted to sink from sight as Elijah stepped up to the tub.

"What's the temperature like?" he asked, still standing on the outside, right behind where I sat. He reached forward to dip his hand in, and his arm brushed my shoulder in the process. I stiffened momentarily.

"What's the matter, Elijah, would you rather just stand outside and watch?" Dan teased. Elijah's face turned very red, and he looked away.

"You're cruel," Cindy scolded and splashed Dan in the face. It turned into a splashing match. Elijah got almost as wet as if he had been inside the tub. I moved to the side, feeling very exposed whenever the water rushed away from me as they created little tidal waves. Once the fun was spent, Elijah got in. With so many bodies in the tub, the seating was squishy, and somehow everyone shifted about so the only open spot was next to me. *They'd planned it that way!* I felt so nervous and shy that I wanted to call out to Toby. *Where was he! Had he fallen asleep?* My only comfort was that Elijah looked just as uncomfortable as I felt. We both stayed quiet as the other five joked and jabbered on. Occasionally we'd end up touching one another. It made me stiffen every time.

When it was time to get out, I was mortified. But the boys left quickly, so I waited until they were gone and got out, hoping I wasn't being watched and they wouldn't see me. I felt the size of a whale. *Where had all my confidence gone?* With a towel over the window in the door, we changed in the guest room. The boys were in the basement bathroom.

Rayla was dressed, and she came to stand close to me. "He really likes you," she said quietly. I nodded, not quite sure what to say. "We dated once; he was a really good kisser…" I subconsciously put my hands to my lips. *The memory of Tony's lips was still alive on them.* Rayla misinterpreted my gesture. "Haven't you ever been kissed before?"

"I have!" I answered a little too quickly and forcefully.

"Oooooo, do tell!" Rayla exclaimed, loud enough to get the attention of the other two. Then she explained what was going on. Now all eyes were on me.

I didn't want to lie for several reasons: one—it was something I'd have to remember I'd told them for the rest of our friendship, two—it would probably backfire like the ant story had, and three—how were we to be good friends if I didn't tell the truth? But most of all because everything I could think of telling them would change their opinion of me…

Finally I said, "It was nothing really, one of my brother's friends." When I was pressed about it, I explained it away as if it were a one-time deal. He'd come to help me in our storage closet, and it just sorta happened. But the memory in the back of my mind was so strong, it made Toby pop back into existence.

"What'd I miss?" he asked groggily. Looking around, he seemed relieved that everyone was fully clothed.

"The boys will be waiting," I said, trying to change the subject.

Rayla grumbled that she thought there was something I wasn't saying, but Charlie shooed her out, then said to me, "This would be a friend of your troubled brother's." She wasn't acting as if she'd caught me. Her words seemed more compassionate, as if she might have understood all too well how the story really went.

I was the last to enter the living room. Cindy's mom, who was just an older looking version of Cindy, explained that we'd get one movie with the boys, then her husband would be taking them home. And she added that we needed to keep our voices low so the other kids wouldn't be disturbed. Then she provided us with popcorn, chips, and fruit juice and left us to ourselves. When I checked, she was sitting at the kitchen table playing solitaire.

Charlie sat on one sofa with Teb, and Rayla sat on the other with Dan. That left me the spot on the third couch with Elijah and Cindy, who was in the kitchen getting cups. Elijah sat in the middle, leaving me a choice of sitting close to him on the left or close to him on the right.

Toby stood beside me as I tried to decide. "I don't get it," he said softly, "you were all over Tony when it was wrong, but now with Elijah, when it's right, you are shy."

I didn't get it either, and the memory of Tony now made me feel slightly dirty. *Yet I knew if I had the chance, I'd do it again, and again! I just didn't understand it…* I finally convinced my feet to move forward and chose to sit on Elijah's left. Cindy returned, poured us all a cup of juice and sat on Elijah's right. He shifted closer to me to give her room. I felt my muscles contract.

I watched as Charlie snuggled with Teb and felt a twinge of jealousy. Then in amazement, I saw Rayla lean against Dan in a friendly sort of way, and I wished Elijah and I could at least do that. He sat next to me casually, and I felt as stiff as a statue. I felt like Elijah wanted to make a move, and I prayed he wouldn't. I just didn't know how I'd react. I felt so dirty, so ugly and unworthy. I tried to relax enough to enjoy the show, but it was no use.

Toby, who stood next to the sofa, twitched a bit from time to time. I knew he knew what I was feeling.

Finally, the movie ended, and the boys said their farewells. Everyone seemed tired. Rayla and Charlie joined Cindy and me on our sofa, and we started to watch the second movie. Toby yawned and disappeared into dreamland. Charlie eventually moved to one of the other sofas with her sleeping bag. Cindy stretched out on the other sofa and dropped off to sleep too.

Rayla and I were the only two left awake. "Listen." She kept her voice low so she wouldn't disturb anyone else. "Elijah really likes you! But you seemed to be withdrawn tonight. You're not worried about what Charlie said earlier? You know, about how if things didn't work out with Elijah, the group would have to pick only one of you to stay in."

I nodded, not wanting to share the truth, even if I knew how. *I had just gotten to a place where I liked having these friends, and already the prospect of losing them was imminent.* That thought made me sad.

"That's not how we work. Besides, we had a meeting yesterday at school, and we've decided that it's not safe for you to go anywhere alone with Effie and her gang of hyenas on the loose. So we all made a pact about being committed to keeping you safe."

I wished Toby were awake so he could hear this—he had suspected it all along. I heard a soft whistle in my ear. "Here's a true group of friends— hold on tight to them."

Suddenly I was worried that I could easily lose this loyalty I'd found with a simple mistake, *or lie*...and I wondered how I had managed to receive it in the first place. "Why are you being so nice to me?" I asked before I could stop myself.

Rayla scratched her head. "Well, I guess partly because I like having you in drama. The class just isn't the same without you; you're really fun to be around." Then she added, "I guess because before you came to the school, it used to be me that was picked on by those jerks, all the way since we were in second grade together, and Cindy and Charlie kinda did the same thing for me."

I smiled even wider. This realization flooded me with exhilaration. *I wasn't alone!* "Why do you think they do that?" I asked.

Rayla leaned back and looked at the ceiling. "Someone once said that there is no real reason—just 'cause they can, I guess."

"I heard this guy say that it was because I was special, somehow, and that scared them," I said with a hint of embarrassment. Toby chuckled in my ear.

"Ya, a counselor once told me it was sorta like a power struggle, before it even became one. Like they wanted to beat you down before you can even stand up. I don't know. I think it just comes down to them deciding that somehow they are better than us, so that gives them the right to act that way." She sat up straighter. "It doesn't matter why! What matters, is you didn't do anything to deserve it. They are wrong." *It wasn't me! There wasn't anything wrong with me.* It was them. They just had to be mean to someone, so they chose me, because I looked like the easiest."

It felt great to hear what Rayla said. I could imagine Toby jumping up and down and applauding, but he stayed quiet.

Feeling satisfied, I leaned my head back next to Rayla. I started to watch the movie again, and Rayla did the same. I became aware of her steady breathing, and looking over, I saw she was sleeping soundly. I looked from her curled up on the same sofa as me to Charlie who lay on the floor with the sleeping bag protectively pulled about her, then at Cindy who slept on the other sofa stretched out with an arm hanging over the edge and her leg propped over the back of the couch. Then I looked at Toby, who appeared on my free side.

He too did a quick scan of the three girls. As he turned to me, he wore a look I couldn't decipher. "What do you think of Elijah?"

I leaned back, thinking about him. The whole night, I had felt ill at ease. With a shrug, I answered, "He's alright, I guess."

"But don't you like him?" Toby scratched his head.

I closed my eyes. *I had liked hearing that he was interested in me, but perhaps that was just because I had never realized that I was admired before…*

"Mariah, Elijah is a nice guy. He wouldn't try to hurt you or force you into anything you wouldn't like. How come with him you are reserved, but with Tony you abandon all reservations?"

I didn't know. All I knew were my feelings. "When I'm with Tony, it feels fun, exciting, a bit dangerous, thrilling…" I whispered.

Toby made a face like someone was forcing him to swallow horrible medicine.

"With Elijah, I feel scared, worried, like what if he doesn't really like me? And I just don't know what he's going to do next. At least with Tony I know. And even though I know it's wrong, it sort of feels more right."

Toby brought his hand down and shifted to face me. "You know, I think I understand. I can remember that feeling: the excitement, the prospect of being caught, the danger, and the thrill of the hunt. I can see it clearly... It was all wrong."

"Does that make me all wrong?" I asked with tears in my voice.

"No," he said with such conviction that I narrowed my eyes. "Absolutely not. Perhaps your wiring is mixed up. Somehow you learned that wrong feels right, bad feels good—and I'd wager that good to you feels bad, or right feels somehow wrong."

Gloom crept in. "Will I ever be able to enjoy myself? Will I never be happy? If something is good, I feel bad, but if it feels good, I know it's bad, so I end up feeling worse!" I shuddered, "Is there no hope for me?"

He pulled me close to his chest with strong hands. "Never give up on hope." Warmth spread from him to me. "I know that if you learned this stuff, then you can most certainly unlearn it!" I closed my eyes as tears cascaded down my cheeks. "I was mixed up too, and being mixed up, I tried so desperately to feel better by chasing my tail in this constant downward spiral, of doing wrong to feel good, only to end up feeling worse..."

"But how do I get out of it then?" *He had tried to fix it by looking to make himself feel better, if only for a moment. I had tried to surrender to the feeling of misery. What was the solution?*

"I'm not positive," he answered, "but I think we're heading in the right direction. It's a process, a journey—there are no quick solutions. If I have learned anything from my life, it's that to try and get instantly better is only a trap. Mariah, give yourself some time. You'll get it soon enough. Just keep it firm in your mind that you are wired this way. Don't let false happiness hinder your quest for true joy."

For a brief moment I felt jealous of him. He didn't have these troubles any more! Then, as I shut my eyes, I felt all of Toby's regrets piling up at the back of my mind like a great mountain. He may not have these problems now, but he also had no way of finding freedom from his mistakes. I fell into a peaceful sleep as the end of the third movie played quietly in the distance.

DAY 14 Sunday...

IT SEEMED LIKE I HAD ONLY CLOSED MY EYES FOR A MOMENT, but when I opened them again it was light out, the TV was off and a young boy stood next to the sofa watching me. He looked to be about five, with a large birthmark on the side of his face.

"She's awake! She's awake," he screamed and ran from the room.

"Well, she'd definitely be awake now." I heard Cindy's voice from the kitchen, then she walked in. "You are one sound sleeper!"

I sat up, rubbing the dust from my eyes. Looking around, I wondered aloud where Charlie and Rayla were. Toby opened his eyes too and looked slightly disorientated.

Cindy took the seat next to me. "Charlie had to go home early. Rayla was just picked up a few minutes ago."

"What time is it?"

"Quarter past one. My mom was beginning to wonder if you'd fallen into a coma, and if she'd have to administer insulin or something." She smiled apologetically.

"Wow," I breathed, filled with shock. "I don't think I've slept this well before."

"Well, you stayed up pretty late." Cindy looked over to the kitchen. "We saved you pancakes."

I ate them hungrily as the house buzzed with activity. Cindy's mom was in charge; there was no mistaking that. She broke up three fights, fixed a scraped knee and managed to get two not too happy girls to start work on dinner. In the midst of all this, she asked me questions about myself and really listened when I answered. I wished I had a mother like Cindy's, and I didn't want to leave. However, no matter how much I stalled, eventually my time came to an end.

As I stood at the door saying goodbye for the third time, Cindy offered to walk me home. I eagerly accepted, and before long we were heading down her front steps and along the street that carried me away from the happiness of her bustling home towards the dreaded silence and loneliness of mine. If Toby hadn't been at my other side, I wouldn't have had the courage to go home.

"I love your house," I said as we walked down the second block.

"Oh ya," Cindy said, shaking her head. "It can be a bit overwhelming sometimes."

"No," I explained, hearing the disbelief in her voice. "It's really nice, and you have a great mom." *I'd trade her with my mom in a heartbeat!*

"Tell me that when she's banned the family from all sugar for a month again."

"She did that?" *I'd still trade with her!*

"Ya, it was terrible! We didn't have any cookies or bars, and let's not even mention the list of goodies I wasn't allowed to buy from the store."

"Why would she do that?"

"Well, sometimes my mom gets it in her head that she wants us to be more healthy, so she removes things like wheat or sugar, and once even milk."

I nodded, but secretly I still wished I had a mother as loving and caring as Cindy had. She might make life feel harder, but at least she really cared about her children.

Cindy seemed to have many small complaints; there were too many siblings, her father was always away at work, and her mother was, as she put it, "a bit of a nut." All in all, it didn't sound like she had anything to really complain about, but I listened, even if I was envious.

"Then again, it's not like I have a mother like Anna," Cindy finally said.

We turned down a lane that would lead into my complex. "Who's Anna?"

"Oh, she's a girl that used to come to my music group on Tuesdays. Now *her* mom was a nut! She wasn't allowed anything but fruit and vegetables! I really felt sorry for her."

Toby had almost tripped over his feet when he had heard the name. "Ask her what Anna's last name was," he begged. I did.

"Miller. Why?"

Toby stopped in his tracks, so I had to stop too. Cindy stopped and looked over at me. Thinking quick, I said, "I think I might know her, what does she look like?"

"Oh, I'm not good at this," Cindy said, "but I guess she had long, wavy blonde hair, brown eyes, and she's kinda your size and height, and..." Cindy gestured with her hands to mean my chest and hips.

Toby's mouth had dropped open.

"Do you know her?" Cindy asked.

"Maybe," I said and started to walk again. I knew now that he had heard the name, Toby wouldn't forget. "You say she used to come to your music group?"

"Ya, she was a sort of a funny girl. Her mother home-schooled her, and she was a bit, I don't know, unique. She liked to wear very bright clothes, and she didn't really listen to the teacher when she told the class it was time to do anything. Anyway, about three weeks ago, Anna came, and she was different, like quieter, then she just didn't come again."

I felt my heart break for this girl. I knew what had happened to her, and I could only try to imagine how it made her feel.

"That's my house," I said, pointing to the one in the centre of seven rows of identical townhouses.

"Do you ever get confused which house is yours?" Cindy asked.

"Oh ya," I giggled, recalling one time. "I was running back in, and I guess I hadn't realized how far I had walked, because I ran up the stairs and burst through the door. It was only then that I figured out I was in the wrong house, and the people sitting at the table weren't my family!"

Cindy laughed so hard she had to stop walking. "Listen, wait for me on Monday, I'll walk down here, and we can go to school together."

"It's a deal!" I thanked her and we parted.

"Anna Miller!" Toby said before I had even shut my front door.

I spent the next two hours looking up the name Miller in every phone book I could find, and even on the online directory. Then I called everyone I found, pretending I was a friend, and I was looking for her. But no one had a daughter named Anna Miller.

Toby sat slumped in the kitchen chair. I looked up to the microwave clock. It was nearing six in the evening. I felt tired and frustrated. The pancakes I'd had five hours earlier were completely digested, and my stomach growled.

"Let's call it a night," Toby said, though he didn't sound happy.

I got up and started to look through the fridge for something to eat. Our supplies were running out, so I pulled together a pitiful supper of Mr. Noodles and some leftover ham slices, and then sat down with the list to write out my requests. I was wondering if I should talk to my mom about doing the shopping myself as I wrote. I made a small note about it at the bottom under apples and "any other fresh fruit you can find."

Taking my food into the living room, I turned the TV on. Toby slumped down next to me but stayed quiet. My mind wandered, and I wondered if there was anything else I could be doing to help him. He gave a little jump seconds before the doorbell rang. I turned to him, but he seemed distracted, so I went to the door to see who it was for myself.

Tony stood on the other side. "What do I do?" I asked in my quietest whisper, expecting Toby to tell me to leave him out there.

Toby looked through the peephole himself. "He brought you flowers?" He scratched the back of his neck and added in an undertone like he was talking to himself, "I've never heard of him bringing flowers."

The doorbell rang again. "What do I do?" I asked again.

Toby stood staring back at me. "I want to ask him a question," he finally answered. *Dread filled my heart.*

"You want me to let him in?" I said, astonished. The memory of Tony's arms all over me on Friday played in my mind. *I wanted to let him in… What would I do if he were in my house? How would I be able to stop him? Would I be able to stop myself? What about the promise I'd made?*

"I need you to ask him about Anna. He's the one who introduced me to her. I need you to get her number from him." I wasn't sure how I was supposed to do this.

Before I could protest, Toby reached out, unlatched the lock and opened the door. Tony wore a tight black shirt and sleek black jeans. He hadn't put any product in his hair, so it curled in loose waves about his head.

As he held out the bouquet of flowers, I noticed that Tony had not worn his school ring. I felt grateful for that. *Maybe he hadn't come to score.* "Good evening," he said as I took the flowers, and he stepped over the threshold to my house. I felt a tingle race down my spine. *I was excited—I was scared.*

I walked into the kitchen. Hearing the door close behind Tony made my heart pound. I found a vase and plopped the flowers into it, then filled it with water. All the while I kept looking at Toby out of the corner of my eye.

"It's so good to see you," Tony said. "I was disappointed when Larry said I'd missed you at the mall. Couldn't you wait around just to say hi?"

With the water still filling the vase, I kept my back to Tony. "Ya, I had to rush home. I had somewhere I needed to go."

"Oh. That's why you weren't home last night."

How did he know that? Had he tried to call? Was that disappointment I heard in his voice? The thought of it made butterflies tickle the inside of my stomach.

I turned around to put the vase on the table and walked into Tony. He embraced me so tightly, I could barely breathe, and brushing his cheek against mine, he said, "There's just something different about you…" It didn't take long for our lips to meet and lock.

I know Toby was watching, and I could almost feel the ice in my veins that he described, but that made the moment feel all the more exciting. *Here I was again.* My mind screamed NO, but my body begged YES. All hope of having a sensible conversation left me. Toby's request fell from my thoughts like leaves off a tree in autumn. Tony took the vase from my hand, put it on the table, and then he guided me out of the kitchen, down the hall and to the living room.

The television happily chattered in the background as Tony laid me on the sofa, and I didn't protest. I felt like I was floating, not quite in my body any more as he came to rest on top of me. I was surprised at how quickly time seemed to move. One moment he had his hand up my shirt, the next my bra was unclasped, and all too quickly his pants were off.

Toby shook my foot and I jumped. For the first time since that fateful night when he'd come into my life, I had completely forgotten that Toby was there. Tony took my jerk as a good thing and moaned into my ear.

"Mariah!" came Toby's voice as he shook my foot harder. "You have to stop."

I couldn't—like someone who'd jumped off a cliff, I was falling, and despite my feeble attempts to slow down, I wasn't able to make anything stop.

"Oh yes," Tony breathed into my ear as his hands found my jeans button and started to unclasp it.

"Mariah, listen." I could hear Toby's voice cut through the fog that clouded my brain. "I know you can hear me. You are in grave danger, but I can help."

"Mmmmm," I responded, though I'm not sure if it was in response to Toby or to what Tony was doing.

"Don't worry, just do exactly what I say, when I say it," Toby instructed.

"I'm not worried," I breathed out.

"Oh, beautiful, neither am I," Tony hummed to me.

That all changed in a heartbeat! The front door opened and slammed shut, and before I could respond—Jake stood over the sofa. Tony didn't know what had hit him; Jake was so quick when he grabbed the collar of his shirt and hauled him off me. Tony landed in a crumpled heap at the end of the sofa.

"Mariah!" Jake said, leaning down to where I lay.

That's when I heard Toby yell, "Run, now!" I didn't hesitate; I scrambled out from under Jake and took off in the direction of the kitchen as I heard someone fall to the floor behind me. I made it safely to the kitchen to find Tony there, looking like a trapped animal. He'd grabbed a knife from the dish rack and held it up like it was a protective sword. In his other hand he held the cordless phone.

I heard the line ringing, then a female voice came on and answered, "Emergency, 911, how can I help you."

"I'm under attack!" Tony said through panicked breaths.

"Get the gun," Toby said. I hesitated. "Mariah, get it now!"

From down the hall I could hear Jake stomping as he headed our way. I dove past Tony and pulled the junk drawer clear out of the cabinet. It crashed to the floor. I was able to locate two bullets, and then I reached into the empty space where the drawer had been and found the revolver stuck to the bottom of the counter, just like my mom had said it would be.

With shaking hands, I pulled it free from the tape and started to load it the way Toby told me to. I could hear the conversation Tony was having with the 911-dispatch operator. He gave my address.

I got the gun loaded, and Toby told me to hand it to Tony. Tony passed me the knife just as Jake came staggering in; he was clearly drunk and probably stoned.

I could hear my heart pound in my ears, and my body shook so badly I wouldn't have been able to stand had I wanted to. Toby stood across the room from me in invisible safety and watched as the events unfolded. Yet as the tension mounted, he swayed as if being knocked across the face.

"It's not your fault!" he cried out, but I was beyond able to register what he said.

"I have a gun," Tony threatened. He danced from one foot to the other just inches from where I was. He looked as if he was protecting me from Jake, whose eyes were glued on me alone.

Only now did Jake seem to stop and take stock of the situation. "Hang up the phone," he said calmly, reaching around his back slowly.

"Jake has a gun too," Toby said in a panicked voice next to my ear. "Tell Tony to shoot!"

"Don't use the gun unless absolutely necessary!" the operator's tinny voice came from the receiver. "The police are on their way."

"Tell Tony to shoot!" Toby yelled.

"But he's my brother," I moaned.

Jake started to pull his hand out from behind his back, revealing a shiny revolver. He was taking aim as he said in a commanding voice, "Hang up the phone, boy, and step away from my sister."

Toby stood up and reached over to Tony's hands that shook as he aimed the gun at Jake. I closed my eyes and yelled "No!" as I heard one shot, then a second. Tony fell onto me and stayed there, covering me. Confusion, worry and fear filled those silent seconds that followed, even though it felt more like a lifetime.

"It's going to be alright," Toby said. "Open your eyes. The cops are here."

I heard an unfamiliar voice speaking. He was reading Jake his rights. I opened my eyes and saw Jake sitting on the kitchen floor less than five feet from me. His right leg was all bloody.

A second cop, a woman, came over to Tony and me. Offering Tony a hand to stand up, she asked if we were alright.

"I'm fine," Tony answered, though his voice sounded anything but fine.

"And you, young lady?" The cop bent down to me.

I just blinked. My mind was swimming. I shook from head to toe and felt nauseous. I could feel a cold sweat trickle down my forehead.

"What's wrong with her?" Tony asked, kneeling next to the cop. He reached out and put his hand on the side of my face. "She's all cold," he said, scanning me up and down.

The cop did a quick check to see if I was hurt, then she too put her hand on my head. "She's going into shock. Are there any blankets we can use to keep her warm?"

Tony jumped up. "Ya, in the living room." He left to get them. Jake was being escorted out of the house as Tony passed.

"And son?" the female cop yelled out, "Put some pants on!" She smiled and looked back down at me. "You're going to be alright."

Toby echoed her words and rubbed my back. I shook so violently that I couldn't breathe properly. My lungs ached, and my fingers tingled with the lack of oxygen.

"Come on, darling," the cop said, pulling me up to a sitting position, "snap out of it."

"Mariah, it's over. You are alright." Toby tried to console me, but I couldn't get the image of Jake's bloody leg out of my head.

Tony returned with blankets, and the cop wrapped them around me. My teeth chattered.

"Stay with her," she said to Tony. "Don't let her go. I'm going to call for medical help. If she doesn't snap out of it quick, we'll have to take her to the hospital." She ran from the room.

"I'm so sorry," Tony whispered into my ear as he hugged me tight and reached around my back to re-clasp my bra. I felt even guiltier as he showed me this kindness.

"Not your fault," Toby choked as he was hurled backwards by my pain and guilt. *If I weren't with Tony, then Jake wouldn't have gotten so angry. He might not have attacked us. It was entirely my fault!*

My stomach lurched, and I was able to bolt to the kitchen sink before everything was expelled. I finished heaving when the female cop returned with a paramedic. Tony held the blanket around my shoulders, and Toby lay on the floor muttering "not your fault" like a broken record. I was ill a second time before I slid back down to the floor, where Tony joined me.

"All better now?" the cop asked.

I nodded weakly, but the paramedic insisted on thoroughly checking over both Tony and me before he left. Sitting on the kitchen floor once more after our mini exams were done, Tony reached over and drew my head down to his chest. I slowly relaxed against him and was soothed by the sound of his heartbeat.

The female cop took a call on her cell phone. "I have to check on something outside," she said as she turned to leave, "but I still need statements from both of you." She stopped at the door. "By the way, my name is Sue. I'll be right back."

Tony nodded and held me a bit closer.

Toby slowly pulled himself off the floor. His face looked like it had been used as a golf tee; he had lumps all about both cheeks and his chin. I watched him from where I lay against Tony's chest.

"He's here, now? Isn't he?" Tony seemed to be looking where I looked.

I slowly nodded.

"I didn't fire the gun, you know?" Tony said in a shaky voice.

I pulled myself off his chest and leaned back against the cabinets. I watched Tony as he tilted his head this way and that.

"I didn't aim it. And I didn't fire it." He looked from where I had said Toby was to me. "And I was pushed down on top of you." His eyes were wide.

Toby nodded. "You weren't telling him to shoot. Tony needed to shoot Jake, or Tony was dead." Past all the bruises that grew on his mangled face, I could tell his skin was pasty white.

"Toby says he saved your life," I stated flatly.

Tony closed his eyes and put his hand up to the back of his neck like Toby always did. Seeing him do it gave me a shiver. "Well," Tony said, "it certainly wouldn't be the first time."

"So you believe me now?" I sat up a little.

Tony looked to the spot where I had told him Toby was sitting and stared long and hard. "It's hard, because I don't see him, but I know what happened tonight, and it wasn't me."

Toby pulled himself up to his knees. "Can you tell Tony something for me?"

I nodded. Tony continued to look from me to the empty space where Toby sat.

"Ask him if he remembers our last night together?"

I relayed the question. Tony said he did.

"Remember that afternoon?"

"Ya man," Tony said, seeming really tense.

"You had said that you thought we got a bad deal?" I worried a little about saying those words to Tony again. The image of him raising his hand to hit me flashed behind my eyes. But I knew that the police were just outside my door, and that gave me the confidence I needed to relay the message.

Tony closed his eyes. "Ya," he answered quietly. "Listen, I'm really sorry I tried to hit you the other night…" he said. Then to Toby, "It was you that stopped me."

Sue walked back in. She held a clipboard in her hands. She came over to us and sat down crosslegged on the floor. "Now, it's clear that what you did was an act of self-defense, and you will not be considered guilty for anything that took place in this house tonight. But I need to understand how the events unfolded so we can have it on our records, and it may be used against the attacker…"

"My brother," I said quietly.

Tony's eyes widened. Sue's face filled with pity.

"Jake Lafont is your brother?" Sue said as Tony breathed, "J-boy."

"How is he?" I asked, ignoring them, almost too afraid of the answer.

"He's high and drunk, but he'll live. You had a pretty good shot, son, clear through his thigh, missing any major arteries. He'll have a good scar to brag about while he spends his next few years in jail."

I wanted to sound shocked as I said, "He's going to jail?"

"Oh, yes, this is just the last in a long list of reasons why we have a warrant for his arrest."

"I don't want to know," I said.

"I couldn't tell you anyway." Sue shifted. "Just to let you know; he will go to jail; the only question will be is if it's for five, ten or twenty years."

I nodded numbly. Tony continued to look at me, shocked.

"Now, I need your statements please." She took them, first Tony's, then mine. I wanted to leave out the way Jake had found us, but Tony didn't seem as embarrassed by it. Sue was supportive and understanding the whole time and only asked questions when it wasn't clear what we were describing to her. Once we were done, she told us that she needed one of our parents to sign us out of the police custody, but I didn't need to worry, my mother was on her way home. Tony, on the other hand, would have to go down to the station, because his parents were unreachable. He didn't seem surprised to hear that. Toby shook his head sadly at the news.

Then Sue left us again, saying she'd return when it was time to take Tony with her. Tony seemed to stiffen at these words, and only once she had left the room did he exhale. Toby shifted around next to me and took my hand in his.

"Sweet Mariah," he said, and his words sounded like it was confession time again. I braced myself. "Yet again I have discovered another way that we seem to be connected." I closed my eyes, but I had a feeling I knew what was coming. "That bad deal…" Toby was saying, but it was Tony who took over his speech.

"Man, I thought J-boy had tracked me down for ratting him out." I looked to my left, where Tony sat. "That bad deal, that was J's," he sighed and rested his head against the cabinets.

Toby just nodded. For some reason I wasn't as mad at Toby. In fact, I wondered for the first time if it was me that should be apologizing.

"Don't suppose you know that eight other kids died in that deal?" Tony said, looking at the spot where Toby had been before.

"I thought nine had died," I said quietly.

"Ya," Tony said. "Toby here, he was the ninth."

I covered my mouth.

"Man, I don't know what I'm going to do without you, Toby," Tony lamented. I looked from Tony to Toby, noting all their similarities once more.

"You'll be better off," Toby replied, but I didn't relay it, because I didn't think Tony was in the place to hear it. Instead he gave me something new to say. "Can you tell Tony I'm trying to fix some of my mistakes?"

"Toby says that he made a lot of mistakes while he was alive, and now he's trying to repair them," I repeated.

"Like what?" Tony asked.

"Well, you for one," I said bluntly.

"What did he do so wrong with me?" Tony asked defensively.

As Toby talked, I tried to explain what he said, about a life filled with frivolous pursuits and empty successes. Tony shook his head, not able to comprehend.

Toby started to get frustrated and finally said, "Just ask him about Anna."

"Never mind then. He was wondering about this girl you hooked him up with—Anna Miller?" It came out a bit edgy, with my frustration over Tony not understanding what Toby was telling him, *or was that Toby's frustration flowing freely through me?*

Tony shook his head, his voice low. "You don't want to know about her…"

"I already do," I said flatly.

Tony shook his head again and gave his neck another rub. It was making me crazy to see him act so much like Toby. "I can't believe he told you about that," Tony whistled. "That's some pretty bad, um…stuff we did."

"At least he can see I was wrong for doing that," Toby commented sadly.

"Its funny how in death you get honest," I said, not quite understanding the way Tony was talking. Toby gave my hand an encouraging squeeze.

Tony brought his hand down from his neck and looked at me. "He's dead, he's really dead." He looked at the spot where Toby had been. "You know, I kept expecting him to show up and tell me it was all one of his huge practical jokes. He used to do all these stupid pranks, big like, and this just felt like it was his style. You know, the deal was bad, and by the end of the evening, we had figured it out. Toby was going to drive this girl home, and it would be convenient if he had this huge wreck then hid out in the woods until all this trouble blew over." Tony shook his head and licked his lips. "Even when his mom told me, at his funeral, that the dental records matched, I didn't want to believe her. She could have been in on the joke too… He was my best friend, the only one who was better than me. I mean, before he came to my school, I was hot shit, excuse me, but he was better than I was, and he had style. If he wanted to hurt someone, they hurt for the rest of their lives. There was this one kid that was causing real trouble for us, so Toby just ordered up a bunch of fire ants from Texas…"

Toby shifted uncomfortably under my weight. I cringed at the story and interrupted. "Ya, fire ants, nasty little buggers, could kill someone if they aren't stopped."

Tony fell silent and looked over to me. I could see him looking at the scabs that were still visible on my neck where the shirt didn't cover them. "I heard about a copy-cat job down at East Ridge High school. You know, I was impressed that Toby's pranks had made that big an impact."

I unconsciously scratched at one of my old wounds. "Interesting how it's not as funny to be on the receiving end."

"Great, I've left a legacy of cruelty," Toby said, dropping my hand and running his hand through his hair.

We sat in an uncomfortable silence until Sue returned. She escorted Tony from the room, and he almost looked glad to be leaving to go sit in the police station. As he was at the doorway, he looked back, scanning the room. I wondered if he was trying one last time to catch sight of his old friend, as if somehow seeing him again would make everything better.

When they were gone, I moved onto the kitchen chair and looked out the window. My mom was standing out on the front walk talking to the officer who had arrested Jake. She looked angry and animated as she spoke. Sue guided Tony past the two of them, and catching sight of him, my mom jerked her head up to me in the window. Then she talked with the officer for several more minutes.

When she finally came in, she headed straight for the liquor cabinet. Returning with a full glass, she inspected the door and wall. "Oh," she sighed heavily, "what are the neighbours going to say." She closed the door. It swung back a few inches, and a huge gap was in the place where the latch used to be. "I guess we'll be needing a new door," she said as she walked away. "I wonder if the super will be able to fix it?" but it was clear she wasn't talking to me any more.

I stared out the window. Dusk was falling and the world seemed to wrap itself in twilight. A quiet breeze made the trees sway gently, and a few leaves fell. The world seemed oblivious to any troubles. Yet inside my head, my life raged on, and I sat with the reality that it was my world that had caused Toby his greatest grief. *My* brother was responsible for his death.

The wind pushed the door open further and made the bouquet on the table flutter. It was then that my thoughts returned to Tony, to our night before it was interrupted, and I wondered how far it would have gone had we not been stopped. I held my hand to my mouth. I could taste the bile at the back of my throat. *Not again.* I silently begged my body to behave.

Toby, who was still sitting on the floor, reached up and took my hand. His warmth seemed to chase away my nausea, but I couldn't stop my thoughts from racing. Toby had said what it felt like when I… I knew that when I abandoned all reason and gave in to my pleasure, his pain just began. I was about to say something when my mom wandered back through the kitchen.

"No, it does not lock! It doesn't even close!" she yelled at someone on the phone. "Well, what do you recommend?" She stood in the archway, tapping her foot. "Then I guess that will have to do!" She pressed the off button and slammed the phone onto the stove. "We're on our own for the night," she snapped, looking over at me.

I didn't know what to say, but I was more scared of my mother than I was over having no lock on the front door for the night.

She stood staring at me through an unfocussed gaze, and then she narrowed her eyes like she was truly noticing me for the first time. Placing her hands on her hips, she asked in an icy voice, "Who was that boy they escorted from our house?"

"Um…" I stammered.

"The police said that you two were necking?"

Like a deer in the headlights, I froze. *What should I say?*

"Mariah, I hope you know how to be safe."

"What?" I asked, feeling as if I'd missed something.

"Safe!" She raised her voice. "I don't want to hear about any accidents happening!"

Accidents? I wondered. *What did she think tonight was? We had no front door! What could be more of an accident?*

Coming over and roughly pulling the chair beside me out, she threw herself into it. "What am I going to do?" she moaned, bringing her hands up to her face and starting to cry. I sat paralyzed, watching her. Her features were accented with fatigue and stress, and as she cried I realized I was even more afraid of her like this than when she was yelling at me.

"He's done for good this time," she sobbed. "No lawyer will be able to get him off now! He'll have to go to jail for at least a year or two. What am I going to do without my boy? I love him."

These last words enraged me! I leapt from my chair, letting Toby's hand drop and yelled, "Your boy KILLED someone else's boy; don't you know that!" Once I started, I didn't know how to stop. "And what about me!" I raged. "Don't you care about me? He almost killed me; he might have if Tony hadn't shot him first! You know he let his friends tie me up, and then they left me, LEFT ME! I was stuck for hours! Don't you care? Don't you care about me?" I shook, but I stayed standing, my chest heaving.

Toby was still sitting on the floor, staring up at me with an awed expression on his face. My mom slowly brought her hands down from her face, and then stood. And before I had a chance to react, she reached out and slapped me across the face. I fell back into the chair.

"Don't you ever, EVER tell such lies about your brother again. He might have been mixed up with the wrong people, but he would NEVER kill anyone, nor do I believe he would tie you up. When was this—how did you get out? Your brother is mixed up in a whole mess of trouble, and he needs our sympathy and support! As for you," she leaned toward me, the scotch on her breath making me cough, "I don't ever want to hear you complain that I don't care enough about you! I feed you, I clothe you, and I give you a nice place to live with all sorts of comforts! If anyone should feel like they are being taken advantage of, it should be me!"

She slowly straightened and went back into the other room. I heard the familiar squeak of the key in her liquor cabinet, then a clink of glass against glass. She returned with a full tumbler of booze. "If you don't like it so much here, you're welcome to leave."

I was tempted to walk out the door; I could see myself going to Cindy's and her mother taking me in. Or helping me to find new parents like Charlie had, but then I wondered if that would be the way things would happen. What if Cindy's mother didn't want me either, and she didn't want to help? Would the police come and take me away? To where?

My mother was staring at me. "Make yourself useful, or go away." She sat at the table again.

I bolted from the room and scampered down to the imagined safety of my room. Then I placed my chair against the door and fell onto my bed.

"I am constantly amazed by you," Toby said. He sat next to me and started to rub my back. "If anyone had an excuse to be mean and unkind to everyone around them, it would be you, yet you are the most loving, caring, considerate girl I've ever met." He gently touched my face. It still stung from the force of my mother's hand.

"I've told you some fairly gruesome things about myself, yet you still accept me and are kind towards me. And I've seen your compassion for Tony…"

The mention of his name made me shiver. "Why did you let him in tonight?" I moaned. "Didn't you know I wasn't able to stop myself?" I punched my pillow.

"I'm sorry, Mariah," Toby said, taking his hand off my cheek. "I am so sorry. I got confused. The longer I'm here, the harder I find it to be sure about what I'm doing. I wanted to find a way to make things right with Anna, and I knew Tony could help. And I guess I just wanted to talk to him…" Toby looked at me and shook his head. "I miss him."

"Do you really?" I asked, sitting up.

"Part of me does."

Suddenly, and for the first time Toby had come into my life, I felt like I couldn't trust him. "But why did you open the door?" I asked more forcefully.

"I…" Toby stammered.

"You are the one who told me how sly your old friend is! You are the one who insisted that I never let him into my house. You said he would only use me! Did you think he had changed?"

Toby shook his head and rubbed his neck.

I felt like he was avoiding answering my question, so I sat up straighter and raised my voice. "Did you set me up?" Toby still didn't answer. "You knew I wouldn't be able to resist! You knew Tony would take advantage! Was I your final gift to Tony?" I shook with rage. *I was used! Toby had tricked me!*

"No!" Toby's voice cracked. He looked ghost-white. "No, please don't think that about me! That was the live me—I'm not that guy any more!"

"Well then, what is it?"

"I don't know! I don't know." Toby had both his hands up and was rubbing his neck so hard, his skin turned bright pink. "Please believe me, I didn't want Tony to touch you like that. I felt so sick that I fell to the ground in pain! And I did know that that's exactly what he would do… But there was something else. Something bigger. Something more important that had to happen, and I had to let Tony in because of that."

"Telling Anna you're sorry was more important that my safety tonight?" I accused.

"No, Mariah. Not Anna. I thought at the time she was important to me, and telling her I'm sorry is important, but not more than you. That wasn't it; there was something else going on. I think... I think I had to let Tony in so he could save you from Jake."

I was baffled. "How did you know Jake was going to come home tonight?"

"I didn't know at the time, but I felt something important was happening." He took my hands in his. "Do you remember how I used to get a sense about things? Well, I haven't noticed it so much lately, but tonight I just felt like Tony needed to be in the house... I didn't understand it, but I couldn't stop myself. You can't know how hard it was for me. I had opened the door, and I wanted to slam it shut in his face. Then he gave you those flowers, and you were hooked, I could tell. He touched you, and I felt like I had pins for blood. I hurt everywhere. Then you went to the living room, and I fell on the floor. I've never experienced pain like that before, not even when my car crashed and exploded the night I died." The car on the news the night Toby came to me flashed into my mind. The flames were several feet high. *He remembered it now?*

"Then suddenly everything changed. I could feel Jake approaching, and I knew he'd be violent. But I also knew that I had the key to save both you and Tony."

I sat back looking at him. He still had a grey tinge to his face. *Could I believe him?* I spent an eternity in that moment...then I leaned forward and hugged him. "I'm glad you came," I said into his chest, "though when you said you'd save me, I had no idea that meant my life would get harder."

We both laughed at this. After that I got ready for bed, aware that my mother was still up prowling the house, refilling her drink and lamenting over her baby boy that would now be in jail. As the evening wore on, I had a crushing realization: my mother would never get it. *She would never be able to love me like I needed. She would never truly see me for who I was.* But as I vowed that I wasn't going to let that make me feel bad about myself any more, something wonderful happened. All the bruises from Toby's face seemed to disappear in that instant.

DAY 15 Monday...

THE NEXT DAY I GOT UP EARLY. Toby was already awake, sitting on the bed looking at me. "What?" I asked as I stretched.

"Have I ever told you how nice it is for me to be with you?" he smiled.

I shrugged.

"You see, I never had a girlfriend in life," he continued. "I never thought of girls that way. I'm just glad I get to experience it now."

I made a face and got up. Our mornings had become quite routine: brush teeth, get dressed with Toby's back turned or his eyes closed, fix hair, apply make-up, go upstairs and clean the mess from the day before, walk to school. Of course, the mess from the previous day was the cupboard I'd pulled out of the wall and the several glasses my mother had used. I returned the contents to the cupboard then found the gun, taped it back to the counter and put the drawer in its place. This almost erased the event from having happened. Then I picked up the blankets, refolded them and put them back in the living room. The only evidence left was the hole in the door and the smaller one in the archway.

I went over to it and put my finger to it. "This would be the shot that went through Jake's leg," I said.

Toby nodded.

"I'm glad you saved us," I said, not taking my eyes off the hole. It felt very special. "And I'm glad you didn't hurt Jake too badly."

Toby smiled. "He is your brother, and as much trouble as he was, you care deeply for him. And in his own way, he loves you." I nodded dully.

Just then there was a knock at the door, which caused it to creak open.

"Anyone home?" Cindy asked timidly.

"Come on in," I said as I stood up.

She rounded the corner with a look of concern and intrigue on her face. "What happened here?" Her hair was pulled back into a ponytail, and she had on a shirt with pictures of bugs all over it.

I didn't want to talk about it while I was still in the house, but once we were on our way to school, I told her most of it. I left out the part about me and Tony making out. *Was I betraying her by omitting it?* Toby didn't say anything about that. It took us almost the whole way to the school for me to tell her the whole account.

Cindy looked horrified, but finally she managed to say, "No wonder you like it at my house so much! And you know you're welcome to come visit or stay whenever you need. I know my mom won't mind."

We went into the school and started our day. Cindy and Rayla walked me to homeroom. Fifteen minutes later, Elijah took me to first period. As the bell rang, he was out of his seat so fast, I hardly had time to stand.

"May I escort you, milady?" he asked with a bow.

Toby laughed. Knowing I'd be safer this way, I swallowed the uncomfortable knot in the pit of my stomach and agreed.

As we entered the crowded halls, Elijah put his hand on my back in a protective way. I felt myself stiffen. Toby tried to help me relax, but I just couldn't. Luckily Elijah didn't seem to notice.

"So what did you get up to yesterday?" he asked as we weaved our way though the packed corridors.

"Shoot," I replied, "not much." Toby laughed so hard, he nearly tripped. Elijah nodded, not knowing the hidden meaning, and then we'd made it to my first class.

After that class was over, Dan met me at the door. All this kindness was starting to wear on me, but Toby told me to calm down. After that class, Charlie met up with me. She tried to make it fun. "Let's just pretend you're a celebrity." Then she asked me questions about my upcoming movie. It worked; I relaxed a bit and even giggled as she walked me to third period. When the lunch bell rang, the whole gang showed up miming that they had cameras, and Rayla impersonated a reporter trying to take an interview all the way to the office. It was so fun, I had a hard time saying goodbye.

As I turned toward the office, happiness seeped out of me like water through a sieve.

I was given several things to photocopy. Toby stood against the wall, deep in thought. "There was this one kid." He rubbed his neck. "I used to tease him relentlessly."

I used the photocopy machine as an excuse to avoid giving Toby my full attention.

"He ended up committing suicide." Glancing at him, I saw tears trickling down his cheeks. I busily unstuck a jam. "But I wonder, I just wonder if he had good friends…" Out of the corner of my eye, I saw him wipe away his tears. "He didn't have friends, that's what made him an easy target, and I made damn sure no one would befriend him."

I stayed quiet. *What could I say?* I was soon finished. It only took fifteen minutes; I was getting exceedingly good at this job. Standing in the hall, just outside the office, Dan's deep voice echoed in my head. "Ms. Lafont, you wait right here until we can get your bodyguards to escort you." I had agreed, but they were nowhere in sight, and after a few minutes, Miss Rose came out and ordered me away. So, taking a deep breath, I headed in that direction. *I could get to the lunchroom alone.*

I turned down one hall, then another, wondering what way my friends would be coming to get me. As I got to the bottom of a flight of stairs, I looked up the hall to see Sara headed towards me. With my pulse quickening, I doubled back to go up the stairs, but I heard someone, and looking up I saw Marika. I was trapped. The only retreat I had was the girls' washroom. I ducked in, even though I had a feeling it was right where they wanted me to go.

Effie stood leaning against the stalls, staring down at a well-creased piece of paper in her hands. She looked up lazily when I entered. I could hear the blood rushing in my ears, and I worried I'd have another panic attack and fall to the ground helpless.

Toby took my hand in his. "Just breathe," he said, trying to calm me. "It's going to be alright." *Did he know that? Or was he just saying it?*

I felt anything but alright. Visions of Toby picking on some poor kid danced in front of me. Yet he squeezed my hand tighter, and I did relax, if only a little, and I immediately started to feel my breath come more easily.

Effie held a note out to me; I hesitated then reached for it. Drawing it closer, I realized the writing was mine. It was the note I'd used to communicate with Toby those first few days he'd been with me. I looked from the paper to Effie and, for the first time, I didn't feel as intimidated by her.

She wore a fearful expression. Her eyes were wide, and she looked pale. "Explain yourself!" she demanded. Her voice gave away her true feelings, and I stood up straighter, drawing my shoulders back.

For whatever reason, I had the upper hand, and I liked it. "Explain what?" I asked, and I was proud that my voice was loud and strong.

"Who were you writing this note to?" she demanded, but somehow her voice didn't carry as much threat as it usually did.

I looked down at the note again. I hadn't written it in any particular order, but trying to see it from Effie's eyes, I silently read: "What did I miss with Effie and her friends? Why would she do that? Are you sure about that? What do you mean by 'wow' him? Do you remember anything else? How do you know this, and are you sure it's true? I really need to hear it again, because it would make me feel better. You know how much Effie hurt me, don't you? I trust your judgment completely, so you tell me what's first. Absolutely, and won't Effie be shocked…" Turning the paper over, I read, "By the way, did I thank you for saving me from my locker," and "What sort of things did I do that made him laugh? Do you see or get those feelings from me too?" At the top corner in printing that was my smallest and was too smudged to read properly was my first note: "Not going to talk to you, don't want to look insane, but smile, this isn't your life."

I could not imagine what Effie was thinking as I turned the note over and over again in my hands, but it could be mistaken to incriminate her…

"Who did you write that letter to?" she asked again.

I was at a loss for an answer.

Toby, who stood next to me, had been reading the note himself. Narrowing his eyes, he looked over at Effie. "She's terrified that you know something about her, something she doesn't want anyone to know. She hasn't even shared this with her friends. Tell her you were writing to Tony."

I didn't feel all that comfortable telling a lie; after all, she could easily find out that I had made it up, but I could see no better way out, so I answered flatly, "Tony Dyphan."

Effie's eyes widened, and she seemed to fall back against the stall. "Tony Dyphan?"

I nodded.

"Did he tell you…?"

"Don't worry," I said quickly, cutting Effie off. For some strange reason, I didn't want to know what she was so terrified about me knowing. Just that she thought I knew it was enough for me. Effie swallowed hard a few times, and I handed her back the note.

"I'm going to go now," I said feeling very powerful. Effie nodded.

Toby wore a huge grin of satisfaction. I walked out of the washroom, passing Sara and Marika, who seemed to be standing guard. They rushed in as I left. One let out a small cry of shock, but neither one tried to call me back. I felt no reason to rush. I wanted to savour this victory, so I took my time walking the rest of the way to the cafeteria.

"You know, that was a really nice thing you did back there," Toby said, keeping pace with me. "You could have used what she was about to tell you to ruin her life." I tried to shrug casually. "This is what I was telling you about the other day. You are kinder than people deserve." I smiled, feeling good about myself. "Even though she's made your life miserable, you've taken the higher road. That shows the quality of your character, and no one can take that from you."

I felt stronger for the rest of the day. I was able to go from class to class with my head held high. When I met up with my friends in the cafeteria, they were blown away by my confidence. I never told them about the strange encounter with Effie. They didn't need to know. Instead I enjoyed the food Cindy had bought for me with the money I had given her in the morning and simply said that today had been a very good day.

I shared my last class of the day with Effie and Sara. I saw them talking from time to time. Toby seemed amused by their chatter, but he kept what they were saying to himself, explaining that it was nothing really. I believed him. I knew that nothing they were talking about could hurt me any more. That knowledge made it easier to concentrate on the lesson and think more clearly about my work. *We had a pop quiz, and for the first time, I got one hundred percent!*

Dan and Elijah met up with me outside my class, and we walked to our lockers, and then hooked up with the rest of the gang. As we headed out of the school, I did a double take at the corner. Tony stood there. Seeing me, he smiled and walked over.

"I was so worried I'd missed you." He pulled me towards him for a friendly hug.

I felt conflicted. I was happy to see him again, and surprised. I looked to Toby and wondered if he thought this was alright, and then I caught sight of my friends, and the looks on some of their faces made me worry.

"Guys, this is Tony," I explained, "a friend of mine." I introduced him to each of the gang. He politely said hello to each. Elijah seemed less than happy to be meeting him. And I kept checking with Toby, but he didn't have anything to say.

"Listen, I was wondering if you wanted a walk home?" Tony said when all the introductions where done.

I agreed, and saying farewell to Rayla, Charlie, Cindy, Teb, Elijah and Dan, I started to walk to the end of the block with Tony. I could feel their eyes following us until we turned down a side street. Tony walked at a medium pace, but he didn't say anything for quite a while.

I kept trying to figure out what Toby was thinking; he seemed distracted by his old pal. Finally, more out of not knowing what else to say, I asked, "Did it take long for your parents to pick you up from the police station last night?"

Tony let out a dry chuckle and rubbed his neck. "Not long." I could hear the sarcasm in his tone. "Just until lunch time today."

"So you had to stay overnight there?" I asked, horrified.

Tony slowed his stride. "Don't worry, beautiful, it's not the first time I've had to spend the night there."

Toby nodded with a sad expression on his face.

"I don't see how that makes it any better," I replied.

Tony stopped and smiled at me. "She is a real sweet thing," he said, his eyes darting everywhere in hopes of catching sight of his old pal.

Toby chuckled and agreed, "You *are* sweet."

I smiled.

"Did he just say something to you?" Tony asked, and I told him that Toby had agreed with him.

Tony started down the street again. "It gave me some time to think," he confessed. "I spent a lot of it recounting all the crazy, stupid, mean things Toby and I did."

"Oh, ya?" I asked. "Did you come to any conclusions?"

"Just a few." Tony reached out and took my hand, and a small tingle raced through my arm. Toby didn't look happy about it, but he still didn't say a word. "If Toby's advice is for me to change my life, then I better find a new way to live."

"Do you believe him?" I asked, turning to Toby.

Toby narrowed his eyes, like he was trying to see something far off. "I think he believes what he's saying."

"What'd he say?" Tony asked, squeezing my hand. *Was he nervous?*

"He believes you," I answered. "And he should know; he has the ability to see into people and know if what they say is true."

"Great superpower."

Then, with me in the middle of the conversation, relaying most of what Toby said, the boys recalled the better times of their friendship. It had started when they were younger, more innocent—at least Tony was. Toby had been a manipulator, even back then, he admitted. But in the beginning, they had hung out and generally had good clean fun. Then they'd started to get bored, and that's when they began to play pranks for amusement. As the years went by, the pranks got bigger and meaner, and eventually more deadly.

As we neared my house, the mood became somber. Toby stopped with my row of houses in sight. I had to stop too. Tony, who was still holding my hand, also stopped.

"What's the matter?" he asked, looking at me.

I shrugged. "It's Toby."

Toby looked from Tony to me, and at our hands clasped together. "Before I will let him into your house again, Tony has to promise that he won't try anything physical."

"What?" Tony asked again.

"Toby says you have to keep your hands to yourself if you are going to come in."

Tony let my hand drop. "I promise," he said.

I felt disappointed. It had felt nice to just hold his hand, and I think Tony felt the same way too, but he crossed his arms in front of his chest and looked about as if to show Toby he meant what he said.

"Alright," Toby said and started towards my house.

As we came to the front door, Tony stopped and whistled. "That's from the police; I had—well Toby had shot Jake, and they blew the latch off to get in. I can't believe they left it broken."

I shrugged. Tony seemed distracted still, but eventually he tore himself away and came to sit at the dinner table. I was in the middle chair with a boy on either side of me. I felt nervous, which caused me to make silly mistakes; when I was filling a glass of water, I dropped it for no reason. Then I tripped over my own feet as I was trying to walk over to my chair. Tony caught me but let go quickly once I was standing again.

Tony held his hands up like it was a robbery. "Keeping my hands to myself."

Toby chuckled loudly, and I let Tony know that.

Tony seemed a little nervous too. He fidgeted with one of the petals on the flowers that still sat in the centre of the table. "You know, even before I believed that Toby had come to you, I thought there was something different about you," he said without looking at me. "You know, at the bowling alley, even that first night I met you. You're the first girl I'd flirted with since Toby's death, and it felt different, but I thought that was because Toby wasn't there, and I didn't have as much competition."

"But he still treated you like he would have any other girl until he believed I was here," Toby accused.

I relayed that message.

Tony nodded. "Ya." He brought his hand to the back of his neck. "And if I wasn't sure that Toby is here right now, I might have started something again." He crossed his arms as if he were holding himself back. "Mariah." Tony's dark eyes filled with remorse, the way I'd seen Toby's look so often. "I know you could never forgive me for what I was trying to do. And I don't want you to. But I have to apologize honestly." He stopped to take a breath while staring at the empty seat. *In his mind, could he see his dead friend encouraging him?* "On Friday, I wore my school ring. I only wear it when I plan to score, big time." He looked away, and I stared at the flowers he'd brought me. "It was this challenge that Toby and I had…" Toby covered his eyes with one hand. "A race to see how many girls we could…"

"I don't want to hear it." I whispered, bringing my hand to my mouth. *I was to be one of those girls.*

Tony fell silent.

"If the girl slept with us, and somewhere in the deal we convinced them to kiss our school ring, then we considered ourselves their masters. We were racing to see who was master over the most girls." Toby said flatly.

"I told you I didn't want to hear it!" I snapped at Toby.

"I'm so sorry," Tony said softly. "I understand if you never forgive me."

Tears were falling down my face. "It's not you, or Toby that I'm mad at, it's me!"

"What!" Tony sputtered. "No!" Toby yelled.

"Yes," I answered. "I knew you were bad, bad news and trouble, and even if I didn't know that, I had Toby telling me every few seconds. But even though I knew it, I still, so desperately, wanted to be with you." *What did that make me?*

We sat quietly for a while. No one knew what to say. It was Toby who broke the silence. "I need to get a hold of that girl, the one you introduced me to. The one I raped." I relayed his words in a whisper.

Tony swallowed hard. "I didn't know Toby would do that… I didn't even find out until later, and I was shocked, really I was. I mean, Stace is an unbalanced girl, and I thought Toby could have some fun with her… But not like that. I figured she would give in easy, she was so needy…" *just like me,* "…and she liked Toby."

"I'm sorry," I interrupted, "Stace? Toby said her name was Anna."

"Na, her name is Stacy; Stacy Ann Miller, formerly Perts."

My breath caught. Stacy Perts, my former best friend.

Toby closed his eyes and nodded. I could imagine him comparing my memories of Stacy to his. "What are the odds?" he asked. *What was she doing out here?*

Tony answered before I even asked. "She moved into our neighbourhood about eight months ago. Her father met mine, and we were introduced.

She's home schooled and didn't have any friends, so her mother thought it would be nice if I helped her to meet some people. I found her kind of annoying. She kept coming over like we were best buds. She's awkward, like she's not good at figuring out when to keep her mouth shut. Her mother had remarried, and she went on and on about her old dad, how much she missed him. I told her once that she should run away back to him. Well, I got really fed up. Then she met Toby once and was obviously into him. So Toby says I should hook them up—he could have some fun with her. I felt bad when I heard what kind of fun Toby had had, but I didn't really lose any sleep over it." Tony rubbed the back of his neck, but I stopped paying attention, as a flood of memories came back, with my old friend the star. Good was overridden by bad, as I actually felt sympathy or caring seep from me. Toby turned green.

Tony continued, oblivious to what I was feeling. But Toby was all too aware; he coughed and wheezed under the pressure of my thoughts.

Stacy, my old friend Stacy, *the girl who had sold me out to everyone else!* I thought back on the pain she would have felt as Toby forced himself upon her, and suddenly I wasn't sad for her, I was glad. *She got what she deserved!*

"You know, I haven't seen her since then; I guess my plan worked." Tony gave a sad chuckle. "I had wanted her to stop coming around, and she did." I recognized the remorse, discovered perhaps for the first time. "We could go see her together, tomorrow. I probably should apologize too. I mean, it was me who set her up." I could hear the regret building in Tony's voice, *but I didn't care! She deserved it.*

Toby fell to the floor.

"What's wrong?" Tony asked, noticing that I was distracted.

"Nothing," I said, watching Toby turn several shades of purple like he couldn't breathe.

"Please, Mariah, this isn't like you!" Toby pleaded, but I wasn't in the mood to listen. "You have a good heart; don't fall into the trap of bitterness and hate."

I felt Tony put his hand on mine, and I turned back to him. "Don't tell me nothing—I can see in your face that something is wrong."

I shrugged, trying to pretend that he was wrong. Having Tony's hand on mine brought back a strong desire to kiss, and without thinking, I leaned towards him. Tony responded to my advance and kissed me back, but only for a few seconds, then he jumped out of his chair and raised his hands again.

"No," he said curtly. "I mean, don't get me wrong, beautiful, I like you... I really like you, and yesterday I would have taken you right here without a second thought. But like I said, I've been thinking, and Toby is right, I need to change."

Toby writhed on the floor, not conscious of anything that was taking place now, but I didn't mention that. "I'm sorry," I said, realizing that I felt awful about Stacy and had used Tony as a distraction from my feelings.

"You know, I think it's time for me to leave," Tony said. Before I could say anything else, he did. The door creaked back open, and I heard him make his way down the steps.

I looked down at Toby. "Mariah?" he begged.

"No!" I said, remembering how mean Stacy had been to me. "She deserves every sadness in her life now!"

It was hard, but I managed to drag Toby around the house. First he stayed on the floor of the kitchen while I made my dinner. Then on the floor in the living room, as I tried to act like nothing was bothering me and watched TV. And finally he lay on my floor when I prepared to go to sleep.

His speech had become slurred, but he tried one last time. "Stacy doesn't deserve this," he managed to convey. "How come you can be so nice to Effie, but you can't bring yourself to show the same kindness to your old friend?"

I sat awake late into the evening pondering this. Stacy had been the one who started it. *She betrayed me.* Effie was never my friend in the first place. And as the night wore on, I started to realize that I blamed Stacy for never having another friend since her. If she hadn't turned her back on me, I might have been able to trust new friends that tried to reach out to me. She was the one I blamed for every misery in my life, and I wasn't going to let her off that easy!

DAY 16 Tuesday...

By the time morning had come, I was set in my convictions. *I would never go to see Stacy, and that was that.* I didn't feel sorry for her one bit, and nothing was going to change my mind.

Reaching over to my alarm, I clicked it off and hopped out of bed. I had made it one step into the hall when an invisible wall stopped me. Turning back, I saw Toby lying on the ground, shaking and convulsing.

"I'm not going to see her!" I exclaimed at his non-responsive body. "If I have to, I'll stay in my room, but I won't go to see her." He didn't respond. He shivered and held himself in a tight ball, his eyes slammed shut.

Unfortunately, that is exactly what I ended up having to do. Toby had become so heavy, I was barely able to move him so I could use the washroom. I was stuck, not able to move more than five feet away from him. He might as well have been a fallen statue as he lay cold, hard and heavy on the floor. I did have a shower, but I couldn't get clean clothes out of my room, so I ended up putting my PJ's back on and sitting in the hallway. Looking past my open door, I was able to watch the numbers on my clock mark off the time as it slowly trickled by.

Over the course of the day, I heard the phone ring several times, but I couldn't answer even if I'd wanted to. With each passing minute, I became angrier and angrier with Stacy. *This was all her fault!* If she hadn't been so mean to me, I wouldn't be stuck here.

At ten in the morning, I yelled at Toby until my voice was hoarse. "I'm not going. You've picked the wrong girl! She was the worst to me; she deserves to be miserable!" But he didn't budge, and when I touched him, he was cold as ice.

At half past twelve, my stomach was growling. I wanted something to eat. "It's not fair." I moaned. "Why me? Why her? I could have gone to any one else. Why couldn't it be a complete stranger? She hurt me so much. She was my friend! Why are you asking this of me? You know how hurt I am!"

Again it was no use. I sat feeling my anger and resolve ebb, but I couldn't relent. I crossed my arms and rested my head on the wall behind me.

Finally, just after four, I broke down sobbing. "I can't go! I can't bear to see her face again. Any time anything bad happens, I see her. She was supposed to be my best friend..."

That's how Tony found me. I hadn't heard him knock. I was too far away. But when he heard my sobs through the broken door, he came rushing in and down the stairs. I looked up as he rounded the corner, and on seeing me, he fell to his knees and hugged me. "What's wrong?" he asked.

I started to explain everything. "Before I moved here, Stacy and I were about as close as you and Toby."

Tony got up to get me some Kleenex, then came back to sit beside me and held my hand as I continued.

"We did everything together, we told each other everything. Then, when my father left I was so sad, and I couldn't explain it to her. She didn't understand, and we drifted apart, I guess. Then one day she was trying to show off to the tough kids, and she made up a mean chant about me. Well, everyone loved it, and we've never been friends since." Tears spilled out from my eyes and flowed down my face. "She got worse after that—she started rumors about me, telling everyone all my secrets, and..."

Tony didn't say anything, but Toby slowly sat up and rubbed his face. His hair was a mess, and he continued to have small tremors, but he was conscious.

"It's not fair." I sniffled and wiped my nose for the umpteenth time. "She's the one who hurt me—why do I have to help her?"

"Life isn't fair," Tony agreed.

I sat up straighter, pulling my hand away from his. Both boys looked at me, but I crossed my arms in front of my chest. *Life was not fair.*

"If life was fair, it would be me in juvenile hall, not Eric."

"Who's Eric?" I asked.

Toby responded. "The night I died, we convinced him to let us use his house for the party." I got the impression that when Toby said convinced, he meant forced. "Ask Tony why he's in juvie." I did.

"The drugs. He was too afraid to tell anyone that it was us who brought them into his house, so he took the rap. Man," Tony said, "He's on death watch: he's tried to take his life twice."

Toby looked sickened. I felt a pang in my chest.

"I need to go see Eric, talk to him." Then looking from where Toby should be to me, Tony asked me meekly, "Can you come with me? I'm afraid to go alone." *Tony was afraid?* "Mariah, just being around you makes me braver." *How?*

"Please," Toby's voice chimed in, "I need to see him too."

Both boys' deep brown eyes were upon me, begging. *They needed me... I was important to them!* I nodded slowly. "I guess I can. His name is Eric? I don't think I know anyone by that name."

Toby insisted that I needed to eat, and Tony suggested that we go out for food. I liked that idea; I had been stuck in my house all day. So I went to my room and got dressed.

On the way, Tony asked, "So you're still planning to go visit Stacy, right?"

I sighed. "Ya," I said, still dreading the idea. "It's what I have to do."

"Alright then." Tony kept his eyes on the road. "I bumped into her mother, and she says that Stacy is busy tonight, so how about Thursday? I have bowling league tomorrow."

How about never, I thought, but I agreed.

Tony took me out to a quaint little Italian restaurant.

It was a small place, serving no more than fifty people at one time. The tables were small, and there were candles in the middle.

I let Tony order our meals. While we waited, I nibbled on a soft sourdough roll. I never knew food could taste so good.

"So how does it work when you need privacy?" Tony asked.

"Privacy?"

"Ya," he said, "like when you are getting dressed or other things."

"Oh." I blushed. "Well he usually just turns around, or he'll close his eyes."

"But honestly," Tony asked Toby, "you do peek, right?"

"Well, if his eyes are closed, he goes invisible, so he can't pretend, or I'd know," I explained.

"Where's the fun in that?" Tony kidded, leaning back in his chair. "I mean if you are going to have to live out eternity stuck to a beautiful girl, you should at least get to enjoy yourself."

"There is no fun in death," Toby said.

"He's not stuck to me for eternity. Just long enough to fix up some things." I didn't feel like saying anything about how I had needed Toby more than he needed me. That time seemed so long ago, even though it had been last week.

"Not forever?" Tony looked crestfallen.

I shook my head. *What had he thought? He could keep his best friend through me?*

"Then what happens to him after?"

"I don't know," Toby said.

"He goes away." I had to stifle a sniffle. *It still hurt to think of him not being with me, but the idea wasn't as scary any more.*

Our food came, and it was delicious. Tony had ordered for me—pasta with chicken and pineapple in a light cream sauce. I would never have suspected something so strange could taste so wonderful before now. He also got a spinach salad with mushrooms. I loved all of it.

Tony explained that he used to be a busboy at this place, and he had fallen in love with the food, but he had never taken anyone here before, not even Toby. "It just didn't feel cool enough," he said, rubbing his neck.

"Would you tell him I'm sorry again?" Toby asked.

Tony looked away as if he were about to cry, but when he looked back, his eyes were clear. "It's alright, man." He shrugged. "Part of it was me. I was never confident enough to stand up to you. I thought you were the best, and that blinded me to everything I sacrificed to be your friend. You know, two days ago I would never have believed what a horrible friend Toby really was, but now I'm beginning to understand, a little."

Tony told me about his life; his mother had left two years before. She'd wanted him to come with her, but Tony felt like someone needed to stay and take care of his dad. When she'd left, he and his father had moved, and Tony didn't like his new home. I could tell that he resented his mother for leaving. His dad could be a great guy. He was self-employed and made good money, but he also had a drug habit and sometimes would go on long binges, so Tony never quite knew what to expect. But he loved his father, who would make it up by buying him almost anything he asked for.

Tony shook his head, "Oh man, this is the most honest I've been with anyone in my life. I've never even told Larry or Toby half of this stuff…" He ran his hand through his hair. "Of course, you've got the human lie detector with you, so I'd be dog meat if I wasn't telling the truth. I don't know why I told you all this. Hopefully you won't hold it against me."

"Have you noticed that when you are honest, it makes you feel closer to that person?" I asked, based on my own experience. "You see, Toby was the first person I was honest with, though let's face it, I had no choice. Now I feel completely connected with him, but of course, I am. And now that you've been truly honest with me, I sorta feel that way with you." *This should be the time where Tony kisses me…* I knew it should, but he wouldn't. He was staring hard at the spot where Toby was supposed to be.

Turning to me, he cocked his head to the side and looked deep into my eyes. "Well," he answered, his voice sounding strained at first, "alright, and boy, do I feel better, somehow." He smiled, and I felt a passion burning in me for him.

I shared more of my history with him; I told him about my dad leaving, and how I felt rejected, my brother and how my mother thought he could do no wrong. Tony scoffed at that. I even shared how I seemed to suddenly put on an enormous amount of weight, and my troubles with Effie and the kids at school. Tony listened and really seemed to care. *I got the impression this was a first for him.*

I was sad when it was time to go home. I didn't want the night to end, even though we had made a plan to get together again on Thursday. He dropped me off at the parking lot, and though he leaned over to kiss me, he stopped, glanced at the rear seat where Toby sat, and said in a choked voice, "Goodnight, beautiful."

In my heart, Thursday couldn't come fast enough. Walking home, Toby stayed quiet. I got to the front door and stopped. It had been replaced, and I didn't have a key. I knocked, filled with apprehension. *Had my mother locked me out? Where would I go...?* Then I thought of Cindy's. My heart fell as my mother yanked the door open and pointed to the kitchen. I went in and took a seat. She stood in a business suit, her hair pulled back into a tight bun.

"You skipped school today!" she bellowed.

"I wasn't feeling good this morning," I answered.

"Well, you seem to be doing much better now!" She started into a long rant about my behavior and her disappointment in me. I sat politely and listened. Toby kept arguing my mother's putdowns, saying, "We know that's not true" or "Do you hear what she's saying? It's ridiculous". It was amusing, and I didn't feel as bad as I usually did sitting there. It was like I was watching a movie about someone else's mother—even when she called me a witch and a slut. Once she was done, I went to my room. I didn't feel that upset, and I certainly didn't feel bad about myself.

"I'm sorry you got into trouble," Toby said, sitting at the foot of my bed.

"Well," I said, crawling under the sheets, "I did skip school. And I didn't have a good excuse."

"I'm still sorry." Toby grabbed my foot.

"But it was my own stubbornness that caused this grief. You told me before not to get hung up on revenge, but I didn't listen to you, again. I deserve the consequences of my actions."

"You know, it may just be that you don't need me any more." I felt his hand tighten around my foot as he said this.

"It's possible that I might be getting to that place," I answered and shifted around in my bed so I could snuggle next to him. "But I'm glad you are here."

"So am I."

DAY 17

Wednesday...

The next day, I left for school at my usual time. When I saw Cindy coming up the block, I rushed toward her. *I'd forgotten my friends.*

"What happened to you yesterday?" she asked.

"I was sorta sick. Did you come to get me?" I worried aloud.

"No, but I tried to call. No one answered. I had a dentist appointment."

I felt a twinge of regret. My stubbornness had cost me time with my friends. Shaking my head clear of this thought and vowing never to let revenge get me again, I asked, "So how'd it go?"

"Oh, it was fun!" Cindy said, but she didn't sound like she meant it. "I've got three cavities, and my mom said that I'm not allowed any more sweets until my next check-up."

We talked all the way to school. As the day progressed, I noticed that I paid less and less attention to Toby. He was truly just becoming a ghost that followed me around. I had friends, and I liked them. I was still escorted to each of my classes, and even if I wasn't completely comfortable, I enjoyed it, and we all laughed a lot... It felt nice to be able to have fun.

Arriving in the office for my lunchtime detention, Miss Rose looked surprised to see me. "Oh," she exclaimed over her sandwich, "Ms. LaKey thought you were home sick again, so she didn't leave anything for you to photocopy." I was able to go to lunch with my friends.

I bolted from the office and ran up the hall to catch up with them. Everyone celebrated my small victory. Sitting at our table, surrounded by my friends, I felt like nothing could go wrong. Then Toby tapped me on the shoulder. I turned a bit to see what he wanted. He pointed out a scene across the cafeteria. It made my heart race.

"Who's that?" I asked Rayla as I watched a girl I'd never seen before being invited to sit at Effie's table by Sara.

The girl had square-shaped glasses that were too big for her face and made her whole head look boxy. Her hair was a mousy brown and fell limply about her face. But what I noticed most was the way she walked and held herself like she didn't want to take up too much space.

Toby leaned close to me and said, "She reminds me of you the night we met." I shivered; I had looked that pathetic, that hopeless. The way she acted was better than any "kick-me" sign someone could have taped to her back. And that's just the way I had been. *No wonder! Was I still like that?* Before I could try and ask, Toby said, "You have come a long way!"

"That's the new girl," Rayla answered, "Mary? No. May... May something." She joined me now as we watched Effie's game played out.

They had snubbed May yesterday at lunch hour, I was told, so today was the day to degrade her. Sara had invited her to come and sit, but as May sat down, Effie and all her hyenas stood up and moved to sit at the next table. Tomorrow would bring outright hostility. I remembered it well. That's how they made sure you knew your social status in the school. You knew it, and so did everyone else. Toby shook his head. May was the loser with no friends, and now no one would ever think of trying to be nice to her. It would mean them risking their own social status!

I was sickened. May was now sitting at an empty table, trying not to look too panicked, while kids from the tables all around her quietly laughed. I stood up.

"What are you doing?" Cindy exclaimed as I climbed to my feet.

"This isn't right," I answered and started over to where May sat. I was glad I had Toby beside me, because I didn't feel as brave as I was pretending to be.

When I got to May's table, I said, "Come and sit with us."

"No, thank you," May replied, and I could tell that she thought it was another trick.

"Really," I insisted, "me and my friends would be glad to have you at our table."

But she wouldn't budge. *I didn't blame her!* So I sat down with her. I hadn't planned on doing that; this side of the lunchroom was way out of my territory, but I just felt compelled to be with her. It didn't take long for Rayla and the rest to figure out what I was doing, and they came over to sit with May and me. Each one looked almost as nervous as I felt. However, we had stopped Effie in her tracks. Though we sat victorious, we weren't as loud or buoyant as we usually were at our usual table. Effie leered at me once or twice, trying to intimidate me, but I glared back. After all, she still thought I knew that secret about her.

It turned out that the girl's name was May-Sue, but she hated it. So we dubbed her "Just May." That made her laugh, and it was contagious. By the end of the day, we all had a new friend. After school we headed to the ice cream parlour and ordered an Earthquake for our victory celebration: ten scoops of ice cream with ten toppings!

"That's so cool the way we annihilated Effie today!" Teb said. "You know, I think we could take her! We could really get her back! After all, there are eight of us now and only three of them!"

Most of the gang agreed, but I had a swooping sensation in the pit of my stomach. I looked at Toby, who stood next to the table watching me; no doubt fearful I'd give in to this trap of revenge.

"I don't know, guys," I said softly. They were all discussing tactics, but they stopped when I spoke.

"What don't you know about?" Rayla exclaimed. "She's been miserable to you. She nearly killed you with those poisonous ants!"

"I know," I said softly. *Was I going to lose my friends over this?* "If we do this, what makes us better than her?"

"We'd be doing if for the right reasons!" Charlie said forcefully. "The way she is isn't right! Someone's gotta teach her a lesson."

"Yes," I said, still keeping my voice quiet, "but repaying meanness with meanness may not be the solution." I was trying not to let this fear of rejection cloud what I knew to be the truth. Toby nodded encouragingly.

Charlie remained adamant that getting even was the only way to truly make her pay. It was Just May who came to my rescue. She was sitting at the end of the booth, and she stood up, picking up her sweater and starting to put it on.

"You're not leaving so soon?" Cindy said, and I realized she'd been quiet the entire time.

"I'm sorry," Just May answered, "but if you guys are really meaning what you are saying, I think I'd be better off without you as friends." Everyone sat in shocked silence. Just May turned towards me. "I'm thankful for your kindness in saving me from that excruciatingly humiliating situation this afternoon, but you're right; plotting and planning these things makes you no better than Effie herself."

"So what should we do then?" The question hung in the air.

Elijah turned to me. "Mariah, did you have a solution?"

I paused and sat up taller. "I think we don't let her push us around. We walk tall, and watch out for each other. She wants to separate, belittle, divide and conquer us. I say we don't let her. If anything will eat at her the most, that will. She's trying to make herself feel better at our expense, but if she fails, then she'll suffer all the more!"

"But what if she tries to attack you again, or for that matter any of us!" Charlie complained.

"We need to be smart," I said. "We need to stick together and not let our guard down around her. But we don't need to walk around in fear—just stay alert."

"That might be easy for you," Charlie said cuttingly.

I felt shocked. "Easy?" I asked, pulling up my sleeve to reveal the scars of my ant spots. "Fifty-five." My voice was still quiet. "For not being smart."

I slid my sleeve back down. "The Effies of this world are never going to go away." I looked at Charlie. "We can't change them. But we can make them a whole lot less effective by not playing into their game."

Charlie's black eyes screamed out untold sorrows. She was right. Our lives had not been that different, and even though she'd been given new parents, she'd never learned to truly trust and let go of the things of the past. I could see that now. *That had been me last week.*

My heart pounded. It was screaming to be accepted. Finally, Elijah said, "Then that sounds like our plan." Everyone nodded. We agreed to stick together and stand up for anyone who found themselves at Effie's mercies, and most of all encourage each other and stay smart and alert. In that little ice cream shop, it sounded easy, but I was sure in our hearts we all knew it would be a long process.

"Mariah, how can you be so cool about this?" Dan asked.

"I know how easy it is to get stuck where Effie is. All it takes is one act of false righteousness, and we'd be no different than her, and from there it's easy to justify way more than we'd originally intended."

"What did I say about her?" Rayla piped in. "She's wise, so when she talks, we all best shut our mouths and open our ears!"

I blushed. *It could have just as easily gone the other way, and I'd be left with no friends…* Everyone laughed, and we ate the rest of our rapidly melting ice cream.

As the afternoon progressed, the boys had sword fights with their spoons, while us girls pretended the ice cream was lip-gloss. We were all extra loud and flamboyant as the sugar set in, and then it was time for some of us to leave. Rayla was the first to go; she had music lessons. Teb and Charlie left us for official "date" business, and May's mother came by to pick her up. Only Cindy, Dan, Elijah and me were left.

"Who was that boy on Monday?" Dan asked.

"Just a friend," I answered absentmindedly, dipping my finger in the melted remnants of our sundae.

"A friend? Or a boyfriend?" Cindy dipped her finger in too. "My mom would have a fit if she knew I'd come here," she added sheepishly.

I leaned back; Toby looked at me closely. "A friend," I repeated.

"So do you have a boyfriend?" Elijah asked, a blush appearing on his cheeks.

"Nope," was all I said. Toby looked from Elijah to me.

"Have you ever?" Cindy asked. "I'm not allowed to date until I'm sixteen…just three more months." She smiled widely, and then returned to the bowl of goop.

"No, I haven't ever, but not because I'm not allowed to…" I felt embarrassed, so I added, "Just haven't found the right guy, I guess."

Toby—who sat in the booth now that there was room—shifted so he could sit up straighter just as Elijah jumped. It looked like Dan had kicked him under the table.

Dan shook his head. "Well then, what sort of guy would be the right kind?" He leaned forward and put his elbows on the table.

I shrugged.

Toby piped up. "If you say Elijah, you'd make everyone's day." Then he put his hand over his mouth to keep from laughing. I was annoyed; *he knew how I felt around Elijah!*

"Let's say," Dan looked all around the shop, pretending to search for someone. Then he turned in his seat and rested his eyes upon Elijah. "My boy Elijah here—would he be the right type?"

"Told you," Toby said smugly. I wanted to kick him.

I didn't know what to say. Cindy looked over at me, anxious to see what I'd do next.

"Just say yes!" Toby gently coaxed. "Come on, Elijah is a nice guy, give him a shot."

But I didn't want to, so I stalled by asking, "Well, tell me about your boy Elijah. What's he like?"

Cindy gasped. Elijah blushed even harder.

"I mean," I added to try and explain, "I don't know him in the boyfriend way." *I felt lame! Why couldn't I say yes?*

Dan took it all in stride. "Well, he's a bit of a soft boy. You know the type; like all those girly movies have in them: thoughtful, passionate. I mean, I'm not saying he's a wuss or anything like that, but he's not all muscle and bronze." Dan scratched his head. "Though he can hold his own…"

"Thanks, man," Elijah said, giving Dan a shove. Then he took a deep breath and said, "Mariah, would you like to go on a date with me this Friday?"

Cindy let out a squeal.

I looked quickly at Toby, and he nodded his head vigorously.

"Um…" I wondered what the harm would be. "Alright." I felt weird accepting. *What was I doing?* I liked Tony; even with everything that I'd been through with him, that only made me like him more than when I first met him, and I felt like I was cheating on Tony by agreeing to go on this date.

Elijah seemed happy enough with my answer. Dan patted him heartily on the back. Then it seemed that it was getting late, and the rest of us needed to go home. Cindy and I took the bus together. She got more nervous; as we neared her stop, she energetically chewed sugarless mint gum and asked three times if I could smell the sugar on her breath. *How could you smell sugar on breath?* As she got off, she looked green.

At home I cleaned a little, then headed to my room. I had a stack of homework to finish, but I found it hard to concentrate as an argument broke out in my mind over Elijah and Tony…

"What's wrong with Elijah?" Toby interrupted.

I put the pencil down. "I really like Tony. I like him more and more, and I really only want to be friends with Elijah. Besides, you've seen how nervous I get around him; that's gotta mean something."

"We talked about your mixed wiring…"

"No, Toby, I think it's more than that! It doesn't matter—I don't like Elijah that way, and I like Tony!"

"But I told you Tony's not boyfriend material."

"Well, *I* think he is!" I argued, and then added feebly, "Or at least he could be."

Toby sat back. "Mariah," he started slowly, "Tony's making a lot of changes." He seemed shocked at his own words, but a happy grin spread across his face. Then he was serious again. "He's nowhere near ready to be a boyfriend. It's just that he's got a lot of work still ahead of him, and he doesn't need the distraction of a girlfriend."

I blinked a few times as his words sank in. "But I really like him."

"I can see that." Toby looked sad. "I'd just hate for you to get your hopes up. He's not going to be ready for a very long time."

"I'll wait." I turned my back to my work, wanting to be done with this conversation.

"Don't do that to yourself!" Toby tried to argue. "I like that you're becoming friends with Tony. He needs a friend like you. But don't close yourself off like this. You've waited so long to really start living, so why couldn't you be Tony's friend while you are Elijah's girlfriend? You can do both." He closed his eyes. I felt him heavy in my mind, and I got a prickly feeling, like he was trying to see my future. "Please keep an open mind."

I agreed, though I thought it could just as easily go the other way. I couldn't imagine wanting to be with anyone but Tony. Elijah made me stiff.

Toby didn't open his eyes, which made my bedtime routine go a lot quicker.

DAY 18

Thursday...

The next day, I was once again accompanied through the halls of the school, and the whole gang was abuzz about my date with Elijah, asking us both a barrage of questions. Toby was in there like a dirty shirt. Someone asked, “Are you excited?” and Toby said, “You should be”. When someone else started talking about how fun it should be, Toby was repeating and backing up what they said. I found it hard to concentrate with Toby’s constant side commentary.

Just May joined us. She was an interesting girl. Her dad took the whole family on business trips, so she had visited China, Greenland and Greece that year alone.

Yet I couldn’t wait for school to be over so I could see Tony again. After the last bell, I bolted from the building and waited at the block where we had planned to meet, but he didn’t come. Finally, feeling defeated, I turned to go as Larry drove up in Tony’s car.

“Mariah!” he called out. He had his hair slicked back, and I could smell cologne. He was dressed in slacks and a designer top. He gave me a huge smile, and he had his arm hanging out of the car. I went over to the window. "Listen, Tony wanted me to come and give you a message."

"Where is he? Is he alright?" I asked, feeling anxious.

"No worries, he's fine." But Larry didn't look like he believed his own words. "He told me to tell you that he's sorry he can't make it, and if it's alright with you, he will come over on Saturday." I nodded numbly. I expected Toby to look smug, but when I caught sight of him, his face mirrored my concerns.

"Would you like a ride somewhere? I've got a full tank of gas and unlimited use of his wheels."

I glanced quickly at Toby. He had no objections, so I accepted and got in. Larry waited patiently for me to get my belt buckled before he put the car in drive. He didn't feel as smooth behind the wheel as Tony, but he was much more cautious and careful.

"Where to?" he asked as he pulled away from the curb, paying close attention to all the students that were leaving school.

"Home," I answered. I couldn't think of any other place to go. As we drove past the front of the school, I caught sight of my friends. Rayla noticed me and waved.

"Well, that's boring." I couldn't tell if he was disappointed or teasing. *Had he wanted to go somewhere with me?* "But your wish is my command," Larry smiled. "I'm under strict orders to treat you well." He asked for directions to get to my townhouse, and I guided him. Toby, who had taken his place in the back seat, was leaning so far forward, his face almost blocked me from seeing Larry, and his elbows were resting on the seat back between us.

As Larry rounded the corner of one of the quiet side streets with a park on it, he slowed the car to the proper speed limit and casually asked me, "What did you do to Tony?"

"Pardon?" I choked. *Was he mad at me?*

"What did you do to him? He's all different." Larry didn't look over, but I saw his lips curl.

"Like what?" I said defensively.

"Well…" Larry concentrated on the road for a moment, "like last night. He got into a fight with the twins."

"About time," Toby interrupted.

Since Larry couldn't hear Toby, he continued. "Tony never disagrees with them. They could suggest the craziest things, and he'd be into it, no questions. But last night, not only did he not go along with it, he also told them it was wrong. I mean, I've never seen him that way."

"Is that bad?"

"Well..." Again Larry was distracted by the traffic. We were close to my house now. "It was actually great that he didn't get into the stuff Sam and Sean were talking about, and it was really good that he didn't. But it was weird. Tony doesn't usually care about that sort of thing, and there he was yelling at the two like they weren't even his friends."

"They're not!" Toby put in.

I smiled shyly.

Larry pulled into the visitor parking and turned off the engine, then turned and looked at me. "You've done something. Said something? Whatever it is, that boy is changed." His eyes, that looked greener today, twinkled.

"But is that bad?" I asked again. *Why was he looking at me like that?*

Larry narrowed his eyes. "Not really." He sat back in the seat and rested his head. "You know, after the fight, Tony quit bowling league."

I gasped, and Toby said, "No."

"Yup." Larry nodded. "Said he had more important things to do with his life."

"I'm sorry." I felt sad that Tony had given up something I knew he loved. *Why would he do that?*

"Ya." Larry turned to face me again. "And he even went up to visit his mom today."

"Well I'll be," Toby said, sitting back in his seat. "I would have never..."

"He hasn't gone to see her since the divorce," Larry said.

"I know, he told me."

Larry narrowed his eyes again. "You know, the first time I saw you at the alley, I thought, no offence, here's another trophy girl for Tony. Then the second time you came, I didn't want to see you end up that way; you're really nice. I was sure Tony would eat you up and spit you out, and he wouldn't care. I felt bad for you. Then you gave me your number, and I was tempted to just throw it out so Tony wouldn't track you down. But I kinda liked you." Larry kept his eyes averted while he said this. "And I wanted to have your number, just in case, I don't know, I felt like talking to you again some time…" He blushed but continued. "Well, Tony took your number. I knew he had the moment I noticed it was gone, and he went and bragged about it that Friday. I was so mad that I had let him get hold of you. I wanted to come and warn you to stay away from him, but I didn't know how to get in touch with you. No way was Tony going to give up once he had you. I thought you were a goner—now I don't know what to think."

I shrugged. "Think that everything seems to have worked itself out," I said, looking sideways at Toby, because at that moment I realized it had, even better than he could have hoped for. I reached for the door and thanked Larry for the ride.

"Hey, do you mind if I come in and use your washroom?" Larry asked, sitting up straighter.

I felt a strange sensation like I shouldn't, but Toby said, "No harm," so I agreed. We walked to the house together, Toby lost in his own thoughts. Larry filled the empty space with conversation. He explained that he was Tony's "sometimes" friend, like if there was no one else to hang with, or if what he was doing weren't too illegal, then he'd invite Larry to join, but that only happened sometimes.

I smiled. "So Tony is your 'sometimes' friend, but you are his 'always' friend. Sounds selfish of Tony."

"A bit." Larry followed me up the stairs to my front door. I stopped at my door, which had been fixed, and realized I still didn't have a key. *This could potentially be very embarrassing if I was locked out now…*

"I don't really mind," Larry went on, "I sorta get lost in books and stuff. If it wasn't for Tony, I wouldn't have any friends."

I smiled, not fully paying attention. I looked from the door to Toby. He shrugged. Then, with a sense of dread, I reached for the handle and turned it. Luckily, it was unlocked. Relieved, I stepped in and told Larry how to get to the washroom. I went over to the kitchen table, where I found a key on a piece of paper with my name on it. I put the key in my jeans pocket.

It was as I realized that I could hear someone coming up the stairs that I figured out I had left the front door open. I went over to it, but my mother stepped in. She held her dry cleaning in one hand and an expensive coffee in the other.

"Mariah," she said curtly as she walked past me and into the kitchen, "I got your note, and I think it's a perfect idea for you to do the shopping.

I don't have time anyway. So I've put some money in an envelope for you; I'll give you something like that every week." She was in control, but for the first time I didn't feel like a toddler around her.

I followed her into the kitchen and saw that the paper with my name on it was actually a sealed envelope. My mother was just dumping the remnants of her coffee in the sink and about to say something more when another voice interrupted her.

"Hey, Mariah…" Larry said as he came bounding into the kitchen. He stopped; I wasn't sure if it was the look on my face or him seeing my mother standing at the sink. "You must be Mrs. Lafont," he said, extending a hand to her.

She turned slowly and scowled. "You," she said, loathing dripping from her voice. "You shot my son!" Her voice became shrill as she advanced upon Larry with her hand raised.

Larry took a step back, looking from my mother to me. In that brief moment, I tried to convey how sorry I was.

"Get out!" my mother bellowed, stepping even closer to Larry.

He didn't hesitate. He bolted from the house, and I watched him run past the kitchen window and out of sight.

I had pushed myself up against the table trying to get out of my mother's way. Finding my voice, I screamed, "Larry didn't shoot Jake!"

She rounded on me quick as lightning. "What were you doing with another boy in the house!" she screamed into my face while grabbing the front of my shirt.

"Nothing," I said, my voice high from panic.

"You slut!" She pushed me backwards, and I fell against the table.

But my reply shocked even me. "No," I said firmly.

Toby, who watched helpless to do anything said, "That's right."

"What!" My mother rounded on me again, only this time I was ready. I ducked and slipped past her to the front door.

"Mariah, don't you walk away when I'm talking to you!" she shouted.

"You're not talking!" I said as I left. I didn't look back for fear that she was following me. I kept walking until I felt my panic subside.

As I calmed down, I started to feel exhilarated as I walked down the path. *I had stood up to my mother, and I had survived.*

Toby took my hand in his. "It's clear you don't need me any more," he said, sorrowfully. I felt sad too, but he was right. I had handled myself against the person I feared the most: my mother. I hadn't needed Toby's help at all. I squeezed his hand tight in mine; the warmth that emanated from him filled me. *But I knew he wasn't leaving yet—he still needed me!*

As I passed the visitor parking, I checked to see if Larry was still there, but he was nowhere in sight. Tony's car was gone. We continued walking until we got to one of the local playgrounds. No one was around, so I took a seat on the swing and slowly rocked myself.

"You know," I said quietly just in case I was intruded upon, "I never would have been able to do any of that if I hadn't met you."

"Thanks." Toby sat in the swing next to me. "Thanks for saying that."

"It's true," I argued.

But Toby only smiled. "You're braver than you give yourself credit for. And you are stronger than you admit."

I pushed off and swung back. Feeling the cool air rush past me, I felt like I could fly. I was free. Nothing could hurt me. Toby watched quietly. I don't know how long we stayed, but the sun was starting to set when I let my swing slow down and come to a stop.

"What now?" Toby asked.

"I don't think I should go home yet," I said more to myself. "I just figure my mom needs some time to calm down. I guess I'll see if I can stay at Cindy's for the night."

It felt like we were running out of things to say, and I wondered how much longer Toby would be with me, but that thought didn't scare me at all. It almost felt like it was right.

One of Cindy's little sisters answered the door. "Cin, it's for you," she hollered and skipped away.

Cindy showed up a moment later. "Mariah, what are you doing here?" she said with concern.

"Well," I started, but as soon as I tried to talk, I felt my throat choke and tears burn the corners of my eyes. "I need someplace to sleep tonight." I hid my face behind my hand.

Cindy took me by the arm and led me into her living room. "I have to go get my mom," she said softly. "You stay here."

I sobbed; it was embarrassing to have to ask for help. *What was wrong with my mom?* Toby put his hand around my shoulder, but he still had nothing to say. I could hear the family at the dinner table. *Why couldn't I have a normal family?*

When Cindy returned, her mother was with her. We talked for a while, and I explained that my mother and I had had a fight; Toby wanted me to tell them my mother had attacked me, but I just couldn't utter those words. Cindy's mother and father said any time I needed a place to stay, their door was open, and if I ever needed to get help, they could assist me. Then I was offered some leftover dinner and given the guest room to sleep in. As I changed with my back to Toby, he gasped and came over to me.

"She bruised you!" he said, touching my lower back lightly. I felt sore and pulled away. "You have to tell someone," he insisted,

"No." I turned toward him with my borrowed pajamas on. "She's upset about Jake. She'll calm down—she did last time."

"She's done this to you before!" Toby was really upset, but I got the impression that it was more because he was shocked that he didn't know this already.

"Only once," I told him. "It was just after my father had left, and I couldn't stop crying, like, for days. She got fed up with my useless tears, so she grabbed me, shook me and threw me against the wall." I put my hand up to my head as I remembered it. "I didn't cry again until I met you."

Toby wrapped his arms around me, careful of my bruised back. "Mariah, that isn't right. No one should ever touch you that way."

"I know." I felt my chest filling with resolve, and I vowed, "And I wont let her do it ever again."

Toby didn't let me go. "Mariah, tell Cindy's mom. She said she could get you help!"

I thought for a moment. A flash of a life with new parents danced enticingly before me, then I answered, "No. I think I'll be okay where I am now." I got into bed, feeling braver than I ever had before. Toby curled up next to me, and I heard his breathing become regular as he slowly sank into sleep.

I knew Cindy's mother could help, but I didn't want it. I was just starting to get comfortable with my life. I was finally getting a handle on it, and I didn't want things to change again! Besides, I knew I could duck better, and my mom wasn't due for another major explosion for another six years, and I'd be way gone by then...

Cindy snuck down after bedtime and crawled into the bed with me. "Are you still going on your date with Elijah tomorrow?" she asked while she got herself comfortable.

"Sure," I answered, "why not?"

"Don't know," she murmured, and then she rolled onto her side and held her head under her hand. "Hey, Mariah, don't you like him?"

"I like him," I said, taking a breath. "I just don't know if I like him like that."

"Oh." She rolled onto her back and looked up at the ceiling. "You do know that *he* likes you like that." Her voice could hardly contain her excitement.

I nodded. I could feel Toby in the back of my mind. I mulled over what he had said about Tony. *Tony; just the mention of his name made my heart flutter.* As I pondered it, I realized again that Tony reminded me in so many ways of Toby—and the truth was I loved Toby. *Did I want Tony so badly only because he was so much like his old friend? Toby was my hero. Was I trying to replace him through Tony? Was there anything wrong with that?*

I was confused, but Cindy was still talking, and her words interrupted my thoughts. "Elijah has liked you from the first day you moved to our school. I don't think he's liked anyone else. Please be gentle with him, okay?"

I promised I would, and sleep came quickly after that.

I dreamed of the meadow again; velvet grass, violet-blue sky and a sun that warmed me inside and out. I noticed Toby. He was pacing back and forth, muttering to himself anxiously. "My time has almost run out! There's so much to do! I need to fix it! I need to fix it." I tried to console him, but he was frantic. "I've done so many bad things! How can I fix them all?"

I walked over to him, but he couldn't see or hear me as I tried to reason with him. "You fixed me! Don't I count for something good?"

"I've left a legacy of misery! My life is forfeit!" He was ranting almost in gibberish and beating his chest.

Seeing him so distraught made me panic. "Stop it!" I yelled, reaching out to him. "Your life may have been forfeit, but look what you've accomplished in mine!" He vanished beneath my fingers.

DAY 19 Friday...

Slowly the dream dissolved around me, and I found myself looking up at an unfamiliar ceiling with bright streams of light pouring in through a large window. It took me a while to remember that I was at Cindy's. She yawned and stretched. Toby opened his eyes and materialized on my right.

"Good morning," Cindy chirped. I sat up. My back was sore and stiff, but I tried hard not to let it show.

The morning went by quickly. Cindy's mom, who didn't believe in cereal, had made everyone oatmeal. She served me a large bowl, and though I had the impression she was watching me carefully, she didn't press me for any information. Cindy spent the entire walk to school putting down her home. I had quite enjoyed it myself, but I got the feeling Cindy didn't dislike it so much, and she was just trying to help me not feel so bad about mine. Toby stayed quiet most of the morning. He looked a bit agitated, but he didn't say anything about it.

I was only escorted to about half my classes, but I didn't feel like I needed it any more. It was becoming more of a company thing than for safety. I showed up for my detention, and the secretary informed me sadly that it would be continuing into the next week. However, I was getting proficient at the job, and even though I was given a huge job, I had it done within twenty minutes. I met up with the gang in the lunchroom. Cindy had ordered me my meal once again. I threw myself down onto the bench and ate it heartily. The gang was buzzed about the weekend and talked excitedly about their plans.

"Of course, we know what Elijah and Mariah are doing!" Rayla said.

Elijah blushed and looked away. I just smiled slyly.

I was at my locker after the last bell had sounded when Elijah approached me. "About tonight," he said shyly. The guys hovered around Elijah, making plans and congratulating him. The girls cornered me, insisting that I remember every detail and give them an accurate play-by-play when we spoke again.

"Yup," I said, turning to look at him. Classmates were rushing all around us.

"Do you want me to pick you up, or meet me at the theatre?" Elijah looked nervous as he fiddled with his books.

"Do you have a car?" I closed my locker.

"No." Elijah looked embarrassed.

I thought for a moment. I tried to imagine what would happen if my mother saw me with another boy. "I think it's best if we meet there," I said.

Elijah nodded, then we worked out the details, and I headed home to get ready. Halfway home, Toby spoke up. His voice seemed rusty as he said, "Elijah is a really nice guy."

"I get that," I answered. I was mildly aware that we were walking down the same street I'd had my first collapse in. I thought back to that day. I was very different; so sad and lonely. I closed my eyes and marveled at how much I had changed.

Toby stopped, causing me to crash into that invisible wall that held us together. I looked back to see him staring at the very tree I had rested against. "You are worth it," he said, not taking his eyes from the spot.

"I am worth what?"

"You're worth it. My time here—you are worth my whole life."

I felt strangely honoured. I went to him and placed my hand on his shoulder. Then with a sinking feeling, I asked, "You're not leaving me yet, are you?"

Toby looked up and smiled at me. "Soon." My breath caught. "But not right now. I just wanted to let you know that you are worth it. If all I accomplished was helping you, then that would be worth it."

"But," I argued, "you've already helped Tony too. And I'm still planning on seeing Stacy, and Eric."

Toby smiled. His eyes sparkled, but they still seemed sad. "Sometimes I feel so overwhelmed with it all," he said, bringing his hand up to my cheek. "There's just so much! I can remember it all now, all of it, and there is no way I could ever make it all right, not even if I had the rest of your lifetime, or even if I was given back my own."

"If my life was fixable, then surely there is hope for yours," I said, trying to cheer him up.

He continued to hold my cheek. "I think that it is far easier to fix things while you are still alive. My deeds are done, and apart from these stolen moments I have, there just isn't enough time to make amends for a lifetime of mistakes."

"Alright then, I'll cancel this date to help you out!" I said with conviction.

"I love you for that," Toby said, letting his hand drop and starting down the street, "but it isn't right to have you put your life on hold for me; it doesn't work that way." He ran his hand through his hair. "You need to keep on living. Go on the date. I'll wait for tomorrow." I wanted to argue more, but he made it clear his mind was set.

We walked the rest of the way home listening to the sounds of the world around us; the breeze making the trees whisper, the birds having animated conversations, and the far off sounds of cars and people and dogs and the business of a Friday afternoon.

I entered the house cautiously, calling out several times to my mother. I was relieved when I didn't find her, but I did find the money on the table in the envelope, just as it had been the day before, and a few used cups. As I cleaned, I wondered if things would ever feel right between her and me. Then I thought back and realized they never had, not even before my father went away. I had always been daddy's girl, and Jake was mommy's boy. No wonder I'd felt so devastated when my father left. *He was my cheering squad.* Without him, I didn't fell very special any more. I realized that Toby had given that back to me! *When Toby left, would I lose it again?*

Trying to put these thoughts out of my head, I started to pick out what I should wear to my date: *a real date, where the boy was actually interested in me.* That raised my spirits, and I started to get excited despite myself.

I spent over an hour trying to put my outfit together. Finally I stood in front of my mirror with a pink top and green pants. "So, you're telling me that these pants make me look good, and so does this top."

Toby stood behind me. I caught his reflection as he nodded.

"But," I added, raising one brow, "they don't look so good together, eh? So which one goes?"

"You pick, beautiful." *I liked being called that.*

I chose the pink top and a new pair of black pants that hugged my hips. I looked at myself from every angle in the full-length mirror. Though the pants were brand new, they felt looser than I remembered. *Had I lost weight? I didn't look so bad any more!* I asked Toby what he thought, and he was so impressed, he went invisible.

"Are you serious?" I asked.

"Absolutely!" came Toby's reply. "And I've decided that tonight is all yours. I'll keep my eyes and mouth shut so you can enjoy it the way it should be."

"But surely you can keep me company while I finish getting ready and on the way there." I was already starting to miss him.

"Nope. You don't need me. I'm only a distraction." I had a feeling that he knew how much he reminded me of Tony, and he didn't want that to be a problem for me.

I finished getting ready alone without a word from Toby, but when I concentrated, I could still feel him at the edge of my consciousness, and I found that calming. As the afternoon progressed, I became preoccupied with thoughts of Elijah and our date. I started to look forward to seeing him and fantasized about how it would be: *would we hold hands? Would he kiss me? Would he be shy? Would I?*

The whole bus ride felt like it took forever. As I disembarked, I checked my watch. I was still ten minutes early. I made my way to the movie theatre, bombarded with a hundred sights, sounds and smells. It was Friday, one of the busiest nights; the arcade games off to one side were being well used, and everywhere I looked there was a lineup. I made my way over to the tables through crowds of people, and getting closer, I caught sight of Elijah. I took a moment to admire him, just like I was preparing for a big game. His hair a mess of unique individual ringlets, his blue eyes that looked like the ocean on a sunny day, his deep red lips and his perfect cheeks. Even the beauty spot halfway along his jaw looked perfect. *Maybe I did like him...*

Elijah waved and rushed over to me. Reaching out, he took my hand then hesitated, looking like he wanted to hug me. Instead he continued to hold my hand and said, "I'm so glad to see you."

I returned the sentiment, marveling at how nice I felt while he held on to me; his hand was warm and smooth. He seemed reluctant to let it go as he escorted me to the lineup for tickets, but he had to let go when it came time to pay for the show. Elijah wanted to see an action movie, so I let him pick, realizing that we'd do more watching than my last "date." *I guess he won't be kissing me like Tony,* I thought, but I didn't know if that was a good thing.

We entered another lineup and did more hand holding while we waited to buy snacks. Elijah filled the space with conversation: he came from a family of five; he was the middle child, but the first boy with two older sisters, a younger brother and a baby sister. It made his life loud, he said happily. His father worked on oilrigs, so he was away for long periods of time, like months. But Elijah didn't mind. He understood that his dad had to work. Even though he missed his dad, the good part was that when he was home, he wasn't running off to the office or anything, so he'd really spend time with his kids.

Elijah surprised me when he told me that he was already thinking of what he wanted to do after he graduated: he wanted to be an architect. He wanted to be able to be some place and say, "I made that." I started to wonder what I wanted to do after I graduated, and that same feeling of not being stuck in my mother's house came to mind. The day was fast approaching when I'd be moving out and able be to live my own life, free of her. *What would I do then? What could I do now to be ready for that day?*

With our hands full of treats, we lined up for the theatre. Elijah turned to me and said, "Your turn—talk."

I felt nervous as I painted him the picture of my life with a crazy single mother and a delinquent brother that was awaiting trial. Elijah seemed uncomfortable, and I wondered how he'd feel about me once I was done telling him my story. But he surprised me again.

"I always knew there was something special about you." He leaned closer to me. "I saw a strength in you that I admired. It doesn't come from a soft life; it's sorta like my mother. She had a rough childhood too, but she's the most a wonderful woman I know, and so kind. I see that in you too." He placed a quick kiss on my cheek. I nearly dropped the popcorn.

When it was time to go in to the movie, Elijah seemed to get shy. *Was he embarrassed by the kiss?* I felt a little light-headed with it all. We followed the crowd into the theatre, and I felt like it was déjà vu as we took our seats, Elijah on my left and our drinks on the outside with the popcorn in the middle. But this time was different; we were sitting only three rows from the front. Elijah said he liked to be as close to the action as his eyes could handle. Clearly he meant to watch the movie and not be too distracted by me—again I couldn't tell if I was disappointed. *I liked the idea of being held and touched, but not forced.*

We talked while snacking on popcorn until the lights dimmed. My mind wandered to Tony; it had been so different with him, and for a moment I missed him. Then Elijah put his arm behind my head, I rested against it, and all thoughts of Tony went away.

The show was better than I would have imagined. It had a good plot and characters I ended up liking, and of course lots of explosions. I was transported to another time and place, and for a moment I forgot all about my life and troubles. Elijah seemed very impressed too. He whooped and hollered at the appropriate times. Halfway through, once the popcorn was finished, I leaned into his shoulder, and he held me more tightly. I found myself wanting him to kiss me, but he never did.

Afterward, Elijah continued to hold my hand as we walked to a local café. It was half a block down from the theatre. He treated me to a slice of cheesecake topped with fresh strawberries and whipped cream, which we shared. In the end it became a fork war that erupted in laughter. I started to wonder why I'd ever felt hesitant around him.

I was having a really good time. We talked about the movie and argued about the probability of it actually happening. Then we settled into a comfortable silence. Looking across the table, I realized I wasn't as attracted to Elijah as I was to Tony. *Why?*

Elijah seemed to sense something. "I've never had a girlfriend before," he said while watching my fork as I chased around the last strawberry in the crumbs from the cake crust. "I was hoping you'd be my first."

I continued to play with the leftovers. "I don't know." I felt horrible for saying that, so I concentrated on the plate, not wanting to see the look on his face.

"You like that other guy," he said after a long pause.

How'd he know? I looked up sharply. Elijah wore a dejected look.

"Well, kinda," I sighed, "but he's not my boyfriend."

"But you wish he was." I was shocked at his boldness. His blue eyes seemed to pierce right through me.

"Ya," I said quietly, then added, "I don't know if it's going to work out, though."

Elijah reached over and placed his hand on mine. "Would you consider giving me a chance anyway? I really like you, and I could never forgive myself if I didn't do all I could to make you mine."

Two conflicting emotions warred in my mind: as Elijah held his hand on mine, I felt good, and I wanted to say yes to him. But I also had a vision of Tony in my head, and I didn't want to give that up.

"You don't have to answer today; just think about it." Elijah gave my hand a squeeze and let go.

I promised him I would. Already the fight between the boys was playing out in my head. He walked me to the bus stop, holding hands again. When he saw my bus approaching, he leaned over and kissed me lightly on the cheek. I put my hand up and held the spot as I boarded the bus. Then I watched as the bus started down the street, taking me away from him. Toby appeared beside me as Elijah and the bus stop went out of sight.

Toby cleared his throat and said, "Now, wasn't that nice."

That's what I was thinking! The bus was relatively empty, but a few passengers were still on board, so I didn't answer.

"Good movie too," Toby continued, "and it could totally happen!" I crossed my arms and leaned back in the seat. "I felt that; you like him. Elijah is nice, and that's how you are supposed to feel with a boy."

It wasn't until I was home in the safety of my room, with the chair against the door, even though my mom wasn't home yet, that I was able to reply. "Ya, I like Elijah," I said, sitting down on my bed with my nightclothes on. Toby sat on top of my desk. "But it doesn't feel exciting. When I was with Tony, I was in constant anticipation about what he would do next!"

Toby winced. "Mariah, that's not right." It was obvious that he was fuming. "Tony ruined it for you to have a healthy relationship with anyone else!"

I shifted so I could lean against the wall. "You might be being too harsh on Tony." I drew my legs to my chest and held onto them. "The more I look at my life, the more I realize I'm really messed up: my father left, my mother's always mad at me, my brother and his friends abused me. I don't think Tony corrupted me. I was already in a destructive cycle. He didn't do anything to me that hadn't already been done."

"Perhaps, but he sure didn't help." Toby came to sit next to me on the bed. "The student surpasses the teacher," he said, placing a hand on my knee. "So what now, beautiful?"

"I was going to ask you that." I leaned my head on his arm. "Things have changed. I have, and Tony is changing. I still really want to be with him… But Elijah is nice. Perhaps if I had never met Tony, I might really like being his girlfriend. But now, I don't know."

"I'm not so sure," Toby said, squeezing my knee. "I'm not sure you would have met Elijah if you didn't meet me, and once I was part of the equation, then Tony was in the mix too." Toby sighed. "You're right, everything is changing, and it's happening so fast, I don't know what to tell you any more. My only question is: can you be with Tony without becoming so physical too quick?"

"Like, take it slow, the same way I would if I was with Elijah?" I repeated, thinking hard about it. I wanted to say I could, then I thought of Tony's face, and my pulse quickened. "I guess we'll find out tomorrow."

DAY 20 Saturday...

My plan had been to get up at my regular time, even though it was the weekend, and leave to shop before my mother got up. I spent the morning debating between the merits of Tony and Elijah, and as the hours wore on, I could tell Tony was coming into the lead. Toby seemed more quiet and reflective, keeping his thoughts to himself, but I could sense his emotions were in knots.

By nine thirty, I was leaving my house. As I walked down the path, someone called out, “Hey beautiful.” It sounded just like Toby, so I stopped and turned to see what he wanted. He shook his head and pointed behind me; I spun around to see Tony.

My heart leapt. “What are you doing here?” My voice made it clear I was happy to see him.

He had been hiding in the bushes half a block from my house. When he jumped out, he still had a leaf stuck in his hair. I reached up to pull it out, but he caught my hand. “Hey, no touchy,” he said, letting go with a playful grin. “You saw that, right Toby, she tried to touch me!” His eyes darted all around, not knowing that Toby stood on the other side of me.

Toby shook his head and rolled his eyes.

I was embarrassed, so I explained, looking into his hair. "You have a leaf."

He brought his own hand up and pulled it out, then handed it to me. "For you, beautiful." His dark eyes danced as he held it out.

I took it and put it in my back pocket, like it was the best gift he could ever give me. "Thanks."

"What are you doing here?" I started to walk, and Tony joined me.

"Waiting for you." He looked sideways at me. "I tried to call last night, but your mom answered, and she gave me an earful… By the way, where were you?"

"On a date," I answered, looking away.

Tony brought his hand around my back then pulled it away, catching himself. Instead he said in a hurt voice, "You went on a date? Toby, you let her go?"

"Of course I let you go—it's not like you have a boyfriend. Tony doesn't own you." Toby sounded upset.

I laughed nervously.

"What? What!" Tony grabbed my hand, and this time he didn't let go.

I loved the way Tony's hand felt around mine, like he was in charge. "Toby is upset. He says I don't belong to you."

"That's true." Tony said with a hint of disappointment. He took a breath, then asked, "So who was this guy? Is he your boyfriend?"

"No, just a boy from my school." I felt weird talking about it with Tony. *Somehow it seemed wrong.*

"Did I meet him?" I jerked my hand nervously at the question. Tony didn't let go, but he held our hands up and asked, "Is this alright?" *It was for me.*

I looked over to Toby. He shrugged, asking, "Is it enough? Or do you want more?" He was right. My body ached to be in Tony's embrace and to kiss him again. But just holding hands was nice too.

"Toby isn't objecting." I tried to sound casual.

"So who's the guy then?" Tony persisted. *Why did he want to know?* "He's from your school, right?" I nodded. "And I met him, right?" I hesitated before I nodded again. Tony let out a sigh. "I bet I could guess who it was." I didn't say anything, so he went on. "It was the boy with brown curly hair and a mole on his cheek."

"How'd you guess?" I was astonished.

"It's a gift," Tony answered while he pulled my hand so our shoulders bumped. "It wasn't that hard to see he liked you." *It had been for me.* Toby stayed quiet, but he watched Tony closely, and I could feel his emotions like little air bubbles at the back of my brain.

"So do you like him?"

I stopped and pulled my hand away, crossing my arms. "I will not answer you."

Tony came in front of me, holding both my upper arms. "No, don't answer that. Instead tell me this; do you like me?"

Toby scowled. "Careful," he warned through clenched teeth. I stood frozen, watching the look on Toby's face.

Tony let my arms go and stepped away quickly. "I've upset Toby, haven't I?"

I nodded.

"Would you believe me if I told you that this is different?" I was staring at Toby, and Tony followed with his eyes to the same spot. "You wanted me to change—can't you see I'm changing? You're the human lie detector! Can't you see?" The anger behind Tony's voice scared me a little. I took a step back.

Tony seemed to deflate and sat down on a low brick wall. "I'm sorry, Mariah," he said, running his hand through his hair. Then, looking deep into my eyes he said, "I am trying. It's just hard, and you're…well, when I'm with you…never mind. I *am* trying."

I felt bad for him. He seemed so sincere. I wanted to fall to my knees and embrace him, but Toby moved so he was standing right in front of Tony, and he asked me to repeat what he was saying. "I see the changes. I see that you've changed, a lot, and I know that this is different." I smiled inwardly at the last statement, as a vision of Tony being my boyfriend played in my head.

"He wants to keep things good for both of us. Can we believe that it's too soon? We both need more time." My inward smile faded before I even relayed the last part.

"Do you believe him?" Tony asked me.

I shrugged. *I did, but I didn't like it.* I told him that. Tony took a deep breath and stood up. Then he told me that he felt that same way. Taking my hand in his and starting to walk again, he asked if he could join me in the rest of the morning. When I told him all I was doing was shopping, he became insistent. *I loved the idea of his company.* Toby also seemed to think it would be fine.

Tony turned out to be a good shopping partner. He explained that he did most of the grocery shopping in his house too, so he was able to help me to find the best produce and in-store deals. But he jokingly threatened that if I let out his secret, he'd hunt me down… he didn't finish that thought. As his eyes darted about, he mouthed, "Where's Toby?" I pointed to behind him, and he pretended to duck. It was highly amusing, especially because Toby wasn't even there. He stood almost glued to my side. But Toby stayed quiet. I felt like he was studying us the entire time.

As we neared the house again, Tony became somber and stopped at the same bush he had jumped out of earlier that morning. "Maybe I should wait for you here." He held out the bags he had been carrying for me. "I mean, after all, it was me who shot your brother, kinda. And if she was that mad at Larry, a stranger, then I just don't want to see how she feels about me."

"How…" I started to ask.

"Larry picked me up from the bus station last night and told me all about your crazy mom."

"Sorry," I said, looking down at the sidewalk. *What was he thinking about me with a mother like that!*

Both Toby and Tony said, "Not your fault." I looked from one to the other. They stood side by side.

"Thanks." I half smiled.

"Listen, don't worry about it; my dad can be a real creep too sometimes," Tony said, going to hide behind the bush again. I looked at Toby and wondered if he was sad that he couldn't hang out with his old friend instead of having to come home with me. He didn't say anything.

I was instantly relieved that Tony hadn't come home as I walked through the door. My mother stood at the counter, chopping some lettuce.

"Hi," I said, trying to determine what her mood was.

"Where were you?" she asked without turning around, but her voice sounded even. *Thankfully.*

I put the three bags of groceries on the table. "Shopping." She quizzed me about all the items I'd purchased, making sure I hadn't missed anything on the list. When I passed her test, she said offhandedly that I'd done a good job and sat at the table to eat her salad while I put the food away. I found it hard to do a good job while she watched and criticized me, but I managed to get everything done, and I started to leave.

"Where are you going?" she asked as she heard the front door opening.

"Out." I took a step outside. *Why did she care?*

"When will you be home?" I heard her voice follow me out the door.

"Later," I called. I went down the stairs and didn't look back. *When did it ever matter to her? Yet in her defence, when did I ever go out before?*

When I got to Tony's hiding place, I crawled into the bush with him and tripping fell into his arms. He caught me.

I looked up into his face. *I wanted to kiss him,* but instead I said breathlessly, "We are so lucky; my mom was still home." I went to stand up, but Tony pulled me closer. *Did he want to kiss me too?* But he brushed my bruise, and I let out a yelp.

Tony's arms dropped to his side. "I didn't do nothing, Toby!"

"It's not Toby," I said, brushing back tears. *It hurt!*

"What is it?" Tony asked.

"Nothing," I lied.

"It doesn't sound like nothing." Tony narrowed his eyes.

"Show him your bruise," Toby said.

I had become so accustomed to talking to Toby in front of Tony that I didn't think twice about answering. "He doesn't need to see my bruise."

"What bruise?" Tony said. I could see Toby smiling.

"It's really nothing."

"Well, if it's nothing, then why don't you show it to me?"

"Show it to him," Toby demanded.

I sighed. "It's not fair; the two of you are ganging up on me." But I turned around and lifted my shirt.

Tony whistled and put his hand lightly on the edge of the bruise. "Yup, that's a good one." Then he pulled up his pant leg and showed me a scar that went the length of his calf. "I fell on a broken bottle while I tried to get away from my father. How'd you get yours?"

I explained about my mother, that it was mostly insults and put-downs, but twice now it had turned physical. It felt nice to be able to tell him, especially because I knew he understood.

When I was done, he took his hand in mine and said, "There's nothing for it, they're our parents, the only ones we get. Just promise me that when she gets like that, you'll stay as far away from her as you can." I nodded and had him promise to do the same with his dad. "Oh, I learned that lesson a long time ago," he said with a smile.

Toby shook his head. I got the impression that he'd hoped something else would come of it. Then he rubbed his neck and asked, "When did Tony get that?"

"Two years ago," Tony replied. "It was the last straw. My mother left three months later."

"That's not how Tony told me it happened," Toby said.

Tony looked away. "No, no it's not. I told Toby that it was in a fight with a kid from our school… Wait a minute…"

But Toby was already telling me the rest of the story. Toby had beaten that kid up, threatened him, and he had transferred within the week. "I see it all now." He moaned, falling to the ground. "Every mistake! Every bad choice! All the hurt and pain I caused. And it's crushing me. I feel it eating away at me from the inside out; I'm afraid that soon there may be nothing of me left!" Then Toby urged us to go see Stacy and at least set one mistake right. The sight of Toby on his knees pulling at his shirt frightened me. I explained to Tony what was going on, and he led me to his car.

I sat in thought as we drove up to her house. I was still apprehensive about seeing her. *How was she going to react? What was I going to say to her?* Then I got distracted, wondering who Toby really was in life; the kind of kid who could rape a girl and beat people up without regard for the person he was hurting. I looked back at him; he seemed so small as he sat with his hands folded on his knees, looking out the window. Well, he felt remorse now. *But would he ever find peace*? I wondered.

Tony pulled the car over to the curb. We were on a middle class street. Most of the homes looked to be the typical three-bedroom type. Tony pointed out Stacy's house, and I studied it for a moment. It was a bungalow. The garage jutted out in front, with a walkway leading to the front door along the side. Beside the door I could see a huge bay window.

"Ready?" Tony asked, pulling on the handle to get out.

"You know," I said, getting an idea, "perhaps it would be best if I just go in alone at first." I could imagine one of Jake's friends showing up at my house. I wouldn't be able to think clearly. *Yes, it would be better this way.*

Tony released the car doorknob. "You think? Fine, I'll wait right here."

As I got out of the car, I tried to calm my squirming gut, and then realized it was Toby's feelings. He looked a wreck, with dark shadows under his eyes, and his cheeks sunken in. I slowly approached the front door and tried to walk casually up the three cement steps, and then I knocked.

It took a moment, and then I heard a small dog barking and someone shushing it on the other side of the door. I stood waiting. Toby looked intently at the door. It almost seemed like he had X-ray vision.

"Here we go," he said, a moment before the door opened a crack.

"Yes?" came a timid voice as the door opened a few more inches. There stood my childhood friend. She was taller and her hair longer. Her body was no longer that of a child, but there was no mistaking it was her! She had the same greasy blonde hair, the same blue-grey eyes, the same flat cheeks and plump lips. As I stood facing her, studying her features, I became aware that she was doing the same, and slowly I saw recognition dawn on her face.

"Mariah?" she breathed. I couldn't tell if she was happy or anxious to see me. There was a long pause. "What are you doing here?" she finally asked, a shy smile playing on her lips.

I looked for a moment at Toby. *How could I explain what I was doing here?* "Well," I started, "I just found out that you moved to town."

"Oh," she said, sounding tired.

"And well," I fumbled for the right words, "well, I had to come see you."

"You did?" I could tell she didn't quite believe me.

"Ya," I said. "I just couldn't not." I smiled widely, for Toby's sake.

Toby gave me a thank-you nod.

"Really, me?" Stacy seemed amazed, but she stepped back opening the door and asked, "Would you like to come in?"

I accepted and followed her into her living room. There were three mismatched sofas, all surrounding a glass-topped olive coffee table, with books and magazines on the lower shelf. Where there would normally be an entertainment centre, I saw a desk with shelves on either side filled with papers and more books. Placed all around the room were plants of different sizes and types.

Stacy sat on the sofa facing away from the hall entrance. It was old-looking and had a blanket draped over it. She picked up a pillow and held it in front of her like it was a protective shield. I sat on the couch in the middle, to the right of Stacy. It faced the window; that way I could look out and watch Tony, who sat in his car waiting for my signal. Toby took a seat beside me, but of course Stacy didn't know that.

She stared at me almost as if this was a dream, and she expected to wake up any moment. I cleared my throat and tried to sound casual, as I asked, "So, how's life been for you these past"—I did a mental count—"six years?"

"Well, my parents divorced," she answered, suddenly seeming interested in the blanket she sat on.

"I'd heard that," I replied. *She was nuts if she expected my sympathy.*

"Careful," Toby cautioned, rubbing his face. "Don't let bitterness get the better of you."

Easy for him to say, I thought. Then I said, "I heard your mother got remarried."

Stacy continued to outline the pattern on the blanket with her finger. "Ya." She told me about her new father. He'd come with a stepbrother that was seven and a sister who was now five. She also had a half-brother who would be two in the next few months. I felt jealous; I would love to have the kind of family that she described. Toby winced, and I worked hard to not let my resentment harden my heart as she complained about how she had a mother that was caring or siblings that annoyingly adored her and a new father that loved her as if she were his own daughter.

"Where are they?" I asked, noticing the quietness of the house while I listened to the soft ticking of the wall clock.

"At some church function." She waved her hand dismissively.

"What about you? Why didn't you go?"

Stacy pushed harder on the blanket as she followed the pattern. "I'm sick."

I noticed the large bags under her eyes and the grey hue to her cheeks and wondered if it was contagious. Toby shifted uncomfortably next to me. I felt a small, strange sensation working its way through my intestines. *Was it coming from him?*

"How long have you been sick?" I asked, wondering if it was something like leukemia or some other life-threatening ailment. I secretly hoped it was for a moment but stopped when Toby nudged me.

"Be nice," he said, glaring at me, and then he turned his attention back to Stacy.

"A week or so, I guess." She sniffled, and in that moment all resentment dissolved. I felt concern for her. She was hiding something painful, but I knew what it was, and looking at her, I realized I wasn't happy it had happened to her. *She didn't deserve it.*

"The only thing good about being sick is not having to do schoolwork," I said, trying to cheer her up.

Stacy looked up at me. "I home school."

"Right," I said, feeling stupid for forgetting that. "Tony told me that."

I could swear I saw Stacy's lip quiver, "You know Tony…Dyphan?"

"Ya, he's the one who told me about you…" I stopped, since Stacy looked like she was going to cry, or be ill. Her eyes were wide, but the rest of her face was scrunched up. I knew that she'd feel this way. I had pictured how I'd react if some girl mentioned Mims to me, and I'd be feeling no different.

"How do you know…Tony?" I noticed she tripped over his name like it hurt her just to say it.

Thinking quickly, I answered, "I've bowled with him." I knew it was a mistake almost instantly. Stacy shuddered. She had stopped tracing the pattern in the blanket, but her finger turned white under the pressure as she kept it there.

"What's wrong?" I asked. *I knew what was wrong. Why did I ask that?*

She looked down. It was taking all her strength to keep herself together. "I hate Tob…Tony," she muttered.

Toby slipped off the couch onto his knees. I reached out to him and felt a wave of remorse engulf me. I pulled my hand back as quickly as I could. "Pardon?" I asked shakily. "Did you say Tony or Toby?"

Stacy's head jerked up while she brought her hand to her mouth then bolted from the room.

I looked at Toby. He was staring at me. "Panic attack?" I asked in a whisper.

"I'm… I'm not sure," Toby said as if he were gasping for air. He put his hand on the coffee table to steady himself. "I feel like my lungs are being crushed."

I tried to touch him again, only to be met with the same overpowering sensation of grief. "But what's wrong with Stacy?" I asked, hoping Toby would have an answer.

"She's really sick." His breath was coming more easily now.

"Oh." I got up and started toward where Stacy had gone, but before I made it to the archway, she reappeared.

She placed one hand on the wall next to her and said curtly, "I think it's time that you leave." She was making room for me to walk past her and out the door.

But I hadn't been able to deliver Toby's message, and I'd promised him I would. Also, I could feel a mounting pressure, like my stomach was about to explode, and looking at Toby, I was certain these sensations were emanating from him. So I stalled by asking, "Why?"

Stacy kept her one hand on the wall and leaned her head against it. "I don't want to think of either of those boys ever again." She stood up straighter, her voice hardening. "I wish they were dead!"

"Toby *is* dead," I said quietly. He covered his eyes with his hand. I watched as Stacy reached out with her other hand like she was hugging the doorframe and slowly slid to the floor.

"Oh God, now what am I going to do?" she wailed.

My heart broke seeing her hurting so bad. I took a step closer. "Why? What's wrong?" Of course, I already knew, but she didn't know that I did, and somehow I felt it would be better if she told me. I waited for her reply.

She gazed up at me, and I could see a familiar look in her eyes. It seemed to ask the question; could she trust me? I sat down beside her. She continued to hug the wall like it was the only thing that kept her from sinking through the floor. Toby crawled closer to us; he looked like a wounded animal.

"You don't know what they did to me." She swallowed hard, like something was caught in her throat.

"Stacy," I started, watching her closely, but I could also see Toby out of the corner of my eye, and inside I felt his regret like a storm raging in my gut. "I came here today because I have a message from Toby." Stacy closed her eyes. Silent tears washed down her face as she leaned her head against the wall. "He wanted me to come and tell you how sorry he was for what he did."

Her whole body shook with her sobs. "You know?" she gasped.

"Yes," I answered, and for a moment I felt guilty, as if somehow I had done something wrong by knowing.

"Tell her I was wrong! I was bad!" Toby choked out urgently. "I bullied her and took advantage of her! I'm the creep."

"Toby was a creep," I said, finding my voice. "He admitted to me that what he did was wrong. He took advantage of you; he was a bully. He was bad."

"But why?" she managed to ask before her sobs overcame her voice.

"Because," I looked at Toby now, "because he could," I said flatly.

"What?" she asked, confused. Her hands stayed wrapped against the wall. *She looked so sad, so scared. I remembered feeling like that.*

I could feel my resolve building. "Because he could. He was a bully, and he could do whatever he wanted. So he did. He didn't need to justify it to anyone. When he wanted something he just took it. Because to him the only thing that mattered was what he wanted. Not you or anyone else." I surprised myself with the amount of anger I heard in my voice.

Toby had sat back on his knees looking awestruck. His eyes were wide in surprise, but he nodded. Stacy closed her eyes and continued to sob. I watched her grip on the wall seem to relax. I gave her the time she needed, but I was distracted by my own thoughts. *I wasn't wrong!* All those time with Mims, then Rock and Nick. *I didn't do anything wrong!* Just like Stacy, I was the victim of their choices. *I had felt so guilty,* and no one had corrected me, but I hadn't told anyone either...

A thought struck me. "Have you told anyone about what happened?" She just shook her head. "What about your mom!" I persisted. *I remembered her mom; she had always seemed nice.*

"She's busy with the other kids." Stacy's voice sounded defeated, like she'd given up before she even tried. "Besides, I don't think they'd believe me."

"Why not?" *That sounded more like the way my mother would react, not hers!*

"Because," the tears started to fall heavily again, "I snuck out that night. It was past my curfew because it was a weeknight, and I snuck out though my window. I even wore clothes that I'm not supposed to; a short skirt and a tight top. My parents would just tell me this is God's way of punishing me."

"No!" Toby protested, pounding the floor with his fist. "No. No. No. NO!"

"No, Stacy," I said softly, pulling some loose hairs from around her face, "I don't think it's that. Your mom cares about you, and she doesn't want to see you get hurt. She wouldn't be glad that this happened. She wouldn't think you deserve this—no one deserves to be treated like this."

"Then why did it happen?" she moaned.

I started slow. "I think it happened because we can't make everyone's choices for them. You may have chosen to sneak out, but you didn't know Toby would choose to do what he did. The world is full of people making their own choices—some good and some bad. You can't be responsible for other people's choices, only your own. So maybe you deserve the consequences for sneaking out; like being grounded, or maybe no TV, but I just don't see how being raped is a reasonable punishment."

"What about being raped and getting pregnant?"

I felt all the air leave me. Toby fell over. "You're pregnant?" I asked, my voice high and squeaky. I felt like the room was spinning.

Stacy looked at me and shrugged. "I might be." Somehow she seemed much calmer now. I watched her as she rubbed the remaining tears off her cheeks. "I've been too scared to go out and buy a pregnancy test, but I'm about a month overdue, and I've been sick almost every morning since that night."

Toby rolled on the floor. Holding his face in his hands, he moaned, "What have I done?"

Stacy was watching me with newfound composure. *What was I supposed to do now?* Toby was no help. I worried that he was falling into despair, and I'd never get him out. I could feel his emotional turmoil, and it made me nauseous.

Stacy didn't blink. *How could she be so calm now?* My stomach felt like I'd jumped out of a plane without a parachute! *How was I supposed to help her?*

"Want to get one with me now?" I finally asked.

She shrugged. "I can't be seen buying a pregnancy test. I'm the pastor's daughter."

"What!" I gasped.

"My mom married a widowed pastor. Didn't I tell you that?"

"I'm going to hell," Toby wailed.

"You skipped the part where you stepdad was a pastor," I said, trying not to be distracted by Toby. Stacy shrugged again. I felt like I needed to take a moment and clear my head. There were way too many new things I was trying to take in. "I could go get you a test and bring it back," I offered, wanting to leave, if only for a little while. Toby had quieted but stayed lying on the ground.

Stacy shifted so her back was to the wall. She stared blankly at the hall in front of her. "The store is too far away." She sounded almost like she didn't care. "How will you get there and back in time?"

"When is your family supposed to be home?" I asked, avoiding her question for the moment. *Could she handle the answer?*

"Oh," she said mildly, "it's a church thing, so probably not until late in the afternoon; at least an hour or two."

I looked at the clock; it was getting close to one o'clock. *What should I do? What should I say?* I felt bad for her. I had already exposed so much. *How will she feel when she finds out Tony is waiting to talk to her?*

"How did you get here?" Stacy asked, helping me decide what to do next.

I tried to answer quietly, "Tony drove me here."

Her voice became small and squeaky. "Who?"

I knew I didn't need to repeat myself. She had heard. Her eyes were still bright from the last cry, but I could see new tears forming in the corners. She wiped them roughly with the back of her shaky arm. I wished more than anything that Toby would tell me what to do now, but he seemed paralyzed watching Stacy.

"He wanted to apologize to you himself," I explained, looking into her face and wondering how I'd feel if Mims had done the same thing to me. Had my brother not come home in time, he would have... *What if this were me?* I now realized just how lucky I had been.

"Do you know what he did to me?" Stacy had drawn her knees as tight against her chest as she could.

"Tony or Toby?" I wasn't sure who she was talking about now.

"Tony, the other one!" Stacy's voice had become hard with anger. "He pimped me out!" Fresh tears escaped from her eyes. She covered her face with her hands and sobbed.

"Stacy," I said, reaching out and laying a hand on her arm. "It's not your fault." *I wasn't sure why I told her this; it somehow seemed to be the right thing to say.*

Toby, who had tried to sit up, now fell forward. "Tony drugged her."

For a moment I felt like I was about to pass out. I thought of Tony, waiting out in the car, and all I wanted to do was march out to him and cut him open with my nails.

Toby kept talking. "It was muscle relaxant—we'd used it before. That way the girl stays conscious but, well, it just worked to our advantage." He wasn't bragging but that didn't diminish my desire to strike him across the face.

Toby shuddered and tumbled to the floor once again. "Mariah, I've done so many things…" I put my hand up. I didn't want to hear any more. *I was glad he was dead! He deserved all the pain and misery he was feeling!*

"How can it not be my fault?" Stacy asked quietly, and I was reminded of that night, when Toby was trying to convince me of the very same thing. It seemed unbelievable now that I too had felt so guilty.

"It's not," I said with conviction, "it's just not." *Why did we feel responsible when it was them that hurt us?*

"But I liked Toby. I met him, and afterward I couldn't think about anything except being his girlfriend." She sniffled. "Tony said I wasn't his type, but I kept badgering him to help me become whatever Toby wanted. I was willing to do anything to be with Toby." She regained control of her tears. "He was so handsome, and when he walked into a room, you could tell he was in control. I wanted him."

"Not this way," I said.

"No." She shook her head sadly. "Not this way." She wiped her nose with the back of her sleeve. "That night Tony planned the whole thing. He got me some clothes that he said Toby would like. I felt naked in them. He even told me how to sneak out so I wouldn't get caught, and he drove me over to the bowling alley. I was so nervous. Tony offered me something— said it would numb my jitters."

I was shocked. *She'd taken it!* Even I knew not to do something as stupid as that. *Even so, it still wasn't her fault.* She had only made it easier…

"But I didn't take them," she continued while playing with a loose thread from her sweater. "When we got to the bowling alley, Tony bought me a drink for while I watched. It was league night." She twisted the string between her thumb and finger. "You know, the pop tasted a little flat, but I still drank it all." She tugged harder on the thread. "I was watching Toby. He was a really good bowler, and he kept looking over at me." The string came loose from her shirt, leaving a frayed hole in its place. Then she started to tie it into knots. "When I got up to use the washroom, my legs were tingling. And when I got out of the washroom, Tony bumped into me, saying that Toby was looking for me. Then he took me to this small closet…"

I closed my eyes. I could see the storage room.

"Toby was waiting." Stacy swallowed hard. "He…"

I looked down at Toby. "I'm sorry. I'm so sorry," he whimpered.

"He did things to me, and I kept begging him to stop. I wanted to leave, but my arms and legs had gone numb."

"Please tell her I'm sorry," Toby cried out in agony.

I kept nodding, hoping that was all she was going to say. *It hurt just listening.* Stacy sat facing me, the knot of string pulled tight between both hands.

"Don't you see? I wanted him so bad. It had to be all my fault."

I swallowed hard. My throat felt dry and sore. "No, it isn't. They set you up, like a trapped animal. They had the whole thing planned well before that night." I remembered how smooth Tony had been, how easy it had been for him. I could picture Toby doing the same, only with drugs that helped, and no one there to stop him. "Listen, what they did was very bad. It was wrong. And I'm really sorry it happened to you." I gave her arm a squeeze. The only thing that kept me from attacking Toby was that I could feel just how deep his remorse ran—it was bottomless.

"Why are you here?" Stacy asked as if she finally realized who I was.

"I came to tell you that Toby's sorry." I looked over at him. *Sorry didn't seem to cover what he was feeling, or what he had done.*

"No, Mariah, why are you here? We haven't seen each other, like you said, in five years, and I was terrible to you."

I took a breath. *I had come so far.* Just days earlier I would never have forgiven her. *Now it hardly seemed like it mattered.* It was so long ago. "Ya, you were," I agreed. "You were really bad."

"No, I was worse," she went on. "You don't know the half of it. For years I was spreading rumors and turning everyone against you."

It was my turn to get emotional; I could feel the tears burning at the back of my eyes. I had suspected that, but it still hurt to hear the truth. I tried to steady my breath and asked, "Why did you do that?"

Stacy pulled her shoulders back and continued without looking at me. "I was mad at you for what you did to me." *This felt like the ultimate insult.* I was the one who was hurt by her; *what did she have to be mad at me for? What right did she have to feel that way?*

Toby seemed to be instantly cured. He sat up and looked from Stacy's face to mine. "Ask her why," he coaxed gently.

It took me a few moments to feel calm enough to repeat his question.

"This is going to sound silly. I've had a long time to think about it now, and I can see how stupid I was." With the string in several knots, she rolled it around in the palm of her hand. "You stopped talking to me." She finally looked at me. "I can see now that I was being childish. But can't you understand? I knew something was wrong, and I was hurt when you didn't tell me? I was supposed to be your best friend, and you had a secret you wouldn't share. That meant that you didn't trust me, and I was mad about that. It made me feel like I wasn't good enough."

I sighed. *I had never thought about it that way.* "Some problems seem so big, like they are swallowing you up whole," I said in my defence. "It's only recently that I discovered, when you share them, they shrink, but I didn't know that then." And I surprised myself by adding, "I'm sorry I didn't trust you with my troubles. It had nothing to do with you and everything to do with me"

"I sorta get that now. I'm sorry too, really sorry!"

I explained how my father had left, and how I had felt worthless with him gone. How he had been the only thing that had kept my life in balance, and without him my mother had become bitter and sad, and there was nothing that could stop my brother from making horrible choices that affected the whole family.

"I'm sorry," Stacy said softly again as I finished. There wasn't much else that could be said. But she shocked me with her own story, how her father was abusive to her mother, and how they had to run away to a shelter. "You know, for everything that went bad, I got madder at you; like if you had still been my friend, it wouldn't have happened. I know it wasn't really your fault."

But I felt differently. I thought back to that time in my life when I had chosen to shut Stacy out and wondered how much better things could have been if I had told her. I would have shared with her, and she could have been supportive of me at a time when I'd really needed it… Then, when things had gone wrong for her, I might have been able to be a good friend back, instead of us having to be so very alone. In some ways she was right; without me in her life, it had been harder; without her in mine, my life had been miserable!

We sat in silence. Toby even seemed more at peace for a while. Stacy made us fresh-squeezed lemonade, the kind that makes your face scrunch up with its real sourness, and we drank it in the living room, catching up on each other's lives as if we'd been best friends all along, and no time had passed.

Toby coughed, and I looked up at the clock, which showed that we had visited for over two hours. It was nearing three. Her family could be returning soon, and we had things we still needed to do. I stood up.

"You're leaving?" An edge of panic crept into her voice.

I looked out the window. Tony's car was still there. I had taken so long I wondered what he'd been doing. "Didn't you want me to get you that test?"

"Right." Her whole body slumped. "I'd forgotten that for a moment… I guess you should go now then, huh?" Stacy looked up to the clock herself. "You said Tony's with you?" I could physically feel the hurt and fear behind her words.

I nodded. "He wanted to apologize, but if you don't want to see him, I completely understand."

Stacy's hands shook while she tried to take a sip of lemonade. I could tell she was trying to act casual. "I don't know." The glass clunked as she set it down on the table. "Let me think about it while you're gone. I'll tell you when you get back."

I didn't want to leave Stacy like this, and I wished with all my heart that Toby could stay to watch over her. He seemed reluctant to leave her too, but he slowly turned to the door, and I followed. My legs felt like dead weight as I headed down her steps, along her walk and across the street. But when I got to the car, I stopped. Tony wasn't there.

"He might have gone home to wait," Toby said, pointing to a house just a little way up the block. "We could go see what's up."

I shook my head and walked around to the passenger side of the car, then leaned heavily on it and held my head in my hands. Every muscle ached. I was so fatigued from the afternoon. I kept rolling Stacy's words around in my head. "They drugged me."

"I understand if you are upset with me," Toby said softly, cutting into my thoughts.

Upset, that word didn't seem to cover it. "You could have warned me," I said in a choked voice. He didn't respond. "You drugged her!" He had slid down beside the car onto his hands and knees. "And she wasn't the only one!" I hissed, feeling rage well up in me. I bent down next to him, but only so I could speak directly into his ear. "How many? How many other girls did you do this to?"

Toby shook, as if it took all his might to stay in that position, or perhaps like a giant hand weighed down upon him, and he fought to not be squished flat.

"Did you rape the rest?" My voice was as cold as ice. I was glad as he continued to struggle. *He deserved to be torn limb from limb.*

"No!" Toby's words came out hard, as if he'd been running a long time and couldn't get enough air. "The others all went willingly…" he huffed a few times. "At least, none of them complained openly."

I wanted more than anything to kick him, but I didn't. I knew it would be useless; my foot would go right through him. "You are a monster." My voice shook and even scared me. Toby trembled like he was losing the fight to stay up, and I was satisfied. I thought of poor Stacy in the storage room, her arms and legs numb, and then I asked, "What did you do after? How did she get home?" *Where did his cruelty end?*

Toby fell flat to the ground, his arms and legs spread out. He convulsed as if someone had attached him to a live wire. "Lar-ry," he breathed between spasms, "Lar-ry f-f-ound her."

I stood up. *Larry found her!* My mind flashed back to the look on Larry's face when he'd discovered me in the storage room, and how careful he'd been after when he'd bought me a drink and kept it sealed. Another question entered my head, and it gave me a chill. I placed my hand over my mouth and slid down the car to the ground…

"When did you remember this?" I asked. "Was it before or after my date with Tony?" *Had Toby known Tony was capable of this and not warned me all those times?*

Toby continued to twitch, but not as violently. When he spoke, his voice was strained, but his words came easier. "That night as Tony brought you home from your date."

"Why didn't you tell me?" I asked, anger welling up, and then I thought of Sunday. Toby had opened the door for Tony. "You knew this about Tony, and you let him into my house anyway!"

Toby didn't get a chance to answer…

"Mariah! What's wrong?" Tony exclaimed and rushed over to me. Before I could respond, he'd pulled me up to my feet.

All the rage I felt toward both boys flared up, and I slapped Tony across the face. He stepped back but didn't say anything. I slapped him again and watched his head jerk back from the force of my blow. His eyes were wide. Then I went to hit him again, and he caught my hand. I raised my other hand, but he caught it easily too. I was livid. *I wanted to tear him apart!*

I kicked out, and Tony sidestepped my leg. Before I knew what was happening, he had somehow managed to get me in a bear hug with my back to him, sitting on the ground. I yelled as he firmly held my hands and kept his legs around mine so I couldn't hurt him or myself. I struggled, but he remained solid. My yells slowly turned to moans, my struggles became feeble jerks, and then I stopped. Resting my head against Tony's chest, I closed my eyes. I could feel my breath coming erratically and the beat of Tony's heart.

Time seemed to dissolve around us. The autumn afternoon was chilly but not uncomfortable. When I opened my eyes, they fell upon Toby. He lay only a foot from me. His eyes were bloodshot, his hair had lost its shine and was a mess, and his skin looked yellowish.

I felt Tony's grip relax, but he didn't let go. Quietly he asked, "What's going on?"

I began to squirm against him again, but he held fast. So I cried out, "You drugged Stacy!"

Tony released me, and I shifted away from him and Toby. Pulling myself into a ball and resting my chin on my knee, I sat staring at the boys. Tony put his hand on his head and grabbed his hair. I watched as his face seemed to go through a multitude of emotions. I swallowed hard. *What was I doing with boys like these?*

"Yes," Tony finally answered, banging his head against the car door.

"You lied to me!" I accused. "You said you had no idea Toby would do that—but you gave her the drugs! What did you think he'd do?"

Tony kept knocking his head on the car door.

"It was me," Toby said, making a move to come closer to me. I put my hand up, and he stopped. "Mariah, it was always me."

I shook my head.

Toby sat up on his knees and continued to try to convince me. "I had coerced Tony into doing it! It's not his fault. Tell Tony it wasn't his fault!" he pleaded.

"I will not!" I snapped back.

Tony stopped banging his head and looked at me, but he didn't ask anything.

"Come on!" Toby begged. "I showed him every trick I knew! I even made him believe that it was cool. I challenged him to be more like me; it's not his fault! I told him to do it!"

"But Tony is the one who chose to do it," I said firmly, with a newfound calm. "You can't take the blame for him choosing to do it. He could have just as easily said no!"

"She's right, man," Tony said, letting go of his hair. "You can't take the blame for what I did. I've got to live with it." Tony's eyes were bright with tears.

"I drugged Stacy. It was me and no one else. She wasn't the first either," he licked his lips, "but I promise she will be the last. They're a type of muscle relaxant prescribed for my father's back pain. He takes them to go to sleep. Three knock him out for the night; one did the trick for our purpose. The deal was supposed to be that if the girl said no then we didn't, because that would be wrong… Usually we didn't slip them the drug until they'd consented. Actually, at first we only gave them some if the girls accepted, but then we started to sneak it into their drinks."

He turned away. "It made it exciting—at least that's what we told ourselves. The girls seemed to like it too. Most of them weren't comfortable with their bodies; this just helped them to relax…easy. And then we could do all sorts of things they normally wouldn't agree to." Tony looked down at his lap. "Please don't look at me."

"Why?" I asked, not turning away.

"Because what I did was hideous, and I really like you. I just can't bear to have you looking at me, knowing who I really am."

"Tough," I said. "I get to know all your dirty little secrets, and you're just going to have to live with it." Not that I liked knowing. It was sickening, but somehow I just knew that was how it was supposed to be.

"How is Stace?"

"She's doing better than I could imagine," I said, sitting up straighter. "But she needs me to get her a pregnancy test." *I loved the panic those words inflicted.*

Tony reached out like he was falling over. "Toby's?"

"Do you think it could be someone else's?"

Tony just shook his head.

The ride to the pharmacy was quiet. It seemed to take all of Tony's concentration to keep the car on the road. Toby looked as if he was shrinking under the mistakes of his life, and I couldn't stop playing the day's events over and over again in my head.

When Tony parked, Toby spoke up. "I need a favour from Tony."

"Anything!" Tony said.

He explained that he wanted Tony to write a confession for him. Their handwriting was very similar, and Tony could forge Toby's signature. If Stacy had a signed letter, then Toby's parents wouldn't argue it; they were the kind of people who would make sure that Stacy and the child were cared for. Tony agreed. So we ended up buying a pregnancy test, a note pad and envelopes. We returned to Stacy's within the hour.

I hid the test in my jacket pocket in case her parents had returned, even though Tony told me their mini-van wasn't there. He waited in the car again. Stacy was quicker to answer the door this time, along with their miniature dachshund that sniffed my toes, then Toby's, snorted and headed back inside. Stacy didn't say anything but moved aside so I could walk in. I handed her the test, and she disappeared into the bathroom. I waited uncomfortably in the front hall.

Toby watched down the hall, as if he were holding his breath. He shook his head sadly and turned to me as we heard the latch of the door open. Stacy stumbled up the hall, the stick with a huge plus sign on it in her hand. She walked right past me and into the living room, where she fell onto the first sofa and sobbed.

I came to sit next to her, putting my hand lightly on her hair. She sobbed and sobbed, and I waited for her to calm down. When she ran out of tears, I quietly said, "Tony wanted to see you; he has something for you. Can I invite him in?"

"Whatever," she said with her head buried in the cushions.

I went to the door, happy to see that Tony was still in the car, and I waved. He got out, took a moment to steady himself, then made his way in.

He looked white as he walked into the house. I pointed to Stacy, and he went over and sat on the coffee table in front of her. "Stacy." His voice sounded strained, and the remaining colour in his face drained. "I'm sorry." She didn't budge. "Listen, there is no excuse for what I did, or for Toby. We were wrong, and I am so sorry." He paused to clear his throat. "I have a confession from Toby. It tells everything that he did to you." My gut squirmed at the thought of it. Toby wanted to explain in-depth what he had done. It had made me ill having to repeat each item to Tony, and he had looked just as sickened writing them down.

"And I'm willing to stay and tell your parents," Tony finished. We had talked it over and agreed that it was the right thing to do. Stacy didn't answer, but she seemed to calm down. Her breathing evened out, and she eventually turned to look at Tony. I moved over to sit on the middle sofa, gazing out the lovely big window at the yard and street.

I wondered how it would feel having done such horrible things and now taking responsibility. Tony seemed nervous yet calm. He'd developed a strong resolve as we'd been shopping. His jaw was set. He knew what he had to do, and now it was just a matter of doing it.

I saw the van pull up. Stacy's mother opened the door and stepped out. She was the same, only older. Her hair was graying, and the wrinkles on her face were set deeper, but she was the same woman I remembered from my childhood, with a warm, cheery smile and soft grey-blue eyes like her daughter.

Mrs. Perts, now Mrs. Miller, was deep in conversation with her new husband. He came around the front of the van to help her unload. He was tall with short black hair. They were both smiling.

As they opened the sliding door, a balloon escaped and floated up to the sky, making a girl who looked to be five years old cry. She had long black hair, neatly braided. Then a boy of about seven climbed out. He too had the same dark hair as the rest of his family.

Finally Mr. Miller leaned in to undo a child in a car seat. I didn't know what to do. Stacy's stepbrother was nearing the front door, and before I could make a plan, he was though it and standing in the front entrance staring at Tony and me.

"Mom!" he yelled—she was making her way up the walk. "Stacy's got friends over!"

Stacy's mother came through the door and looked into the living room. She must have missed Stacy lying on the couch because she asked, "Where's Stacy?" Stacy hid her face as she began to cry once more.

I pointed to her, so her mother took a step into the room and looked over the back of the sofa. That's when her husband entered carrying a cute little boy with light blond hair and grey-blue eyes.

"Evening, Tony," Mr. Miller said, putting the toddler down. The kid scampered off in the direction of the bedrooms. Mrs. Miller and the two older children stood stock still in the archway to the living room.

"Good evening, sir," Tony replied.

"Who's your friend?" Mr. Miller asked, ignoring his stunned wife and children. He removed his jacket casually, like everything was quite normal.

"This is Mariah Lafont," Tony said, but I could tell the suspense was driving him nuts. *Soon this man will not be so polite to you or me,* I thought.

"Mariah?" Mrs. Miller said, as if she had been jolted from a trance.

Mr. Miller came to stand beside his wife, placing a hand around her waist. Then he noticed Stacy and breathed, "Oh dear, what's wrong?"

"Could we speak to you alone?" I asked, aware of Stacy's brother and sister, who stood mouths agape behind their parents.

"Of course," Mr. Miller said and escorted his children away. Mrs. Miller stood as if frozen to the spot studying me. *Did she hate me for letting her daughter down?*

"Mariah Lafont, Stacy's childhood friend?" Mrs. Miller asked when her husband returned.

I nodded. Mr. Miller brought the chair from the desk and placed it next to the sofa where Stacy was. Mrs. Miller stiffly sat on the other end of the couch with me. "It's nice to see you again," she said, though she was understandably distracted by the state of her daughter.

"I wish it were under better circumstances," I admitted.

Toby leaned in over my shoulder and said shakily, "I can't thank you enough for doing this."

Bracing myself, I started. "Last weekend, I found out that you'd moved to the city." Mrs. Miller smiled. "But not in a good way. It was during something like a confession." It was like the whole room was holding its breath. "I was told about a girl who'd…who had been…" I couldn't bare to say the last word. I watched as Stacy pulled herself into a ball, and I heard Toby fall to the floor behind me.

Tony, who was so white he might have been mistaken for the ghost, finished for me. "A girl who'd been raped."

Mr. Miller looked from Tony to Stacy, then he went to his knees in front of her, and leaning over, he talked softly into her ear. She nodded and began to wail.

Mrs. Miller brought her hand to cover her mouth and gasped, "My Stace?"

Tony lowered his head and looked at the letter in his hands, but I looked straight at her and nodded. Stacy refused to look at anyone. Mr. Miller stayed by her side with his hand lovingly on her back. Mrs. Miller brought her other hand to her mouth and rocked as she started to cry.

"Thank you for informing us," Mr. Miller said to me. "I too wish that you had come under better circumstances, but it's good that you came nonetheless."

I felt like he was trying to politely dismiss us.

Toby lay next to the sofa, "Tell him the rest, quickly, please!"

"There's more…" Mr. Miller's hand tightened into a fist on Stacy's back. "When I came to see Stacy she said, well, see…" Again my voice failed me.

Tony sat on the edge of the sofa like he was preparing to run, "Sir," he said in a small, shaky voice, "Stacy's pregnant." His statement was met with eerie silence. "I have a letter from a boy named Toby Studdem; it explains everything he did." Tony seemed to be gathering strength, and then he went on. "And I've added what I have done to the list."

"Are you really pregnant?" Mrs. Miller asked shrilly. "Surely God wouldn't do that! Jon?" She turned to her husband.

Stacy pulled her arm out from under her. Clutched in her hand was the positive pregnancy test.

"God does things that we don't understand, Hazel." Mr. Miller's voice was kind as he patted Stacy's heaving back. "He also allows things to happen for reasons that don't make sense to us." He stood up and put his hand out to Tony for the letter. Tony stood slowly, and though it looked as if he wanted to run, he didn't. He handed the envelope to Mr. Miller. With great slowness, Mr. Miller opened the seal and took the letter out to read it.

Toby lay in a ball on the floor, and I could feel him at the back of my thoughts. *I couldn't do anything for him.* Tony stood, waiting, but I saw that he was shaking too. I felt so bad for him that I went to stand beside him. *I didn't care what anyone thought about me now.* Every muscle in Tony's body was flexed. I slid my hand into his, and he squeezed it in response. Toby crawled over to us on the floor. He looked so wretched, he reminded me of a wet cat.

Mrs. Miller was dissolving into a puddle of tears. Mr. Miller looked over the top of the paper at us then went back to reading. Stacy seemed to have run out of tears for the moment, but she kept her face hidden. Mrs. Miller kept rocking. I could hear the children playing in a bedroom down the hall. They shouted and giggled, and the dog barked.

Finally Mr. Miller neatly folded up the note and put it with the envelope onto the coffee table. "I think it is time for you two to be going." He didn't sound angry, but his voice made it clear we were to leave.

Tony led the way, and I followed, with Mr. Miller not far behind me. Toby managed to crawl along the floor at my feet. Tony got to the front door and reached for the knob.

"Young man," Mr. Miller said in a quiet voice that wouldn't carry back to the living room. "God still loves you." He looked like he was going to put his hand on Tony's shoulder, but he stopped and looked down at the floor.

"Mr. Miller." I was reminded of what Stacy had said earlier; I explained how she felt God was punishing her.

Mr. Miller's eyes filled with sorrow. "If that were true, then that poor girl has been punished for ten lifetimes of sin! No, I don't believe that. Often those that deserve punishment, as you call it, seem to get away scot-free, while the innocent have to suffer."

Toby pulled himself to standing and hooked his arms around my neck just as I stepped out the door. I felt like the ground had disappeared under me, and it took all my strength to make it down the steps using the railing as my guide and support. I caught Tony's arm as I made it to the bottom of the last step. I might have fallen if I hadn't. The world seemed to be getting dim, and my breathing felt hard, like I was trying to breathe under water. Tony guided me to his car, and Toby fell into the back seat with relief.

I felt shaken but stronger now that Toby had let go. Tony seamed oblivious. I took my seat beside him while he put the key into the ignition but didn't turn it on. Instead he gripped the steering wheel with both hands and stared out the front windshield. I leaned back and shut my eyes. Dusk would soon be approaching. I could feel the dark of night creeping closer, making the world seem bleak and unpleasant.

I thought of Stacy's life; past, present, and future, and how it wasn't all that different from mine. We both had our share of heartaches. In fact, I now knew that Tony's story was the same too. In fact, the more I thought about it, the more I realized that none of our stories were that different. Yet for all the bad, there were bits of good.

I tried to count mine up. Toby came to mind, despite all his mistakes, as did my friends at school, and now Stacy, but also Tony, and even Larry. Then I thought of Molly; yes even my hairdresser was a bit of good I could count on.

I felt Tony brush my cheek as he said, "Hey beautiful, I don't want to be alone tonight. Would you come to dinner with me?" He sounded so desperate. Even though I was exhausted, I agreed.

This time he took me to an authentic Mexican restaurant, and although it was a Saturday night, they found us a private booth. The table was topped with a Mexican blanket covered by clear glass. They had a real musician singing a song in Spanish. Toby managed to walk himself in and flopped down onto the bench opposite us.

There was a bowl of chips and salsa to dip into as a starter. Tony warned me that the splash of green in the middle was hotter than a volcano exploding, so I made a mental note to avoid it. The waiter came dressed in a Mexican poncho, and Tony ordered the platter for two. It had a selection of several items from the menu, so we could try a bit of everything.

I reached out and took a chip more for something to do. Only when I swallowed did I realize how hungry I was. After that I couldn't get the chips into my mouth fast enough!

Tony was watching me. "Hungry?" he asked, amused.

I couldn't remember when I'd eaten last.

"Just save some room for the main course."

For the first time in a week, I felt self-consciously big. I turned away from Tony and watched the other customers. They were laughing and talking loudly. There was a couple that was probably on a date. They looked like they were oblivious to anything around them. *I wished I were them.* I heard Tony munch on a few chips.

My emotions were frayed. I couldn't seem to control them. *I felt black, hopeless.* Toby sighed. I looked over to see his upper shoulder just above the top of the table; he looked like he was having an asthma attack. *How much of what I was feeling was me and how much him?* I felt so alone; I threw my head against the seat and shut my eyes.

"Mariah," Toby whispered, and I felt his hand on my knee as he reached under the table. Overwhelming darkness seemed to consume me. *I was falling!*

I felt like I was drowning in it. "Stop it," I choked.

Toby let go of my knee, and I fell over onto Tony. "Mariah," he gasped as he caught me. There was a look of fear in his eyes. "What's wrong?"

"Toby," I whimpered. "Something's wrong with him." I pressed myself against Tony. *I was safe now*

Tony leaned in and asked with urgency, "What?"

"I don't know." Though the darkness had dissipated, and I could breathe again, I still felt my stomach was sinking like I was in some supercharged merry-go-round. "Whatever it is, when he touches me, it gets way worse."

Tony nodded. "You went white. I thought you were going to pass out." He was talking into my ear, and his lips tickled. I got a shiver.

Sitting up straighter, I agreed. "I felt like it."

"Do you need to go home?" The question hung in the air, and I could tell Tony didn't even like asking it. *I didn't want to go home. Then I'd be alone with Toby and his remorse.*

Toby continued to gasp and moan. "I don't think he'd be any better off there, and you've already ordered." *Even though I felt waves of sickness, and I wasn't sure how much I'd enjoy staying, I knew it was best.*

Our meal arriving interrupted us. I had to eat extra slow and chew each bite carefully, as the sinking feeling in my stomach didn't improve. Through most of the meal Tony and I talked about the food. We also discussed the music and my favourite topic: the other people in the restaurant. Tony liked to make up wild stories about who they might be. It reminded me of Toby on the first morning back to school after my ant attack.

"That girl is an aspiring actress," he said looking at an attractive girl with three gentlemen. "Those are the producers of a movie she wants to star in, and she's trying to convince them she's the right gal for the job."

"You and Toby are really alike—I love you." I had meant to say, "I love that."

Tony put down the chip he'd loaded up with salsa, sour cream and guacamole and turned towards me. "Listen Mariah, I really like you. I've never felt this way about anyone else. I could see spending the rest of my life with you." He took my hands in both of his. *Did he say spend the rest of his life with me?* "But not right now. I, being so much like Toby, have some fairly big mistakes I have to set right. And it wouldn't be good having you wait until I get my life in order. I don't want you to, and I'm gonna feel horrible if I found out you were. I want you to be my good friend." Tony brought one hand up to my cheek. "Go out with that guy from your school; he seemed really nice."

I pulled away from him. *This just made me like him more! Why couldn't we be together? It made sense.*

"Mariah, please, I can't lose you. I need you."

"You won't lose me! You can have me. All of me! I'll be your girlfriend, and you won't have to worry about needing me again—I'll be yours." I took a bite and looked over at Toby; he was completely oblivious to our conversation. *I knew he'd have something else to say.*

"I'm afraid I'd lose you if I tried to be your boyfriend. I don't know how to have a girlfriend. Don't you understand, I don't even know how to be a good friend? I'm trying to learn that first. Trust me, it would go wrong if we dated. Maybe later, but please, for now let's just be friends. Promise me you will consider dating that other guy…" His eyes begged me, and he waited for my response.

I reluctantly agreed. *I hated it.* Yet when I agreed, Tony relaxed, and so did I. We were soon teasing each other and joking, and the rest of the evening was good fun. Tony would push my shoulder or hold my hand, but it was meant as nothing more than a friendly gesture. Toby was struggling greatly, but if I didn't dwell on it, it wasn't too bad.

At the end of the meal, Tony and I walked slowly so Toby could crawl behind us. We had to stop several times, pretending to tie a shoe or to pick something up, and once to hug each other so Toby could catch up.

"Couldn't you just keep walking?" Tony asked as he embraced me at the front door.

I shook my head. "We seem to be stuck to each other, and we can't go past seven feet," I explained.

"Like an invisible rope." Tony was leaning with his cheek next to mine. "Couldn't you just pull him along?"

"It's more like a box." I rested my head on his shoulder for a moment. "If I try to go too far, I hit a wall."

Tony asked, "Why don't you just carry him?"

"Too painful."

"But why do you think this is happening?"

"My guess is because Toby did some really bad things, and right now there is nothing left for him but his regrets."

Tony didn't say any more as we made it to his car. Toby sighed as he took the back bench. Tony waited until I was buckled then started the engine and headed home. Toby became more and more verbal as the car neared home. He called out like he was having a bad dream and uttered regrets with increased urgency. I felt that weight upon my thoughts, and I couldn't tell if it was that the sun had set or that Toby had made the world seem to be darker.

When we were in the visitor parking, Tony tuned off the engine and looked into the back seat. Even though he couldn't see Toby, he started to talk to him. "You know, Toby, I believe you now. You were a terrible friend. Mariah," he added, "please forgive me. I've just got to say this!" Tony went on to describe every dirty deed he had ever committed with, for, or on the behalf of his old pal. I closed my eyes as he listed insults, pranks, fights, and all types of illegal activities. There was the ant prank, the girls and the drugs and several other dirty things I wished I didn't have to listen to. Even when tears rolled down his face and he choked over his words, he went on…

This was the second time today. *Why did I have to hear this?* Just listening to him made me feel dirty and guilty. But since Tony was honest, not only about what he had done, but how he felt then and how he felt now, I sensed a new emotion—hope. I started to cry, only not so much from what Tony was saying, as horrible as it was, but because I knew this was his closure. This was the end. These things were done; he could not go back and undo them, but he would never do them again. Tony was making a choice—no, a commitment to never be that way again. *He would change!*

He finished by saying, "You were the worst friend I could have had, but now man, you've just changed all that. Now I will forever remember you as my best pal. You've changed my life, man, and in a good way. Mariah, I'm sorry you had to hear all that."

"I'm not going to lie to you," I said, trying to sound lighthearted, even though I could feel my skin crawling. "I'm sorry I had to hear it too."

Tony smiled. "Did he hear me?"

I looked in the back seat. There was no way for me to tell if he had. Toby looked no better than before. The nausea mounted, and I held my mouth. I wasn't sure it if was coming from me or Toby.

Though I thought he might be disheartened that Toby hadn't reacted, Tony didn't seem to mind. "I had to say those things," he explained. "I had to be honest. I'm sure he heard, even if you can't tell. He needed to hear it, so I'm certain. But I got to ask; will you please still come with me to visit Eric tomorrow?" I nodded. *Toby needed to go, I knew it, and I wanted to be there for Tony.* "I'm so glad… There is no way to explain how glad I am that Toby brought you into my life."

I smiled, even though the blackness was starting to pull me down. Toby rolled onto the floor of the car, whimpering. I felt my whole body shudder. "Toby's getting worse," I said. "I need to go home."

"How can I help?"

Toby's eyes were rolling into the back of his head. *I didn't know how I was going to get home.* Tony came up with the plan; I had to guide Toby. He was almost completely unreachable unless I held his hand and showed him where to go. But as soon as I touched him, the world seemed to disappear for me too. So Tony held on to me. I could feel his hand, and it was the only thing that kept me from giving up as he guided me back to my house. Before we started, I explained how he could go to my bedroom window, around the back of the building. That way he'd avoid my mother, and I would be able to make it into the house.

I took Toby's hand, only to discover the longer I held on to him, the deeper the misery and pain became. I was blind, and my skin was on fire. I couldn't feel my feet, or anything apart from pain, and Tony's hand. I became mildly aware that Tony was now carrying me. Then he put me down. The darkness grew and engulfed me.

"Help," I yelped, reaching out to anything I could. Toby had his hands wrapped tightly around me.

"Toby, stop it!" Tony said, drawing me into his arms again. "This is yours to carry! Not Mariah's. You've got to stop it, you're hurting her!"

All the pressure, the plummeting, the spinning, the prickles and fire and darkness—stopped. I was standing under the living room window outside my bedroom, being held up by Tony's strong hands.

"Thank you," I said, tears of relief running down my face. Looking down, I saw that Toby was no better off. The only difference was that I was no longer affected by it. I didn't feel him at all, not a hint or a whisper in the back of my thoughts. He was gone, yet there he lay at my feet, and in a small way I felt sad that I couldn't sense him any more.

Tony helped me into my room. Toby crawled through after and fell to the floor. He seemed more aware of where he was now. After it was clear that I was alright, Tony excused himself. He gave my hand a squeeze before he hopped out the window and walked down the path without looking back. I watched until he was out of sight. Then I looked down at Toby. He was rubbing his eyes, and it looked like his fit had ended. Eventually he pulled himself onto my bed and over to his usual spot. I stayed kneeling at the head of my bed.

"Mariah?" he said softly. It was strange being able to see him but not feel connected to him.

"Are you better now?"

He shook his head. "Not really. Just getting used to it, I guess."

"What is this? Why is it happening? Why did it affect me? And why doesn't it any more?" I felt like I needed answers.

Toby rubbed his eyes. Deep circles accented them, his hair had lost all its shine, and his cheeks looked sunken. "What you told Tony is mostly right. I've remembered it all… ALL. And it's not pretty, and there is nothing I can do to change it. I guess I just feel so guilty, so bad; it sort of physically manifests itself. You are connected to me, we share this odd bond, and I guess some of my feelings transferred over."

"Some," I said sarcastically.

He smiled at me. "Okay, more than some. I'm sorry. I was oblivious to how much I was affecting you until Tony called me on it."

"How did you turn it off?" I asked, wondering if he could turn it back on as easily.

"I didn't." Toby shook his head sadly. "But what I did do was let go of you. Ever since we met, I've been holding on to you in my mind. Sometimes that's all that I have to feel good about. When Tony pointed it out to me, I realized what I needed to do." He looked sad, *as sad as I felt.*

"Can you get it back?" I didn't want to remain unconnected. *It felt strange and lonely somehow.*

"I don't know. It might not be a good thing right now. You could end up getting hurt again." Toby ran his hand through his hair and gave me a half-hearted smile. "Besides, I don't have that much time left. Listen, I wanted to let you know you have helped so much." *I didn't believe him*, but he persisted. "Just knowing that you're better off makes a huge difference to me, but now with Tony, and even Stacy." He fell silent, looking at me with a smile on his lips.

"Perhaps you've erased your legacy of misery now," I offered hopefully.

"I wish." He licked his lips, and I noticed how dry and cracked they had become. "There's not much I can do for my lifetime legacy of misery. It will always be there. I can't erase it, and neither can you. Yet somehow I've been blessed with this opportunity to start a new legacy through you—one of hope, kindness and love."

We stayed in my room for a while, Toby in quiet contemplation, while I tried to get some homework done. Every so often I would turn in my chair to see if he was still there. I had to see him, since I had lost even the slightest sensation of him. Every time I checked, I felt relieved that he was still there.

Later we headed upstairs to get me a drink. I almost fell when I tripped on the two laundry baskets in the hallway. My mother had left a note on the kitchen table. She needed her clothes cleaned by tomorrow evening. It was already quite late, but I didn't know if I'd have time to do it the next day, so I transferred my mom's clothes into a bag, added some of my own then trudged down to the laundry room.

We had a room where we could put a washing machine and dryer right in the house, but it sat filled with storage items. My mother refused to buy machines when she felt it was perfectly easy to use the co-op's. I disagreed; it meant I had to carry the clothes down through the underground parking then stay while it was being washed and dryed, and all the time I had to share with the other tenants who used it too. It was a boring and time-consuming project. I usually brought something to read.

Toby's ability to move about had improved, but he still looked wretched. I led the way with a full bag slung over my shoulder. He was quiet for our whole walk. Once we were in the room, he sat on a washer while I loaded up three and put the money in to start them. The room had ten washers and eight dryers, but they seemed to keep breaking down. The nice thing about doing it so late at night was that apart from one dryer, none of other machines were being used, and no one was there to bother us.

Toby was playing with his sock. I was sitting in a spare chair reading when he said, "I remember my parents…" He started to tell me all about his mother and father, and the way he told it, he actually had a very nice father and a loving mother. They both worked—that was his biggest complaint—so he didn't see them much, but he said that was no excuse for his behavior. He didn't have any siblings, so he was spoiled. He'd traveled quite a bit. He'd been a terrible student, but mostly because he didn't care about learning. He remembered the sports that he was good at, but he didn't realize how good he'd been until now, even with all the trophies he brought home. He realized now that he'd been given so much, and he'd wasted it all.

"What do you miss the most?" I asked, trying not to sound too envious of his life. I was folding the clean clothes now.

Toby looked up from his sock. "This, right now."

"Laundry?" I said jokingly.

He picked up a towel and tossed it at me. "Not this! Just being with friends."

"Like talking?" I wasn't sure what he meant.

"Ya, talking, hanging, just being friends. I never knew how important that was until now. There is nothing more important than making a connection with another human being. You've taught me that." *Me?*

Once all the laundry was clean, I took it home and put mine away, then did my nighttime chores. It was now early in the morning. I was glad that it was still the weekend, and I could sleep in. As I lay in bed, I reached out with my toe to Toby. I was afraid his regrets would touch me, so I was prepared to pull away, but I didn't have to; instead I felt the familiar warmth, and I fell asleep feeling safe.

DAY 21 Sunday...

"Hey, beautiful." Someone tugged on my arm. As I came to my senses, I thought it was Toby. I looked over at the clock. Seeing that it was only eight in the morning, I rolled over, mumbling, "Too early."

"Come on," he said, kneeling on my bed next to me. I felt the mattress give under his weight. "I'm hungry; I want you to come to breakfast."

It was a combination of his words, "hungry" and the realization that he had physical substance that alerted me that it wasn't Toby. I sat bolt up, holding the bed sheets tight to my chest. Tony sat on the edge of my bed wearing a wide grin.

"What are you doing here?" I demanded.

"I'm sorry. I've scared you." Tony slid from my bed and took a seat at my desk. "I knocked, but you didn't hear me, so I snuck in through your window. I came to take you out for breakfast."

I looked all around the rest of my room, suddenly realizing that I couldn't see or feel Toby. "Toby?" I called, swinging my head back and forth. "Toby!" I was starting to feel panicked. *What if he'd left, and I didn't get to say goodbye!* Tony also looked around, though I wasn't sure why he did.

"I'm here, Mariah," came Toby's voice in my ear moments before he appeared beside me. *Thank goodness.* Relief flooded me.

"Is he gone?" Tony asked, watching me closely.

"Don't leave yet," I begged Toby.

"Not today, beautiful," he said and softly pushed my chin with his fist.

Tony cleared his throat, muttering about starting over, then he said, "Good morning, beautiful. Want to come to breakfast?"

"Let's, it should be fun." Toby said. He sounded like he was doing much better. *What had changed?* I said I would go.

Tony waited outside my window for me to get ready. I took just over half an hour, feeling pressured to hurry, which made me clumsy. I ended up trying to put my shirt on backwards and my underwear inside out. When I crawled out, I saw Tony in the bush, hiding so he wouldn't accidentally be seen from the living room window. He walked me to the car. The air was cooler, and dew covered the grass. Soon it would be frost. I was surprised to see Larry in the back seat; he looked sleep-deprived, but he smiled and told me he was glad to see me again. I climbed into the front seat, and Toby slipped in the back next to Larry.

Tony took us to a quiet diner with only one other customer. It was no bigger than a trailer. It had a long counter with stools along it and only seven tables against the wall, with a bright window every foot or so. Tony picked out a table next to a window but far enough away from the door, so we wouldn't catch the fall breeze when it opened.

"He always orders the food," Larry commented as I followed Tony with my eyes.

"Always?"

Larry nodded. He was sitting across from me with Toby beside him and this left room for Tony to take the seat next to me.

"Always," Toby answered. "Even when I was around. He actually has a gift for knowing exactly what to order for each person he's with."

Larry leaned his elbows on the table and rested heavily on them. "You're looking lovely this morning."

I narrowed my eyes while turning toward him. "Really? I didn't have time to shower, and I know my hair is a mess."

Toby looked at Larry for a moment, then at me and chuckled, shaking his head.

"Well, you still look great." *The way Larry looked at me made me feel shy and a little stiff inside.*

I thanked him, averting my eyes, then commented on how tired he looked.

"Yup." He leaned back in his chair, and stretched out, his foot only a few inches from my toe. "Tony came to my house last night and kept me up talking."

"All night?" I yawned, the very thought of it making me feel sleepy.

Larry yawned too, then smiled. "All night! But it was good. And I just want to let you know: I blame you, and so does Tony, though he won't tell me how you did it." Before I could respond, he went on. "Well, whatever, you did, it's a good thing. That boy is changing so much, I hardly recognize him. It's all good. So thank you; whatever your secret is, it's worked." I leaned back and smiled; but I was smiling at Toby, who nodded in agreement.

Tony returned, carrying all our food. The waitress brought cups and filled them with coffee for the boys. I got a hot chocolate. Tony bought Larry a huge breakfast omelet, pancakes with a whipped cream smiley face on it for me, and bacon, eggs and toast for himself. Toby had been right. Tony had somehow sensed what would be best for each of us.

We settled into a relaxed conversation about all sorts of unimportant things while we enjoyed our breakfast. *This was what Toby had said he'd miss the most.* He looked content, happy even, as he watched Larry and Tony debate the finer points of race-car driving.

As the morning progressed and breakfast came to an end, Tony's mood slowly became sombre. The lady behind the counter had come to take our dishes away and refill the boys' coffee. With the mood change, the conversation fizzled out.

Tony slowly stirred a third creamer into his cup. "I want to go visit Eric. I know it's the right thing to do, but man am I nervous."

Larry reached across the table and gave Tony a friendly nudge. "Well, Tone, after our talk last night, I know you're gonna do just fine."

"Ya," I said, putting my hand on Tony's, "and I'll be there with you."

"I wouldn't be able to do it without you," Tony said.

He stayed quiet while he drove us up to South View Juvenile Hall. It was nearing noon as he pulled into the guest parking. I got out and moved so Larry could open his door, but he just got comfortable and pulled out a novel from his back pocket. "See ya," he said with a wave.

"You're not coming?" I asked as the fall breeze played with my loose strands of hair. Tony was coming around to my side of the car to walk with me.

"Three's a crowd," Larry answered, finding his place in his book and holding it up to start reading. *What was that supposed to mean?*

"It's not his fight; he's got no part in this," Tony said holding his hand out to me. I accepted it, and we walked together up to the entrance. Toby was just a few paces behind us. Tony's grip tightened as we walked into the building and up to the front receptionist. She was in a booth behind glass, and the front waiting area was a small room with two lines of benches.

"Can I help you?" She looked up. Her hair was pulled tight behind her head, and she wore huge glasses. There was only a small screened hole for her to talk through.

Tony explained that we were there to visit a friend. The receptionist asked us to wait, but it didn't take long for a short, balding man to come through a door into our side of the reception area. He introduced himself as Eric's counselor, Carl, and asked a few basic questions, such as how did we know Eric and how long had we been friends. If Tony was nervous, he didn't show it. Toby, however, wore an expression of mingled fear and pain.

Eric's counselor finished talking to us and escorted us to what he called a meeting room. He had us go in, explaining that the doors locked but we would be safe. There were guards, and he'd be watching through the window, which looked like a mirror. We were also told that Eric might not be cooperative. So far he'd had no guests, but he seemed anti-social when it came to the rest of the residents.

Sitting on the edge of his chair, Tony looked anxious, but not nearly as bad as Toby, who fell into the seat next to him. The meeting room was about the size of my living room, with bare off-white walls and some folding chairs, a long mirrored window along one wall and two doors, the one we'd come through and another that opened a few minutes later, with a young boy being escorted by a large guard.

As soon as my eyes fell upon Eric, my heart broke. He wore an expression of complete brokenness; his hazel eyes looked dull and lifeless, like they had lost all hope. His hair was shoulder-length and dirty blond, and was matted and tangled. His shirt was wrinkled and his pants stained.

Eric saw me first and seemed confused, but when Tony sat up straighter, his face hardened, and his eyes seemed to come to life. He stopped walking and turned to the guard. "I don't want to see him," he said loudly. "Take me back to my room."

Tony gazed at Eric with a look of mingled disgust and compassion. *This was the monster he'd created through his actions.* Toby shivered.

"Sorry, Eric," the guard said in a hushed voice. "Carl says you need to take visitors." The guard was large and bulky. He could have easily picked Eric up and carried him over to us.

"Not them," Eric argued, trying to push the guard back through the door.

"Why?" the guard asked, standing firm against Eric's attempts to move him back. When Eric didn't come up with an answer, the guard swung Eric around and sat him in a chair opposite Tony. Then he turned, left the room and shut the door firmly behind him.

Eric scowled at Tony, his eyes ablaze, which seemed to breathe life into the rest of his body. Tony looked down at his hands. Toby sat wide-eyed, staring at Eric. I stood, feeling absolutely foolish and useless. I wished more than anything that I had sat down, but I felt too shy, and I didn't want to interrupt this interaction.

Eric drew himself up, folding his arms in front of himself. He seemed to grow in stature. "Heard your pal Toby died." Tony looked up. With a scowl on his face, Eric continued, "I'm glad."

Toby winced like he'd been hit but didn't say anything. I continued to stand uncomfortably. Tony lowered his gaze again. He seemed lost for words.

"What do you want?" Eric spat. I saw his fists clench and unclench.

Quietly, Tony started. "I came to tell you how sorry I am..."

"Save it!" Eric said, leaning forward. "I don't want to hear it!" Every muscle seemed to flex like a bull preparing to charge.

Tony moved back in his chair, grabbing the armrests and holding tight. He looked terrified, and I wanted to help somehow, *but what should I do?*

Tony tried again, "Eric, I know you got a..."

"Shut it!" Eric said, uncrossing his arms and making fists. "I told you I don't want to hear it." As terrified as I was to see Eric like this, something told me it was healthy for him to be enraged, better than when he'd entered in despair.

Tony pulled back more but didn't seem to want to stop trying. "But I feel awful…" His face reflected his emotions, but Eric seemed blind to it.

"What do you know about feeling awful?" He was balancing on the edge of his seat, his voice a low, shaky yell, and I got the impression he was about to jump on Tony if he tried to speak again.

"Listen, I know…" but Tony didn't get to finish. Eric had lunged out of his chair towards Tony like a cat pouncing on a mouse. I yelled out as I watched Tony's chair tumble over backwards, with Tony in it and Eric on top of him. I felt someone grab me and pull me out of the way while three guards came rushing in, one from the door that we'd used and two from the other. Two guards grabbed Eric, hauling him off Tony and holding him firmly. The other bent down to where Tony lay and checked to see if he was alright. His nose was bleeding, but not badly. He wiped it on the back of his sleeve and assured the guard that he would be fine. I didn't realize until the guards had taken Eric away that I was crying.

The guard stayed and talked with Tony a bit. I missed most of it trying to calm myself down. Toby, who had pulled me away from the commotion, didn't help. As he held me, I felt darkness, remorse and pain pouring into me. Toby must have figured this out, because he quickly released me. The third guard left, closing the door behind him, and Tony came over to my side.

He asked if I was alright, touching his nose gingerly. He tried to convince me that his nose didn't hurt, he'd felt worse. He pushed my hand away. Then, drawing me into his arms he said, "Aw, beautiful, I'm so sorry."

"You know," I said, feeling stiff next to him, "this really isn't my fight either. I had no part in this…"

"I know," he said, giving me a tight squeeze, and then he let me go. "You're the best."

Toby, who still stood behind me, whispered, "I'm so sorry I dragged you into all of this." Then he collapsed on the floor and shook uncontrollably.

Tony had to talk with the counselor again, so I sat while Tony paced back and forth. He seemed consumed with a great dilemma, but when Carl walked in, Tony quickly took a seat and talked calmly with him. Tony was asked a whole bunch of questions about his relationship with Eric. They wanted to know if Tony knew anything about the night Eric had thrown the party, or if Eric had told him anything about the drugs or dealer. However, Tony was never asked directly about his own involvement in any of the events, and he never volunteered any information or fessed up to any of it either.

As Tony was talking, Toby seemed to gather himself together. He sat up and rubbed his eyes, then watched intently. I got the feeling something more was going on that I wasn't aware of, but no one said any more. The counselor finished and allowed us to leave. Tony didn't say anything on the way back to the car; he just held my hand and walked. At the car, I looked into the back seat to see Larry asleep across the bench. I was starting to feel overwhelmed by these boy's lives and wondered if I'd always be so deeply involved with them. I sighed.

Tony got in and chuckled. "It's been a long morning for all of us."

Toby slid in between Tony and me.

"Where to?" I asked as Tony fumbled with his car key. Eventually he discovered he'd been trying to use the wrong one. He started the engine, looking like he was trying to sort out all his thoughts.

"I guess we should take Larry home," he answered, and then asked, "How's Toby?" He reached out and put his hand right through his old friend when I indicated that he was there. Toby jumped, but Tony didn't react.

"Anything?" I asked.

"No." Tony shook his head, disappointed. "How is he?"

"Hanging in," I answered honestly. Toby still looked miserable; in fact, he looked worse since Tony had touched him. "How are you?"

"That didn't go as well as I'd hoped." He forced a smile.

"What did you expect?" I was trying to be very careful not to let Toby touch me, so I pressed myself against the car door.

"I'm not sure." Tony shook his head and started the car up. But he didn't drive. Instead he gazed out the front of the car at the building. Finally, he nodded as if I'd asked him a question, then he turned to me and smiled. "Thanks for everything." His eyes held mine for a moment, and I knew he just couldn't put into words what he wanted to say.

The ride to Larry's was quiet, yet Toby seemed to improve as we went. Tony turned the radio on softly to try and distract us from Larry's snores. I watched out the window. I might have dozed off a bit.

Tony turned the car up a long driveway lined with trees. The grass was lush, green and perfectly trimmed. When Larry's house came into view, I let out a small gasp. It looked more like a small hotel.

"Ya," Tony agreed. "Forty-eight-hundred square feet on two-and-a-half acres."

My eyes popped as I took in the monstrosity—two stories with a balcony on the roof, and several large windows with fancy curtains. "It's bigger than my entire row of townhouses."

"I used to live just down the way," Tony said, pointing off to the right of the car, but I couldn't see anything through the trees. "You can see it from the media room on the top floor."

"My house was next to Tony's," Toby said, looking in the direction himself.

"Is your house as big as this?" I had been asking Toby, but I forgot Tony didn't know that. Toby said it was, and Tony with a hint of bitterness told me his was about the same.

"Wow," was all I could say. I couldn't imagine living in such a big place. I think I'd get lost, and somehow I knew I'd feel small.

Tony parked the car near the front door and turned it off. Turning in his seat, he shook Larry until he woke up. "Home, buddy."

Larry sat up and rubbed his face. "Want to come in?" When he didn't get an immediate answer, he added, "We could have some lunch."

I got the impression that Tony wanted to be doing something else, but he agreed. Toby told me he'd never set foot in Larry's house and was curious what it looked like. Putting jealousy aside, I decided it would be fun. We all climbed out of the car and made our way to the five cement steps leading up to those huge double doors. Larry looked at Tony's bloodstained shirt and swelling nose but made no comment.

The front hall was huge. You could fit my whole house into it! There was a large staircase off to the right and a formal living room to the left. As we walked down the hall, we passed through double swinging doors that opened up to a bright kitchen. All the appliances were made of chrome that sparkled and shone. It was somewhat blinding. There was a large island in the centre of the room with pots hanging from a rack attached to the high ceiling. I felt a bit like a midget among giant things.

Larry made his way to the fridge and rummaged through, then brought an assortment of items over to the island counter. He prepared three deli sandwiches with pickles, olives and radish flowers on the side. Handing us each a plate, he led the way into his "breakfast room." *They had a whole room just for breakfast!* It was spacious, with ten soft chairs around a low polished wooden table, with a fireplace in the corner that had five more chairs, with their own matching footrests and a wall with three large seat windows.

Larry sat at the head of the table, but instead of putting his plate on it, he brought his feet up and rested the plate in his lap. Tony sat two chairs down from him in the same manner. I took a seat across from Tony, but unlike the boys, I felt uncomfortable and out of place. Toby sat perched next to me. I noticed his colour had returned, and his eyes shone again.

As he finished his sandwich, Larry asked, "So, how's Eric?"

Like a cloud blocking the sun, the mood in the room changed.

"Not good," Tony replied, then stood up and headed back to the kitchen. Toby followed him with his eyes. Larry turned to look at me, looking for an explanation.

"Eric wouldn't talk to him, he wouldn't even listen. And he attacked Tony when he was trying to say how sorry he was."

Larry looked up to the ceiling. "That explains the nose." Then he smiled sadly. "I'm not that surprised." He sighed. "I know Tone wanted to make things right, but there's some things that just can't be undone." I nodded. Out of the corner of my eye I saw Toby jerk his head away from the doorway to the kitchen. He looked at me as if he was about to say something, but Larry cut him off. "This is one of those times."

"He's trying," I said in Tony's defense.

"Oh, I know he's trying, but honestly, it really wasn't him who did the most damage."

"Toby?" I said, watching Toby out of the corner of my eye. Toby brought both his hands up to his hair and ran them through, slowly nodding.

Larry stayed quiet.

"What happened that night?" I asked, but it was more of a demand. Toby shook his head. I ignored him.

Larry hesitated, not wanting to tell me, but I persisted. *I felt I deserved to know. I'd been thrown into this mess, and I might as well know it all.* Larry said, "This is all secondhand, but the best I can figure out is Toby discovered Eric's parents were going out of town, so he convinced Eric, and I mean threatened him, to hold a party. Toby took Tony to get some drugs, to make the night more fun, and they invited all their important friends to it. Now, seeing as Eric was the host, he was allowed to choose one guest. Toby didn't want a bunch of losers at his party, and in the end that might have been a saving grace for Eric's friend… Yes, Eric had friends; at least that was the case until this night. So Eric decided to invite his girlfriend. He figured he'd hide out with her until the night wound down and T and T went home. I guess Eric didn't know about Toby's animal magnetism, or his competitive spirit." All of Larry's contempt for Toby came out as he spoke. I didn't look at Toby as I listened.

"So the way I hear it," Larry continued, "is that Tony and Toby made a challenge that evening for themselves, because the parties and drugs just weren't exciting enough. They decided to compete over who could win Eric's girlfriend away from him, and the winner would be the first of them to convince her to sleep with him. It wasn't the first time they'd done that… Toby won, as usual. Here's how: when things started to turn ugly, and the first guest passed out, Toby offered to take her home, and the way the story goes is he tucked her into bed that night, and the next day she told Eric she never wanted to see him again…"

"No wonder Eric feels so hopeless," I breathed. "Why doesn't he tell someone what really happened?" I think I was getting used to these tales. This one didn't shock me so badly.

"My guess is he doesn't think anyone will believe him," Larry said. "Even though Toby is dead, Tony isn't, and as much as a pal as he is to me, Eric is probably still terrified of him." Larry sat up, putting his plate down on the table. "One thing I don't get is you." I stared at him. "You said you were friends with Toby, but that just doesn't make sense. And now that you've come along, and I see Tony, he's really turning things around. Who are you? And where did you come from?"

I didn't know how to answer. "You know, I didn't really know Toby all that well. We met that night when he died, but I didn't know much about him."

"You were at that party?"

"No," I said, feeling trapped. I turned to Toby to see if he could help, but he was too busy looking down at his hands in his lap. "Toby bought the drugs from my brother."

Comprehension dawned on Larry's face. "That explains your mother's response to me." I told him I was sorry for that, but he shrugged it off, saying the same thing Tony had said about his dad. "But really, who are you?"

I leaned back in my chair. "Just a lost girl who really needed a friend."

Larry shook his head. "I don't believe you for a second. You knew what you were doing." He smiled, and his eyes twinkled. *I wish he wouldn't look at me that way!* "But that doesn't matter; whatever the truth is, it's all good." He stood, picking up his plate, then, taking mine as well, he went into the kitchen.

"Toby," I whispered out of the corner of my mouth, "what can I do to fix this for you?"

"Nothing," he said as he stood up awkwardly, as though he'd forgotten how to use his legs.

"There's got to be something!" I said more forcefully, standing too. "Write another confession, or I could talk to this girl."

"It wouldn't work." Toby's voice was calm and steady. "I can't do anything more now. She wouldn't want to talk to you anyway. What we did, she was a willing partner. She'd made her choice long before, and there is nothing I, or you, can do to reverse the role I played in these events. I've done all I was able to do." He took a few steps towards the kitchen to let me know that the subject was closed. I wasn't willing to give up so easily, so when he couldn't take another step, he turned back to me and added, "Mariah, you've been a lifesaver, but it's time for you stop worrying about my mistakes now." Though he still looked wretched, he seemed to be more at peace. He looked like he had the first night he'd shown up in my room.

As we entered the kitchen, I felt a tingle at the back of my mind. Toby was smiling. *I could sense him again! It felt so nice.* Larry and Tony were cleaning up and goofing around. I stood at the back counter and watched. Toby reached out and put his arm around me. Soapsuds were flying as they whipped each other with the towels, but slowly the mess was taken care of.

Tony came over to me and took my hand. "Want to play some pool?" Larry was excited about it, and when I told them I didn't know how to play, they insisted I come and learn.

We walked down to the games room, Larry leading the way. It was huge. It had a pool table and an area for darts, but there was also air hockey, foosball, a dance machine, ping-pong and an assortment of pinball machines. There was also a bar off to one side, from which Larry got us each a soda, and some couches dispersed throughout the room.

I was taught, mostly by Larry, how to hold a cue for pool, how to hit a flying ball in table tennis, how to toss a dart, and the finer points of air hockey. Tony gave pointers, but he stood back to let Larry guide me when I needed more help. The afternoon seemed to fly by. I wasn't the best player, but Tony seemed to think with a little practice I'd be able to hold my own. Toby seemed preoccupied with Tony, smiling as he studied him, but I'd also catch him doing the same with Larry or me.

I really enjoyed it when Larry and Tony horsed around; they'd slap each other on the back or slam into one another, trying to knock each other over. It was all in fun, and I wished I could join them. Instead I stood back with Toby.

It was getting late, and I was starting to feel tired. Tony had gone off to play pinball, while Larry and I had one last game of pool. I sank the eight ball, taking the game. Larry congratulated me, then went off to watch Tony. He was taking the high score. I watched as Tony won and entered T.O.N.E. Then I came over as he played another two games, but he wasn't as successful as the first.

Finally Tony seemed to lose interest in playing, and after those two unsuccessful games and a round of darts where he lost to both Larry and me, he said it might be time to leave.

"No!" Larry protested loudly. He turned to me and asked, "You don't want to go, do you?"

I didn't know how to answer. I was having fun, but Tony had something on his mind, and I didn't want to feel like I was getting in his way. *It was late. Maybe I should go home.*

"Mariah can still stay if she feels like it," Tony suggested, leaning up against the bar. "I don't need to be here for her to stay." He looked between Larry and me, a sly smile playing on his lips.

Larry's mouth fell open. Even Toby seemed shocked by it. I wasn't sure. *After all, I didn't know Larry or this neighbourhood.* I knew it would be fine if I decided to stay, but I didn't want to without Tony.

"But how's she supposed to get home?" Larry protested. "If you don't remember, my parents still haven't given me my own car! It would take over two hours for her to bus back."

Tony shrugged. "I'll leave you my car." When he ran his hand through his hair, I got a chill. *Still so much like Toby.*

I didn't know what I wanted—but I was starting to feel uncomfortable, so I spoke up. "If you want to leave, Tony, then I'm alright with going too. I'm getting sorta tired, and I have homework."

"No," Larry said again. He looked at the clock. "Alright, you two are tired. Well, it's suppertime, let's order a pizza and watch a movie. Come on? Please."

Tony softened to the idea, so after a quick stop in the kitchen to order the food, Larry led the way up to the entertainment room on the second floor. It was as big as a small movie theatre, with a very large sectional leather sofa perfectly centered in front of the largest screen TV I'd ever seen. On a raised part of the room were a polished piano and several chairs around another large table with all sorts of games behind it in a glass cabinet. Larry gestured for Tony and me to wait, and he walked over to the couch. The TV was showing a commercial for breakfast cereal.

Larry looked annoyed, putting his hands on his hips. He gazed down, saying, "Sara, what are you doing home? You're supposed to be visiting grandma with Mom and Dad."

"Ya, well I'm not," she retorted, standing up. When she turned and saw me, her voice became shrill. "What's *she* doing here?" Just seeing her made all my confidence disappear. I felt my knees wobble. *What was I doing on her turf? I was asking for trouble.*

Larry looked at me apologetically, but Tony looked perplexed. I took a step back and ended up bumping into Toby, who stood behind me. Panic was rising in my chest, and in my mind I could see Tony and Larry turning on me any moment, *once they knew how uncool I was.*

"She's my guest!" Larry said, crossing his arms in front of himself and adding, "And what's *she* doing here?" He nodded at someone I couldn't see sitting with Sara.

Then Sara's guest stood. It was Effie, who blocked out a quarter of the screen now showing a carpet shampoo commercial. With a murderous look in her eyes, she made her way around the couch and the twenty feet to where I stood, her hands on her hips. "Who invited her?" she hissed, but I thought I heard a slight quiver.

"I did," Tony answered, taking a step in front of me protectively.

I breathed out, feeling relieved, but even so, I continued to press myself against Toby as Effie scowled at me.

"Do you have a problem?" Tony leaned threateningly towards her. Sara let out a soft panicked noise as she watched from a distance.

"No." Effie's hands quivered on her hips and stepped back. "Not my problem if you want to hang out with losers." She glared at me.

Tony made a move like he was going to hit Effie, and she moved to the side, her glare turning scared. "Let's go somewhere else," she said to Sara. This time I was certain I heard a quiver.

Sara took a few minutes to gather up their stuff, protesting all the time, and walked out. Effie managed to bump me as she passed. I'd turned to the side so they could get by. When she clipped me, I was knocked off my feet. Tony caught me and righted me then yelled something ugly after Effie. For a second he looked like he regretted it, but the moment passed.

Then he went to the sofa and flopped himself down. I sat next to him, and Larry came to sit on the other side of me. Toby stood behind leaning against the back. It was a big couch, enough space for Sara and Effie to have joined us, and we still would have had room to spare, *though I was glad they hadn't.* Larry picked up the remote and went to the movie-listing channel.

As the name of an action movie passed, Toby said excitedly, "That one!"

I jumped slightly at his voice but told them I'd like to watch what he'd picked. Larry seemed surprised and impressed at my choice. He flipped to the channel and settled back as the opening credits started.

Tony leaned over and whispered, "Toby?" with an amused grin on his face. I nodded. "Figured," he said, but he didn't move back. Instead he stayed leaning into me and eventually rested his head on my arm.

The pizza arrived; we all enjoyed the deep dish, cheesy meat lovers special with sodas. Later as I went to stretch out, Larry caught my feet and offered to let them rest across his lap, and he even massaged them too. This felt odd. *Was it wrong?* I tried to check with Toby, but he was distracted by the movie. Eventually I relaxed and just watched the show too. After the movie, we ended up watching some TV shows, and by the time Tony insisted we had to go, it was late in the evening.

Before we left, Larry called me over to the huge bay of windows behind the piano. Tony had stepped out of the room. Pointing, he showed me the roof of Tony's old place. It looked just as large and impressive.

Then he turned to me. "I really like you," he said in a constrained voice. "I'm so glad I got to meet you."

I felt oddly stiff, but before I could say anything, Tony returned and we started to walk back to the front door. Tony held my hand all the way to the car. *It felt nice*, partly because I was fearful that we'd cross paths with Effie again, and also because of the way I was now feeling shy around Larry. Larry said he'd be in touch; I wasn't sure whom he was talking to. He had been looking at me, but Tony had returned his remark with the same promise. *Did he even have my number?*

All the way home, Tony was quiet and stone-faced. I had no clue what was going on in his head. Toby was also very quiet, and as we had passed his house, he said something about goodbye to it, then he didn't say anything else, but I felt him in the back of my mind.

Tony walked me to my bedroom window. Checking to ensure the coast was clear, I invited him in. He sat on my bed, right where Toby had appeared that first night almost three weeks earlier. Toby stood at my door like a security guard.

I sat down next to Tony and took his hand in mine. As though being interrupted from a good thought, Tony turned to me. Toby turned his head away, so I leaned in and kissed Tony full on the lips.

He returned my kiss, embracing me passionately but not with the same urgency he had before. It was more tender, considerate, real. Tony drew back and kissed my hand, then looked down but kept holding me.

"Mariah, I meant what I said." His eyes were filled with such turmoil. "Date that other boy."

"But I want you," I said, my voice small from too much emotion.

Tony smiled and kissed my hand again. "I love you," he said, "but I need some time to fix things."

"I'll wait. I don't want anyone but you, so it doesn't matter!" I felt desperate.

"Oh, beautiful, don't." he leaned over to kiss me on the forehead, but I pulled away. *I was hurt! Why didn't he want me?* I bowed my head so Tony wouldn't see my tears.

Toby came and knelt in front of me. "Just give him a chance to explain," he said gently, so I turned back.

He reached out and caught a tear as it rolled down my cheek. "Mariah, please, say we can be friends." I drew my shoulders into a shrug. "Like really good friends," he persisted. "Please." *I wanted more.*

"But Tony, we're already really good friends." I couldn't know all I did about him and still be talking to him unless we were.

He sighed with relief and pulled me into a long hug. "Thank you," he whispered into my hair. "You don't know how much this means to me." And with one final kiss on the cheek, he left, stopping briefly to look back into my room. He waved, took a deep breath and was gone.

I fell onto my bed and cried.

Toby stayed kneeling on the floor so his face was only inches from mine. "Mariah, I know you're sad, but this is best for now." He pulled some loose hair away from my face. "Maybe in a while, you never know. I am so proud of you."

Proud—what had I done?

"You did one of the hardest things in the world; you stayed just friends."

Once I had collected myself together, I got ready for bed. It was nearing midnight. Thoughts of the next day ran in my mind. It would be nice to see Cindy, Rayla, Charlie, Just May and the boys again. *I had missed them.* Then I thought about Elijah. I wasn't sure I'd date him yet. *He was no Tony,* but the idea might have been growing on me.

"Mariah?" Toby interrupted. Something in his voice made me stop. He sat in his spot on my bed. I had just put my PJ's on and was starting to crawl under my blankets, the sheets still in my hand.

"When you wake up tomorrow, I won't be here." *The world stopped!*

I couldn't breathe! I fell onto my pillow. I felt blackness, and my mind spun. *This was a panic attack...* Slowly I started to feel my heartbeat, and it soothed me a little. Eventually I pulled myself together. Toby was watching me. *He hadn't tried to help at all; I'd ended up calming myself.*

"Are you sure?" I protested. He nodded sadly. "Then this is our last night?" I felt arguments explode in my head: *He can't leave! I'm not ready! I need him! I can't live without him!* Yet even as I thought them, I knew they weren't true. I wiped my tears with the back of my hand. *Had I known this was going to be our last night, I would have spent it differently.* I crawled over to Toby and snuggled into him. "Where will you go?" I asked quietly.

"I don't know."

"Are you sad?"

"Not any more." His chest heaved, but he still lacked a heartbeat. "Not now."

I held him tighter. The thought of him gone filled me with immense sadness. "So what's going to happen to me now?"

"You'll be just fine." He put his hand on my hair. "I'm sure of it. So will Tony, and even Stacy and Eric."

"How do you know this?" I still felt so sad that I had to take long, deep breaths to keep my emotions from overwhelming me.

"I just know," he said, a slight chuckle in his voice. He pulled me closer to him. *What did it matter—he'd be gone.*

We stayed like this, his arms around me, my hands holding so tight to his black shirt that it stretched out.

"Mariah, are you going to date Elijah?" It seemed like such a strange question for our last moments together.

"I don't know," I answered, not even wanting to think about it.

"If you don't, you could date Larry." This comment surprised me so much, I sat back to look at his face. *Was he kidding?* He looked serious enough. I wrinkled my nose—*Larry?*

"You've changed so much." His eyes danced. "It makes me so happy to see you now. I remember when I first saw you, you were so scared of the world and so sad, but…"

"I'm still sad and scared of the world," I interrupted, pulling close to him again.

He patted my back. "It's not the same."

I knew he was right. And looking back, I couldn't tell you what had changed, but I could see that I had. I gave Toby an extra squeeze.

"Hey beautiful, do me one last favour?"

I closed my eyes and promised, "Anything."

"Never stop being who you are. You are special—one of a kind. Don't let yourself get stuck like you were ever again. Add up all the good and never let it go. Never let anyone kill your compassion—it's one of your biggest assets. And when things get bad, or feel bleak or hopeless, just remember me and live, because that in itself is a gift that I sorely miss, and I'll never get it back, because when it's gone—it's gone."

I let his words wash over me. My voice wouldn't have worked even if I had something to say. Time continued to move forward to the moment when Toby would be taken from me. *I couldn't stop it*, no matter how hard I tried. Soon I felt my body relax, and slowly my eyes became heavy.

"Do you promise?" he asked softly, but his voice sounded like it was fading.

"That's more than one last favour," I sleepily replied.

He chuckled, and then I felt his lips on my forehead, warm and soft.

"Yes," I answered as I surrendered to sleep.

We stood in the meadow, the sun bright, and the grass soft under our feet. Toby looked at me as if trying to fix my image in his mind. And I studied him: from his short brown hair spiked up in front, to his deep, passionate chocolate-brown eyes, perfect nose, high cheekbones, and even his ears. His bronze complexion, that black shirt with "The Fray" written across it, his baggy faded black jeans, and most of all, his innocence and carefree smile.

Though neither of us moved, the gap between us grew, until I looked at him from such a distance, I couldn't make out his features any more. The sun was setting behind him, and as it slipped past the horizon, Toby disappeared.

DAY 22

Monday...

I WOKE PANTING LIKE I COULDN'T CATCH MY BREATH, and my heart beat so hard in my chest, it felt like it might break out. My hands shook, and I couldn't focus my eyes. I wanted to call out to Toby, but I knew he was gone. I did a mental check; there was an empty space where I'd usually feel him.

I continued to fight for air, and the room began to swim, so I closed my eyes. *This is a panic attack.* There in the darkness of my mind, as I felt as if I was being pressed from all sides, like I was in a box that was rapidly shrinking, I found something. Words that echoed back to me from a time with Toby: "Be sad now, for soon you will have no reason to be." Like magical words that opened a secret passage, I started to choke out sobs, and a floodgate of tears released. *He was gone.* Though I felt like my tears would never cease, they slowly did.

It was still early, but not too early to have a shower; the soothing water running over my body warmed me and reminded me of Toby. Fresh tears were shed, but I didn't try to stop them. Then I got dressed and had to stop again, because Toby had helped me buy the shirt I wore. Afterwards I fixed my hair and finally was ready to go up to the kitchen. It was quiet and lonely, and I missed Toby all the more. But as the hour approached to go to school, I collected myself and headed out the door. *This is how it had been just three short weeks ago. Only it hadn't been anything like this…*

Cindy met up with me as I was leaving home. She had been skipping along, but she came to a halt and said, "You've been crying." *She was a good friend. I had friends. That was a big difference.*

I nodded, and even though I was fearful of sharing, I didn't want to keep things from her. *I had made that mistake last time!* But I still didn't know how to explain my sorrow. *What would she think of me if I told her I had a ghost friend, and I'd lost him?* So all I said was, "Bad morning," and she accepted it.

She looped her arm around my back as we started for school. Within a block or two, Cindy was into one of her great stories of her adventures from the weekend. As she talked, I actually started to feel better. *At least I didn't feel so alone.*

"I'm so glad we're friends," I said.

Cindy casually threw her arm over my shoulders "Thanks," she replied. "I'm glad we're friends too."

By the time we got to the school, I didn't feel so consumed by sadness, but I'm sure I still looked pretty bad. We met up with the gang, and while waiting for the first bell, everyone caught the others up on their weekend. When the question came to me, I stammered. *This was it, just like last time—only it wasn't; at the very least I wasn't the same, and I wouldn't make the same mistake.*

Trying to control my sobs, I said, "Someone close to me died." *In so many ways, that was the truth.* I'm not sure who hugged me first, but in the end seven pairs of arms were wrapped around me. *Yup, this time was definitely different.*

They didn't ask many questions. Somehow it was enough to just comfort me in my sorrow. They took turns consoling me. Elijah walked with me to our lockers then to homeroom. I was sure he was anxious to hear if I had an answer for him, but he didn't say anything. He did, however, catch my hand and hold it lovingly. *What would I tell him? Should I go out with him?*

The first three classes went by in a blur. I was reminiscing about the first day Toby had been with me. I'd been so uncomfortable with him shadowing me, but also with myself. Even with him gone, I sat taller, more confidently. When lunch came, I went to the office for my detention. I got my orders from Miss Rose and went into the secluded copying room. Alone, I cried openly, being careful not to get my tears on the freshly duplicated papers, but even as I cried, I noticed that the pain didn't feel as deep or as bleak. When I finished, I wiped my face dry and left for lunch.

Elijah met me right outside the office. He took my hand as we started toward the lunchroom. "I know you're sad today. I can't imagine what it would feel like, but I just have to ask you if you've thought about my question at all? You don't need to answer, though, if you're not able to."

I had, and I still didn't know what to say, but I found his persistence adorable.

He stopped me and turned me to face him in the almost deserted hall. "Listen, I'm not asking you to spend the rest of your life with me. Just try dating me, for now, and if it doesn't work, then we'll go back to being friends."

I closed my eyes. I could imagine Toby standing next to me. He'd be telling me to say yes. *And this is the way Tony wanted it.* Before I could come up with any reasons why I shouldn't, I said, "Yes."

Elijah did a jump and whooped, and then he put his hand behind my neck and leaned forward to kiss me. As our lips met, I knew that this was the right choice. Elijah would make a good first boyfriend. Even though I still loved Tony, it was best that we stayed friends. *He was right, he wasn't ready for forever, and neither was I.* I was only fifteen. It was good to have a boyfriend who was only for now. Who knew about someday? But at this very moment, I was happy with Elijah. *I mean, how many first boyfriends last forever?*

Elijah wrapped his arm around me, and we walked the rest of the way to the lunchroom. Of course, showing up like that created quite the commotion among our friends. There were squeals of excitement from the girls and congratulatory gestures from the boys. Charlie told me that she'd always thought we'd make a good couple; I was confused and reminded her about what she'd told me at the sleepover. She explained that she did mean it, but she felt the risks were worthwhile, and she just wanted me to understand them before I made my decision. I didn't really understand, but she smiled and we laughed together.

We ate and talked and had fun for the rest of the lunch hour. I barely thought of Toby. Elijah hardly took his eyes off me. It made me feel special, and when I returned his gaze, his smile would grow to cover his whole face. He walked me to my locker, making plans for a date on Wednesday. He just couldn't wait until Friday but already had plans for Tuesday, and tonight was too soon. We made plans for Friday, too, of course.

In all the excitement, I'd forgotten to use the bathroom. I got permission from the teacher and hurried so I wouldn't miss too much of the class. As I stood gazing into the mirror, still marveling at my reflection, I could kinda see how guys found me attractive… *kinda.* I finished washing my hands and turned to leave when Sara walked in, followed by Effie. I instantly felt panic in my chest, like a bird trying to escape from a cage, *but it quickly faded!* They said nothing, so after a steadying breath, I started to walk toward the door. Sara's foot tripped me. *I should've seen that coming.*

"I'm sorry," she said falsely as she leaned over taking my arm under the pretense of assisting me up. Once I was standing, she didn't let go.

Effie stood in front of me. "I don't care what you know or who you're friends with—you are not welcome to EVER be seen at Sara's again!"

Sara continued to hold my arm, tight. I stood with my back to the counter and Effie barring my way out. I missed Toby. *He'd know what to do to get me out of this!* Somehow, just the thought of him made me feel stronger.

"And I suppose you are going to stop me?" I was so happy, and my voice didn't shake.

"No," Effie answered, and her eyes danced. "Sara will."

With her free hand, Sara made a threatening fist.

But it didn't work. I wasn't convinced. "How's that going to stop me?" I challenged. "If either of you hit me, I'll have proof, then you'll be suspended."

"Ya," Effie said, shoving me against the counter, "but you'll still hurt!"

When my back hit the counter, it was in the same place as the bruise I'd gotten from my mom shoving me against the table. With the pain, it caused my feet to buckle, and I fell to the floor just as Sara was swinging at me with her fist. I figure she was aiming for my stomach with the hope of not leaving a mark, then it would have been their word against mine, but I fell, and her fist collided with my face.

I shut my eyes. The pain was excruciating, and I could feel hot sticky blood pouring from my nose. I yelped in pain.

Sara swore twice, and then in a whiny voice, she turned on Effie. "You promised no one would find out!"

Effie's voice shook, but she wasn't talking to Sara. "Oh, Mrs. Kellee, Mariah tripped."

"That's quite enough." Mrs. Kellee's voice was shrill with rage. "Sara, Effie, you two will come with me to the office immediately. Rayla and Cindy, please stay with Mariah. Elijah's gone to fetch the nurse." I heard them leave and Rayla and Cindy sobbing. They came to me and helped me up. Cindy wetted some paper towels, and Rayla didn't leave my side. They both helped clean me up as best as they could. My shirt was bloodstained, and it made me sad because it was my favourite that Toby had helped me buy. But as Rayla and Cindy worked on getting the bleeding to stop, I didn't miss him so much—how could I with such good friends?

Mrs. Kristy came in and took me down to her office, where I spent the rest of the afternoon resting. There was concern about a concussion, but luckily Sara hadn't broken my nose, just nicked it. I was told that I would have a black eye. Even though the nurse spent the afternoon trying to get a hold of my mother, she was unsuccessful, and as the end of the day came, she eventually said she would have to let me go home alone. Elijah showed up after the last bell and promised to make sure I got home safely. *My boyfriend! My hero.*

Before I left her office, the nurse assured me that things were going to be different now. Not only had Effie and Sara been suspended for at least the current week, but also because of this incident, the staff had held a meeting to consider an anti-bullying program, to be implemented as soon as possible. I had my doubts, but I kept them to myself. *Besides, things already were different for me.*

As Elijah walked me home, my hand in his, I noticed the air had developed a bit of a nip; autumn was quickly fading, and winter would soon be here. This winter, however, didn't feel quite as dark and dreary as the ones before. I had friends, and despite this day's events, I still felt hopeful for the future.

Elijah and I talked all the way home. It seemed we had the same taste in music, movies, and we shared a warped/twisted sense of humor. We ended up talking a little about Tony. I'm not sure how we got onto the subject, but Elijah was curious about my relationship with him. I explained that Tony was trying to change his ways, and I was helping. I couldn't tell if Elijah was more or less happy to hear the truth. Then he quizzed me about my other friend, Larry. I assured him we were nothing more than friends. Elijah seemed doubtful, but he said he'd believe me and made me promise to tell him if things changed.

I had almost completely forgotten about Toby. Now my thoughts returned to missing him, and as we neared my home, I became aware of a mounting dread.

When we got to my complex, I was torn. I wanted to invite Elijah over for two reasons. I was having tons of fun with him, and also because I knew he would ease the lonely feeling in my house. But I didn't want my mother catching him over, and it didn't feel right to sneak him into my room. I started to explain why I couldn't have him come over unless my mom was out, and Elijah was embarrassed at the idea of visiting me alone. *I had never thought about that.* So we parted with a kiss.

I turned with a heavy heart. I didn't want to say goodbye to him, and now I was faced with the reality of missing Toby and no distractions from it. My heart filled with sorrow with each step that brought me closer to home. Finally I found myself standing at the bottom of the stairs without the strength to walk up them. *I couldn't stay at home; it would be far too quiet and depressing without Toby!* So I decided to walk around for a bit. When I passed the park where Toby and I had sat on the swings, tears blurred my vision, but I kept walking.

I had no idea, no plan. I just walked. Then, looking up, I recognized a small hairdressing shop in the mini-mall. With new determination I went over to it and entered.

I was greeted by Molly's joyful voice. "Have a seat, I'm just finishing up." She didn't look up as she worked on a young man's hair. He looked to be in his mid-twenties. I sat on a soft stool and picked up a magazine. Molly and the man were talking about the weather. I wasn't paying much attention to the conversation or the book; I was simply enjoying the atmosphere of warmth and safety.

Once she was done with her customer and he had left, she came over to me. "Now, sweet thing, what can I do for you?" I looked up, and a gasp escaped from Molly's mouth. "What happened?" I ended up telling her a lot more than I'd thought I would. It started with my black eye and worked backwards. In the end, I told her about Toby and all the adventures I'd had over the past three weeks.

For the first while we talked in her shop, but as the time passed she invited me upstairs to her apartment. It was directly above the store, and it wasn't much different. It had several lamps, most of which were dimmed with coloured scarves. We entered into the kitchen from a back door that had stairs leading down to her shop. Her kitchen was about the same size as mine, only it didn't have any windows, but it seemed much more inviting. She had a tall table that was the right height to stand at, or you could use one of the two bar stools to sit on. Through the kitchen was a homely looking living room with soft sofas and more lamps. There were two doors: one that led into her bedroom, and the other a small but functional bathroom.

I talked, and Molly only interrupted to clarify bits and pieces. Otherwise she was a very good listener. I told her everything I could think of and ended with, "I don't think I'll ever be able to go home! I just can't—I miss him too much." I sat in her living room holding a cup of tea, the scent of honey and chamomile wafting up to my nose.

Molly sipped slowly on her tea. When I didn't say any more, she looked over her cup at me. "First of all, thank you for trusting me and sharing you adventures. And I want you to know I do believe you, every bit of it. But I would be very selective about who you share this with."

I smiled. *I already knew that!* Then I realized: *she'd said she believed me!* That felt great. *And I believed her.*

"Now, about you going home to an empty house. Well, Toby was sent to you to help. It wouldn't make sense for him to leave you worse off. So I think that you will go home, and though it will feel sad and hard, you'll be just fine. It does seem that everything Toby said and did worked out well in the end." I nodded. "You helped him with Stacy, and now you have a new start with an old friend. You wore more daring clothes and even trusted him on cutting your hair, and you feel better about yourself." I nodded again. "So I'd trust him with what he told you about the boys too. Don't fret; enjoy yourself with Elijah, be friends with Tony and even Larry. What was it Toby said? Larry likes you too? That's not a bad thing. I'd just relax; you aren't doing anything wrong. Continue to be as honest as you can with all your new friends and enjoy yourself. I'd trust that everything will work itself out just like Toby told you it would."

She invited me to stay for dinner, and though it was some strange dish with sprouts, tofu, beans and something called quinoa, I actually enjoyed it. But I enjoyed Molly's company even more. Later she found me a top to borrow and kept my blood-covered shirt, promising she'd do all she could to remove the stain.

I used Molly's phone to call Stacy. She was overjoyed to hear from me and shared with me how things were going for her: she'd met with Toby's parents on Sunday, and they'd been really nice. They accepted the contents of the letter and what their son had done and offered her and the child financial assistance, including all of Toby's old trust funds. "I'm rich," she said. Then today she'd had her first doctor's appointment, and both her and baby were doing great. They'd even scheduled an ultrasound in a few weeks, and she couldn't wait to see the little sucker. Stacy expressed how scared she still felt to be having a child, but somehow it was all going to be fine. Her parents had been a wonderful support. She was surprised that they weren't mad; they had set her up for some counseling to try and help. Before we said goodbye, we made plans to go to the mall together on Saturday. She wanted to treat me to a show and even a small shopping spree. We both said how happy we were to be friends again. *I knew things weren't going to be perfect for her, but they would be better.*

I stood at the door to leave. It was nearing eight at night, and it would take about thirty minutes to walk home. Molly had hugged me three times already, but as I turned to leave, she called out, "You know, my sister lives so far away, and she really doesn't have time for me…" Her eyes danced. "Could I adopt you as my little sister?"

It sounded great! I beamed at the idea. We exchanged numbers and made plans for Sunday. After that, the walk home didn't seem as long or lonely. When I walked into my house, I knew that what Molly had said was true; even though my whole body resounded with sorrow, I didn't feel hopeless, and I knew I'd get over this loss.

I was down in my room trying to get my homework finished, still missing Toby a little, when the phone rang. It was late, and I almost decided not to answer. On the second ring, I reluctantly put my pencil down and raced up the stairs to the kitchen.

"Mariah?" came Larry's voice. His voice was thick, like he might have been crying.

"What's wrong?" I braced myself. *Was it bad news?*

He paused, and then said through chokes, "Tony's in South View."

"The jail." I fell onto the kitchen chair from the shock. *Hadn't Tony changed?*

"Well, S.V. Juvenile Hall."

I watched out my window; the sky was clear and blue, with the last rays of light before the sun slipped over the horizon, but darkness was falling fast, and I could see the odd star shining though. "What happened?" I asked, still shocked that Tony would have gone and messed everything up.

"He turned himself in." Larry's voice showed his shock.

He'd turned himself in! I was relieved. *At least it wasn't for something new.* It took a while for Larry to calm down and explain the whole story. Tony had picked him up for school as usual, but when he got there, he'd handed Larry the car keys and said he had to take care of something, and to keep the car until he got back. From there, Tony had ordered a cab that drove him to juvenile hall, where he'd confessed to everything he had ever done wrong. He even had a signed letter. After school, Tony had called Larry to tell him all this and also that Eric had been released. Neither one knew how long Tony would end up staying in juvie, but he didn't seem upset by it. In fact, he said something about this being the time he needed to get himself together.

Larry seemed to be at a loss. "I want you to know that I still blame you." *Was he teasing?* Taking a deep breath, he went on. "Honestly, I'm really proud of what Tony decided to do, so like I said, whatever you did to him was good."

The sun had fully set, stars were littering the sky, and a peaceful, happy feeling entered my heart. "Do you think he'll be alright in there?" *Now that he'd changed, would it be good for him to be surrounded by other delinquents?*

Larry chuckled. "You know, after the other night, when Tony told me everything… I wanted to turn him in myself, but he's my pal. No, he said he would be fine, and this is the first time I believe him. Mariah, you should have heard him, he sounded so calm, even happy…"

It made sense. It was the same relief I'd seen and felt in Toby at the end. What he'd done was horrible, but now things were being set right. Justice was being served and the innocent cared for. Now Tony could start to feel better about himself without a guilty conscience. *He'd have a clean slate.*

Larry said his only regret was selfish; he was going to miss Tony, because no matter what he was to everyone else, he'd always been a good friend.

Then he invited me to go visit Tony with him the next day after school. I agreed, and we talked a little longer about school. He'd heard about Sara punching someone and wasn't completely surprised it had been me. He made some unkind remarks about his sister and her Effin friend. I enjoyed talking with him and thought about what Toby and Molly had said, but I knew I wasn't doing anything wrong.

After we'd said our farewells, I made my way back down to my room and sat at my desk, pulling out a notebook. Then I spent a long time recounting all the shards of good I'd had in the last twenty-one days. *I made a promise to myself to do this every night!* I worried that I wouldn't be able to get to sleep without Toby, but in the end that wasn't a problem. I had hoped I would see him again in my dreams. *I didn't*, but I wasn't sure if that was good or bad.

DAY 23 Tuesday...

And the rest of my life...

I WOKE EARLY AGAIN. The feeling of loss was easier to handle this morning. When I went upstairs, I found my mother sitting at the kitchen table. She looked miserable, as though she had cried all night long. Her hair was loose and frizzled, her eyes bloodshot, and when she turned her head to look at me, it seemed as if it took all her energy. Through chokes, she said, "They sentenced your brother yesterday."

What a relief! I tried not to let my feelings show through. I really wasn't surprised. "How long?" I asked carefully.

"Five years!" she sobbed, grabbing a Kleenex from the half-empty box on the table. "He'll be eligible for a review if he serves three years with good behavior." *Somehow five years just didn't sound like enough*, but I kept my mouth shut.

"He was my baby!" My mother continued to wallow.

As I watched her, I wondered why she felt such a loss. Jake hadn't been very nice to her, yet for some reason she couldn't bare the thought of losing him. I knew she had lost him long before today, but for her, that was what she finally faced. I felt pity for her, not anger any more—more like sadness.

She couldn't see the truth. I tried to find some consoling words, though I'm not even sure she was listening. Then I finished my chores and left for school. *She might never get it—she would probably never change.* Yet, as I walked, I knew that had no effect on my value.

Cindy ran to hug me as we met up. We walked to school, and I told her what had happened with my brother. It felt nice to be able to share this burden with her. She didn't know what to say, but she listened and tried to empathize. Then she told me my eye was looking better and about her brother needing braces and her mom's plan to take away the candies once again. I had to laugh.

At the school, I again felt like a celebrity as I was asked to tell and retell about what had happened in the girls' washroom. I was commended for my bravery. *How had I been brave?* But it wasn't just my friends; several other students came to me and asked me to tell them about the incident. I also got high-fives and congratulations. I thought about it. Those same kids that had taunted me about ants were now cheering for me. *How had I gone from butt of the jokes to school hero?* It was beyond me. I tried not to take it too seriously—who knew what tomorrow could bring? I might end up the "loser" again—though I highly doubted it.

At lunch, I went to the office to serve my standing detention, but instead of having a stack of pages ready to be copied, the secretary informed me that Ms. LaKey wanted to see me in her office.

She sat at her desk; her chair swiveled to face the wall behind her. As I stood waiting, she slowly turned it to face me. "I want to make it clear that I don't agree with the rest of the staff. I don't care what you've told them—I know the truth." She narrowed her eyes, "Mrs. Roosofe and I are good friends, we grew up together, and I know she would never raise a kid to be mean." She leaned forward in her chair. "Now, you may have everyone else fooled, but I know the truth. You need to toughen up! I saw that from the first day you came here, walking around like the world is against you…"

I felt a twinge of remorse that Toby wasn't with me. *I needed him now…* Ms. LaKey told me about how I played victim and I invited kids to be mean. I was pleased, as I slowly felt strengthened inside. Even though he wasn't here—I couldn't see him or sense him—I knew he was still with me. Knowing that gave me a strength that welled up from within, helping me to square my shoulders and look Ms. LaKey straight in the eye.

She faltered for a second. "Anyway, because you seem to have the wool pulled over everyone else's eyes, I am, for now, revoking your detention. But I warn you: you do one thing wrong, I will be there ready to reinstate it and make your life miserable for the rest of your days at this school."

I had no problem believing her. I knew she meant it. Yet it somehow didn't bother me. I left her office with my head held high. I realized that the world was gonna keep on going with good and bad. That was never going to change. But I had; and so had the way I handled things. I was no longer weak, afraid or alone.

I enjoyed the rest of the lunch hour with my friends, Elijah next to me with his arm around my back. *He was a good boyfriend.* The rest of the day flew by after that. Larry met me after school, marveling at my eye and using some choice words about Effie. Elijah came to meet Larry. When I introduced Elijah as my boyfriend, I saw something flicker in Larry's eyes. I squeezed Elijah and kissed him goodbye, and he reluctantly let me go.

"You gonna tell Tony about your boyfriend?" Larry asked while keeping his eyes glued to the road.

"Yup." *I hadn't done anything wrong!* I answered, "You know, he's the one who told me to date Elijah."

Larry swerved but stayed in the lines. "Wow," was all he said.

Worrying that Larry was upset somehow, I asked, "This doesn't change things with us, does it?"

For the first time he looked at me, very briefly. I saw disappointment, but he told me that all was well, we were friends, and a boyfriend didn't change that.

Once we got to S.V., Larry stayed out. He wanted to give Tony and me some time alone, he said. Tony rushed in. The guard was almost knocked over in his haste. I got up and he embraced me. The guard stayed just inside the door, watching.

"I was hoping you'd come! You're the only thought that's kept me going." He stepped back, and looking at me he gasped, "What happened to your eye!" I was gong to ask Tony the same thing. But I explained first. Tony seemed shocked but gave me a huge hug again and commended me on my bravery.

"Tony, I'm dating that other boy."

Tony slowly let me go. *Was he angry? Was he sad?* He sat, and I sat next to him. "I'm glad," he said, giving me a sad smile.

"Really?" *I didn't believe him.*

He took my hand in his. "Absolutely." Then he added, searching around the room with his eyes, "It's the right thing, and I'm sure Toby would agree."

"Toby's gone," I whispered. The tears burned at the corner of my eyes.

"Really? Like for real?" *He understood my pain; it was reflected in his face.*

I told Tony about our last night together, my brother's sentence and my mother's grief. I talked until I was all out of things to say, and then I asked him about his eye.

He chuckled while rubbing the back of his neck. "You know that brother of yours?" I stiffened. "He was in here yesterday before they sentenced him. Well, he's really ticked about his leg, but that's not why I got this…" Tony grinned, his dark eyes shining. "He got extra mad when I told him he was wasting his life…"

I gasped. *Why would Tony say that!*

"I don't know why I felt compelled to talk to him. I guess I was thinking of Toby and how he had set me straight." Tony chuckled again. "Jake didn't take the news so well, but I can't say much. I wasn't really any better when you told me." Taking my hand in his, he kissed it lightly. "Didn't I try and hit you over it? I'm so sorry for that."

I smiled. *I knew Tony was going to be just fine…*

"Well, I'm not giving up. I plan on telling everyone I get a chance to about the dangers of making the wrong choices." He went on, but I thought about Toby's legacy: *his new legacy, the one he'd created through me. It felt nice being part of something that special.*

I listened as Tony told me about all the details of his life in jail—how he was going to have a hearing to discuss how long he should be held in custody. His mother was going to come down, and he was glad she'd be there. He hadn't seen his father since Wednesday, but that didn't matter. When he was released, he was going to move in with his mother. He talked about the counselor he'd have to see daily, but he also said how much better he felt, and it showed on his face.

Eventually Larry came in and we all visited, spending over an hour just talking, and I remembered to enjoy every minute of it, because I knew this was the good stuff.

We planned to make it a regular thing to meet every Tuesday and Thursday. Larry took me out for dinner on the way home, and sitting opposite him in Dave's Deep Dish Pizza Parlour, I thought, Toby was right, it did have the best pizzas, but also that the best part of life was the time spent in the company of friends. I realized then that all those tiny shards of good had somehow grown! I could see clearly that the good outweighed the bad.

When Larry took me home, even though the house was empty when I got in, I knew I'd be alright; soon enough I'd be moving away from my mother, and starting the next chapter of my life. But how sad for her—I could see that she'd be stuck here, and with me gone, she'd truly be alone.

I wish I could tell you that I lived happily ever after, but there is no such thing. As long as you are living, there will be something that could trouble you. What I can tell you is that I lived, and there were sorrows as well as great happiness. I promise, though, that I held on to the good forever after, and it always outweighed the bad!

You see, it's not what happens to you that makes your life better or worse; it's how you deal with it… I choose happiness. In that I can be safe.

About the Author

As a teen, Aviva was a bit of a social misfit, so she had plenty of time to create characters and worlds away from her reality. Now, at thirty something years of age, she's finally able to report that things are looking up.

Happily married with four children, Aviva and her family live just outside Calgary, Alberta. At this stage of her life, she feels fortunate to be able to devote much of her time to doing what she loves—writing.

My other books -

CHiP

Blood Matters

Stuck - Facing Forward

Acknowledgments

My thanks are extended first to my oldest and dearest of friends, Larissa, who has, since the age of twelve, listened patiently as I told and retold my story ideas—always the plot, or synopsis of the plot, and myriad excerpts from whatever happened to be my latest creation—all when I knew you'd rather have been gossiping about cute guys!

To every other friend I've made over the interim years, each of whom has similarly put up with my obsession; my thanks to each one of you for your ear and for giving me the strength to carry on writing. Especially Lori Guildemiester who told me to stop worrying about whether I could or couldn't write and just do it—I might not have done it without you.

For my husband Dave Harold—you are my anchor (my Toby). Thank you for not only putting up with this writing quirk, but also my many others.

To my children Amally, Zandr, Aubyn and Andrew—for simultaneously assisting me in recalling my youth and innocence as well as challenging me to grow up as a parent and mother.

Especially for this book, I thank Terri for being my first editor and cheerleader. My thanks also to Allister Thompson, my professional editor, for illuminating the rough edges in my writing—I'm henceforth a better writer for all that I have learned with you.

To Heather Reinhardt, both for your wonderful artistic talents and for your complete professionalism; your flexibility and patience in working with me to create the illustration for the cover of Safe is much appreciated.

To Jeremy Drought of Last Impression Publishing for consultation services and guidance throughout the process of publishing a book and for his technical skills and expertise in publication design, print management, publicity and marketing.

To Barbara Russo, my final proofreader. Many thanks. I came up with the story but you made sure it was presentable.

To my mom, sister, and members of extended family, all of whom kept assuring me that I have a talent for writing. Perhaps, maybe, I do…

To all the teenagers (friends of my children—those who attended the church youth group as well as the ones I drove to and from school every day) who made themselves available, willingly read early drafts of the manuscript, and freely offered their honest opinions of my efforts, I wouldn't have stopped driving you to school if you had said it was no good.

And to all the others who've helped and supported me in my journey to get to this point—my most sincere thanks to you all…